CURRENT LEGAL PROBLEMS 1994

Volume 47
Part 2: Collected Papers

EDITORIAL BOARD

CURRENT LEGAL
PROBLEMS
1994

Volume 47

Part 2: Collected Papers

Edited by

M. D. A. FREEMAN

with

R. HALSON

as

Assistant Editor

OXFORD UNIVERSITY PRESS
1994

Oxford University Press, Walton Street, Oxford OX2 6DP

Oxford New York
Athens Auckland Bangkok Bombay
Calcutta Cape Town Dar es Salaam Delhi
Florence Hong Kong Istanbul Karachi
Kuala Lumpur Madras Madrid Melbourne
Mexico City Nairobi Paris Singapore
Taipei Tokyo Toronto

and associated companies in
Berlin Ibadan

Oxford is a trade mark of Oxford University Press

Published in the United States
by Oxford University Press Inc., New York

British Library Cataloguing in Publication Data
Data available

Library of Congress Cataloging in Publication Data
Data available
ISBN 0-19-826000-8

1 3 5 7 9 10 8 6 4 2

Set by Hope Services (Abingdon) Ltd.
Printed in Great Britain
on acid-free paper by
Biddles Ltd.,
Guildford & King's Lynn

PREFACE

This year's volume contains the revised texts of ten lectures delivered at University College London between November 1993 and March 1994. Four of the lectures were 'special': an inaugural (Palmer), two memorial lectures (the Dennis Lloyd Memorial lecture delivered by Jeffrey Jowell, his successor as Head of Department, and the annual J.A.C. Thomas lecture, this year given by someone with whom he was especially associated, Sir John Smith), and Lord Wolff's address to the Bentham Club, offering thoughts on reform of the civil process in advance of his report. The volume also contains two commissioned papers by Richard Gardiner on patent law and Jane Holder on the Sellafield litigation.

The currency of the volume may be judged by the fact that three of the contributions have by the time the volume goes to press assumed new significance. Diane Birch's article was waiting for a case like that of Colin Stagg to happen. Anyone who has read the extracts from his trial which appeared in *The Independent on Sunday* (18 October 1994) will have been confronted with the grossest encouragement by the police to admit to a crime that we are likely to encounter. The right to silence too, explored by Sanders and Young, takes on a new significance in the light of the European Commission on Human Rights' ruling in the   Ernest Saunders case. But will the Government take note or prefer to await an inevitable challenge to its proposals in the Criminal Justice and Public Order Bill? Conor Gearty's article also acquires a new meaning in the light of the I.R.A. ceasefire and the events which have followed this.

A number of themes jostle for attention in this year's volume. The scope and importance of civil liberties figures prominently (Gearty, Feldman, Birch, Smith, Sanders and Young). Four of these essays examine police powers: the fifth, that of David Feldman, asks important questions about the privacy interest.

The changing constitution comes in for critical scrutiny. Jeffrey

Jowell asks whether equality is a constitutional principle. Conor Gearty is sceptical of the value of entrenching human rights within a constitutional framework and less than enthusiastic about the judiciary's role in such a structure. Andrew Sanders and Richard Young ask whether the rule of law has any meaning in the context of decision-making in the criminal justice process.

A number of the articles explore the boundaries of property. Richard Gardiner examines the elusiveness of what is involved in 'invention'. Norman Palmer explores theft in an arena where normal conceptions of this fit uneasily. And Kevin Gray, in what is likely to become a seminal paper, explores the relationship between property and empowerment, examining the 'new property' in three key areas (quasi-public places, raising in yet another context civil liberties issues, traditional country and the natural environment).

And, to add to new civil liberties and new property, we have in Andrew Grubb's article an examination of the possibility of construing a new relationship—a fiduciary relationship—between doctor and patient, and in Jane Holder's an exploration of a new toxic tort. In her essay a novel precautionary principle is described, an import from the European Union and international law. But this will not surprise readers of this volume who will find throughout it examples of the impact of Europe and the lessons and insights to be drawn from other systems of law, in particular the U.S.A. (in Gray, Palmer and Jowell), Canada (Grubb) and Australia (in particular Gray's discussion of the *Mabo* litigation). One of the lessons of this volume is that as the legal world expands it becomes at the same time smaller! A paradox that merits an explanation but this is not, I think, an appropriate place to speculate upon it further.

M. D. A. Freeman
September 1994.

CONTENTS

TABLE OF CASES

TABLE OF STATUTES, TREATIES AND OTHER SOURCES

IS EQUALITY A CONSTITUTIONAL PRINCIPLE?

*Jeffrey Jowell**
(Dennis Lloyd Memorial Lecture)

English public law has displayed a remarkable vigour over the past 25 years. Whatever the state of our other public institutions, or other parts of our law, our courts have, over this period, addressed the most intractable problem of our unwritten constitution and come up with a definitive answer. That problem is the extent to which the exercise of governmental power is constrained by legal principle. The answer, which the courts have firmly asserted, is that it is so constrained, and that individuals have the right, in their dealings with the state, to be treated legally, fairly, and, if not reasonably, then at least not unreasonably.

Last year saw a further decisive step in this direction. A unanimous House of Lords held that a local authority, the Derbyshire County Council, was not entitled to bring a libel action against Times Newspapers. The reason given was that 'it is of the highest public importance that a democratically elected body should be open to uninhibited public criticism. The threat of a civil action for defamation must inevitably have an inhibiting effect on free speech'.[1]

The House of Lords did not reach this conclusion by resting it upon our obligations in international law. Freedom of speech has thus been judicially recognised as a right implied in our domestic common law. As was made clear, it is a right that is derived from the principle that, in a democracy, necessary criticism of government should not be unjustifiably restrained.

* QC, Professor of Public Law and Vice Provost, University College London. The author would like to thank Stephen Guest, Bob Hepple, Martin Loughlin, Anthony Lester, Jeffrey Barnes and Daniel Jowell for their helpful assistance with the preparation of the lecture.

[1] *Derbyshire County Council* v. *Times Newspapers Ltd* [1993] AC 534.

In other recent cases, other rights, such as the right to life,[2] and the right of unimpeded access to courts[3] have been mentioned as meriting especially 'anxious' judicial scrutiny when threatened.

If these rights exist, what others? And, the question I shall now address, what of equality? Is equality a constitutional principle?

It might seem self evident that equality is a fundamental principle in a democracy, as I believe it to be, but the evidence from the literature on that point is sparse. Working through the index of all the leading English works on constitutional and administrative law published over the past 10 years there is barely a mention of equality.[4] Most have no reference to it at all. Books on Civil Liberty do deal with our law outlawing certain forms of race and sex discrimination, but rarely with other forms of discrimination.[5] Contrast the books on the public law of most other countries, where equality takes up at least as many inches in their indexes as are allotted in ours to Professor Albert Venn Dicey and his book *The Law of the Constitution*, which was published 109 years ago.[6]

Dicey's formidable Victorian figure still looms over the law of the British constitution. It brings to mind the image of the Albert Memorial as it exists today, encased in scaffolding and wrapped in protective sheeting. The powers that be cannot decide whether to restore it to its former glory or to acknowledge that its fabric, ravaged by twentieth century elements not foreseen at the time of its Victorian construction, is frankly beyond repair.

On balance I would vote to restore Dicey's monument, not to demolish it. Not in order to elevate his work to the order of unimpeachable doctrine, nor to provide our scholars with a perpetually revolving grindstone on which to sharpen their critical faculties, but to have the opportunity from time to time to salute some (although by no means all) of his insights into the British constitution, and his method of determining its elusive patterns and practices.

[2] *R. v. Secretary of State for the Home Department ex parte Khawaja* [1984] AC 74; *Bugdacay v. Secretary of State for the Home Department* [1987] AC 514.

[3] *Raymond v. Honey* [1983] AC 1. And see the recent case of *R. v. Secretary of State for the Home Department, ex parte Leech* (No.2) [1993] 3 WLR 1125.

[4] A singular exception is the recent book by T. R. S. Allen, *Law, Liberty and Justice* (1993).

[5] But see the excellent chapter on equality in the context of decisions about sentencing in A. Ashworth, *Sentencing and Criminal Justice* (1992), ch.7. See also D. Feldman, *Civil Liberties and Human Rights in England and Wales* (1993).

[6] In 1885; referred to here in its 10th edn. (1959), edited by E. C. S. Wade (reprinted 1960).

Although many of Dicey's dogmas delayed the development in this country of a coherent public law, his abiding insight was that our constitution, albeit unwritten, is guided by principles. Some of these principles, together with what he called Conventions, *enable* power to be exercised by government, and specify the manner of its exercise. Dicey also however identified the fact that principles also *disable* government from abusing its power. The essential disabling principle is the Rule of Law, which acts as a practical constraint on the way power is exercised. The content of The Rule of Law is broad: it requires laws as enacted by Parliament to be faithfully executed by officials; individuals wishing to enforce the law should have access to courts; no person should be condemned unheard; power should not be arbitrarily exercised. Perhaps above all, and in order to achieve the aims just mentioned, the Rule of Law requires law to be certain, that is, predictable and not retrospective in its application. These constraints inherent in the Rule of Law have provided the background justification for much of our developing rules of public law.

The practical effect of a disabling constitutional principle, like the Rule of Law, is seen when an alleged breach of the principle is challenged in the courts. The courts make the assumption that individuals have a right to be treated in accordance with the principle. In interpreting the scope of a statutory power, the implication is made that Parliament intended the law to conform to the principle. If the scope of the power is ambiguous, the principle applies. It is only excluded where clearly stated to the contrary. That of course means that a principle like the Rule of Law *can* be expressly overridden by Parliament—in our system the prior principle of the Sovereignty of Parliament has up to now prevailed, as Dicey required. But the absence of judicial review of primary legislation is by no means fatal to the principle. It will still always provide the basis for evaluation of all governmental action.

It serves as a critical focus not only for judicial review, but also for public debate. The government may succeed in enacting a law providing for detention without trial, or may enact retroactive legislation, but strong justification is needed for such laws to withstand the Rule of Law's moral strictures. It is this conception of a constitutional principle that I seek for equality.

Now it may be that we do not need a separate and distinct constitutional principle of equality, because it is already contained within the Rule of Law. In elaborating the Rule of Law Dicey said that 'With us every official, from the Prime Minister down to a constable or a collector of taxes, is under the same responsibility for every act done without legal justification as any other citizen.'[7] Dicey is here espousing a concept of what has been called formal equality, by which he meant that no person is exempt from the enforcement of the law. Rich and poor, revenue official and individual taxpayer are all within the equal reach of the arm of the law.

This kind of equality has been derided[8] but it is important. It is inherent in the very notion of law, and in the integrity of law's application, that like cases be treated alike over time.[9] Its reach however is limited because its primary concern is not with the content of the law but with its *enforcement* and *application* alone. The Rule of Law is satisfied as long as laws are applied or enforced equally, that is, evenhandedly, free of bias and without irrational distinction. The Rule of Law requires formal equality which prohibits laws from being enforced unequally, but it does not require substantive equality. It does not therefore prohibit unequal laws. It constrains, say, racially-biased enforcement of laws, but does not inhibit apartheid-style laws from being enacted.[10] Dicey's supporters such as Maitland and, later, Hayek freely admitted that certain laws are much more important than 'bad' or 'unjust' laws.[11] The

---

[7] Dicey, *The Law of the Constitution*, above n. 6, p. 193.

[8] See e.g. Morton Horwitz' review of E. P. Thompson's *Whigs and Hunters: The Origin of the Black Act* (1975). Although Horwitz agrees that the Rule of Law (claimed by Thompson to be an 'unqualified human good') creates formal equality which Horwitz regards as a 'a not inconsiderable virtue', he claims that 'it promotes substantive inequality by creating a consciousness that radically separates law from politics, means from ends, processes from outcomes.'. (1977) 86 *Yale LJ* 561.

[9] See R. Dworkin, *Law's Empire* (1986). Compare J. Raz, *The Morality of Freedom* (1986), ch. 9. For a clear account of the debate about equality's role in relation to justice and judicial reasoning see S. Guest, *Ronald Dworkin* (1992), chs. 9 and 10.

[10] Compare T. R. S. Allen, *supra*, note 4, who claims that both formal and substantive equality are inherent in the Rule of Law. For an extended discussion of different concepts of equality see P. G. Polyviou, *The Equal Protection of the Laws* (1980), ch. 1. See also Bernard Williams, 'The Idea of Equality', in Laslett and Runciman eds. *Philosophy, Politics and Society*, (1962) p.125.

[11] Maitland wrote that 'Known general laws, however bad, interfere less with freedom than decisions based on no previously known rule' *Collected Papers*, vol.i [1911], p.81. Maitland equated arbitrary power with power that is 'uncertain' or 'incalculable'. *Ibid.*, p.80. Hayek wrote that 'it does not matter whether we all drive on the left or on the right-hand side of the road so long as we all do the same. The

role of equality in the Rule of Law is merely instrumental. It is espoused not as a virtue for its own sake. Its place is to buttress the Rule of Law's supreme quality; that of legal certainty.

A very different conception of equality was advanced by Dicey's critics in the 1930s. Professors Ivor Jennings and Harold Laski unleashed attacks on the Rule of Law which were almost fatal. They accused Dicey's thin concept of formal equality, together with his concern not to permit wide discretionary powers, as devices to perpetuate inequalities in society and to inhibit the redistribution of wealth.[12] Jennings and others were interested therefore in unshackling our officials from the constraints imposed by this kind of Rule of Law so as to give them a freer hand to promote social and economic equality.

But can a *constitution* foster social and economic equality? If we seek a theory of equality suitable for a modern constitution, there are important contenders more convincing by far than those that simply advance the equal distribution of wealth.

A great deal of attention has been focused upon John Rawls' 'Difference Principle',[13] under which social and economic inequalities are permitted only to the extent that they are to the greatest benefit of the least advantaged members of society. By contrast, writers of a more libertarian point of view, such as Robert Nozick[14] and Peter Bauer,[15] tend to support economic equality in the sense of the equal right freely to enter into contracts or the equal opportunity to enjoy one's property or the fruits of one's labour.

important thing is that the rule enables us to predict other people's behaviour correctly, and this requires that it should apply in all cases—even if in a particular instance we feel it to be unjust' F.Hayek, *The Road to Serfdom* (1943), p. 60.

[12] See Sir W. Ivor Jennings, *The Law and the Constitution (1933)*. William Robson's celebrated criticism of Dicey in 1928 did not take issue with the Rule of Law as such. However, Robson listed a number of 'judicial virtues', among which are the need for consistency, for certainty *and* for equality. W. A. Robson, *Justice and Administrative Law* (1928), ch.5.

[13] J. Rawls, *Political Liberalism* (1993), p.6. In other words, if the least advantaged members of society can be made better off in *absolute* terms only by the existence of greater *relative* inequality between themselves and the more advantaged members of society then this form of inequality is permissible. Rawls' view concentrates on equality of 'primary goods'. By contrast, other theories of economic equality focus on equality of 'welfare' or equality of 'capabilities'. Under these theories for example a disabled person is entitled to more resources in order to conpensate for his disablity. See e.g. Amartya Sen, *Inequality Reexamined* (1992), who defines equality as the equal 'freedom to achieve' or 'capability to function'.

[14] R. Nozick, *Anarchy, State and Utopia* (1974).

[15] P. Bauer, *Equality, The Third World and Economic Delusion* (1981).

Should any of these conceptions of equality qualify as the constitutional principle of equality that we are seeking? John Ely gave
one answer to this question when he responded to a plea by
Ronald Dworkin to employ the writings of Rawls as a way
towards fusing constitutional law and moral theory. Ely replied as
follows: 'Rawls's book *is* fine. But how are judges to react to
Dworkin's invitation when almost all the commentators on Rawls's
work have expressed reservations about his conclusions? The
Constitution may follow the flag, but is it really supposed to keep
up with the *New York Review of Books?*'[16]

Ely's jibe too lightly dismisses the riches for law in the work of
Rawls, but there is a related point which is valid; that a constitution ought not to be in itself an instrument of policy. It provides
the framework for the implementation of policies by an elected
government. It is not the function of a constitution to predetermine
the allocation of resources or the distribution or redistribution of
wealth, or the proper place of the market. A government duly
elected by the people should be free to pursue Rawls' or Nozick's
vision of equality, and the constitution should ensure its freedom
to do so.

[As an aside, it is interesting to note that in the recent debate
about the South African Constitution the African National
Congress initially proposed that certain social and economic rights
(such as the right to a health service and guaranteed shelter) be
contained in the constitutional text. In the end these were not
included, although the right to 'freely engage in economic activity'[17] is balanced by the right to form and join trade unions, and
the right to strike.[18]]

If formal equality is too thin a concept to deal with substantive

---

[16] John Hart Ely, *Democracy and Distrust* (1980), p. 58. There has been an extensive debate in the USA in the context of the equal protection clause as to whether
or not equality in itself is an 'empty idea'. The proposal was mooted in P. Westen,
'The Empty Idea of Equality', 95 *Harv. L. Rev.* 537 (1982). For some of the replies
see Greenawalt, 83 *Col. L. Rev.* 1167 (1983); Chemerisky, 81 *Mich. L. Rev.* 575
(1983); D'Amato, 81 *Mich. L. Rev.* 600 (1983). Westen's reply is at 81 *Mich. L. Rev.*
604 (1983).

[17] *Constitution of the Republic of South Africa* 1994, Chapter 3, Article 26.

[18] *Id*. Article 27. The South African Constitution also has a general 'equality
clause' which also permits affirmative action. *Id*. Article 8. Some constitutions e.g.
India, Brazil, Namibia, do contain social and economic rights, but these are
expressed as 'directive principles of state policy' and expressly excluded from judicial enforcement. See e.g. The Constitution of India, Part IV.

inequality, and if broad theories of social equality disqualify themselves as constitutional principles (however attractive we may find them as social policies), is there any other notion of equality which might limit government's power to treat people unequally in a substantive sense?

Put in this negative way, seeking a *principle* to limit governmental power, rather than seeking a policy to promote a particular conception of the social good, a positive answer is suggested by a conception of equality that requires government not to treat people unequally without justification. In other words, government should not discriminate. Such a principle does not require or predetermine any particular social and economic programme Yet it is directed not only to the way law is applied but also to the content of the laws themselves. It forbids not only the unequal application of equal laws, but also forbids unequal laws. Just like free speech, it is a principle that derives from the nature of democracy itself. Basic to democracy is the requirement that every citizen has an equal vote, and therefore an equal opportunity to influence the composition of the government. The notion of equal worth is thus a fundamental precept of our constitution.[19] It gains its ultimate justification from a notion of the way individuals should be treated in a democracy. It is constitutive of democracy.

This conception of equality of course allows differential treatment (between adults and children, the elderly and the young, aliens and citizens) but it prevents distinctions that are not properly justified. Distinctions between individuals or groups must be reasonably related to government's legitimate purposes. Under our system, equality may be expressly violated if Parliament clearly so requires. Like the Rule of Law however, its apparent violation will provoke strong questioning and require rational justification. We see this debate today on the question of different ages of consent for homosexuals or on the question of the possible withdrawal of some forms of hospital treatment from habitual smokers or from the elderly.

Now where do we find this conception of equality in our law? How do we test whether it is a constitutional principle?

We could start with that growing element of our law which involves the application of 'directly effective' European Community

[19] See Ronald Dworkin, 'Equality, Democracy and the Constitution', (1990) *Alberta L. Rev.* 324.

law. Certain provisions of the European Community Treaty provide for the principle of equal treatment with regard to specific matters. Discrimination is prohibited on the ground of nationality,[20] in pay on the grounds of sex[21] (though not race) and between consumers and producers in the application of the Common Agricultural Policy.[22] The European Court has however ruled that each of these prohibitions on discrimination is 'merely a specific enunciation of the general principle of equality which is one of the fundamental principles of Community law.'[23] The principle of equality in Community law requires that similar situations shall not be treated differently, and that different situations not be treated equally, unless the distinction or lack of distinction is 'objectively justified'—a concept of equality which is compatible with that which I have just outlined.

Many of the cases in which the equality principle is applied under Community law may not be exactly rivetting to civil libertarians. One important case, for example, dealt with unjustified discrimination in subsidising two kinds of maize, quellmehl and grits, while continuing to pay the refunds on the maize used to make starch. The producers of the two former products successfully argued that the distinction between their products and starch could not be objectively justified.[24] Important of course if you happen to produce quellmehl, starch or grits, but the same principle has been enunciated in cases involving equal pay between men and women,[25] or the discrimination against Mrs. Johnston by the Royal Ulster Constabulary (although the latter case was decided on other grounds).[26]

It should be added that, although the Treaty of Rome does not provide for a catalogue of fundamental human rights, the Court of Justice has held in the case of *Nold*[27] that it cannot uphold mea-

---

[20] Article 7.   [21] Article 119.   [22] Article 40(3).
[23] Joined Cases 103, 145/77 *Royal Scholten-honig* v. *IBAP* [1978] ECR 2037 at 2072. See also Joined Cases 117/76 and 16/77 *Ruckdeschel* [1977] ECR 1753.
[24] *Ruckdeschel, supra,* at 1769.
[25] E.G. Case 1/72 *Frilli* v. *Belgium* [1972] ECR 457.
[26] *Johnston* v. *Chief Constable of the RUC*, Case 222/84 [1986] ECR 1651; [1986] 3 CMLR 240. See generally, D. Wyatt and A. Dashwood, *European Community Law*, (1993) p. 95–98.
[27] *Nold* v. *Commission* Case 4/73 [1974] ECR 491 at 507. Now see Article F(2) of the Treaty on European Union 1993 (the Maastricht Treaty): 'The Union shall respect fundamental rights, as guaranteed by the European Convention . . . as general principles of Commuity law'. However, this provision is not justiciable by the

sures which are incompatible with fundamental rights, and subsequent cases have accepted that the European Convention on Human Rights has a special significance in this respect. Article 14 of the Convention outlaws discrimination on a number of grounds namely, sex, race, colour, language, religion, political opinion, national or social origins, association with a national minority, property, birth or 'other status.' The case law of the European Commission and Court of Human Rights has included under 'other status' a variety of grounds, including marital status, and the distinction between 'foster' and 'natural' children, and illegitimates.[28]

In cases in which Community law is directly effective in the United Kingdom, equality of this kind—preventing discrimination without 'objective justification'—is one of the principles which our courts must apply as governing not only our administrative action, but also our primary legislation.

Turning now to English common law, we find some ancient duties placed upon the likes of inn-keepers, common carriers and some monopoly enterprises such as ports and harbours, to accept all travellers and others who are 'in a reasonably fit condition to be received'.[29] The reach of these laws was not sufficient to prevent racial discrimination in other public places and therefore, in the 1960's, legislation outlawing discrimination first on racial grounds, and later on grounds of sex, was introduced.[30] These laws cover discrimination in employment, education, the provision of goods and services, and some other areas in relation to racial discrimination.[31]

Does this specific enunciation of forbidden discrimination imply that other forms of discrimination are permissible? To answer this question we have to turn to our administrative law. Here we find

European Court. See Article L of the Treaty on European Union. And see S. Weatherill and P. Beaumont *E C Law* (1993) pp. 220–23.

[28] *Danning* v. *The Netherlands* (Communication no. 196/1984); and *Sprenger* v. *the Netherlands* (Communication no. 395/1990).

[29] *Rothfield* v. *N. B. Railway*, (1920) S.C. 805; *Pidgeon* v. *Legge* (1857) 21 J.P. 743. The services of some utilities are also required to be offered without discrimination. See e.g. *South of Scotland Electricity Board* v. *British Oxygen Ltd* [1959] 1 WLR 587.

[30] See generally, A. Lester and G. Bindman, *Race and the Law* (1972); The governing statutes are now the Race Relations Act 1976 and the Sex Discrimination Act 1975. See also the Equal Pay Act 1970.

[31] Membership of associations and the exercise by local authorities of their planning functions.

first that the courts imply that decisions of public officials should not be taken in 'bad faith'. Decisions should not therefore be infected with motives such as malice, fraud, dishonesty or personal animosity. Such motives are impermissible because they bias or distort the decision-maker's approach to the applicant.[32] The applicant is therefore in a sense subject to unfair discrimination, in breach of the principle of formal equality.

In other cases the courts have invoked the notion of ' public policy' to strike down discriminatory provisions. In *Nagle* v. *Fielden*[33] a decision of the Jockey club to refuse a woman a horse trainer's licence was held to be against public policy and in *Edwards* v. *Sogat*,[34] a case involving the withdrawal of trade union rights, Lord Denning said: 'The courts of this country will not allow so great a power to be exercised arbitrarily or capriciously or with unfair discrimination, neither in the making of rules or in the enforcement of them' (thereby addressing himself both to substantive and formal equality).

Most decisions invoking substantive inequality have been struck down under the ground of judicial review known as 'unreasonableness'. In cases of this kind, wide discretionary power has normally been conferred on the decision-maker, and the courts—through judicial review—must be careful to allow the decision-maker a sufficiently wide margin of discretion. Courts therefore intervene under the formula set out by Lord Greene in the 1947 case of *Wednesbury* only when the decision is 'so unreasonable that no reasonable decision-maker would so act'.[35] Incidentally, the example of a clearly unreasonable decision provided in the *Wednesbury* case was that of a teacher dismissed from her post on the ground of her red hair alone.

Unease with the tautologous *Wednesbury* formulation of unreasonableness has recently resulted in some attempts at redefinition. The term 'irrationality' is currently in vogue—it was suggested by Lord Diplock—in the *GCHQ* case in 1984.[36] His extended definition of irrationality incorporates situations defying 'accepted moral

---

[32] S. de Smith, *Judicial Review of Administrative Action* (1979), p. 335.

[33] [1966] 2 QB 633.

[34] [1971] Ch. 354.

[35] *Associated Provincial Picture Houses Ltd.* v. *Wednesbury Corporation* [1948] 1 KB 223.

[36] *Council of Civil Service Unions* v. *Minister for the Civil Service* [1985] AC 374.

standards'.[37] Other definitions employ terms such as 'absurdity' and 'perversity' so as to prevent the courts interfering with a decision unless the official has 'taken leave of his senses'.[38] Lord Donaldson recently rejected all the above definitions, preferring that of an unreasonable decision as one that elicits the exclamation: 'My goodness, that is certainly wrong!'.[39]

The courts tend to avoid defining criteria of unreasonableness more specific than any of those above. There are advantages to vagueness and judges may be concerned to disguise the fact that judicial review allows the courts to strike not only at procedural defects and cases of illegality, but also at defects in the substance of the decision itself. Underneath the *Wednesbury* camouflage, however, a principle of equality can be discerned.

A century ago the notion of unreasonableness was less obscure. In 1898 in the case of *Kruse* v. *Johnson* Lord Russell of Killowen was asked to invalidate a by-law for unreasonableness. 'Unreasonable in what sense?' he asked, and then proceeded to provide some relatively specific examples including the following: The by-laws would be unreasonable, he said 'if, for instance, they were found to be partial and unequal in their operation as between different classes'.[40]

In 1925 in the famous case of *Roberts* v. *Hopwood*[41] the House of Lords confirmed the view of the district auditor that the attempt of Poplar Borough Council to raise the level of the wages of both their men and women employees to an equal level was unlawful. Lord Atkinson fulminated against the council for allowing themselves to be guided by 'eccentric principles of socialistic philanthropy, or by feminist ambition to secure the equality of sexes'. This case is often produced as an exhibit of a typically blatant example of judicial opposition towards social equality. No doubt Lord Atkinson was not one of its more ardent supporters, but the ratio of the case was based upon a more sober consideration of the

---

[37] Irrationality was defined by Lord Diplock, supra, as applying to 'a decision which is so outrageous in its defiance of logic or of accepted moral standards that no sensible person who had applied his mind to the question to be decided could have arrived at it.'

[38] See *Pulhofer* v. *Hillingdon L.B.C.* [1986] AC 484, 518; *R* v. *Secretary of State for the Environment ex. parte Notts C.C.* [1986] AC 240, 247–48.

[39] *Piggott Brothers and Co. Ltd.* v. *Jackson*, *The Times* May 20 1991. See also May LJ in *Neale* v. *Hereford and Worcester C.C.* [1986] 1 CR 471, 483.

[40] [1889] 2 QB 291.   [41] [1925] AC 578.

lack of 'rational proportion' between the rates paid to the women and the going market rate (a ground of review which has a more modern ring).[42]

In 1955 in *Prescott* v. *Birmingham Corporation*[43] the local authority, which had power to 'charge such fares as they may think fit' on their public transport services introduced a scheme for free bus travel for the elderly. The decision was declared to be unlawful because it conferred out of rates' 'a special benefit on some particular *class* of inhabitants . . . at the expense of the general body of ratepayers'.[44] The reasoning in *Prescott* might have benefited from attention to a more sophisticated conception of equality, but its approach was followed in other cases involving differential transport fares schemes, each of which grapples with some notion of equality. In the GLC Fares Fair case,[45] for example, justification was required for the differential costs and benefits of the transport fare cut to the inhabitants of Bromley, other ratepayers in London, and travellers from outside London using London's public transport.

Looking behind recent applications of *Wednesbury* unreasonableness we do see stark examples of the application of the principle of equality. In 1988 a councillor in Port Talbot was allowed to jump the housing queue in order to put her in a better position to fight the local election from her own constituency.[46] The decision was held unlawful because unfair to others on the housing waiting list, adversely discriminated against. The principle of equality was not mentioned, but surely applied.

It has recently been held that schools may not discriminate in the allocation of school places against children living outside the school's catchment area. In *R.* v. *Hertfordshire County Council ex parte Cheung*[47] the Master of the Rolls Lord Donaldson held that the Home Secretary, in considering the remission of a prisoner's

---

[42] As pointed out by Ormrod LJ in *Pickwell* v. *Camden L.B.C.* [1983] QB 962 at 999–1000.

[43] [1955] Ch. 210.   [44] Per Jenkins LJ at 235–36.

[45] *Bromley LBC* v. *GLC.* [1983] 1 AC 768. In *Board of Education* v. *Rice* [1911] AC 179, oft cited in connection with natural justice, the decision of the Board was quashed by the House of Lords on the ground that the Board had failed properly to determine whether teachers in church schools should be paid the same rate as teachers in the authority's own schools.

[46] *R.* v. *Port Talbot BC ex parte Jones* [1988] 2 All ER 207.

[47] *The Times*, 4 April 1986.

sentence, must have regard to the length of time served by the applicant's co-defendants. He said that: 'It is a cardinal principle of good public adminstration that all persons in a similar position should be treated similarly'.

Some of these cases provide examples of formal equality, but there are many other cases where, whether explicitly mentioned or not, substantive equality was the standard by which administrative decisions have been tested. Planning conditions that insist that local businesses only have access to new office premises have been upheld on the ground that their primary intent was to fuel the local economy—a legitimate planning consideration. On the other hand, conditions attached to planning permissions requiring local people only to occupy new or converted housing in the area (and thus discriminating against second home owners, or indeed anyone from outside the area) are of more doubtful validity.[48] In *Great Portland Estates* v. *Westminster Council*[49] the council's local district plan was challenged on the ground that it favoured the retention in the area of certain small industries only. The plan was upheld but the apparent discrimination had indeed to be carefully justified.[50]

The clearest recent articulation of equality as a substantive standard was applied by Mr Justice Simon Brown in the case of *R.* v. *Immigration Appeal Tribunal, ex parte Manshoora Begum*,[51] when he struck down part of immigration regulations promulgated by the Home Secretary. The regulation made provision for a dependent parent to be admitted to the United Kingdom in exceptional and compassionate circumstances, but required as one such circumstance that the parent should have a standard of living 'substantially below that of his or her own country'. Citing Lord Russell's formulation of unreasonableness as, inter alia, involving 'partial and unequal' treatment, it was held that these regulations would

---

[48] See generally Malcolm Grant, *Urban Planning Law* (1982) pp. 349–51. See also *Alnatt* v. *Kingston on Thames BC* [1991] JPL 744. Discrimination in the allocation of school places to children living outside a school's catchment area has been held to be unlawful. See *R.* v. *Greenwich LBC ex parte Governors of the John Ball Primary School* [1989] 88 LGR 589; *R.* v. *Devon County Council ex parte G.* [1988] 3 WLR 49.

[49] [1985] AC 661.

[50] By showing the linkages between those industries and other economic activities. There is some doubt as to whether provisions in structure plans requiring preference to the Welsh language can be reqarded as material planning considerations. See Huw Thomas, *Planning*, 22 October 1993 p. 20.

[51] [1986] Imm. AR 385.

benefit immigrants from affluent countries and discriminate against those from those from poor countries. The particular provision was however struck down on the explicit ground that it was 'manifestly unjust and unreasonable'.

Sometimes, in our administrative law, we see the principle of legal certainty, of formal equality, the Rule of Law value, in conflict with the principle of substantive equality I have outlined, involving treatment as equals. The doctrine of the fettering of discretion is a case in point.[52] Public officials are permitted to make rules that make it easier for them to exercise their discretion and which have the benefit of making their policy clear to the public. For example, local authorities devise a points system for the allocation of council housing. But the decision-maker must always be prepared to listen to someone with something new to say. Discretion may not be fettered. The decision-maker must be willing to depart from a rule aimed at all equally (that is, seeking formal equality), by allowing the applicant to show that difference in treatment is justified in the particular case (that is, in order to achieve substantive equality).

There is no doubt that equality is used as a test of official action in our law. But is it wise for it to be explicitly articulated and declared—to be elevated to the status of lion under the throne, and not just a well-disguised rabbit to be hauled occasionally out of the *Wednesbury* hat? The jurisprudence of equality in international law, in European Community law, and in places with equal protection of the law enshrined in their constitutions—like the USA and Canada—give us fair warning of the kinds of problems with which our courts may have to grapple:

The first is the question of *direct and indirect discrimination*. Our anti-discrimination law is familiar with the concepts of direct and indirect discrimination (known in America as 'disparate treatment' discrimination): Direct discrimination involves the less favourable treatment of the complainant than someone else on prohibited grounds and in comparable circumstances. 'Indirect' discrimination arises when a seemingly neutral provision has a disproportionate impact on a particular group without any objective justification. For example, a height requirement, or requirement to work full time, may disproportionately disadvantage women. European Community

---

[52] See generally D. J. Galligan *Discretionary Powers* (1986).

law outlaws indirect discrimination,[53] but in the USA the situation is patchy. In the area of racial discrimination in employment, indirect or disparate impact discrimination was outlawed by the US Supreme Court in *Griggs* v. *Duke Power Co.*[54] Subsequent case law reversed the *Griggs* position,[55] which legislation then clearly endorsed.[56] Disparate impact discrimination is not however covered under the Equal Protection Clause (The 14th Amendment to the Constitution)—even in respect of racial discrimination.[57]

The second question concerns the scope of *affirmative action.* Under European Community law, affirmative action—positive discrimination for the special protection of socially, economically or culturally deprived groups—is regarded as a derogation from the fundamental right to equal treatment. As such it is strictly construed, in accordance with the principle of proportionality, and must therefore be within the limits of what is appropriate to achieve the aim in view.[58] International human rights law goes further and even requires affirmative action in order to diminish conditions which help to perpetuate prohibited discrimination.[59]

A third question is about the *intensity of review*—or the margin of discretion or appreciation allowed to the decision-maker. The approach of the United States Supreme Court is instructive on this point: The Fourteenth Amendment to the United States Constitution guarantees that '[n]o State shall make or enforce any law which shall deny to any person within its jurisdiction the equal protection of the laws'. While it had initially been argued that the Equal Protection Clause was intended only to require equal

---

[53] For example, Article 119 of the EEC Treaty and the Equal Pay and Equal Treatment Directives. See e.g. *Bilka* v. *Weber von Harz* [1986] ECR 1607; *Commission* v. *Belgium* [1991] ECR 1–2205.

[54] 401 US 424 (1971).   [55] *Wards Cove Packing Co.* v. *Antonio* 490 US 642.

[56] Title VII, Civil Rights Act 1991.

[57] See e.g. *Washington* v. *Davis* 426 US 229 (1976).

[58] Such as measures for the special protection of women, in pregnancy and childbirth. See e.g. *Ministère Public* v. *A. Stoeckel*, Case 345/89 (25 July 1991)—(equal Treatment Directive obliges Member States not to prohibit night work from being done by women).

[59] See generally, W. McKean, *Equality and Discrimination under International Law* (1983); I. Brownlie, *Principles of Public International Law*, (1990), p. 598–601. See the Human Rights Committee's General Comment on 'Non-Discrimination', No. 18, UN doc HRI/GEN/1, 4 September, 1992, which requires specific action by states to correct conditions which prevent or impair a certain part of the population from their enjoyment of human rights. See also General Comment no.4 and *Stalla Costa* v. *Uruguay*, Communication no 198/1985, paragraph 10.

enforcement of the laws (that is, Diceyan formal equality), it is accepted now that the Clause is a guarantee of 'equal laws', that is, State legislation may be challenged as violating equal protection. A legal classification will however survive a challenge if it is 'reasonable in relation to the objectives of the law'.[60]

In developing the conception of reasonableness the Supreme Court has employed a threefold standard of review. In matters involving social and economic policy, or where the matter is not easily 'justiciable' because a question of opinion or taste, the threshold of discretion is high and the courts will tend to defer to the administrative agency. Differentiation will in this kind of case survive challenge if it is 'rationally related to furthering a legitimate government objective'.[61] In such cases therefore the law is accorded a strong presumption of validity and a classification must be upheld if there is 'any reasonably conceivable state of affairs that could provide a rational basis' for the classification. For example a 'grandfather clause', exempting two vendors from a ban on pushcart dealers in the French Quarter of New Orleans was sustained because the City could rationally conclude that the exempted vendors had become part of the 'discrete charm' of the area.[62]

When, however, the law employs what the Supreme Court has called a 'suspect classification', such as race or 'immutable traits or stereotypes', or when the classification burdens 'fundamental rights', *strict* scrutiny is applied. 'Suspect classifications' include those which 'imply inferiority in civil society' and include race or national origin. Judicial deference here is not appropriate. In *Palmore* v. *Sidoti*[63] the Supreme Court overturned a state rule allowing child custody to be refused to a white mother cohabiting with a black male.

In between these two extremes there is a third category, that of a 'quasi-suspect classification.' Sex discrimination—against men or women, comes under this head at present. In California, where a man challenged the rape legislation, which he said was discrimina-

---

[60] See Tussman and Ten Broek, 'The Equal Protection of the Laws', 37 *Calif. L. Rev.* 341 (1944).

[61] *Massachusetts Board of Retirement* v. *Murgia* 427 US 307 (1976).

[62] *City of New Orleans* v. *Dukes* 427 US 297 (1976) (*cf. Great Portland Estates* note 49, *supra*).

[63] 466 US 429 (1984).

tory because aimed at men and not women, Justice Rehnquist has said that the courts will uphold gender classification which 'realistically reflects the fact that the sexes are not similarly situated in certain circumstances'. 'Men as a class' the Court has held, 'are not in need of the special solicitude of the courts'.[64]

Do we really want our already overloaded courts to grapple with these kinds of problems? They are by no means foreign to our system. Our courts are already familiar with many of these questions through the interpretation of our laws against race and sex discrimination. What is particularly striking is the extent to which the approach of the House of Lords, in recent cases about substantive review, is so similar to that of the US Supreme Court on the subject of equal protection. In cases involving allegations of unreasonableness the House of Lords have made the distinction between two types of decision. First are decisions which involve social or economic policy-making or the allocation of resources. In this type of decision, for example by a minister to penalise local authorities for 'excessive expenditure',[65] the courts will only intervene if the decision-maker has acted 'perversely', to the extent of his having 'taken leave of his senses'. Like US-style rationality review, this test permits a very wide margin of discretion to the decision-maker.

In a second type of case the margin of discretion is less and the courts are less deferential towards the administration. These are decisions concerning fundamental human rights. In the case of *Brind*,[66] involving the challenge to the Home Secretary's ban on broadcasting the direct words of members of certain terrorist organisations, the majority of the House of Lords was prepared to impose 'more anxious scrutiny' upon a provision interfering with a fundamental human right, and required evidence that the infringement is justified by a competing public interest (such as the need to prevent terrorism). This test is very similar to US-style 'strict scrutiny'.

Fears that equality as an articulated principle will undermine our conventions of judicial review are therefore highly exaggerated. In respect of directly effective European law—covering virtually all

---

[64] *Michael M. v. Superior Court of Sonoma County* 450 US 464 (1981).

[65] *R. v. Secretary of State for the Environment ex parte Hammersmith and Fulham L.B.C.* [1991] 1 AC 521.

[66] *R. v. Secretary of State for the Home Department ex parte Brind* [1991] 1 AC 696.

economic activity, equality is a concept which our courts will have to treat expressly and which our textbooks on 'English' administrative law will no longer be able to ignore. In respect of other law, equality is there to be found.[67]

Our constitution rests upon an assumption that government should not impose upon any citizen any burden that depends upon an argument that ultimately forces the citizen to relinquish her or his sense of equal worth. This principle is deeply embedded in our law, although it is rarely made explicit.

The scope of equality is too great to be contained within the interstices of the Rule of Law. Its aims are too important to be obscured under vague definitions of irrationality. These aims summon far more than nebulous conceptions of reasonableness; they are integral to our democratic system.

---

[67] A striking example of judicial attention to equality was provided in the recent Australian case of *Leeth* v. *Commonwealth* (1992) 107 ALR 672. A challenge was made in that case to legislation which had the effect of creating different periods of non-parole detention for sentences for the same offence in different States and Territories. Although the Australian Constitution does not possess an express equal protection clause, Deane, Toohey, Gaudron and (perhaps) Brennan JJ all acknowledged the force of equality as a common law doctrine or concept.

THE COST OF HUMAN RIGHTS: ENGLISH JUDGES AND THE NORTHERN IRISH TROUBLES

*Conor Gearty**

Introduction

The title of this evening's lecture is 'The Cost of Human Rights'. If we were the Monday Club, or a High Tory think-tank, none of us would be in the least doubt about what would be about to happen—a tirade against the very existence of human rights or a vast exegesis on the futility of rights without responsibility. But we are in a law school distinguished for—it would not be going too far to say famous for—its commitment to human rights and fundamental freedoms. The Faculty's members include many of Britain's most dedicated human rights lawyers, and a legal philosopher whose first path-breaking collection of essays was entitled, *Taking Rights Seriously*.[1] With such a title preying on the mind it might be thought frivolous even to suggest that there are costs to what most of us would intuitively want to favour and to support.

Much depends of course on what we mean by human rights. In the early days of the modern era—the period of the enlightenment—the idea was as simple as it was subversive. Human rights involved the liberty, the equality and the dignity of each and every one of us regardless of our wealth, our education, our status or our family origins. Rousseau, for example, was contemptuous of authoritarian rule or of any government not firmly rooted in the popular will. But his version of freedom led him also unequivocally

* Reader in Law, School of Law, Kings College London. The author is grateful to Mr Justice Stephen Sedley, Professor K. D. Ewing, Dr Brian Bix and Mr A. Tomkins for comments on an earlier draft.

[1] R. Dworkin, *Taking Rights Seriously* (Duckworth, London, 1977).

to reject the distribution of power and of property in the society in which he found himself.[2] The French revolution of 1789 demonstrated that Rousseau and his ideas could be as cataclysmically radical a political message as any of the ideologies that have followed it. Indeed, the mere fear that this egalitarian bug would infect Britain with revolutionary zeal was sufficient to provoke the authorities of the day into a repressive rampage, what Trevelyan described as the 'angry fright' that 'obscured' for a generation the humanitarian spirit that had been engendered by Eighteenth Century England.[3]

It is hard for us to understand all this, and in particular to enter into the minds of those who regarded human rights with such hostility. Not even the greatest ally of such rights in Britain today would claim on their behalf that they are as subversive of established authority as they obviously were in the time of Pitt and Lord Liverpool.[4] In their modern form, they draw the support of such unlikely revolutionaries as the Lord Chief Justice of England[5] and the Master of the Rolls,[6] and the official opposition's support for 'human rights' is seen—rightly—as a move away from rather than towards political radicalism.[7] This change in the nature of the human rights debate is partly due to the obvious fact that society itself has changed, has become less unequal, with more of an emphasis being placed on human dignity and the quality of life than was apparent at the height of the industrial revolution. But it is also the case that what we mean by human rights has itself undergone a remarkable transformation. Gone are the subversive simplicity of Rousseau and the revolutionary clarity of the slogans of 1789. In their place are complex formulae balancing the individ-

---

[2] See generally J. Rousseau, *The Social Contract and Discourses* (J. M. Dent Ltd., London, 1973).

[3] G. M. Trevelyan, *English Social History* (Longman, London, 1973), 466.

[4] For an historical account of civil liberties in this period, see generally E. P. Thompson, *The Making of the English Working Class* (Victor Gollancz, London, 1963).

[5] Lord Taylor, 'The Judiciary in the Nineties', *Richard Dimbleby Lecture*, BBC TV, 30 Nov. 1992.

[6] T. H. Bingham, 'The European Convention on Human Rights: Time to Incorporate' (1993) 109 *LQR* 390. One of the earliest and most influential judicial contributions to the bill of rights debate came from Lord Scarman, *English Law: The New Dimension* (Stevens, London, 1974).

[7] See the speech of John Smith QC, Leader of the Labour Party, to a Charter 88 meeting on 1 March 1993, discussed in J. Rozenberg, *The Search for Justice* (Hodder and Stoughton, London, 1994), 215–17.

ual against the State; long legal documents which are concerned with human rights certainly but which are also engaged in the delineation of situations in which human rights may be legitimately confiscated by the State. The subject has been forgotten by the revolutionaries and captured by the lawyers. Pre-eminent amongst these documents is the European Convention on Human Rights,[8] and it is to this that the judges mentioned earlier and the Labour Party are committed.

The European Convention on Human Rights has many fine features. Its castigation of torture,[9] slavery[10] and forced labour[11] and its qualified prohibition of discrimination[12] are admirable. Its very existence, however flawed, has got people (particularly those who have not read it) enthusiastic about human rights. Viewed as a whole however, the document would be unrecognisable as a human rights charter to Rousseau or to any of his generation. Many of its provisions tell a quite different but depressing story: of a great revolutionary slogan that has been appropriated by the powerful, largely emptied of radical content and transformed into a bulwark of inequality.[13] The Convention contains no guarantee of equality. It accords the same 'human rights' to corporations as to the rest of us.[14] It largely accepts and protects the pre-ordained allocation of property in society by presuming that '[e]very natural or legal person' should be 'entitled to the peaceful enjoyment of his [or her] possessions.'[15] The provisions of its protocol on education suggest that even to withdraw charitible status from our private schools would be an infringement of 'human rights'.[16] To the extent

---

[8] Convention for the Protection of Human Rights and Fundamental Freedoms of 4 Nov. 1950. The Convention came into force on 3 Sept. 1953.

[9] Article 3.   [10] Article 4(1).   [11] Article 4(2).

[12] Article 14. The prohibition is qualified because it only covers discrimination in the enjoyment of the other rights and freedoms set out in Convention.

[13] For a powerful statement of radical opposition to incorporation of the European Convention on Human Rights, see J. Griffith, 'The Rights Stuff' [1993] *Socialist Register* 106.

[14] There are many examples from the case-law to illustrate this point, but see in particular the following decisions on the freedom of expression guarantee in article 10: *Markt Intern and Beerman* v. *Federal Republic of Germany* (1989) 12 EHRR 161; *Groppera Radio A.G.* v. *Switzerland* (1990) 12 EHRR 737; *Autronic A.G.* v. *Switzerland* (1990) 12 EHRR 485.

[15] Article One of the First Protocol to the European Convention on Human Rights and Fundamental Freedoms, signed on 20 March 1952.

[16] Article Two of the First Protocol, as interpreted in Independent Schools Information Service, *Independent Schools: The Legal Case* (A Joint Opinion by

that it guarantees the classic liberties of thought,[17] religion,[18] expression,[19] association[20] and assembly,[21] then it does so only with a whole variety of restrictions said to be 'necessary in a democratic society'. Rousseau would surely have protested that it is the rights—not the exceptions—that are necessary in a democratic society, but the Convention clearly views necessity as a relative concept.[22]

Central to this emaciated version of human rights is the fact that in the ECHR our rights are not inherent in us but are rather achieved for us by the judges. They are our guardians, the guarantors of our humanity. This is because it falls to the judges to determine whether a restriction on our freedom is 'necessary in a democratic society', a somewhat ironical task given their own lack of accountability and their manifestly unrepresentative nature. This lecture is not however concerned with these criticisms of the judges, important though they certainly are. Our subject is the way in which the judges in this country have generally acted not as the defenders of our freedom but as the legitimisers of the state's repression of our civil liberties. They have not so much protected freedom as all too often sanctioned its demise. Allied to this central idea is a second theme directly connected with our title, namely the great mistake it would be to incorporate the European Convention on Human Rights into our law, since the effect of such an explicit 'human rights' vocabulary would be to do little more than to add a further weapon to the judges' arsenal of state-conformity.

It is not possible in the confines of a single lecture to establish this thesis as a matter of empirical fact across the whole spectrum of our civil liberties, not that such a task would be impossible. When one thinks of the decisions against left-wing activists in the 1930s,[23] the deferential case-law during the second world war,[24]

Anthony Lester QC and David Pannick, with a foreword by Lord Scarman, ISIS, 1991).

[17] Article 9.   [18] Ibid.   [19] Article 10.
[20] Article 11.   [21] Ibid.

[22] For a powerful critique, see K. D. Ewing, 'The Bill of Rights Debate: Democracy or Juristocracy in Britain?' in K. D. Ewing, C. A. Gearty and B. A. Hepple (eds.) *Human Rights and Labour Law. Essays for Paul O'Higgins* (Mansell, London, 1994), 147.

[23] Most famously *Elias* v. *Passmore* [1934] 2 KB 164; *Thomas* v. *Sawkins* [1935] 2 KB 249 and *Duncan* v. *Jones* [1936] 1 KB 218.

[24] *Liversidge* v. *Anderson* [1942] AC 206 is the most well-known example.

the disgraceful series of decisions during the miners' strike[25] and most recently the upholding of what was effectively executive detention via our deportation law during the Gulf War,[26] it seems reasonably clear that in moments of crisis—whether contrived or genuine—no executive has found its judges to be wanting. To say that there are liberal decisions in quieter times is merely to state the obvious, namely that the judges can be as courageous as the rest of us when courage is neither required nor punished.

The focus this evening is specifically on Northern Ireland. Despite its scant treatment in many of the standard works on civil liberties,[27] the Province provides (with trade union rights)[28] the key area of civil liberties law this century. It has been responsible for much of the transformation of the relationship between the individual and the State which has been so marked over the past twenty-five years. The Home Secretary's recent call at the 1993 Conservative Party conference to abolish the right to silence because of the 'fight against terrorism' fits into a longer tradition than perhaps even he knows.[29] And throughout this period, the role of English judges in the Province has been of vital importance and of enduring value to the executive. In this lecture, we will consider first the judicial record as it is reflected in the case-law. This will lead on to a discussion of whether that record would have been improved by—or the future record could be improved by—incorporation of the European Convention. Following from this we will examine the record of the English judges when they have not been restricted by the narrowness of our laws, when they have been engaged in the tribunals of inquiry, the commissions of inquiry, the legislative reviews and so on that have been such a characteristic of 'the troubles'. Through these three strands to the

[25] On which see K. D. Ewing and C. A. Gearty, *Freedom Under Thatcher, Civil Liberties in Modern Britain* (Oxford University Press, Oxford, 1989), 103–8.

[26] *R. v. Secretary of State for the Home Department, ex parte Cheblak* [1991] 2 All ER 319.

[27] Neither G. Robertson, *Freedom, the Individual and the Law*, 6th edn.; earlier edns. by H. Street (Penguin, Harmondsworth, 1989) nor D. Feldman, *Civil Liberties and Human Rights in England and Wales* (Clarendon Press, Oxford, 1993) deal directly with the law in the Province.

[28] See K. D. Ewing, *Britain and the ILO* (Institute of Employment Rights, London, 1989).

[29] See the Criminal Justice and Public Order Bill, published in December 1993 and at the time of writing under scrutiny in Parliament.

argument, it is hoped to be able to establish the truth of the case
at least insofar as it applies to Northern Ireland—namely that far
from upholding civil liberties, the role of the British judges is generally to rubber-stamp their erosion.

The British case-law

We would expect those who argue for the introduction of a judge-
reliant human rights code to be able to point with pride to the
courageous way in which the judges have upheld civil liberties in
Northern Ireland despite the executive's determination to win its
self-styled 'war against terrorism'. The Northern Irish judges at
least partly fit this bill; the civil libertarian contribution of a number of members of that embattled bench deserves our highest admi-
ration.[30] Their weakness lies in their vulnerability to appeal to
London. If we look specifically at the role of the House of Lords in
the case-law that has arisen since the outbreak of civil disorder in
1968, we encounter a most depressing picture. It is not an exaggeration to say that every single civil libertarian challenge to executive
action that has been misfortunate enough to reach this court of
final appeal has been unsuccessful.[31]

We shall briefly refer here to just a few of the major cases, the
drab highlights in a dismal record that will be familiar to many of
you. In *McEldowney* v. *Forde*,[32] a pivotal case decided at a time
when Nationalist radicals still believed that they could use the courts
in the way that civil rights campaigners had in the United States, the
House upheld the then Unionist government's ban on 'republican
clubs' or on 'any like organization howsoever described'. The majority did not think these words vague. Lord Guest, writing in 1971,
said that he did not 'know what significance the word "republican"
[had] in Northern Ireland.'[33] The matter he said was one for the
Minister. What we do not learn from the report is that the Minister
was William Craig, a rather controversial figure who was particularly well known for his sectarian views. On one occasion he had

---

[30] See B. Dickson, 'Northern Ireland's Troubles and the Judges' in B. Hadfield
(ed.), *Northern Ireland: Politics and the Constitution* (Open University Press,
Buckingham, 1992) 130.

[31] See S. Livingstone, 'The House of Lords and the Northern Ireland Conflict'
(1994) *57 MLR 333.*

[32] [1971] AC 632.   [33] Ibid., at p. 649.

justified discrimination against Catholic lawyers, arguing that they were 'educationally and socially inferior'.[34]

In a later case decided in 1977, reported as an *Attorney-General for Northern Ireland's Reference* for that year,[35] the House unanimously accepted that a soldier who had shot and killed an unarmed man who had run away when challenged could properly be acquitted of murder. Lord Diplock admitted that the victim had been 'entirely innocent'[36] but nevertheless accepted that the soldier—who did not of course know this—could reasonably have apprehended what Lord Diplock described as an 'imminent danger to himself and other members of the patrol if the deceased were allowed to get away and join armed fellow-members of the Provisional IRA who might be lurking in the neighbourhood' since this could lead to the 'killing or wounding of members of the patrol by terrorists in ambush', thereby ensuring 'the continuance of the armed insurrection.'[37]

These two cases cannot be written off as relics from a time of past judicial conservatism. Similar to *AG Reference* is *Farrell* v. *Secretary of State for Defence* decided in 1980[38] in which the House accepted that the killing of three men by the army at a bank in Newry was reasonable force in the prevention of crime notwithstanding evidence that the army planning had been such that the only possible way of stopping the men had been by shooting them. And as recently as 1990, a unanimous House overturned the Northern Irish Court of Appeal to restore inquest rules, unique to the Province, the effect of which is to allow members of the security forces to refuse to give evidence at or even to attend inquests into the deaths of civilians in which they are known to have been involved.[39] This reduces such inquests to farcical occasions, and this is all the more serious for the fact that the deaths are often not dealt with through the normal process of prosecution.

These cases, and others similar to them, not only maintain the illiberal status quo; they legitimize that status quo. They give the executive position the stamp of judicial approval. Mr Craig is

---

[34] J. J. Lee, *Ireland 1912–85: Politics and Society* (Cambridge University Press, Cambridge, 1989), 418.

[35] *Attorney-General for Northern Ireland's Reference (No. 1 of 1975)* [1977] AC 105.

[36] Ibid., at p. 136.   [37] Ibid., at p. 138.   [38] [1980] 1 WLR 172.

[39] *McKerr* v. *Armagh Coroner* [1990] 1 WLR 649.

entitled summarily to ban the opposition. The soldiers may shoot people who run away as long as they have the right mistaken frame of mind, and so on. The same was true of the Court of Appeal's decision in early 1988 dismissing the appeal against their conviction by the Birmingham Six.[40] Lord Lane's memorable declaration that the longer the case had proceeded the more convinced he had become of the guilt of the applicants became the official mantra for years afterwards. The Home Secretary refused calls for a fresh inquiry by declaring that the 'Court of Appeal ha[d] carefully reviewed the convictions in this case and ha[d] concluded that they [were] safe.'[41] His Minister of State John Patten was more robust on the floor of the House the following day, when he responded to pressure from the campaigning parliamentarian Chris Mullin by emphasising that after 'long and careful deliberation the Court of Appeal gave its judgment.' Mr Patten went on:

[Mr Mullin] cannot now, in the absence of any indications from the court that he should do so, intervene in these convictions. It is not for him to seek to pass further judgment, quite rightly. He is not a court of law; nor am I; nor, in the strict sense, if I may say so, is the House.[42]

Eventually of course the overwhelming nature of the evidence of the innocence of the men compelled yet another reference to the Court. Their subsequent release more than three years later was a credit to the politicians and the journalists who had fought for their freedom, rather than to the judges who had been instrumental in ensuring that they were kept behind bars. But the protection of the reputation of Lord Lane and his colleagues was not high on the government's agenda when their enthusiastic deference to executive illiberalism had become an embarrassing political liability.

Would the European Convention on Human Rights be an improvement?

Moving on now to the second part of this lecture, the abjectly bad record of the senior British judiciary in this and other areas has led many to argue that the country should incorporate the European

---

[40] R. v. *Callaghan, Independent*, 29 Jan. 1988. The full transcript of the judgment is in the February 1988 issue of the Irish current affairs monthly magazine, *Magill*.
[41] 127 HC Debs. 436 (15 Feb. 1988) (Mr Hurd) (written answer).
[42] 127 HC Debs. 956 (16 Feb. 1988).

Convention on Human Rights into its domestic law.[43] How a problem of judicial weakness can be overcome by putting even more weight on this admittedly weak link is not at all clear. The argument this evening is that—even with the Convention—British judicial decision-making would continue to be negative as regards civil liberties in Northern Ireland. Moreover, it is also argued that the maintenance of illiberal and restrictive laws would be a far more serious matter if it could be done by reference to a human rights charter as famous and as highly regarded as the European Convention on Human Rights. The decisions we have discussed so far have dealt with their own specific points of law; they have not claimed either to be supportive of or inimical to freedom and liberty. But if we were to have the European Convention as part of our law, then the judges would be able to justify executive action by reference not to this or that statute or common law rule but to something much grander—the requirements of 'human rights'. In an inversion of linguistic reality that would have Rousseau turning in his grave, restrictions on our freedom could be presented as *necessitated* by our *commitment* to human rights.

It may be that there are doubts about the evidence for anticipating such a depressing scenario. But we have already had a foretaste of this approach in those cases in which the House of Lords has considered the impact of the Convention, has pretended as it were that it is already part of the law. In *Brind*,[44] for example, in which their lordships unanimously upheld the media ban on Sinn Féin and others, it was quite clear that the ban would still have been upheld even if article 10 had been part of UK law because it would have been considered by the judges to have been 'necessary in a democratic society.' This had already happened in *Spycatcher*[45] and in other illiberal decisions.[46] The strong words employed by the Court in favour of the ban in *Brind* made it that much more

---

[43] There is a good though brief summary of the current debate in J. Rozenberg, *The Search for Justice*, op. cit., 213–17.

[44] *R. v. Secretary of State for the Home Department, ex parte Brind* [1991] 1 AC 696.

[45] *Attorney-General v. Guardian Newspapers Ltd.; Attorney-General v. Observer Ltd.; Attorney-General v. Times Newspapers Ltd.* [1987] 1 WLR 1248, especially Lord Templeman at pp. 1296–1300. The eventual decision in Strasbourg on the first two of these cases resulted in a qualified victory for the newspapers: *Observer and Guardian v. United Kingdom* (1991) 14 EHRR 153.

[46] See for example *In Re an Inquiry under the Company Securities (Insider Dealing) Act 1985* [1988] AC 660, especially Lord Griffiths at p. 706.

difficult to get rid of. If its supporters could have invoked in its favour a judicial determination that it was 'necessary in a democratic society' it might well have been even more difficult to remove.

Nor when we turn to the actual words in the Convention and the European case-law that has accompanied it do we find much scope for hoping that incorporation would compel the judges to take a more liberal line. It is almost certain for example that the House of Lords in *Brind* was right and that the media ban was not an infringment of article 10. In *Purcell v. Ireland*,[47] a TV and radio ban on Sinn Féin even more draconian than our own was held to be so obviously in compliance with article 10 that the case was thrown out at the Commission stage as manifestly ill-founded. So a ban on political speech did not even raise an arguable case under the Convention's freedom of expression clause! Various experts are currently ransacking the Convention for evidence of a right to silence, and the following dicta from a customs' case in Strasbourg, *Funke v. France*,[48] appears to offer some promising ground:

The special features of customs law cannot justify such an infringment of the right of anyone 'charged with a criminal offence' within the autonomous meaning of this expression in Article 6, to remain silent and not to contribute to incriminating itself (*sic*).[49]

It remains to be seen how this *dicta* will be applied in the context of Northern Ireland. The truth is that the Convention is an open-textured document which is rarely unequivocal or unstinting in its support for freedom and liberty. It should not surprise us therefore that the record both of the European Commission and the European Court on Northern Ireland is distinctly mixed. Of course there is the celebrated case of *Ireland v. United Kingdom*,[50] which held that sensory deprivation when used as an aid to interrogation violated article 3's prohibition of 'inhuman or degrading treatment or punishment'. The Court and particularly the Commission have been rightly applauded by the human rights community for this courageous stand. But not nearly enough of the credit had been given to the Irish Government which withstood immense diplomatic pressure from Britain to take their close neighbour to Strasbourg on an issue of principle. The effect of this was that the case was one in which a State was bound to lose. It was

---

[47] (1991) 12 HRLJ 254. [48] (1993) 16 EHRR 297. [49] Ibid., at para. 44.
[50] (1978) 2 EHRR 25.

not a normal individual v. State case. Neither the Commission nor the Court could avoid offending a Government; it was a question of which one.

In stark contrast to *Ireland* v. *UK* is *Donnelly* v. *UK*[51] decided three years before in which the complaint by seven applicants of a 'continuing administrative practice' of ill-treatment whilst in detention in Northern Ireland was rejected because of the availability of domestic remedies. The applicants in the case had sued the Crown and four of them had received damages when the case was decided by the Commission, with the other three cases pending before the local courts. So an individual trying to make the same points as in *Ireland* v. *UK* would have been told to sue the authorities in the local courts. This would surely have destroyed any individual applicant trying to make the same case as was made on their behalf by the Irish Government in the Inter-State application. Donnelly did not get past the Commission and this is often the stage at which Northern Irish applications fall.[52] In *X* v. *UK*[53] an IRA prisoner was held in solitary confinement for approximately 760 days. The Commission held this practice to be 'unusual' and 'undesirable'[54] but not to be in breach of article 3. The case was rejected as manifestly ill-founded. In a later case, the Commission upheld a law which allowed a prison officer to listen in on conversations between a prisoner and his wife on a prison visit—it was an interference with privacy which was necessary in a democratic society in the interests of public safety, for the prevention of disorder or crime or for the protection of the rights and freedoms of others.[55] In *Stewart* v. *UK*,[56] the Commission held the death of a thirteen year old as a result of being hit by a plastic bullet fired by the army to be justified under article 2, having regard to all the circumstances of the case.

When one turns to the judgments of the Court in this area, one finds a record that is if anything even more depressing. In *Fox, Campbell and Hartley* v. *United Kingdom*,[57] two of the applicants

---

[51] (1975) 4 D & R 4.
[52] See generally B. Dickson, 'The European Convention on Human Rights and Northern Ireland' in J. Velu (ed.), *Présence du Droit Public et des Droits de L'Homme* (University of Brussels, Brussels, 1992), 1407.
[53] (1980) 21 D & R 95. [54] Ibid., at para. 11.
[55] *X* v. *United Kingdom* (1978) 14 D & R 246.
[56] Application No. 10044/82 reported at (1984) 7 EHRR 409.
[57] (1990) 13 EHRR 157.

were arrested at 3.40pm and questioned between 8.15pm and
10pm. The third was arrested at 7.55am and questioned between
11.05am and 12.15pm. All three naturally relied on article 5(2) of
the Convention which declares that '[e]veryone who is arrested
shall be informed promptly . . . of the reasons for his arrest,' since
it was admitted that no such reasons had been given in these cases.
Despite this, the court found that that there had been no breach of
article 5(2). This is how they justified their decision:

[F]ollowing their arrest all of the applicants were interrogated by the
police about their suspected involvement in specific criminal acts and their
suspected membership of proscribed organisations. There is no ground to
suppose that these interrogations were not such as to enable the applicants
to understand why they had been arrested. The reasons why they were
suspected of being terrorists were thereby brought to their attention during
their interrogation.[58]

This creative approach to communication still left the long
period after arrest and before interrogation during which no adequate information had been conveyed. All that the Court said
about this was that 'In the context of the present case these inter-
vals of a few hours cannot be regarded as falling outside the constraints of time imposed by the notion of promptness in article
5(2).'[59] That was the extent of the reasoning offered in favour of
the Court's upholding of the Government's argument.

Now there are two aspects to this case which are of particular
interest. First, the Court's decision on this point overturned the
Commission's findings which had been in the applicants' favour.
So even where the Commission is unfavourable to a State, its
lawyers are allowed this important second bite at the legal cherry.
No such opportunity is accorded to applicants who fall at the first
hurdle. Secondly, the Court ruled against the Government on a
subsidiary issue, namely the requirement that an arrest should be
based on a 'reasonable suspicion' rather than on an honest belief
which was all that was then required by the Northern Irish law.
But this decision is less path-breaking than it appears when one
takes into account the fact that the law had been modified before
the *Fox* case so as to require just such a reasonable suspicion.[60]
What looks like courageous judicial intervention is in fact little

[58] (1990) 13 EHRR 157, at para. 41.   [59] Ibid., at para. 42.
[60] The domestic legal background is set out at ibid., para. 22.

more than a confirmation that a reform in the law that had already taken place was required—hardly the stuff of civil libertarian dreams. The meat of this case was in the article 5(2) point about reasons, and here it is submitted that the judgment of the Court was found severely wanting.

The version of the meaning of 'promptness' offered in *Fox* seems at odds with the earlier and justly celebrated decision in *Brogan* v. *United Kingdom*,[61] in which the Court had held by a majority of twelve to seven that seven day detention under the prevention of terrorism legislation was a breach of article 5(3)'s requirement that arrested persons be brought 'promptly before a judge or other officer authorised by law to exercise judicial power.' But look at the sequel to *Brogan*. The Government derogated from the Convention, arguing under article 15 that seven day detention was necessitated by a 'public emergency threatening the life of the nation'. In a decision in May 1993, *Brannigan and McBride* v. *United Kingdom*[62] (which incidentally received almost no publicity in the national press in contrast to the lavish praise heaped on *Brogan* by the various journalist-advocates of incorporation), the Court upheld the Government's action by twenty-two votes to four. This was an area in which the national authorities were—according to the Court—to be accorded a 'wide margin of appreciation'. It was left to Judge Walsh in dissent to argue that the life of the nation as opposed to a region was not under threat and that there was no evidence that the operation of the courts in either Northern Ireland or Great Britain had been restricted or affected by the 'war or public emergency'. It was merely in his view the case that the executive wished 'to restrict the operation of the courts'.[63] The upshot of this case is that seven day detention has been rubber-stamped by the highest Human Rights Court in Europe. It may be in the form of a derogation certainly, but nevertheless the Government has the high-minded excuse for the maintenance of this illiberal law— namely that they are preserving the life of their nation. And we no longer have to take their word for it—twenty-two human rights judges have legitimized their action, by finding in their favour in a challenge to their authority. It was not surprising that, in the first

---

[61] (1989) 11 EHRR 117.

[62] *Brannigan and McBride* v. *United Kingdom*, Decision of the European Court of Human Rights, 26 May 1993.

[63] Ibid., at para. 3 of Judge Walsh's dissenting judgment.

debate on the renewal of the prevention of terrorism legislation to take place after the ruling, the Home Secretary Mr Howard should have drawn liberally from the majority judgement.[64]

The British judges and the politics of Northern Ireland

We do not even need to speculate on which side of the line most British judges would have found themselves in *Fox, Brogan* and *Brannigan*. But if Britain were to incorporate the Convention, then domestic judgments adverse to liberty would be that much harder to unravel in Strasbourg not only on account of the conservatism of the Strasbourg court but also because of the respect that Court shows to domestic courts, both through their requirement that local remedies be exhausted (which would make challenges very much more expensive) and through the operation of their 'margin of appreciation'. So incorporation would make the slight chance of success in Strasbourg that bit more remote. And at the same time it would of course greatly increase the opportunities for the judicial legitimization of illiberalism.

In trying to guess at how good our judges would be at applying the Convention domestically, we do not have to restrict ourselves to speculation about cases that have not yet been decided. There is evidence right at our doorstep, empirical evidence, of the attitude of the British judges when confronted by issues of human rights in Northern Ireland. Moreover it is evidence of how the judges behave when freed from the constraints imposed on them by precedent, by statute and by the narrowness of the common law, in other words when they are liberated from the supposed 'ethical aimlessness' of the common law. What is being referred to here, of course, are the many judicial inquiries that have been undertaken since the troubles first broke out. The United Kingdom had long had a fondness for judicial involvement in politics. It is judges who oversee the security services[65] and official telephone tapping.[66] Lord Scarman has inves-

---

[64] The debate is at 239 HC Debs. 291–338 (9 March 1994). Mr. Howard's comments are at ibid., 297.

[65] See for examples of such reports *Report of the Security Commission*, Cmnd. 8876 (1983); *Report of the Security Commission*, Cmnd. 9514 (1985).

[66] See for examples of such reports *Interception of Communications Act 1985. Report by the Commissioner for 1986*, Cm. 108 (1987); *Interception of Communications Act 1985. Report by the Commissioner for 1987*, Cm. 351 (1988).

tigated the origins of inner city rioting,[67] and Lord Woolf has analysed the cause of prison disturbances.[68] It was to a judge, Lord Denning, that Harold Macmillan turned during the Profumo scandal,[69] when he needed 'kindness . . . at a very difficult and delicate time', as he explained in a letter to the judge on his retirement from the bench.[70] Such a letter could equally well have been penned by any of Britain's last five Prime Minister's to the many judges that have investigated Northern Ireland. One of the first significant examples of this form of executive dependency on the judiciary came after the disaster of Bloody Sunday on 30 January 1972, when thirteen civilians were killed and a like number injured when the army opened fire during a demonstration in Derry. The key question was why the army had fired. The day after the event, the Home Secretary Mr Maudling explained to the Commons that there had been disorder at the march and that the General Officer Commanding had reported that 'when the Army [had]advanced to make arrests among the trouble-makers they [had come] under fire from a block of flats and other quarters'.[71] Returning this fire the army had 'inflicted a number of casualties on those who were attacking them with firearms and with bombs'.[72]

This statement was extremely controversial and Mr Maudling conceded the need for an inquiry which Merlyn Rees for the opposition stressed had to be 'impartial' and—in his words—'entirely judicial'.[73] The next day the Prime Minister Mr Heath announced in the Commons that '[t]he House [would] be glad to know that the Lord Chief Justice of England, Lord Widgery, ha[d] consented to undertake the inquiry'[74] and that he would sit alone. Mr Wilson for Labour welcomed his appointment, and the Liberal leader declared that the involvement of Lord Widgery would 'guarantee a full, impartial, judicial inquiry'.[75] The establishment of the inquiry as a Tribunal of Enquiry under the 1921 Act had the consequence, convenient to Government, that the law of contempt immediately applied to the whole issue, thereby preventing any further public discussion of the incident pending the Lord Chief Justice's

---

[67] Lord Scarman *The Brixton Disorders, 10–12 April 1981: Report of an Inquiry by the Rt. Hon. Lord Scarman*, Cmnd. 8427 (1981).

[68] Lord Woolf, *Prison Disturbances, April 1990*, Cm. 1456 (1991).

[69] Lord Denning, *Lord Denning's Report*, Cmnd. 2152 (1963).

[70] I. Freeman, *Lord Denning: A Life* (Hutchinson, London, 1993), 298.

[71] 830 HC Debs. 32 (31 Jan. 1972).   [72] Ibid., 33.   [73] Ibid.

[74] Ibid., 241 (1 Feb. 1972).   [75] Ibid., 243 (Mr Thorpe).

Report.[76] Efforts to raise Bloody Sunday in Parliament in the weeks after its occurrence were ruled out of order by the Speaker[77] and the public were similarly constrained. A vital political issue was thereby effectively removed from public debate. In the event, Lord Widgery's report[78] declared the judge to be 'entirely satisfied that the first firing . . . was directed at the soldiers'.[79] In a line evocative of Lord Denning's later infamous 'appalling vista' statement in the appeal of the Guildford Four,[80] the Lord Chief Justice declared that '[i]f the soldiers are wrong they were parties in a lying conspiracy which must have come to light in the rigorous cross-examination to which they were subjected'.[81] There was 'no reason to suppose that the soldiers would have opened fire if they had not been fired upon first'.[82] Moreover, while some of the dead and injured were clearly innocent, Lord Widgery considered that there was 'a strong suspicion that some others had been firing weapons or handling bombs in the course of the afternoon and that yet others had been closely supporting them'.[83]

For present purposes, there are two points of interest about Lord Widgery's report. First, it effectively finished Bloody Sunday as a party political issue at Westminster. The Government of course accepted his findings.[84] The shadow Home Secretary Mr Callaghan commented in the House that '[t]hese tragic events belong in the past.'[85] A Unionist member suggested that the report had 'exploded some of the myths surrounding the so-called "Bloody Sunday"'.[86] When a Nationalist MP suggested that the Report was a 'spurious and desperate attempt' at 'whitewash', he was interrupted from all sides of the House with members shouting 'Have you read the Report?'[87] The second interesting thing about Widgery is that what

---

[76] See Mr Heath's remarks at ibid., 244. On the contempt law relating to such tribunals, see the *Report of the Interdepartmental Committee on the Law of Contempt as it affects Tribunals of Enquiry*, (Chairman: Salmon LJ), Cmnd. 4078 (1969).

[77] See the interchange between the Speaker and two members of the House, Mr A. E. P. Duffy and Mr J. Biggs-Davison, at 831 HC Debs. 594–6 (17 Feb. 1972).

[78] Lord Widgery, *Report of the Tribunal Appointed to Inquire into the Events on Sunday, 30 January 1972, which Led to Loss of Life in Connection with the Procession in Londonderry on that day* (HL 101; HC 220 of 1972).

[79] Ibid., para. 54.

[80] *McIlkenny v. Chief Constable of the West Midlands* [1980] 2 WLR 689.

[81] Widgery, *Report*, para. 54.

[82] Ibid., para. 7 of the summary of conclusions.

[83] Ibid., para 10 of the summary of conclusions.

[84] 835 HC Debs. 519 (19 April 1972) (Mr Heath).   [85] Ibid., 521.

[86] Ibid., 522.   [87] Ibid., 526. The member was Mr Frank McManus.

is still called by many nationalists the Widgery whitewash did more to alienate nationalist opinion from the rule of law than almost any other single judicial or (in this case) quasi-judicial event. The insinuation that some of the dead had been attacking the soldiers was regarded as peculiarly offensive and insulting to the relatives of the deceased, and this finding has since been disowned by the Government. In a letter to the MP for the area, John Hume, the present Prime Minister has acknowledged that all those shot 'should be regarded as innocent of any allegation that they were shot while handling firearms and explosives'.[88] As was the case with Lord Lane, the executive has paid less attention to the (in this case posthumous) reputation of a Lord Chief Justice than was paid by the same man to the army's reputation twenty years before.

The Widgery Report was by no means a one-off event. An inquiry the previous year into allegations of the ill-treatment of internees had been headed by the Parliamentary Commissioner (or ombudsman), Sir Edmund Compton, a man whose independence was established in Parliament by the Prime Minister's assurance that 'his capacity [was] that of a judge.'[89] The report duly found the various practices of sensory deprivation then engaged in by the army to be 'physical ill-treatment' but not 'brutality'.[90] This permitted the Home Secretary to declare in Parliament that he could not 'think of any country in the world where such a standard of thoroughness and impartiality would have been maintained'.[91] As if to prove this, a further report was commissioned on the general appropriateness of these interrogation procedures, which we should remind ourselves involved wall-standing, hooding, continuous noise, deprivation of food and deprivation of sleep. This inquiry was headed by the former Lord Chief Justice Lord Parker who together with J. A. Boyd-Carpenter concluded that such sensory deprivation might well amount to criminal and civil assaults[92] but

[88] See the statement by Michael Mates MP, issued by the Northern Ireland Information Service on 28 Jan. 1993, which quotes from the Prime Minister's letter to Mr Hume.

[89] 823 HC Debs. 324 (23 Sept. 1971).

[90] Sir Edmund Compton, *Report of the Enquiry into Allegations against the Security Forces of Physical Brutality in Northern Ireland Arising out of the Events on 9 August 1971*, Cmnd. 4823 (1971), para. 105.

[91] 826 HC Debs. 438 (17 Nov. 1971).

[92] Lord Parker, *Report of the Committee of Privy Counsellors Appointed to Consider Authorised Procedures for the Interrogation of Persons Suspected of Terrorism*, Cmnd. 4901 (1972), para. 2.

that 'there [was] no reason to rule out these techniques on moral grounds'[93] and that it was 'possible to operate them in a manner consistent with the highest standards of our society'.[94] It was left to the sole dissentient, Lord Gardiner, to condemn such conduct as 'secret, illegal, not morally justifiable and alien to the traditions of what' he believed 'still to be the greatest democracy in the world'.[95] When the Parker report was published, the Government gave an undertaking that it would not in future engage in such practices.[96] It was reacting to international pressure, to the Strasbourg court action that had just been initiated by the Irish government and to the widespread public revulsion to such practices being carried out within the United Kingdom. The 'moral guidance' offered by the majority Parker report was no part of that pressure. Again as with Lord Widgery in 1972, and Lord Lane with the Birmingham Six, the executive was resiling from the illiberal option that had been presented to it by a Lord Chief Justice.

Our last example of judicial involvement in politics from the early 1970s is the most famous of all, the Diplock Commission,[97] established in 1972 when it had become apparent to the executive that internment was not a long term solution to Northern Ireland's security problems and that there was a need therefore for a fresh way of tackling violent subversion. Usually a judicial report adopts a 'balanced' lawyerly approach, accepting the status quo in principle with this or that minor recommendation for change to prove at least a little radical mettle and justify its existence. Diplock was different. The Commission favoured the continuation of internment (now renamed executive detention and with—predictably—a former Lord Justice of Appeal Sir Gordon Willmer as chair of the newly established Detention Appeal Tribunal). But Diplock also suggested a series of radical changes to the criminal justice system in Northern Ireland so as to facilitate the conviction of accused persons—abolition of the right to trial by jury for a whole range of serious offences, the reversal of the burden of proof for many offences, restrictions on the right to bail, new powers of arrest,

[93] Lord Parker, *Report of the Committee of Privy Counsellors Appointed to Consider Authorised Procedures for the Interrogation of Persons Suspected of Terrorism*, Cmnd. 4901 (1972), para 34.
[94] Ibid.   [95] Ibid., para. 21 of the Minority Report.
[96] 832 HC Debs. 743–9 (2 March 1972) (Mr Heath).
[97] Lord Diplock, *Report of the Commission to Consider Legal Procedures to Deal with Terrorist Activities in Northern Ireland*, Cmnd. 5185 (1972).

and a dilution of the rule on the admissibility of confession evidence. The Dictionary of National Biography suggests that the 'speed and certainty of the[se] recommendations were principally due to the guidance and clarity of the . . . Chairman'.[98] Speed there certainly was—the Commission took less than two months to report and Lord Diplock made no more than two visits to Northern Ireland, meeting only security forces personnel on each occasion.

We need make just two observations about these revolutionary proposals. First, Lord Diplock rationalised his recommendations explicitly by reference to the European Convention on Human Rights. He modified the law on confession evidence by invoking article 3 in his support.[99] He drew attention to article 6 which guaranteed what he referred to as the 'minimum requirements for a criminal trial in normal times.'[100] Since it covered none of the rights which he proposed to dispense with, they could in his view therefore all the more legitimately be jettisoned. In the hands of Lord Diplock, the Convention was turned from a charter of rights into a yardstick of repression. Secondly, the magic name of Lord Diplock made the dramatic changes in the law which followed his Report much easier to steer through Parliament. The Secretary of State for Northern Ireland, Mr Whitelaw, thought strong reasons were needed to abolish trial by jury and it was 'not with pleasure that we have concluded that those reasons are convincingly' set-out in Diplock.[101] The changes to the law on confession evidence were necessary for what Mr Whitelaw called 'technical reasons' which were he said 'fully explained' in Diplock.[102] The Attorney-General intervened to say that Lord Diplock was 'not a man who would be slow to uphold the principles of law'.[103] Even the opposition was stymied, with Merlyn Rees being reduced to saying that the report was 'extremely valuable to us today'.[104] It was left to Bernadette Devlin to remind the House that Diplock was 'only one learned Gentleman.'[105]

This last point seems the key one. The House was debating

---

[98] *Dictionary of National Biography, 1981–85*, 115.

[99] Diplock, Report, para. 90.   [100] Ibid., para. 12.

[101] 855 HC Debs. 281 (17 April 1973) (Mr Whitelaw). The second reading Commons debate on the Northern Ireland (Emergency Provisions) Act 1973 is at ibid., 275–392.

[102] Ibid., 283.   [103] Ibid., 380 (Sir Peter Rawlinson).

[104] Ibid., 294.   [105] Ibid., 305.

Diplock, not the merits of the changes he proposed, just as the House had earlier 'debated' Widgery and Parker. Diplock's recommendations may or may not have been right but their pseudo-judicial status protected them from proper political scrutiny. Far from dying out with time, this pattern of executive dependence on judicial approval has become institutionalised in recent years. The secret services are regularly strengthened by judicial inquiries exonerating them of any wrongdoing and the prevention of terrorism legislation and emergency provisions law have been legitimized for years now by the circuit judge Lord Colville, whose terms of reference require him to accept the need for both Acts but whose annual reports are routinely trumpeted by the executive as evidence of independent scrutiny.[106] Any suggestions for broadening the law that the judge makes are invariably acted upon by government, but most of his substantive civil libertarian points are summarily dismissed. Thus neither of his recommendations in relation to the ending of the internment[107] and exclusion order powers[108] has been accepted and when he advised that a tribunal should oversee seven day detention,[109] the Home Secretary publicly snubbed him by declaring in Parliament simply that 'the Government's answer [was] no'.[110] But his idea of a new offence of 'going equipped for terrorism' was gratefully seized upon and placed (in an expanded form) in the 1991 Act.[111] Parliamentary debates in the House of Commons are absurd games in which both sides ransack Lord Colville's reports for evidence to underpin their predetermined arguments.

---

[106] The most important Colville reports are *Review of the Operation of the Prevention of Terrorism (Temporary Provisions) Act 1984*, Cm. 264 (1987) and *Review of the Northern Ireland (Emergency Provisions) Acts 1978 and 1987*, Cm. 1115 (1990). Lord Colville has recently been replaced as the annual reviewer of anti-terrorism legislation by J. J. Rowe QC, whose first report on the operation in 1993 of the Prevention of Terrorism (Temporary Provisions) Act 1989 was presented to the Home Secretary early in 1994.

[107] Contained in *Review*, Cm. 1115 (1990), para. 11.9.

[108] Contained in *Review*, Cm. 264 (1987), para. 11.6.1.

[109] In his *Report on the Operation in 1990 of the Prevention of Terrorism (Temporary Provisions) Act 1989*, presented to the Home Secretary in 1991.

[110] 187 HC Debs. 24 (4 Mar. 1991) (Mr Baker).

[111] Northern Ireland (Emergency Provisions) Act 1991, s. 30. The original recommendation is in Colville, Review, Cm. 1115 (1990), para. 2.7.

Conclusion

The central thesis of this lecture may be summarised by way of an anecdote. Last year I made many of these points at a weekend conference in Northern Ireland sponsored by the Standing Advisory Commission on Human Rights. As you may know the Commission is keen on incorporating the Convention,[112] and all the constitutional parties in the Province are in favour of some sort of bill of rights. I only convinced one person in the room—but in an unexpected way. This was the Northern Ireland Office's senior civil servant on law and order issues. He intervened directly after my presentation to say that I had gone a long way towards persuading him of the *value* of incorporation. Then turning to the human rights advocates in the room he said that the lesson of my talk was that the civil libertarians had to take the rough with the smooth, and accept their defeats as well as their victories.

There are three further points by way of conclusion. First, it may be tempting to dismiss the pessimistic analysis provided here because of the subject that has been chosen. Certainly, Northern Ireland is a special case, a 'difficult' area, to which different considerations will always apply. But surely it is in precisely the difficult areas that civil liberties—or 'human rights'—matter most? What good is this whole subject if it is strong on protecting corporate interests and great when it comes to one-off examples of misguided or absurd state repression, but unavailable in situations of real civil libertarian crisis? And that is often the case with human rights as exemplified in the ECHR—look at the record of defeat for asylum seekers, for trade unions, or for supporters of communist parties.[113] Northern Ireland is central to civil liberties; it is only embarrassment at the leeway we give the executive that leads us to describe it as peripheral.

Secondly, the fact that the judges and the cases described here have operated as legitimizers of state restriction should not blind us to the gains that have been achieved. We live in a pluralist not an authoritarian society. Government needs legitimization, and their wonderful weakness in this respect is our democratic

[112] See its *Bill of Rights: A Discussion Paper* (1976) and its influential *The Protection of Human Rights by Law in Northern Ireland*, Cmnd. 7009 (1977).

[113] See generally C. A. Gearty, 'The European Court of Human Rights and the Protection of Civil Liberties: An Overview' [1993] *CLJ* 89.

strength.[114] Lord Gardiner's marvellous dissent in the Parker Report[115] was of vital importance, as was his own report some years later.[116] His Honour Judge Bennett bravely took on the police in the late seventies in the area of police brutality.[117] Lord Colville has added to the pressure that has produced some give from Government, in the form of codes of practices regulating the behaviour of the security forces[118] and the appointment of an overseer of army complaints[119] and an independent visitor to holding centres to check on detention practices in Northern Ireland.[120] But these advances for liberty result from pressure being put on government from many quarters—the opposition, the press, bodies such as the Standing Advisory Commission, brave individual police officers who tell the truth, police surgeons who do likewise. Of course the fact that the Government looks to judges to legitimize its activities occasionally adds to the pressure for reform which is part and parcel of our democratic culture. But the general truth remains, that the judges invariably deliver what the executive of the day requires.

Finally it might be thought that this lecture amounts to a strong criticism of the judiciary. This is not entirely the case. It is the job of judges to uphold the status quo. They are schooled in law and order. To expect them to subvert authority is like asking the headmaster to disrupt a teacher's class. The real critics of the judiciary are those liberals who see the judges as the route to a magically just and fair society, as capable, if only they flexed their creative muscles, of transforming the relationship between the individual and the State. It is these people who must be bitter and crestfallen at being so consistently and apparently wilfully let down. I do not believe that this constitutional nirvana—or anything like it—is around the corner. Human rights are 'human' and they are ours to fight for—they are not for others to guarantee on our behalf. To believe that they are is to create a system in which the costs of human rights outweigh the benefits.

[114] E. P. Thompson, *Whigs and Hunters* (Penguin, London, 1990), ch. 10.

[115] Lord Parker, *Report*, op. cit.

[116] Lord Gardiner, *Report of a Committee to Consider, in the Context of Civil Liberties and Human Rights, Measures to Deal with Terrorism in Northern Ireland*, Cmnd. 5847 (1975).

[117] His Honour H. G. Bennett QC, *Report of a Committee of Inquiry into Police Interrogation Procedures in Northern Ireland*, Cmnd. 7497 (1979).

[118] Northern Ireland (Emergency Provisions) Act 1991, ss. 61, 62.

[119] Northern Ireland (Emergency Provisions) Act 1991, s. 60.

[120] Sir Louis Blom-Cooper, *First Annual Report of the Independent Commissioner for the Holding Centres* (Northern Ireland Office, Belfast, 1994).

SECRECY, DIGNITY, OR AUTONOMY? VIEWS OF PRIVACY AS A CIVIL LIBERTY

David Feldman[1]

In a well-known poem, we are told of an Ancyent Marinere who stops a guest on the way to a wedding, and insists on telling him a story.

> He holds him with a skinny hand,
>   Quoth he, there was a Ship—
> 'Now get thee hence, thou grey-beard Loon!
>   Or my Staff shall make thee skip.[']
>
> He holds him with his glittering eye—
>   The wedding guest stood still
> And listens like a three year's child;
>   The Marinere hath his will.
>
> The wedding-guest sate on a stone,
>   He cannot chuse but hear;
> And thus spake on that ancyent man,
>   The bright-eyed Marinere.[2]

Did this breach of good manners on the part of the Marinere also amount to an infringement of the wedding-guest's privacy? True, it

[1] Barber Professor of Jurisprudence, University of Birmingham. I am grateful to Lord Lester of Herne Hill QC, Bernadette Lynch, and Michael Thomson for their comments and for suggesting a number of additional issues and sources, and to the participants at the Annual Conference of the University of Wales Law Departments in November 1993 and at a seminar in the University of Birmingham in January 1994 for the opportunity to clarify some of my views. Remaining errors and obscurities are my responsibility.

[2] Samuel Taylor Coleridge, 'The Rime of the Ancyent Marinere', in William Wordsworth and Samuel Taylor Coleridge, *Lyrical Ballads* (edited by W. J. B. Owen, in *Wordsworth and Coleridge: Lyrical Ballands 1798*, corrected reprint of 2nd edn. [Oxford: Oxford University Press, 1971], pp. 7–32), lines 9–20.

all happened in a public place, and the guest had earlier consented to listen to a 'laughsome tale'. But he was then prevented from choosing to leave, and the tale turned out to be anything but laughsome. It was so harrowing that after it:

> He went, like one that hath been stunn'd
> And is of sense forlorn[.][3]

To assess the scope of the wedding-guest's legitimate expectation of privacy, we need a theoretical framework by which to evaluate privacy-related interests and decide how far the law should protect them. The discussion which follows offers such a framework. This has practical importance because, despite the general reluctance of judges in England and Wales to recognize a right to privacy as such, there is already a considerable body of privacy law, albeit under-theorized. Its rapid growth may soon be further spurred on by legislation, and a sound basis of principle is needed to guide its development.

Privacy in the law

In its classic formulation as a right to be let alone,[4] privacy comes closer than any other right to the essence of liberty itself. In the United States of America it has been developed to enable the Supreme Court to strike down laws banning the sale of contraceptives to married couples,[5] and forbidding, or imposing undue burdens on, the exercise of a woman's freedom to obtain an abortion;[6]

[3] 'Rime', lines 655–656.

[4] The expression was adopted by Gray J. in *Union Pacific Railway Co. v. Botsford*, 141 US 250 (1891) at p. 251 from Thomas Cooley, *The Law of Torts*, 2nd edn., 1888, p. 29. Cooley derived the right to be let alone largely from English common law, particularly nineteenth-century cases on medical treatment. This suggests that it would have been possible to develop a comprehensive right to privacy at common law in England, embracing rights to space, personal integrity and dignity, as well as control over information on the basis of *Prince Albert v. Strange* (1849) 2 De Gex & Sm. 652; 1 Mac. & G. 25 (the case on which Warren and Brandeis principally relied). However, the US Supreme Court, by a majority, refused to extend the right to be free of unwanted medical treatment into a constitutional guarantee that patients in a persistent vegetative state would not be treated and nourished against their presumed wishes: *Cruzan v. Director, Missouri Department of Health*, 497 US 261, 111 L. Ed. 2d 224 (1990).

[5] *Griswold v. Connecticut*, 381 US 479 (1965).

[6] *Roe v. Wade*, 410 US 113 (1973); *Webster v. Reproductive Health Services*, 109 S. Ct. 3040 (1989); *Planned Parenthood of South East Pennsylvania v. Casey*, 122 S. Ct. 2791 (1992).

and to impose due process requirements on wiretapping.[7] Controls on unreasonable search and seizure, originally protecting private property, have been re-theorized on the basis of privacy rights in both the USA and Canada.[8] Although the U.S. Supreme Court decided against using privacy to invalidate statutes forbidding buggery (at least as between males),[9] the European Court of Human Rights has deployed the right to respect for private life under Article 8 of the European Convention on Human Rights to uphold both a right for consenting adults to participate privately in homosexual practices[10] and, in certain circumstances, a right to have a surgical reassignment of sex recognized by the state for official purposes.[11]

State respect for privacy rights, required under the European Convention on Human Rights, is an important driving force behind the development of both common law and statute in this country. While statute does not generally create rights to privacy, it can and increasingly does provide a regime for protecting privacy interests against unjustified intrusion. For example, the Interception of Communications Act 1985 imposed a statutory regime for controlling and monitoring the authorization of telephone and mail interceptions. The Act did not confer a right to privacy, but imposed criminal sanctions on those who conduct unauthorized interceptions, and established mechanisms—a Tribunal and a Commissioner—for reviewing allegations that warrants for interceptions have been improperly issued. The Act was passed in response to the decision of the European Court of Human Rights in *Malone* v. *United Kingdom*[12] that the previous procedural controls on interceptions had failed to meet the criteria for justifying infringements of the right to respect for private life and correspondence under

---

[7] *Katz* v. *United States*, 389 US 347 (1969).

[8] Ibid.; *Hunter* v. *Southam Inc.* (1984) 11 DLR (4th) 641; *Kokesch* v. *R* (1990) 1 CR (4th) 62.

[9] *Bowers* v. *Hardwick*, 478 US 186 (1986).

[10] *Dudgeon* v. *United Kingdom*, Eur. Ct. HR, Series A, No. 45, Judgment of 23 September 1981; 4 EHRR 149. See Sheldon Leader, 'The Right to Privacy, the Enforcement of Morals, and the Judicial Function: An Argument' (1990) 43 *Current Legal Problems* 115–34; Robert Wintemute, 'Sexual Orientation Discrimination', in Christopher McCrudden and Gerald Chambers (eds.), *Individual Rights and the Law in Britain* (Oxford: Clarendon Press and The Law Society, 1994), pp. 491–533.

[11] *B.* v. *France*, Eur. Ct. HR, Series A, No. 232-C, Judgment of 25 March 1992, 16 EHRR 1. On the caselaw of the Court on this subject see David Feldman, *Civil Liberties and Human Rights in England and Wales* (Oxford: Clarendon Press, 1993), pp. 495–510.

[12] Eur. Ct. HR, Series A, No. 82, Judgment of 2 August 1984, 7 EHRR 14.

Article 8 of the European Convention on Human Rights. While the common law had accepted that there was a legitimate interest in maintaining privacy in telephone and mail communications, the constraints had not been placed on an adequate legal footing, and no legal remedy was offered for abuse.[13] As Lord Jauncey has said, 'The mischief which the Act was intended to deal with was accordingly the lack of a clear statutory framework within which telephone-tapping could take place and the lack of any form of redress for someone claiming that his telephone had been wrongly tapped.'[14] It can therefore properly be regarded as part of the UK's law of privacy, because recognizing a legitimate interest in privacy either at common law or by way of the European Convention on Human Rights was a necessary condition, both before the Act and after it, for justifying legal controls over interference with it.

Similarly, the need for an effective remedy for infringements of the right to respect for private life, the home, and family life, justified (if, indeed, it did not require) making it feasible to obtain substantial exemplary damages in County Courts for unlawful eviction and harassment by landlords by replacing a £5,000 limit on damages awards in the County Court with a £50,000 limit.[15] It also justified the provision in the Housing Act 1988, sections 27 and 28, of damages assessed on the basis of the gain to the landlord, rather than loss to the tenant, where tenants are illegally evicted from premises or leave because of harassment.[16]

Common law, too, recognizes privacy. The growth of tortious pri-

---

[13] In *Malone* v. *Commissioner of Police of the Metropolis* [1979] Ch. 344 Megarry V-C had accepted the legitimacy of such an interest, particularly in the light of the European Convention on Human Rights, but held that English law provided no remedy for its infringement. In *R.* v. *Secretary of State for the Home Department, ex parte Ruddock* [1987] 1 WLR 1482 it was held that the privacy interest potentially justified requiring the executive to honour its published statements as to the circumstances in which interceptions would be authorized. Remedies would have been available in judicial review proceedings on the basis of the doctrine of legitimate expectations, although the applicants failed to establish their claim on the evidence. (In the light of the Act, no such remedy would now be available.)

[14] *R.* v. *Preston* [1993] 4 All ER 638 at p. 645. Lord Mustill said, 'We thus see the mischief against which the 1985 Act was aimed: to clarify and place on a sound statutory footing a system of interception whose existing tight constraints were not to be weakened.' (Ibid., at p. 650.)

[15] High Court and County Courts Jurisdiction Order 1991, SI 1991 No. 724, Art. 2, para. 1(1).

[16] For discussion, see Law Commission Consultation Paper No. 132, *Aggravated, Exemplary and Restitutionary Damages* (London: HMSO, 1993), pp. 61–2.

vacy rights in the USA stemmed largely from English decisions, not only in *Prince Albert* v. *Strange*,[17] on which Warren and Brandeis relied heavily in their 1890 article,[18] but also in a number of nineteenth-century cases on medical treatment which led the American academic and judge Thomas Cooley to formulate a right to be let alone as a common law right.[19] The creativity with which American judges built on these cases has not in the past been mirrored in England and Wales, where judges have persistently refused to recognize a right to privacy as such. In *Kaye* v. *Robertson*,[20] the Court of Appeal held that it had no power to grant a remedy for infringement of privacy where journalists intruded on a well-known actor in hospital, taking photographs of him in a severely injured state for publication, without his consent, although the court granted an injunction on the not wholly convincing ground that the publication represented an injurious falsehood. In *Airedale NHS Trust* v. *Bland*,[21] Anthony Lester QC as *amicus curiae* argued that the courts should settle questions concerning the termination of care of patients in persistent vegetative state on the basis that such patients retain the rights to privacy, dignity, and bodily integrity, and that these might be infringed by continuing care to a patient where no therapeutic purposes was served thereby. Counsel called in aid the European Convention on Human Rights, Article 8, and the International Covenant on Civil and Political Rights, Article 17. The House of Lords concluded that care might be terminated in that case, without committing itself to a privacy-based rationale for the decision.

Nevertheless, the common law is becoming more accommodating to privacy interests, and Anthony Lester QC has suggested that common law principles protecting personal privacy could be developed 'interstitially and by molecular rather than molar motions, case by case, without usurping the functions of Parliament, and avoiding the dangers of broad legislative generalizations in this complex and sensitive area.'[22] The law of private nuisance provides

---

[17] (1848) 2 De G. & Sm. 652.

[18] Samuel D. Warren and Louis D. Brandeis, 'The Right to Privacy', 4 *Harvard L. Rev.* 193–220 (1890).

[19] Cooley, *Torts* 2nd edn., p. 29. [20] [1991] FSR 62.

[21] [1993] AC 789 at pp. 846–55.

[22] Anthony Lester QC, 'English Judges as Law Makers' [1993] P.L. 269–90 at p. 286. Lester points out at p. 284 that Lord Keith had suggested in the second *Spycatcher* case, *Attorney-General* v. *Guardian Newspapers* (No. 2) [1990] 1 AC 109 at pp. 255–6, that a common law right to privacy might exist.

a recent example of privacy-related principles powerfully influencing both the substance and the method of common law development. In *Khorasandjian* v. *Bush*,[23] the Court of Appeal, by a majority, held that harassment by a campaign of vexatious telephone calls interfered with a person's quiet enjoyment of property in such a way as to constitute the tort of private nuisance. The court could therefore grant an injunction to restrain it. The defendant, however, argued that the right to a remedy for private nuisance was limited to the owner of the property. The plaintiff was the owner's daughter, not the owner. Nevertheless, Dillon LJ (with whom Rose LJ agreed) held that the daughter, too, could obtain an injunction. They seem to have justified this on the basis (although this is not entirely clear)[24] that they were free to adapt the law to modern problems (in this case, telephone harassment) by treating nuisance as a tort concerned with rights to use and enjoy property, not simply rights of ownership in property.[25] That being so, they were free to give remedies for nuisance to all whose status in the household accorded them the right to use the property.

This extension of the protection offered by the law of nuisance involved departing from two previous Court of Appeal decisions. The first was *Burnett* v. *George*,[26] where the court felt unable to grant an injunction to restrain harassing telephone calls unless they caused an impairment of the plaintiff's health. In *Khorasandjian*'s case, Dillon and Rose LJJ felt that they were not bound by this, because the court in *Burnett*'s case had been referred only to a line of cases concerning intentionally false statements causing impairment to health in the form of nervous shock.[27] (Peter Gibson J. felt

---

[23] [1993] QB 727, [1993] 3 All ER 669, CA. For discussion, see Joanne Conaghan, 'Harassment and the law of torts: *Khorasandjian* v. *Bush*' (1993) 1 *Feminist Legal Studies* 189–97.

[24] See [1993] QB at p. 735, [1993] 3 All ER at pp. 675–6 (Dillon LJ), and at pp. 740, 680 respectively (Rose LJ).

[25] The majority of the Court of Appeal in *Khorasandjian* preferred not to rely on the tort of intentionally inflicting mental distress, under *Wilkinson* v. *Downton* [1897] 2 QB 57, because that tort required medical harm to be caused by the distress. It was therefore to be regarded as a protection for physical integrity rather than privacy. Peter Gibson J. preferred to rely on *Wilkinson* v. *Downton*, and would therefore have given an injunction restraining harassment only if calculated to cause harm.

[26] (1986) [1992] 1 FLR 525, CA.

[27] *Wilkinson* v. *Downton* [1897] 2 QB 57; *Janvier* v. *Sweeney* [1919] 2 KB 316.

bound by those cases, but was prepared to grant an injunction because the telephone harassment in *Khorasandjian*'s case was intended to cause distress which was likely to impair the plaintiff's health.)

The other troublesome Court of Appeal decision was *Malone* v. *Laskey*,[28] in which a bracket, which had been fitted to stabilise an unsafe toilet cistern, came adrift, falling onto the head of the wife of an employee of the sub-lessees of the house, who had been given permission as a perquisite of his employment to live in it. The wife claimed damages in nuisance. The Court of Appeal ruled against her, partly on the ground that she had no independent interest in the property which would enable her to maintain an action in nuisance. On this point, the case can be regarded as having been wrongly decided, because (as Peter Gibson J, dissenting, pointed out in *Khorasandjian* v. *Bush*) it had been well-established law, even in 1907 when *Malone* v. *Laskey* was decided, that anyone in de facto possession of land may sue in nuisance.[29] But it was still necessary to extend the right to a remedy in nuisance from a wife of the person with a right of occupancy to adult offspring living at home with her parents under a bare licence. Dillon LJ felt justified in doing so, because of the need to respond to altered social conditions. He adopted the argument of the Appellate Division of the Alberta Supreme Court in *Motherwell* v. *Motherwell*:[30] the common law retained the power to 'note new ills arising in a growing and changing society and pragmatically to establish a principle to meet the need for control and remedy; and then by categories to develop the principle as the interests of justice make themselves apparent.'[31] In *Motherwell*'s case the Appellate Division, in a judgment delivered by Clement JA, had held that, notwithstanding the decision of the English Court of Appeal in *Malone* v. *Laskey*,[32] the wife of the owner of property was entitled to an injunction restraining harassing telephone calls, directed towards her, which interfered with her peaceful use of the property. The wife, said Clement JA, 'has a status, a right to live there with her husband and children. I find it absurd to say that her occupancy of the

---

[28] [1907] 2 KB 141, CA.
[29] See [1993] QB at p. 745, [1993] 3 All ER at p. 684 *per* Peter Gibson J., citing *Foster* v. *Warblington* [1906] 1 KB 648, CA.
[30] (1976) 73 DLR (3d) 62.   [31] Ibid. at p. 67.
[32] [1907] 2 KB 141, CA.

matrimonial home is insufficient to found an action in nuisance.'[33]
In *Khorasandjian* v. *Bush*, Dillon and Rose LJJ extended the principle to children living at home with their parents, in order to
respond to changed social perceptions of the seriousness of telephone harassment and the increased significance of privacy interests independent of interests in property.[34]

This, for Peter Gibson J., was a step too far, because, he
thought, the daughter living at home as a bare licensee had no sufficient right of occupancy to justify allowing her to claim in nuisance.[35] Unlike Dillon and Rose LJJ, he considered that the scope
of the entitlement of adult children to occupy the family home was
relevantly different from that of wives: in his view, the right to sue
in nuisance must be linked to a right to use the property which
does not depend on the will of the owner. The approach of the
majority is indeed hard to accommodate within the usual situations
in which the Court of Appeal (Civil Division) is free to depart
from its own previous decisions, as laid down in *Young* v. *Bristol
Aeroplane Co. Ltd.*[36] In *Langley* v. *North West Water Authority*[37]
Lord Donaldson MR, while noting that the rules permit rare
exceptions,[38] said: 'Any departure from previous decisions of this
court is in principle undesirable and should only be considered if
the previous decision is manifestly wrong. Even then it will be necessary to take account of whether the decision purports to be
one of general application and whether there is any other way of
remedying the error, for example by encouraging an appeal to the
House of Lords.'[39]

---

[33] (1987) 73 DLR (3d) at p. 78.
[34] [1993] QB at pp. 735, 740; [1993] 3 All ER at pp. 676, 680.
[35] [1993] QB at p. 745, [1993] 3 All ER at p. 685.
[36] [1944] KB 718, CA, affirmed [1946] AC 163, HL The Court of Appeal laid
down three grounds on which the it might depart from an earler decision: (1) where
it is necessary to choose between two conflicting authorities or lines of authority;
(2) where an earlier Court of Appeal decision is inconsistent with a (later) House of
Lords decision; and (3) where an earlier decision (or line of decisions) was reached
per incuriam. In addition, it has subsequently been held (4) that an interlocutory
decision by a court consisting of two Lords Justices is not binding on subsequent
Courts of Appeal: *Boys* v. *Chaplin* [1968] 2 QB 1, [1968] 1 All ER 283, CA,
although this has more recently been doubted, *obiter*, in *Langley* v. *North West
Water Authority* [1991] 3 All ER 610, CA, at pp. 621–2 *per* Lord Donaldson MR.
[37] [1991] 3 All ER 610, CA.
[38] *Williams* v. *Fawcett* [1986] QB 604, [1985] 1 All ER 787, CA; *Boys* v. *Chaplin*,
above, at pp. 36, 296 *per* Diplock LJ.
[39] [1991] 3 All ER at p. 622.

Yet the majority of the Court of Appeal in *Khorasandjian* v. *Bush* departed from *Malone* v. *Laskey* in order to adapt the common law to remedy 'new ills arising in a growing and changing society'. *Khorasandjian* is a piece of judicial legislation which shows that, despite the reluctance of judges to develop a right to a remedy for infringement of privacy as such,[40] privacy-related interests, such as that in being free from harassment in the home, may be significant in re-theorizing and re-conceptualizing torts which, like private nuisance, were originally designed to protect property interests. Indeed, some judges are willing to be fairly free in their application of the principles of stare decisis when necessary to protect significant privacy-related interests. The issue which divided Dillon and Rose LJJ from Peter Gibson J. in *Khorasandjian* v. *Bush* was whether judges should exercise their lawmaking power to give effect to privacy-related rights.

The problem is that the right to privacy is controversial. The very breadth of the idea, and its tendency to merge with the idea of liberty itself, produces a lack of definition which weakens its force in moral and political discourse. In particular, when privacy takes the form of a right to liberty it is doubtful whether it can support arguments for more specific liberties or rights.[41] In 1971, commenting on *Griswold* v. *Connecticut*, Hyman Gross wrote: 'Hopefully, further developments will make clear that while an offense to privacy is an offense to autonomy, not every curtailment of autonomy is a compromise of privacy.'[42] The later cases, including *Roe* v. *Wade* and its progeny, have illustrated the problems which Gross anticipated, and have attracted criticisms from those who argue that the indeterminate scope of privacy rights, which have no direct textual basis in the US Constitution, draws judges into conducting constitutional review on over-broad and illegitimate grounds.[43] Claims to privacy may be set up to prevent fair comment on matters of public concern, or to thwart the investigation of crime. As H. W. Arndt pointed out, a 'cult of privacy' may

[40] *Malone* v. *Commissioner of Police of the Metropolis* [1979] Ch. 344; *Kaye* v. *Robertson* [1991] FSR 62.

[41] Ronald Dworkin, *Taking Rights Seriously* (London: Duckworth, 1977), pp. 266–78.

[42] 'Privacy and Autonomy', in J. Roland Pennock and John W. Chapman (eds.), *Privacy: NOMOS XIII* (New York: Atherton Press, 1971), pp. 169–81 at p. 181.

[43] John Hart Ely, 'The Wages of Crying Wolf: A Comment on *Roe* v. *Wade*', 82 *Yale LJ* 920 (1974).

merely be a cloak for protecting unbridled individualism and anti-social behaviour.[44] Privacy, as a weapon in the protection of civil liberties, is like a shotgun spraying pellets somewhat indiscriminately over a wide area of human endeavour, rather than a rifle delivering a powerful blow at a well-defined target.

The malleability of privacy reasoning has led Raymond Wacks to speak of the poverty of privacy.[45] If privacy is to be used as a basis for legal developments to contain harassment of all sorts, we need to know when the courts or Parliament should regard a person's privacy-related interest as being sufficiently weighty to justify not just state neutrality towards it but state support for it: in other words, treating it as giving rise to a civil liberty. Treating freedom to undertake an activity as a civil liberty involves two moral claims. First, it entails a claim that the activity is a significant one for one's capacity for flourishing, and that the state should therefore not use a judgment as to the merits or demerits of the activity as a moral justification for interfering with it (in the absence of special circumstances). Any such interference would constitute a failure of the respect which is due from the state for the person concerned.[46] Secondly, while the state should be neutral as between visions of the good life, it should not be neutral as between those who wish to give effect to their own vision of the good life and those who wish to impose it on others. The claim that something is a civil liberty is intended to impose on the state an obligation to respect it by protecting citizens against those who would interfere with it, and to provide legal remedies for infringements. Civil liberties, then, are those freedoms which are so significant for particular people that we claim not only that others should, as a matter of political morality, show tolerance towards them, but also that government should make laws to protect against intolerance.

But when will it be proper for the law to be developed (either by Parliament or the judges) to protect privacy-related civil liberties? This can be approached in three stages. First, is the interest really related to privacy? Secondly, how significant is the interest to the

---

[44] H. W. Arndt, 'The Cult of Privacy', XXI:3 *Australian Quarterly* 69 (September 1949).

[45] Raymond Wacks, 'The Poverty of "Privacy"' (1980) 96 *LQR* 73.

[46] Dworkin, *Taking Rights Seriously* pp. 272–4; Ronald Dworkin, *Life's Dominion: An Argument about Abortion and Euthanasia* (London: Harper Collins, 1993), pp. 233–7.

maintenance of a justifiable claim to privacy, both generally and in the particular circumstances of the case? Thirdly, how serious is the infringement of the interest? The first question must be capable of being answered 'yes' before the other two questions can arise. Questions two and three, by contrast, are matters of degree, requiring courts and legislators to balance the weight of privacy interests against other, competing, claims of a private- or public-interest nature.

How can privacy best be conceived?

In search of an account of privacy as a civil liberty, we can usefully start by thinking about its social meaning. In my view, the virtue of privacy is conditioned by the nature of social life. Privacy rights are distinctive because they give control over the boundaries of the spheres of social existence. They express the fact that, in modern, western societies at any rate, individuals live their lives in a number of social spheres, which interlock, and in each of which they have different responsibilities, and have to work with people in relationships of varying degrees of intimacy. I am a citizen of the United Kingdom, and a council-tax-payer in the District of Wyre Forest; a member of a nuclear family and an extended family, of a cricket club and a synagogue, of a faculty and a university. In each of these spheres (in all of which I operate simultaneously), I join different people for different purposes, which dictate the degree of intimacy between us, and also limit the extent to which outsiders can intrude on our activities.[47] Privacy is largely a matter of being able to choose where, when, and with whom to co-operate or to withhold co-operation, in pursuit of defined objectives.

---

[47] This notion was suggested by W. L. Weinstein, 'The Private and the Free: A Conceptual Inquiry', in Pennock and Chapman, *Privacy: NOMOS XIII*, pp. 27–55, especially at p. 34: private and public 'are probably best seen as layers of onion skin, any given layer potentially counting as private in relation to one or more outer layers, that is, various publics'; Michael A. Weinstein, 'The Uses of Privacy in the Good Life', ibid., pp. 88–104, especially at p. 94: 'Privacy demands that there are relevant others with whom communication is possible. If there are no relevant others and communication is limited voluntarily, the condition is one of hermitic isolation. If limitation is involuntary, the condition is one of simple isolation'; and the comparative historical and anthropological surveys in Barrington Moore, Jr., *Privacy: Studies in Social and Cultural History* (Armonk, New York: M. E. Sharpe, Inc., 1984).

The responsibilities which we have in each sphere in which we participate, and the objectives which we pursue in each sphere and which shape our responsibilities, are likely to make privacy interests relatively unimportant in regulating our relationships with other people within our own spheres. Typically, while we mark off each sphere from the others, we individually have relatively little privacy as against people operating in our sphere for the purposes of that sphere. For instance, while I assert a right to be private in my home, it is a communal privacy: it is claimed on behalf of my whole family, and I normally enjoy relatively little protection within the home against intrusion on my space and activities by other members of the family.

Within each sphere, privacy operates in four dimensions: space (in which I include access to and control over material goods); time; action; and information. The privacy rights which can be claimed depend on the circumstances, and particularly whether the focus of attention is the spatial, active, or informational dimension. For instance, a claim to privacy in one's work-place has a spatial element—a claim to control who can enter or watch;[48] a temporal element—the claim to set limits on the times when one is available to customers, suppliers, or colleagues; an active element—a claim to control what goes on there without coercion from outside; and an informational element—a claim to control the dissemination of information about what goes on there. This model of privacy as relating to the control over access to various dimensions of social spheres shared with other people can be contrasted with models which seek to identify the notion of privacy more or less arbitrarily with a limited range of protected interests.[49] The interaction of the

[48] It is on this basis that it is possible to justify the cases which excluded private members' clubs from the application of the race and sex anti-discrimination legislation: *Charter* v. *Race Relations Board* [1973] AC 868, [1973] 1 All ER 512, HL; *Dockers' Labour Club and Institute Ltd.* v. *Race Relations Board* [1976] AC 285, [1974] 3 All ER 592, HL. See now also Race Relations Act 1976, s. 25, of which there is no equivalent in the sex discrimination legislation.

[49] For example, David J. Seipp, 'English Judicial Recognition of a Right to Privacy' (1983) 3 *Oxford J. of Legal Studies* 325–70 treats privacy law as drawing boundaries round three sets of interests, in private property, confidential information, and personal information. Ruth Gavison, 'Privacy and the Limits of Law', 89 *Yale LJ* 421–71 (1980) at pp. 428–9 identifies three elements in what she calls a 'complex concept' of privacy: secrecy, anonymity, and solitude. Gavison's list is more easily able to rebut the charge that privacy can be reduced to other interests, but still does not take account of the full complexity of the social situations in which privacy-related claims are advanced.

spheres and the various dimensions of privacy affect the weight
which different values will have in influencing the development of
the law. I will illustrate this by reference to three such values,
namely secrecy, dignity, and autonomy.

Secrecy, dignity, autonomy

Raymond Wacks has concentrated attention on personal information, which, he argues, is the core sense of privacy and the only
interest which it is proper for the law to protect in the name of
privacy. Maintaining the confidentiality of personal information is
important because there are some things about us which, put simply, are nobody else's business unless we choose to make them
such. This is what, in the title of this lecture, I called 'secrecy'.[50]
However, concentrating on secrecy misrepresents the nature of privacy, by suggesting that it refers to cloistered or hole-in-the-corner
activities. Controlling the flow of information within the circle to
which it relates is, therefore, always difficult, and might even
defeat the purposes which the circle is designed to advance.
Controlling the flow of information can best be described not a
secrecy but in terms of 'selective discloure'.[51] The right to disclose
personal information selectively or not at all is inevitably an aspect
of privacy when it is in harmony with the the social idea of privacy which I have outlined. We ought to be free to choose the circles in which to live, and be compelled to disseminate information
about ourselves only so far as necessary to live in the circles. Of
course, we may choose to disclose information more widely,
putting it into the public sphere for profit (the inside story of the
personalities at the heart of a *cause célèbre* can be very profitable),
or to bolster self-respect or make a political point (revealing that
one is gay may advance either aim). But we feel a need to protect

---

[50] The usage is derived from Ruth Gavison, 'Privacy and the Limits of Law', 89
Yale LJ 421–71 at p. 428, identifying three elements in privacy as secrecy,
anonymity, and solitude. As will become clear, I adopt a rather different characteri-
zation. Hyman Gross, op. cit., n. 42 above, also concentrates attention on secrecy in
this sense, although (as Gavison notes at p. 426 n. 20 of her article) Gross had earlier adopted a view of privacy as incorporating solitude as well as secrecy: see 'The
Concept of Privacy', 42 *NYUL Rev.* 34 at pp. 35–6.

[51] I have borrowed this term from Elizabeth L. Beardsley, 'Privacy: Autonomy
and Selective Disclosure', in Pennock and Chapman, *Privacy: NOMOS XIII* pp.
56–70.

ourselves and our circle against coerced disclosure in order to maintain the mutual respect which holds social circles together, so upholding the ordinary structures of social life.

Control over personal information is instrumentally valuable as a support for privacy interests. It helps us to forge and conduct personal and social relationships which form an important part of the construction of social life. It also protects individual choice, preventing people from being diverted from their chosen path by the knowledge that others will be offended by it or might try to bring pressure to bear on them to abandon it. However, we should not arbitrarily undervalue other aspects of privacy which, historically and culturally, are probably at least as important. Enabling family life to flourish in a secure home is a significant concern of privacy-based reasoning. Freedom to communicate privately with one's friends and relations is another. Enabling people to indulge their personal preferences in sex, play, reading-matter, religious worship, food, or dress, in settings where they are not visible to (and therefore do not offend) others is important. The ability to control the boundaries of the social spheres in which we carry on those activities is particularly significant for people who, like us, live in the political and moral traditions of liberal individualism.

This mention of liberal individualism brings us to the idea of autonomy, which is central to liberal theory. Autonomy in its Kantian form involves a capacity for self-determination, and a willingness to act according to principles which one accepts as rational, and regards as appropriate to guide one's own and other people's behaviour. The autonomous person enjoys a certain level of moral and physical capability, reflectiveness, and self-awareness, which presupposes access to a decent level of social and moral education, and perhaps also to health care and other facilities.[52] The notion of autonomy is tied to that of dignity. In order to develop and exercise a capacity for self-determination, one needs to take oneself and others seriously as moral agents. One aspect of dignity is self-respect, which (as Thomas Hill has convincingly argued) includes respect for one's own and other people's moral rights, and a commitment to our own personal standards, below which we do not

---

[52] Joseph Raz, *The Morality of Freedom* (Oxford: Clarendon Press, 1986), pp. 205–7 has argued that, in addition, there must be a sufficient range of options available to the individual in question for there to be real choice. This, however, lies outside the sphere of this lecture.

wish to fall even if our generalizable moral obligations to others do not extend that far. Dignity also encompasses a desire to be esteemed by others according to the standards of which we approve.[53] These attributes make it possible and worthwhile for people to regard their own choices as important, and this is, in turn, a necessary condition for the exercise of autonomy.

The combination of the idea of a right to be respected as a moral agent with the idea of social spheres of decision-making within which people or groups are entitled to regard themselves as free from outside coercion are, I suggest, of the essence of the notion of privacy as a civil liberty. An assertion of privacy entails a moral claim that, within the circle in question, one is *prima facie* entitled to be free of outside coercion in the choice of values and standards, and to have that freedom protected by law, while recognizing that these entitlements are subject to the right of the wider society to protect the interests of vulnerable individuals within the circle and the interests of society as a whole outside it. The core of privacy as a civil liberty, then, is this entitlement to dignity and autonomy within a social circle. Secrecy, the control over information, serves, but does not exhaust, that entitlement.

Dignity, then, is essential to the forms of human flourishing which depend on the exercise of autonomy. This is why the European Court and the Commission of Human Rights treat dignity as being sufficiently central to human flourishing to justify holding that the prohibition on degrading treatment or punishment under Article 3 of the European Convention on Human Rights forbids any treatment which degrades a person in his or her own eyes, whether or not it also degrades that person in the eyes of others.[54] Medical treatment imposed on a person without consent, even if thought to be in the patient's best interests, is capable of constituting both degrading treatment and an infringement of privacy, as

[53] Thomas E. Hill Jr., *Autonomy and Self-Respect* (Cambridge: Cambridge University Press, 1991), chapters 1 and 2. I am inclined to accept the argument of Edward J. Bloustein, 'Privacy as an Aspect of Human Dignity: A Reply to Dean Prosser', 39 *NYULRev.* 962 (1964) at p. 971 that all infringements of privacy are violations of dignity, although not all violations of dignity are infringements of privacy.

[54] See P. J. Duffy, 'Article 3 of the European Convention on Human Rights' (1983) 32 *ICLQ* 316–46. The Court has recognized that a sufficiently serious assault on the dignity of a victim could constitute degrading treatment or punishment within Article 3: *Tyrer* v. *United Kingdom*, Eur. Ct. HR, Series A, No. 26, Judgment of 25 April 1978, 2 EHRR 1, at para. 33 of the Judgment.

Anthony Lester QC argued in the *Bland* case. The importance of dignity to autonomy also explains why Article 17 of the International Covenant on Civil and Political Rights lumps rights to honour and reputation together with privacy, family, home or correspondence.[55] It seems odd to treat honour and reputation, which appear on the surface to be public assets relating to other people's views about one, as related to privacy.[56] Yet on reflection it seems that honour and reputation together are akin to dignity in allowing one to develop a flourishing social and business life, and honour is a particularly significant contributor to the self-respect and dignity which form a major part of one's view of oneself.

The interest in dignity is only partly protected by the tort of libel. A right to dignity would protect one's reputation against assault on the ground of allegations which, whether true or false, should be regarded as immaterial to anyone but oneself. In English civil law, an action for defamation will not succeed where the defendant can establish the truth of the defamatory statement: people are not entitled to be compensated in tort for loss of a reputation which they do not deserve.[57] Yet the importance of the interest in dignity explains why truth has never been a defence to a charge of criminal libel. The impact on private life and self-respect, as well as on public order, of unrestrained publication of unpleasant personal truths led to the saying, attributed to Lord Mansfield, 'The greater the truth, the greater the libel.'[58] It is therefore not unreasonable to treat the interests in honour and reputation as privacy-related. Manfred Nowak has written of the meaning of 'honour' and 'reputation':[59]

Whereas the word "honour" tends to give expression more to this person's subjective opinion of himself or herself (subjective feeling of honour), the

[55] Article 16 CRC expressly guarantees to children rights expressed in similar terms to those set out in Article 17 ICCPR.

[56] Tony Weir, *A Casebook on Tort* 7th edn. (London: Sweet & Maxwell, 1992), pp. 24–5, commenting on *Kaye* v. *Robertson* [1991] FSR 62, CA, observes: 'to give a right of privacy which can be vindicated only by publicity can benefit only publicity-seekers . . . who are indignant that being vulgarly exposed by others has prevented them making a profit by vulgar self-exposure.'

[57] *M'Pherson* v. *Daniels* (1829) 10 B & C 263 at p. 272 per Littledale J.

[58] John G. Fleming, *The Law of Torts*, 8th edn. (Sydney: Law Book Co., 1992), p. 554.

[59] Manfred Nowak, *UN Covenant on Civil and Political Rights—C.C.P.R. Commentary* (N. P. Engel: Kehl am Rhein, 1993), p. 306.

word 'reputation' describes his or her appraisal by others.[60] Since an attack on a person's honour can thus impair his or her self-esteem, it interferes more severely with his or her dignity, integrity and privacy than the mere injury to his or her reputation. . . . Finally, a person's reputation can be impaired only by an attack accessible to the public, whereas honour may also be violated by degrading treatment face-to-face.

Where an aspect of a person's private life is likely to be held up to ridicule or contempt, there should be legal remedies for the harm done to reputation, dignity, and self-respect by publication of true information (including pictures) unless there is some other pressing interest which justifies disclosure. If people are free to release that sort of information with impunity, it might have the effect of illegitimately constraining a person's choices as to his or her private behaviour, interfering in a major way with his or her autonomy.

The discussion so far prompts the following reflections. A person is entitled to protect his or her dignity, including both self-respect and the esteem of others, from assault on the basis of activities which are nobody else's business. Saying that certain areas of life, or types of activity, are nobody else's business certainly asserts that that other people have no right to know what is going on, but also goes a good deal further. In particular, it asserts that the activity in question should be regarded as being irrelevant to the esteem in which a person is held by those who, in other spheres of life, enter into relationships (whether business or social) with us. People ought to tolerate, if not respect, choices which we make in those circles of social life to which they are not privy. Although privacy is sometimes regarded as a poor substitute for toleration, being a protection against being watched over by the intolerant rather than an assertion of the wrongfulness of intolerance, they actually go together inseparably. A right to privacy represents an institutional limit on people's capacity to make one

---

[60] Footnote refers to Volio, 'Legal personality, privacy, and the family', in Louis Henkin (ed.), *The International Bill of Rights—The Covenant on Civil and Political Rights* (New York, 1981), at 198f. Thus the Human Rights Committee found unlawful attacks on honour and reputation in *Tshesekedi* v. *Zaire*, Communication No. 242/1987, § 13(b), where the government of Zaire had circulated suggestions that an opposition leader was in a disturbed mental state it was held to violate Article 17. See Nowak, *op. cit.*, p. 307.

suffer from their intolerance.[61] Since the liberal tradition demands
that we respect other people's exercise of freedom of religion,
expression, and conscience, which inevitably will sometimes lead
them to the conclusion that our own beliefs and activities are
wrong and offensive, we need some special principle limiting their
freedom to give effect to their beliefs by restricting our freedom.
Toleration may be incompatible with their beliefs. Liberal theory
cannot insist on toleration if that is incompatible with the exercise
of freedom of conscience and religion. Intolerance cannot be
treated as a wrong, in liberal theory, because to do so would
undervalue important rights and would lead to the conclusion,
incompatible with the idea of liberalism itself, that people's choices
are less important than the need to accommodate those choices to
the demands of others. Liberalism can, however, limit people's
freedom to give effect to their beliefs if that would interfere with a
weightier right-based interest. A right-based argument is therefore needed to justify restraining them from interfering with us. A
theory of privacy supplies such arguments.

What is distinctive about privacy? It is autonomy-related, but
then so are all civil liberties. It is also dignity-related, but then so
are many other civil liberties. Identifying these underlying values
does not give a rounded account of the nature of the concept to
which they relate. Concentrating on a single value is likely to be
positively misleading, since values always operate in combination
rather than singly. Yet privacy rights are different from freedom of
expression, religion, and conscience, even though (as David
Richards has pointed out) privacy may help to supply the conditions for the full enjoyment of those other rights.[62] Privacy protects
the area within defined spheres of social activity (family, business,
or leisure groups) against interference from outside the sphere.
Rights to free expression, and other political rights, are essentially
outward-looking, asserting a claim to participate in, and influence,
a wider community by advancing ideas to other social groups.
Nevertheless, privacy interests may be affected even where an
activity is conducted in a public place, because even when done in
public it is not the proper concern of the general public. Because

[61] Compare Stanley I. Benn, 'Privacy, Freedom and Respect for Persons', in
Pennock and Chapman (eds.), *Privacy: NOMOS XIII*, pp. 1–26 at p. 24.
[62] David A. J. Richards, *Toleration and the Constitution* (New York: Oxford
University Press, 1986), chapter 8.

privacy is not one right, but a bundle of rights and responsibilities relating to different spheres of one's social life, one can maintain some aspects against certain people even if other aspects are overridden, and one can maintain one aspect against someone even if they have overridden other aspects by reason of powerful social interests.

Privacy in public

The discussion so far has implications for the notion of privacy rights in public places. There has recently been increasing concern about the civil liberties implications of surveillance in public places. The routine surveillance of shoppers and passers-by in shopping areas, banks, and building societies, and of sports supporters and drivers, has been made a great deal easier by technological developments such as the remote control video camera. Does this constitute an infringement of privacy? At one time I thought that the fact that one chose to do things in public automatically negated any claim to privacy rights in respect of them. Now, however, I think that the position is more complicated. The implication of the model of spheres of privacy outlined earlier is that most spheres involve relationships with other people, and privacy concerns the extent to which we can legitimately claim to control space, action, and information in the context in question. An appeal to privacy therefore always presupposes a conflict of our interests with those of others, and when we speak of public places we really mean 'more public than others'. Surveillance, even in public or semi-public places, may threaten dignity and autonomy. Privacy claims should therefore still be capable of being asserted, although the degree of publicness will affect their weight.

But to what extent? Privacy in public places is less extensive than in private spaces, because we cannot normally claim to control who shares the public space with us, and we acknowledge that we owe duties to fellow-users not to behave in ways which are gratuitously offensive to them. It is likely to be easier to justify interfering with people in public places than in private, because privacy interests, while still operative in public, are less weighty than they are in private. This explains why, in the USA, the constitutional controls over searches of cars on the street under the Fourth Amendment are less stringent than those which relate to searches of homes.[63] There is also a possibility that we may lose at least part of our right to control information when we discuss it in public spaces, or when the information concerns what we do in public. When delivering a public lecture, I can assert no privacy-related interest in controlling access to the lecture, stopping you from listening to it, or make whatever use you like of information about anything which I say or do.

One may therefore ask why, if I do not think that what I am doing is wrong, I should be entitled to object to other people watching me do it. The nature of my objection depends on whether the surveillance is covert or overt. Secret surveillance (where the object of surveillance is unaware of being watched, and so does not adjust his or her decision-making), in Stanley Benn's words, 'deliberately deceives a person about his world, thwarting, for reasons that *cannot* be his reasons, his attempts to make a rational choice.'[64] After the Princess of Wales had been clandestinely photographed while working out at a gymnasium, a semi-private, semi-public setting, Bryce Taylor, the owner of the gymnasium who had photographed her, was reported to have said: 'What was Princess Diana doing there in the first place if she didn't want to be seen? How many women do you know who work out in full make-up? How many do you know who supposedly work out hard and then don't sweat?'[65] In fact, many of my acquaintances regard it as undignified to go out of the house, even if only to take the children to school, without making themselves look at least respectable, and preferably attractive. It is a matter of maintaining the standards of personal appearance and hygiene which one expects of oneself, and which others expect. Failing to live up to one's own standards disappoints one's own and others' expectations, and so damages one's dignity (all the more if one is royalty, of whom particularly high standards are expected). Apart from that, Mr. Taylor's argument seems to be based on the idea of implied consent to being photographed. In fact, consent is impossible when the surveillance is secret, because the victim, who cannot know of the surveillance and is being deceived as to the reality of

---

[63] *California* v. *Carny*, 471 US 386 (1985); *New York* v. *Class*, 475 US 106 (1986). See also *California* v. *Acevedo*, 114 L. Ed. 2d 619 (1991).

[64] See Benn, op. cit., n. 61 above, at p. 10 (emphasis in original).

[65] *The Independent*, Wednesday 17 November 1993, p. 11, reporting an interview first published in London's *Evening Standard*.

the situation, cannot consent to that about which she could not have known.

If the surveillance is overt, it carries with it a clearly implied threat that the fruits of the surveillance may be used for purposes adverse to the interests of the person being watched. This is calculated to undermine people's commitments to their own plans and values. It thus represents a failure of respect for people's dignity and autonomy. This can be justified, but the onus of justification lies on the watcher, not on the watched. Even if some intrusion on privacy is justified, the fact that privacy rights might be to some degree compromised does not entail the notion that they are altogether lost. A person who loses some part of the right to privacy, such as the right to be free from surveillance, when in public, may retain other privacy-related rights, such as a right to control the unauthorized or illicit use of the information gleaned from that surveillance. Privacy involves a bundle of interests, rather than a single right, so loss of part of the bundle does not entail loss of the whole. The common law has recognized that bundles of rights may be restricted to an extent, without being lost entirely, as recent cases concerning the rights of prisoners show.[66] When we are forced to act in public in order to further our private lives, for instance by travelling, speaking on the telephone, using public mail services, or availing ourselves of publicly-funded medical or education services, our right to privacy is inevitably to some extent compromised, but should not be regarded as lost except to the extent necessary for the service to operate and for the public to be protected against abuse of the facilities. The Court of Appeal recognized this in *Francome* v. *Mirror Group Newspapers Ltd.*,[67] when it granted an injunction restraining publication in a newspaper of recordings which were alleged to show unlawful behaviour by a jockey. Even if the public interest in the detection of crime justified

---

[66] *Raymond* v. *Honey* [1983] 1 AC 1, [1982] 1 All ER 756, HL; *Leech* v. *Deputy Governor of Parkhurst Prison* [1988] AC 533, [1988] 1 All ER 485, HL; *R.* v. *Deputy Governor of Parkhurst Prison, ex parte Hague*; *Weldon* v. *Home Office* [1991] 3 All ER 733, HL; *R.* v. *Secretary of State for the Home Department, ex parte Leech* [1993] 4 All ER 539, CA; *Racz* v. *Home Office* [1994] 1 All ER 97, HL; Genevra Richardson, 'Prisoners and the Law: Beyond Rights', in McCrudden and Chambers, *Individual Rights and the Law in Britain*, pp. 179–205.

[67] [1984] 1 WLR 892. The decision is inconsistent with that of Sir Robert Megarry V-C in *Malone* v. *Metropolitan Police Commissioner* [1979] Ch. 344, holding that there was no confidentiality in a telephone conversation.

some interference with the confidentiality of telephone conversations, the public interest required publication to the police, not to
the public at large.

Surveillance in private

If my decision to indulge in some form of activity in public places
might be overborne by the knowledge that others would hold me
up to ridicule if they found out about them, the danger of infringing autonomy and dignity is greater, and requires far weightier justifications, when surveillance covers private places. Privacy provides
a protected sphere in which I can do as I choose (within limits)
without regard to how it will affect other people's opinion of me.
This is an argument from autonomy as well as dignity or self-
respect. Watching people against their will, as Benn has written,
forces them to see themselves and their plans through the eyes of
another, as object rather than subject, undermining their self-
respect and evincing a lack of respect for their freedom to make
choices without pressure from outside.[68] This is perhaps why the
behaviour of the Ancyent Marinere, or a particularly repulsive
advertisement by a clothing company, or other indecent displays in
public, can be seen as an infringement of the dignity which is central to privacy. They are assaults on the mind which seek to over-
bear our normal critical and defensive faculties. This is, perhaps,
what Robert Nozick meant in the context of philosophy when he
wrote, 'Why are philosophers intent on forcing others to believe
things? Is that a nice way to behave towards someone? I think we
cannot improve people that way—the means frustrate the end.'[69]
This may be true of philosophers, but the means do not frustrate
the ends of advertisers, the Ancyent Marinere, or many political
and religious evangelists, because such people are not philosophi-
cally committed to nice ways of behaving towards people: they
regard their own objectives as more important.

One is entitled, as against such people, to insist on respect for
the self-governing nature of the various circles of one's social life.
But the state may have a duty to interfere in order to protect other
people's interests or further social goals. The physical and emo-

[68] Benn, op. cit., n. 61 above, at pp. 8–10.
[69] Robert Nozick, *Philosophical Explanations* (Oxford: Oxford University Press,
1981), p. 5.

tional space in which each of us conducts much private life is likely to be shared with others, either permanently or intermittently: family, partners, friends, lodgers, or pets. The demarcation of a private sphere therefore influences, but does not exclude, two sets of tensions: those between individuals and outsiders, including the state; and those between individuals within what may for convenience be described as the private realm. As Georges Duby has written:[70]

An indoor business, . . . private life might seem to be walled off from prying eyes. But, on either side of that 'wall,' . . . battles constantly rage. Private individuals must use what power they have to fend off the encroachment of the public authorities on their domain. And inside that domain the desire for independence must be contained within bounds, for every private dwelling shelters a group, a complex social organism, within which inequalities and contradictions present in the larger society are brought to a head. Here the clash between male and female power is fiercer than it is outside, the old and the young are locked in struggle, and overbearing masters must cope with impudent servants.

So far as the state is concerned with controlling these tensions, it is likely that law will be one of the main tools employed to regulate them in accordance with criteria developed through political negotiation or legal argument. The state or other agencies (such as the press) may also have a social duty to stop crime, advance democracy, reveal political malpractice, protect the public against a serious danger (if necessary by bringing to bear the spotlight of publicity) or protect the rights or welfare of others. In child care law, the balance between the privacy rights of members of the family and the needs of children to be protected against abuse is hard to strike, but everyone accepts that, subject to appropriate procedural safeguards, the privacy of the family must sometimes give way. Sometimes the law will even intervene to try to prevent activities in private between consenting adults where those activities are regarded as particularly harmful or immoral. In *R. v. Brown*,[71] a majority of the House of Lords decided that it was impossible in law to consent to actual bodily harm, at least when that is inflicted

---

[70] Georges Duby, 'A Foreword to A History of Private Life', in Paul Veyne (ed.), *A History of Private Life Vol. 1: From Rome to Byzantium*, translated by Arthur Goldhammer (Cambridge, Mass. and London: Harvard University Press, 1987), p. viii.
[71] [1993] 2 WLR 556.

in private for the purposes of sado-masochistic sexual gratification. Such was the emotiveness of the subject that the members of the majority refused to regard it as a case concerning sexuality or privacy, preferring to treat it as pure violence. Only Lord Mustill, dissenting, said that he would have preferred to see the case classified as one of privacy. Even where only the actor is directly affected, events and general public interests might make it necessary to permit some infringement of secrecy. If a person (like the late Stephen Milligan MP) decides to seek self-fulfilment through auto-erotic behaviour in private, that is nobody else's business. However, if, by some mischance death ensues, the public interest in investigating sudden deaths inevitably means that secrecy cannot be maintained. Privacy interests are overridden, not solely because the beneficiary of the right is dead,[72] but because public interest considerations justify a limited relaxation of the normal protection for privacy.

But privacy may be interfered with only for a legitimate purpose, and only to an extent that is proportionate to that objective. Although it was inevitable, given the circumstances of Mr Milligan's death, that his sexual behaviour could not remain secret, one can criticise the press and, perhaps, the police for making the publicity as extensive and detailed as it was, when no public interest was served thereby. Politicians do not lose their privacy interests merely by reason of being politicians, although the weight of those interests may be reduced by their political behaviour, including the policies which they espouse or for which they are responsible. A politician who advances a policy or programme which concerns the way in which people should manage their lives in private spheres, we are entitled to test his or her commitment to the policy by asking whether it is one which he or she personally operates. But where a politician has not put his or her character in issue (as criminal evidence lawyers might say) in this way, privacy interests should be unaffected.

Privacy and related rights thus advance a number of different values. As with any normative concept, these justifying values operate in combination, not alone, and clash (sometimes in unpre-

---

[72] Although privacy interests based on self-determination rights are inevitably of far less importance once one's capacity for self-respect and autonomy has ceased, there are some secrets which we are normally entitled to expect will be buried with us because the dead and the friends and family who survive them have a continuing interest in maintaining their dignity and reputation.

dictable ways) with other values. For example, privacy interests frequently and notoriously come into conflict with the interest in a free press. It is in this context that much of the current agitation for a right of privacy, to protect against unjustified press intrusion, has arisen. The relative weights of these different interests cannot be determined by a theory of privacy. As Benn wrote, 'General principles do not *determine* solutions to moral problems of this kind. They indicate what needs to be justified, where the onus of justification lies, and what can count as a justification.'[73] The remainder of this paper looks briefly at these matters.

The weight of privacy and other interests

The weight of privacy-related interests is related to the *significance* of the interest and the *seriousness* of an infringement. *Significance* relates to the significance of the interest which is interfered with. In particular, how central is it to the ability to carry on a reasonably free and pleasant personal and business life in the spheres of activity which one has helped to define? On this dimension, intrusive telephone calls score quite highly, together with interferences with a huge range of other interests relating to one's intimate and personal life. This is why under the ECHR (though not the US Constitution) the right to respect for private life makes it impermissible for the state to impose undue burdens on the private performance of acts expressing a person's homosexuality.[74] The dimension of *seriousness* refers to the nature and gravity of the intrusion or infringement.

When should an infringed interest be regarded as significant? There are two sets of criteria, which can be used together or separately. First, there is the guidance offered by the international human rights instruments, which encapsulate the essence of those interests which are generally regarded, in western societies at any rate, as arising from legitimate expectations of privacy. The UK is under the following obligations, by virtue of being party to the European Convention on Human Rights (ECHR), the International

[73] Benn, 'Privacy, freedom', note 60 above, at p. 13.
[74] *Dudgeon* v. *United Kingdom*, Eur. Ct. HR, Series A, No. 45, Judgment of 23 September 1981, 4 EHRR 149; *Norris* v. *Ireland*, Eur. Ct. HR, Series A, No. 142, Judgment of 26 October 1988, 13 EHR 186; Feldman, *Civil Liberties and Human Rights*, pp. 364, 510–2; Wintemute, 'Sexual Orientation', above, n. 10.

Covenant on Civil and Political Rights (ICCPR), and the UN Convention on the Rights of the Child (CRC):

(i) an obligation to ensure that everyone (including, under the caselaw of the European Court of Human Rights, commercial organisations) is accorded respect for[75] private and family life, home and correspondence (Article 8(1) ECHR);

(ii) an obligation to ensure that no one is subjected to arbitrary or unlawful interference with privacy, family, home or correspondence, or unlawful attacks on honour or reputation (Article 17(1) ICCPR; Article 16(1) CRC); and

(iii) an obligation to provide legal protections against, and effective remedies for, such interference or attacks (Articles 2(2) and (3) and 17(2) ICCPR; Article 16(2) CRC; Article 13 ECHR).

These international obligations form part, at least, of the background against which claims to protection for interests in the area of privacy should be evaluated by judges. An infringement of any of these should be regarded as breach of a significant and particularly weighty privacy-related interest, for which the state has an obligation in international law to offer a remedy. Furthermore, where a party seeks to justify an infringement of a right, the grounds of justification, to be acceptable, must meet the criteria set out in the international instruments. The law must not permit interference (by anyone) with privacy, family, home or correspondence which is either arbitrary or unlawful (ICCPR/ CRC). Interference by public authorities with the right to respect for private and family life, home and correspondence must meet the ECHR requirements that the infringement must be prescribed by law (importing rule-of-law requirements) for one of the objectives prescribed as legitimate by the Convention, and must be necessary in a democratic society (importing requirements of proportionality and pressing social need). In addition, a failure to make adequate provision for legal remedies for interference with the protected interests may constitute an interference by a public authority, which may be disproportionate even if it furthers a legitimate objective.[76]

---

[75] For criticism of the drafting of Art. 8(1) E.C.H.R. on this point, see Sir James Fawcett, *The Application of the European Convention on Human Rights* 2nd edn. (Oxford: Clarendon Press, 1987), p. 211.

[76] See for example *Malone* v. *United Kingdom* Eur. Ct. HR, Series A, No. 82, Judgment of 2 August 1984, 7 EHRR 14; O. v. *United Kingdom*, Eur. Ct. HR,

Such privacy-related interests are clearly capable of operating in relatively public settings. For example, one has privacy interests in public hospitals, in public lavatories, and in one's car when it is in a public place. To some extent, it is reasonable to say that, if one chooses to conduct one's affairs in the open, one has waived part, at least, of the protection for the privacy of those affairs which would otherwise be appropriate, and this may reduce the weight of these interests in public settings. But people cannot live all their lives in a cocoon. Sometimes private affairs must be carried on in public, or using public facilities.

Although choosing to use a public medium for one's activities implies a limitation on the extent to which one can claim protection for privacy interests in respect of those activities, where one has to carry out activities which can only be conducted in public, but which affect one's intimate relationships or private life, there is no implied waiver of privacy rights except in so far as a limitation of those rights is inevitable given the nature of the activity. Where the infringement of privacy interests occurs in relation to public activity or the use of a public medium, it is likely to be easier to justify than an infringement in respect of similar behaviour behind closed doors. But justification, by reference to weighty and legitimately competing interests, is still needed. One cannot, therefore, accept that a person waives privacy rights in communications merely by communicating through a medium which is known to be open to overhearing or surveillance, as Sir Robert Megarry suggested in *Malone* v. *Commissioner of Police of the Metropolis*.[77] To hold that one loses privacy rights when using a telephone is analogous to saying that one loses rights of property in respect of one's baggage when one takes it on an aeroplane, because we all know that bags are sometimes lost or stolen in transit.

Secondly, in assessing the weight attaching to a privacy-related

---

Series A, No. 120, Judgment of 8 July 1987, 10 EHRR 82; *Olsson* v. *Sweden*, Eur. Ct. HR, Series A, No. 130, Judgment of 24 March 1988, 11 EHRR 259; *Eriksson* v. *Sweden*, Eur. Ct. HR, Series A, No. 156, Judgment of 22 June 1989, 12 EHRR183; *Andersson* v. *Sweden*, Eur. Ct. HR, Series A, No. 226, Judgment of 25 February 1992, 14 EHRR 615.

[77] [1979] Ch. 344. For criticism, see Vaughan Bevan, 'Is there anybody there?' [1980] PL 431–53; Law Commission, Report No. 110, *Breach of Confidence*, Cmnd. 8288 (London: HMSO, 1981), para. 6.35; Raymond Wacks, *Personal Information: Privacy and the Law* (Oxford: Clarendon Press, 1989), p. 258; Feldman, *Civil Liberties and Human Rights*, pp. 383–6.

interest we are entitled to ask whether the person asserting the interest is, in the circumstances of the case, using it to discharge his or her responsibilities in the social sphere to which the claim relates. Privacy should not be seen as a wholly selfish or self-indulgent matter. As suggested earlier, privacy interests serve in large part to maintain the semi-permeable membranes at the boundaries of spheres of social action, and the social relationships which operate within each sphere impose responsibilities on members of the circle, as well as conferring rights on them. Privacy-related interests which help people to discharge their responsibilities normally deserve greater weight than those which are used in an entirely self-serving way, and this factor should be taken into account when deciding how to resolve conflicts between interests.

When assessing the seriousness of an infringement of privacy for the purpose of weighing it against competing interests, a number of factors should be regarded as relevant. Four are particularly important: the relationship between the infringement and the core values which privacy protects; the extent to which the infringement interferes with a person's ordinary enjoyment of life; the extent to which the protected interest survives the infringement; and the unlawfulness or oppressiveness of the means adopted by the infringer.

First, an infringement which directly impinges on one of the core values underpinning privacy law is to be regarded as more serious than one which affects a more peripheral interest. It was argued earlier that dignity and autonomy are central to privacy. Accordingly, disregard for an individual's right to control action, access to space, and access to and dissemination of information, in a sphere of privacy are particularly offensive when the disregard affects personal interests in dignity and autonomy.

Secondly, one must take account of the distress, and loss of quality of life, which the victim suffers from the infringement. Even if an infringement merely reduces the utility to the victim of a privacy-related interest, the more severe the reduction, the more serious will be the infringement. Harassing telephone calls have a major impact on the quality of a victim's home life, and so should be regarded (as in *Khorasandjian* v. *Bush*, discussed earlier) as constituting a serious breach of a significant interest. Harassing victims of disasters for interviews and photographs, a journalistic technique singled out for particular censure by the National Heritage

Select Committee,[78] is another intrusion which seriously exacerbates the distress which the victims are in any case bound to suffer, and which should be regarded as a serious infringement of privacy interests.

Thirdly, if the infringement destroys the utility of the privacy-related interest, as wide publication of confidential information might be said to do, it will be a particularly serious infringement.

Fourthly, unlawfulness and oppressiveness in the techniques of infringement may make an intrusion more serious. Where they are violent, or involve harassment or induce fear in the victim, any intrusion is always likely to be considered serious, as is a substantial infringement involving trespass to land, unlawful interference with property, or criminal interception of communications. Where the means adopted are clandestine, but not illegal, as in the photographs of Princess Diana mentioned earlier, or the recordings made of telephone calls from David Mellor (then Secretary of State for National Heritage) to his girl-friend which were made with her consent (and so lawfully) but without his knowledge, the seriousness of the intrusion will be aggravated, although it may depend on the extent to which the victim had a legitimate expectation of respect for privacy. Although this expectation is limited in highly public places, people can reasonably expect not to be spied on in certain ways, even when in certain places to which the public have access (such as the cubicles of public toilets). This expectation is therefore properly protected to a greater or lesser extent in the privacy statutes of various American states.[79] There are certain situations which are in a sense public (in the sense of being places of public resort, or places dedicated to public purposes under the control of a public authority) but where people properly expect a reasonable level of seclusion. Examples include the sites of disasters, hospital wards, and school premises. The same applies to the cubicles of public conveniences. In such relatively public settings, people conduct parts of their lives which are distinctly private. There

[78] National Heritage Committee, Fourth Report, *Privacy and Media Intrusion*, HC 294–I of 1992–93, paras. 30–37.

[79] National Heritage Committee, HC 294–I of 1992–93, Annex 1: Utah defines 'private place' as 'a place where one may reasonably expect to be safe from casual or hostile intrusion or surveillance.' The Maine legislation is less protective, defining 'private place' as 'a place where one may reasonably expect to be safe from surveillance but does not include a place to which the public or a substantial group has access.'

is clearly a legitimate expectation of substantial privacy, and infringements of it are likely to be considered serious. Compliance with the terms of Article 8 ECHR and Article 17 ICCPR demands legal protection against intrusions on privacy in those public or semi-public settings where there is a legitimate expectation of seclusion. Such protection would give a remedy in, for instance, the circumstances of *Kaye* v. *Robertson*,[80] where a well-known actor was intruded on while in hospital suffering from a serious injury and photographs and a spurious account of an interview were published. It would also help in situations where journalists intrude, after being asked to desist, on the shock and grief of witnesses to disasters and the relations of those injured or killed. Such a right of action would, I suggest, be a useful protection to people's legitimate privacy interests.

Conclusion

Privacy is a necessary condition for the exercise of many civil liberties, and is compatible both with the nature of our social lives and with the obligations of the state towards society as a whole. Legislation and developments in the common law to protect privacy interests should be welcome. However, the proper form of the protection depends on the importance of the interest protected, the way in which it connects with other interests, and the duties which we and the state bear to respect each other's dignity. The respect for dignity may require us to say that certain matters are *prima facie* not our concern, giving rise to a civil libertarian claim to protection against interference by anyone, unless there is a more powerful countervailing interest which it is legitimate to take into account.[81] Even in public, a person deserves to be protected in the name of privacy against behaviour which shows a lack of respect for his or her capacity as a free agent to make decisions.

To return to my starting point, the Ancyent Marinere is, in my view, guilty of an infringement of the wedding-guest's privacy. He was on a private errand: his task, on which he was embarking by agreement with the parties to the marriage, was to attend the nup-

[80] [1991] FSR 62, CA.
[81] Jeremy Waldron, *Liberal Rights: Collected Papers 1981–1991* (Cambridge: Cambridge University Press, 1993), pp. 203–24, offers a persuasive account of why this balancing act is required and how it can be performed.

tials and participate in an important social rite of passage. To achieve his goal, he had to go some way in public. The way in which the Ancyent Marinere derailed him from his intended course was a denial of his right to respect for his autonomy and dignity. The Marinere ignored the wedding-guest's protests and overrode his will. This was an infringement of privacy, albeit in a public place. Of the wedding-guest, Coleridge says:

> A sadder and a wiser man
> He rose the morrow morn.[82]

The Marinere deprived the wedding-guest of his happiness, and the bride and groom of a cheerful guest. We are entitled to be protected against such behaviour. As in many cases of infringement of privacy, one may doubt whether the wisdom or knowledge gained was sufficient to compensate for the loss of happiness to the victim and his social circle.

[82] 'Rime', lines 657–8.

EXCLUDING EVIDENCE FROM ENTRAPMENT: WHAT IS A 'FAIR COP'?

*Diane Birch**

In April 1992 two young men, Gary Williams and Ted O'Hare, were passing through a busy shopping area in Woodford, Essex, when they caught sight of a delivery van, in the open rear of which they saw what seemed to be a load of valuable cigarette cartons. The van appeared to be unattended, and after taking their time to weigh up the situation Williams and O'Hare went into action, helping themselves to a number of cartons. After that, things happened very quickly. Police officers appeared out of nowhere and, after a struggle, the two were arrested.

Gary and Ted had stumbled upon 'Operation Rover': a trap set by the police in an area of high motor vehicle crime. Although they admitted taking the boxes, they objected strongly to the propriety of Operation Rover both in court and out of it. In court they met with little success: their convictions for offences of vehicle interference were upheld by an unsympathetic Divisional Court,[1] which considered them the victims, not of a trick, but of their own dishonesty. Out of court, on a television documentary entitled '*Fair Cops*', Gary said that the conduct of the police had been like dangling a carrot in front of a donkey which was bound to try to bite it. Ted, although he realised that some might regard him as 'fair game' because he had a criminal record for theft, was concerned that a normally honest person who was really hard up, such as a single mother passing by with her children, might have found herself tempted beyond endurance.

A few months earlier, Keith Smurthwaite, a 39-year-old married builder, sought help with a personal problem. His marriage was no longer a source of unmitigated joy, but divorce would have

* Professor of Criminal Justice and Evidence, University of Nottingham.
[1] *Williams and Another* v. *Director of Public Prosecutions* [1993] 3 All ER 365.

resulted in the exposure of his financial affairs about which the
Inland Revenue were blissfully unaware. Keith Smurthwaite did
what any red-blooded English tax evader would do. He resolved to
murder his wife. He made inquiries for a contract killer which
resulted eventually in a meeting with one, Webster, who was a hit-
man with a difference. He was an undercover police officer whose
only concealed weapon was a tape-recorder on which the 'deal' he
struck with Smurthwaite was preserved for S's subsequent prosecution for solicitation to murder. Again, the defendant's cry of
'unfair cop!' cut no ice in court. S was thought to have 'made the
running throughout' with W, and the Court of Appeal could find
no ground for criticising the trial judge's decision to allow the
recorded conversations to be used in evidence.[2]

Both *Williams & O'Hare* and *Smurthwaite* raise the question of
the propriety of official involvement in criminal activity. In fact,
the level of involvement in both cases was marginal, with the
defendants having being afforded only the opportunity (in *Williams
& O'Hare*) or the means (in the case of *Smurthwaite*) to achieve a
criminal purpose which could properly be said to have been of
their own devising. But cases may readily be imagined where the
police employ more active methods of persuasion or pressure, up
to the point where the accused may no longer be said to be a free
agent.

The devices available at the trial of defendants lured into crime
for viewing some types of police involvement as 'unfair cops' range
in theory from a complete stay of proceedings for abuse of process,
through a criminal defence of entrapment, to the exclusion of evidence regarded as 'unfair', to mitigation of penalty after conviction.[3] Until comparatively recently, English law recognised only the
last of these devices, with the decision of the House of Lords in
Sang[4] being thought to provide an obstacle to the use of the other
three. However the third option has now been made available, as
Smurthwaite is authority for the proposition that the court's statutory discretion to exclude 'unfair' evidence, conferred by section 78
of the Police and Criminal Evidence Act 1984 after *Sang* was
decided, may be invoked in cases involving entrapment. And recent

[2] *R. v. Smurthwaite*; *R. v. Gill* [1994] 1 All ER 898.
[3] Entrapment may also be controlled by prosecuting the entrapper, which falls
outside the scope of this paper.
[4] [1980] AC 402.

developments in both abuse of process and substantive criminal law potentially increase the options open to an entrapped defendant.

Against this background it is proposed to examine the notion of a 'fair cop' in cases involving an element of official entrapment, concentrating primarily on the use of the statutory discretion under section 78 of the Police and Criminal Evidence Act 1984 to exclude unfair evidence. It will be considered whether this power is properly regarded as available in cases involving entrapment, and, if it is, the basis (both in theory and in practical terms) on which it should be exercised. It will be necessary also to bear in mind the relationship between evidential exclusion and the other possible strategies of stay of proceedings and substantive defence.

What is entrapment?

In its strict sense entrapment requires the activity of one whose function is so dastardly that it can only be described in French: the 'agent provocateur'. The most frequently-cited English definition of the agent's role is taken from the Report of the Royal Commission on Criminal Procedure in 1929, and runs as follows:

a person who entices another to commit an express breach of the law which he would not otherwise have committed and then proceeds or informs against him in respect of such offence.[5]

A broader definition appeared recently in *Williams & O'Hare*, in which Wright J. said:

. . . the police officers were not acting as agents provocateurs. In no sense were they participating in or inciting, procuring or counselling the commission of any crime. That phraseology[6] . . . [describes] the essential characteristics of an agent provocateur. The police did nothing to force, persuade, encourage or coerce the appellants to do what they did.

Where these views diverge is that while the latter focuses exclusively on the conduct of the agent, the former asks the further question whether the offence would have occurred at all but for

---

[5] A definition approved as 'neat' in *Mealey & Sheridan* (1974) 60 Cr App R 59 at 61. See also e.g. *Birtles* (1969) 53 Cr App R 469 at 473.

[6] Which was taken from the *Home Office Circular to the Police on Crime and Kindred Matters* 97/1969: 'No member of a police force, and no police informant, should counsel, incite or procure the definition of a crime'.

the agent's intervention.[7] Common to both views is that the official activity, whatever form it takes, must occur prior to the commission of the offence. Thus the leading case of *Christou & Wright*[8] is not a case of entrapment, because the operation set up by the police in that case, which involved undercover officers posing as shady jewellers in order to recover stolen property from the thieves and handlers did not, as the Court of Appeal rightly pointed out, involve the use of agents provocateurs: the police did not themselves participate in, or incite, the commission of any offence. Any trickery which took place occurred after the commission of the offence, and in order to get evidence of it. Such stratagems may or may not be objectionable, (in *Christou & Wright* they were not), but they do not constitute entrapment.

In some recent English decisions, however, there has been a tendency to use the term entrapment in a wider sense. In *Jelen & Katz*[9] for example, the obtaining of confession evidence by the surreptitious tape recording of telephone conversations was said to contain 'an element of entrapment'. More significantly, in *Smurthwaite*, Lord Taylor CJ clearly distinguished between evidence obtained by entrapment and by the use of an agent provocateur. In deciding whether to exclude the evidence of Webster the undercover officer, his Lordship considered that the trial judge should give separate consideration to the questions:

Was the officer acting as an agent provocateur in the sense that he was enticing the defendant to commit an offence he would not otherwise have committed?

and

What was the nature of any entrapment? Does the evidence consist of admissions to a completed offence, or does it consist of the actual commission of an offence?

While Lord Taylor was 'not persuaded' that Webster was an agent provocateur, he went on to hold:

There was, of course, as the learned judge recognised, an element of entrapment and a trick inherent in the use of an undercover officer to pose as a killer.

---

[7] The former view being closer to the classic American definition propounded in *Sorrells* v. *US* 287 US 435 (1932): 'Entrapment is the conception and planning of an offence by an officer, and his procurement of its commission by one who would not have perpetrated it except for the trickery, persuasion or fraud of the officer'.

[8] [1992] QB 979.   [9] (1990) 90 Cr App R 456.

'Entrapment' in this wider sense seems to mean no more than a trick or snare, and to be capable of referring equally to conduct prior to and after the offence. The evidence in *Christou & Wright* was, in this sense, obtained by entrapment. The shift in meaning probably derives from the courts' present policy of applying the same considerations to the exercise of their section 78 discretion wherever deception is alleged: the rules formulated in *Christou & Wright* were used to resolve the appeals in both *Williams & O'Hare* and *Smurthwaite*. The use of entrapment in its new, wide sense suggests an underlying unity, whereas the history of entrapment in its strict sense suggests anything but. In the following discussion, entrapment will be used to connote the activities of an agent provocateur in the sense of one who at least incites or participates in an offence. This does not mean that there is anything necessarily wrong in the result achieved by applying the *Christou & Wright* rules to entrapment cases: merely that to assert that they raise identical issues is begging the question.

Should the courts control entrapment?

In *Sang* the House of Lords stated that the function of a judge was to ensure that the accused has a 'fair trial according to law'. Although there was some divergence of opinion as to the exact scope of this power, there was general adherence to a basic proposition that the judge was not directly concerned with how investigators had behaved. Lord Diplock put it strongly:

It is no part of a judge's function to exercise disciplinary powers over the police or prosecution as respects the way in which evidence to be used at trial is obtained by them. If it was obtained illegally there will be a right in civil law; if it was obtained legally but in breach of the rules of conduct for the police, this is a matter for the appropriate disciplinary authority to deal with.[10]

Because the facts of *Sang* did not in his opinion involve entrapment, Lord Salmon advanced an illustration of what he hoped was an 'unusual case' which did. A 'dishonest policeman, anxious to improve his detection record, tries very hard with the help of an agent provocateur to induce a young man with no criminal tendencies to commit a serious crime; and ultimately the young man

---

[10] [1980] AC 402 at 436.

reluctantly succumbs to the inducement'.[11] According to Lord Salmon, the most the judge could do for the young man was to impose a mild penalty upon him, although he did express the view that the instigators ought to be prosecuted too.

Changes in the way in which the criminal justice system is viewed, and in how it views itself, mean that such an abdication of interest in the background of a case is unacceptable today. Public interest in miscarriages of justice, and the high profile accorded to cases in which pre-trial misconduct has led to unjustified and lengthy imprisonment, must have played an important part in the courts' changed perception of their role, which now clearly extends to voicing a view on the illegal or improper way in which evidence was obtained,[12] and includes the assumption of broad powers to control the pre-trial stage by monitoring, for example, disclosure[13] and delay and abuse of power in bringing cases to court.[14]

Much of this activity, which in some respects parallels the growth of Administrative Law as a means of controlling executive action,[15] would have seemed excessive and improper twenty years ago, but is now regarded as necessary to command public respect for the criminal trial and to avoid the impression that the courts are colluding in impropriety. It would be odd if the descent by officials to the forms of illegality which entrapment may involve were to be regarded as exempt from judicial scrutiny at trial. The appropriate question is how, not whether, the courts should exercise some control.

Entrapment and stay of proceedings for abuse of process

All courts, including magistrates' courts, have a power to stay proceedings which are an abuse of the process of the court. Even in *Sang* Lord Scarman recognised[16] that this was an exception to the

---

[11] [1980] AC 402 at 443.

[12] See the cases discussed in the later part of this paper, and cf the comment by Zuckerman: 'Illegally Obtained Evidence: Discretion as a Guardian of Legitimacy' [1987] CLP 55 at 56 who argues that the investigative process is now seen as part of the administration of justice, and that judicial attitudes to unlawfully obtained evidence must be publicly acceptable.

[13] See e.g. *Ward* [1993] 1 WLR 619; *Davis* [1993] 1 WLR 613.

[14] Cf. *Horseferry Road Magistrates Court, ex parte Bennett* [1993] 3 WLR 90 and cases therein cited.

[15] Ibid, at 104 per Lord Griffiths.   [16] [1980] AC 402 at 454–5.

supposed' rule that the judge is concerned only with the conduct of the trial. The power, which is to be exercised sparingly, has been most in evidence in cases of prosecutorial delay, and there is no English authority for its application in entrapment cases. *Sang* is largely silent on the point,[17] which, given the House's out-and-out rejection of a defence of entrapment or an exclusionary discretion in such cases, is not a hopeful sign, although some commentators relied upon the absence of express rejection as a possible indication that the option remains open.[18]

The recent decision of the House of Lords in *Horseferry Road Magistrates Court, ex parte Bennett*[19] significantly increases the chances that the power can be invoked. B, a New Zealander, was alleged to have been involved in an offence of deception relating to the purchase of a helicopter in England. He left the country and was eventually apprehended in South Africa. There was no extradition treaty between the two countries, but B claimed that instead the South African police, in collusion with police and prosecutors in England, deported him to his native land on board a plane which conveniently stopped en route at Heathrow, where B was taken off the plane. B challenged the jurisdiction of the English courts to try him, and the House of Lords held, contrary to what had previously been thought, that the High Court's inherent supervisory jurisdiction[20] extended to a consideration of the circumstances in which B had arrived within the jurisdiction and that deliberate abuse of extradition procedures would afford grounds for staying proceedings.

The argument against the power to stay in *ex parte Bennett* relied on *Sang* as authority that the judge's concern is to see only that the accused has a fair trial, and that 'wider issues of the rule of law and the behaviour of those charged with its enforcement, be

[17] Except for the ambiguous comment of Lord Scarman that the case of *Sang* did not itself involve an abuse of process, which as Choo points out ('A Defence of Entrapment (1990) 53 *MLR* 435) might merely be a reference to the finding that there was no entrapment on the facts of the case.

[18] Choo op. cit. at 464, Lanham DJ, 'Entrapment, Qualified Defences and Codification' (1984) 4 *OJLS* 437 at 442.

[19] [1993] 3 WLR 90.

[20] The jurisdiction of magistrates in abuse of process cases was said to be limited to matters directly affecting the fairness of the defendant's trial. Ibid., at 106–7 per Lord Griffiths, with whom the other members of the house concurred on this point.

they police or prosecuting authority, are not the concern of the judiciary unless they impinge directly on the trial process'.[21] That argument was accepted by Lord Oliver (dissenting),[22] but must be taken to have been rejected by the other members of the House. Lord Griffiths, with whom Lord Slynn agreed, identified a general function of the High Court in criminal cases to ensure that executive action is exercised responsibly and as Parliament intended. The court should express its disapproval of a 'serious abuse of power' by refusing to act upon it. This would seem to open the door to a similar argument in entrapment cases.

Lords Bridge and Lowry were more cautious, drawing attention to the impact on the rule of law if the court were to turn a blind eye to the breaches of international law and foreign law involved.[23] Lord Lowry went so far as to distinguish *Sang* on the basis that it concerned a common law rule of evidence and not wrongful conduct by the executive in an international context. But it is nowhere made clear why the rule of law is not threatened by purely domestic executive abuses, and indeed Lord Lowry's summary of Lord Bridge's objection to proceedings against B seems almost to have been formulated with entrapment in mind:

the court, in order to protect its own process from being degraded and misused, must have the power to stay proceedings which come before it and have only been made possible by acts which offend the court's conscience as being contrary to the rule of law. Those acts by providing a morally unacceptable foundation for the exercise of jurisdiction over the suspect taint the proposed trial and if tolerated will mean that the court's process has been abused . . . I respectfully cannot agree that the facts relied on in cases such as the present case (as alleged) 'have nothing to do with that process' just because they are not part of the process. They are the indispensable foundation for the holding of the trial'.[24]

[21] [1993] 3 WLR 90, at 102 per Lord Griffiths, citing Lord Diplock [1980] AC, 402 at 436–7, and Lord Scarman at 454–5.

[22] [1993] 3 WLR 90 at 113: 'Those words [Lord Scarman's] were used in the context of a suggested discretion to prevent a prosecution because of judicial disapproval of the way in which admissible evidence has been obtained, but they are equally applicable to other executive acts which may incur judicial disapprobation'.

[23] Ibid., at 109–110 per Lord Bridge: 'When it is shown that the law enforcement agency responsible for bringing a prosecution has only been enabled to do so by participating in violations of international law and the laws of another state in order to secure the presence of the accused within the territorial jurisdiction of the court, I think that respect for the rule of law demands that the court take cognisance of that circumstance.'

[24] [1990] WLR at 118–19.

If this be true of involvement of the executive in breaches of international law that affect the conscience of the court, why not of breaches of domestic law? If, as seems likely, the distinction is untenable, we now have a foundation for the exercise of the power in entrapment cases.

It has been said that the power to stay proceedings is the most appropriate response in entrapment cases: more appropriate than a substantive defence because it is flexible enough to discriminate between different kinds of official involvement in the way that only a discretion can,[25] and more appropriate than a discretion to exclude evidence obtained by entrapment because it strikes down the whole of the prosecution case, not merely those parts of it which are dependent on the evidence of an agent provocateur.[26] (The latter argument may assume too much in the light of what will be argued about the court's powers under section 78). The disadvantages of using the power to stay as the only method of control are that the injunction to use it sparingly may result in it not being used at all, and that it is not entirely clear whether it will be considered an unacceptable device to be placed in the hands of magistrates.[27] It is certainly too early to give up on other possible control mechanisms.

Entrapment and defences to crime

That entrapment provides no defence to a criminal charge was said to be 'well settled'[28] by the House of Lords in *Sang* in 1979, and indeed was conceded on appeal, counsel's timorous view being that earlier Court of Appeal authority made clear that no such defence

---

[25] Lanham, op. cit. at 443.

[26] Choo op. cit. at 63; Allen 'Entrapment, Time for Reconsideration' (1984) 13 *Anglo-American Law Review* 57 at 64.

[27] Cf. the limitation of the jurisdiction described in *Horseferry Road Magistrates Court, ex parte Bennett* [1993] 3 WLR 90 to the High Court.

[28] [1980] AC 402 per Lord Salmon at 443. See also Lord Diplock at 432: CA decisions described as 'clearly right'; at 441 per Viscount Dilhorne: 'It has been held, rightly in my opinion, that entrapment does not constitute a defence to a charge'; Lord Fraser at 445: CA decisions 'right in principle'; Lord Scarman at 451: previous authorities 'soundly based'.

existed.[29] However the reasons given for disallowing a defence of entrapment lack conviction.[30]

The first is that the entrapped defendant still merits conviction as he commits the *actus reus* of the offence with *mens rea*. This is so, but it is also true of defendants acting under some recognised excusatory defence, such as duress or that recently-recognised form of necessity known as duress of circumstances. Indeed, extreme forms of entrapment might be brought under one of these excuses: if there had been any evidence that Webster had used physical threats against Smurthwaite, duress would have been a plausible line of defence.[31] Similarly, if, as has happened in other jurisdictions, an agent sought to play on the sympathy of the defendant to the extent of fabricating debilitating symptoms of withdrawal from drugs to persuade D to act as supplier, duress of circumstances might conceivably succeed: in *Martin*,[32] M's wife's threat of suicide if M refused to drive her son to work was held to be capable of giving rise to the defence.

The presence or otherwise of *mens rea* is not then sufficient reason for ruling out entrapment. A more plausible distinction is that the rationale of defences based on duress is excusatory; a concession to human frailty where the will is overborne,[33] whereas the case for entrapment rests in public policy and the proposition that crime manufactured by the state does not properly fall within the criminal sanction.[34] Although entrapment as a defence often reflects the notion that 'but for' the entrapment there would have been no crime, so that the effect on the will of D is relevant, this would logically seem to provide the basis for an excuse only if D is equally excused when he is pressured to commit an offence by an ordinary criminal, as it may safely be assumed that D, being

[29] *McEvilly & Lee* (1973) 60 Cr App R 150; *Mealey & Sheridan* (1974) 60 Cr App R 59.

[30] Despite following closely the arguments advanced in the previous year by the Law Commission in its Report No. 83 on Defences of General Application at 32–54, criticised by Ashworth, 'Entrapment' [1978] Crim LR 137.

[31] In fact the evidence of the tapes showed S was relaxed and laughing when the deal was struck, and the jury unanimously rejected the defence.

[32] [1989] 1 All ER 653. The threat, as in duress, would have to be of death or serious injury, and the circumstances such that a person of reasonable firmness with the characteristics of the accused would have responded as the accused did: ibid at 653–4.

[33] *Howe* [1987] AC 417.

[34] Cf. Williams, *Criminal Law, The General Part* (1961) at 786.

unaware of the true identity of the agent provocateur, would have behaved in precisely the same way in response to ordinary criminal solicitation. The House of Lords in *Sang* noted that many defendants become involved in crime only because of pressure brought to bear by others, and it is not suggested that this provides an excuse, so that official involvement in the use of such pressure creates no special distinguishing feature.[35]

A counter-argument not yet fully considered in England would be to say that the criminal law draws a line between inclination to wrongdoing, which is not punishable, and the wrongdoing itself, which is, and the state expects a certain amount of self-restraint on the part of its citizens in resisting the temptation to cross the line. Where one citizen for his own criminal purpose causes another to yield to temptation the state has the right to claim that both should be punished, but where the state itself lures D across the line, the state is quasi-estopped from asserting that the purposes of the criminal law now requires that he be punished for it.

The use of the language of estoppel in this context may seem misplaced, but it is really only another way of saying that the state should be disabled from relying on the presence of a mental element which it has deliberately created. Coincidentally, the House of Lords recently employed similar language in order to justify a disability which applies to the defendant in a criminal trial: the rule that voluntary intoxication provides no general defence was said by Lord Mustill to have as one of its roots that the defendant is 'estopped' from relying on his self-induced incapacity.[36]

---

[35] [1980] AC 402 at 432 per Lord Diplock; a point also taken by the Law Commission Report No. 83 on Defences of General Application at 47.

[36] *Kingston* [1994] 3 WLR 519 at 530. The decision of the Court of Appeal in this case [1993] 4 All ER 373 seemed to open the door to a defence of involuntary intoxication based on a broad understanding of the purpose of criminal law which might have helped provide a theoretical basis for an entrapment defence, but it was subsequently overturned by the House of Lords. K claimed that, as a result of being clandestinely drugged by P, he had indulged an underlying inclination to acts of paedophilia which he normally managed to control. The Court of Appeal considered that the purposes of the criminal law were not served by holding a person guilty for an act which, though accompanied by the intent proscribed by law, occurred only as a result of the removal of K's inhibitions by P's act. The House of Lords, allowing the prosecutor's appeal, restated the traditional doctrine that liability for an act done whilst involuntarily intoxicated depends only on the presence of *mens rea* at the time the act is done. The House considered it undesirable to develop the law in the direction favoured by the Court of Appeal, *inter alia* because of the risk of spurious assertions that the defendant was not the sort of person to have

If entrapment were ever to become a defence (which does not seem likely in the present political climate),[37] it would, in the light of *Sang*, probably require legislation, and it has rightly been observed that the problems of drafting would be enormous. First and foremost, as Lanham succinctly puts it,

The problem with entrapment is that sometimes it is necessary, desirable and lawful and sometimes it is oppressive, unwarranted and illegal[38]

Any defence would thus have to distinguish between good and bad entrapment. This is not easy to do with precision, although in loose terms it may be said that there are some offences which would be difficult to detect without entrapment (such as dealing in drugs, prostitution, unlawful sales of alcohol and other 'victimless' offences in respect of which complainants are unlikely to come forward); and some situations in which evidence is unlikely to be yielded by other methods of detection because offences take place in secret leaving behind little or no trace (again, victimless crimes are often cited in this context).

This could be said to suggest a starting point that, if there are other ways of going about detection, entrapment is bad because unnecessary.[39] But this does not work because there are crimes which, though they could be dealt with by other means, might be better dealt with by a measure of entrapment, for example for reasons of public safety. This might be said to be true of the 'hit-man' situation, where it is better that D is introduced to a fake killer than that he should make contact with the real thing, with possibly disastrous consequences for the intended victim. A different example concerns the 'rat-trap' car used by some police forces: a clever device

done this kind of thing, and the difficulty of deciding whether the drug had 'turned the scale' in causing the deed to be done (per Lord Mustill]1994] 3 WLR 519 at 537). No doubt similar difficulties could be said to arise in the context of an entrapment defence.

[37] It seems more likely that the Law Commission will press ahead with plans to provide a defence to the entrapper who acts to frustrate a criminal enterprise: Consultation Paper no. 131 'Assisting and Encouraging Crime' (1993) at 120.

[38] Op cit at 438. See also Friedland, 'Controlling Entrapment' (1982) 32 *U. Tor. LJ* 1; Heydon 'The Problem of Entrapment [1973] CLJ 268; Barlow, 'Entrapment and the Common Law: Is There a Place for the American Doctrine of Entrapment?' [1978] 41 *MLR* 266.

[39] Estey J., in his important dissent in *Amato* (1982) 140 DLR (3d) 405 at 445 was of the view that certain offences by their detectable nature rendered entrapment unnecessary.

which means that youngsters who are tempted to joy-ride find that upon trying to do so they are securely locked in and 'arrested' by the car until released by the police.[40] Insofar as an element of entrapment is involved, it prevents the taking of other vehicles which experience suggests might only be recovered after damage has been done and perhaps a high-speed chase has occurred.

Again, any definition of the situations in which entrapment may be permitted would have to be flexible enough to cope with change in trends of crime: the rat-trap car is a good example of a response to a problem which is of comparatively modern origin, whilst we seem to have overcome the social evil of fake fortune tellers who used to be detected by entrapment.[41]

In jurisdictions where entrapment is a recognised defence, the question has arisen of how far to take account of D's predisposition to the offence.[42] This would be a problem in England if we began with the Royal Commission's notion of an agent provocateur as one who entices D to commit a crime which he would not otherwise have committed: if D has a criminal record there is a real risk that the police would go further in enticing him than if he has not;[43] and if D sought to challenge the misconduct at his trial the prosecution's proof that he would have committed the crime without the entrapment (or would have done something like it if predisposition is understood in a wider sense) might include reference to his criminal background, with, in all probability, disastrous consequences.[44]

For these amongst other reasons it seems that discrimination between good and bad entrapment might more suitably be dealt with through a discretion rather than a defence.[45] The matter being one for the court not the jury, reference to D's record could be made (if it has to) without risk of prejudice. And the court, in locating the dividing line between what is and is not permissible

---

[40] Cf. *Dawes* v. *DPP* (1994) *The Times* 2 March.

[41] Williams, Criminal Law, The General Part (1961) at 783.

[42] The American experience is discussed e.g. by Allen op. cit.. at 69 et seq, by Choo op. cit. at 57 et seq, and by Friedland op cit at p. 12 et seq. See also Whelan, 'Lead Us Not Into Unwarranted Temptation' (1985) 133 U Penn L Rev 1193.

[43] Allen op. cit. at 62, 70.   [44] Whelan op. cit. at 1206.

[45] Allen op. cit. at 72 concludes in favour of a defence, although a complex one. Friedland op. cit. at 25 ultimately favours a defence which is simplified at the expense of leaving enormous questions of reasonableness to the jury. Heydon op. cit. at 285 and Lanham op. cit. at 443 argue against.

could be as sensitive as need be to the fact that, as Friedland says, the line 'will vary from crime to crime and from fact situation to fact situation'.[46]

Discretionary exclusion of evidence

The use of discretion to exclude evidence in entrapment cases raises three issues. First, is the rule of substantive law that there is no defence of entrapment inconsistent with the use of discretion to exclude evidence so obtained? Second, are the powers conferred on the courts apt to cover entrapment cases? Third, if a discretion exists, on what principles should it be exercised?

DISCRETION INCONSISTENT WITH ABSENCE OF DEFENCE?

According to *Sang*, the common law afforded the court of trial (whether Crown Court or magistrates) no discretion to exclude evidence on the basis that it was obtained by entrapment. It was regarded as inconsistent[47] to permit a defence to operate by the backdoor of judicial discretion which was denied access via the front door of substantive criminal law. It does not, of course, necessarily follow that to make provision for a discretion would be inconsistent with the absence of a general defence, any more than it is inconsistent with the absence of any right of acquittal where evidence has been improperly obtained to say that the court may achieve 'the same result' by excluding such evidence on grounds of fairness. What would be unacceptable would be to have a rule of evidence which excludes *all* material obtained by entrapment, rather than one which seeks to discriminate, as it has been submitted is necessary, between 'good' and 'bad' entrapment devices; between 'fair' and 'unfair' outcomes.

Section 78 of PACE addresses the fairness issue directly by providing that a court may exclude 'any evidence on which the prosecution proposes to rely' if it appears that, 'having regard to all the circumstances, including the circumstances in which the evidence was obtained, the admission of the evidence would have such an adverse effect on the fairness of the proceedings that the court

[46] Op. cit. at 4.
[47] [1980] AC per Lord Diplock ar 432–3, Viscount Dilhorne at 441, Lord Salmon at 443, Lord Fraser at 446 and Lord Scarman at 455.

ought not to admit it'. In *Smurthwaite* the Court of Appeal, rightly in my opinion, took the view that the section, whilst not requiring the exclusion of all evidence obtained by entrapment, nevertheless requires the court to take account of entrapment as a factor bearing upon the circumstances in which the evidence was obtained and the fairness of using it in the proceedings.

The risk of section 78 being used as a 'backdoor' defence of entrapment has, it seems, carried weight only once in the Court of Appeal, in *Harwood*[48] where it was said, obiter, that the section should be interpreted to give effect to *Sang* on this point. In *Gill*[49] reservations were expressed about the correctness of this attempt to limit the section. The trend in most of the cases, including *Gill*, and *Governor of Pentonville Prison, ex parte Chinoy*,[50] an extradition case, has been for the prosecution to concede that the fact of entrapment can be taken into account, and to fight instead on the basis that there was no entrapment.

This in itself may be a dangerous approach as it may lead the court to give too much weight to entrapment where it is shown to have occurred. In *Edwards*[51] a police informer took an undercover officer to E's home, where the officer indicated his interest in purchasing a large quantity of amphetamine. According to the officer, E understood all the drug slang employed in the conversation, and willingly fell in with the sale, suggesting he was well used to doing such business, but the plan collapsed when E proved unable to supply the amount requested. E was charged instead with a general conspiracy relating to supply to persons unknown, and the evidence of the officer was held not to be that of an agent provocateur in relation to the supply of drugs to such persons, in which he had of course played no part. It seems that the court also thought that, had the sale to the officer gone through and had E been charged with that supply, the officer would have been an agent provocateur enticing that offence, so that his evidence ought to have been excluded.[52] This approach cannot be right, for it affords a backdoor defence which gives the court no opportunity to investigate whether this type of entrapment is justified (as it probably is); and furthermore the outcome turns inexplicably on the selection of the charge against E.

---

[48] [1989] *Crim. LR* 285.   [49] [1989] *Crim. LR* 358.
[50] [1992] 1 All ER 317.   [51] [1991] *Crim. LR* 45.
[52] See commentary by Professor Smith at [1991] *Crim. LR* 46.

ARE THE COURT'S POWERS APT TO DEAL WITH ENTRAPMENT?

According to *Sang* the common law did not recognise a general fairness discretion except in the sense that the court had power to exclude evidence the prejudicial effect of which outweighed its probative value. Such discretion as existed to exclude reliable evidence which had been obtained in an unfair manner was said by Lord Diplock[53] to be limited to evidence analogous to confession evidence obtained from the accused himself after the commission of the offence in breach of his privilege against self-incrimination.

The arguments for and against this oddly constructed and very limited discretion, and whether it truly represented the views of the other Lords who purported to concur in it, are no longer of interest as there can be little doubt that section 78 does confer a general fairness discretion.[54] The court is directed to consider the circumstances in which the evidence was obtained in deciding the effect on the fairness of the proceedings if it were to be admitted, and in *Smurthwaite* the Court of Appeal was prepared to regard the section as part of a codifying Act which should be given its natural meaning and not strained either to reassert or alter the pre-existing law.

A possible source of difficulty which was canvassed in *Sang*[55] in relation to the common law is that a power to exclude evidence can bite only on material obtained subsequent to the commission of the offence which it is unfair to use, while the problem in entrapment cases is that the accused has been unfairly induced to commit the offence which the evidence proves. This topsy-turvy argument, as Michael Allen says, neglects to mention that the aim of the entrapper is to prove a crime by all unfair means at his disposal, including getting the crime committed in the first place. The difficulty (if there is one) in relation to s. 78 may be overcome either by holding all the evidence to have been unfairly obtained, or by pointing out that unfairness in the obtaining of the evidence is but one of the circumstances the court is directed to take into account in calculating the effect on the fairness of the proceedings.

[53] [1980] AC 402 at 437.

[54] For further discussion of the common law position see Heydon, 'Entrapment and Unfairly Obtained Evidence in the House of Lords' [1980] Crim LR 129; Polyviou, 'Illegally Obtained Evidence and *R. v. Sang*' in *Crime Proof and Punishment* (London 1981) 226.

[55] [1980] AC 402 at 446 per Lord Fraser.

If section 78 is available in entrapment cases the courts will have to meet the argument that arbitrary results would be achieved if the courts were prepared only to exclude the evidence of the entrapper, and not, e.g. the evidence of an eye-witness or the confession of the defendant.[56] Using the argument canvassed above the wider use of the discretion should be possible (it was so used at common law before *Sang* put a stop to it)[57] but if it is not then the discretion will require to be backed up with other strategies, such as staying proceedings for abuse of process, if true fairness is to be achieved.

GROUNDS FOR EXERCISE

From what has been said thus far it can be seen that there are grounds to welcome the availability of the section 78 discretion, but also reason for caution lest an uncertain, 'mushy'[58] concept of fairness undermines the substantive law. Further, it is open to criticism, as are all discretionary powers, on the ground that it will be difficult to ensure consistency in its exercise.

The more principled the discretion can be said to be, and the more its underlying aims can be articulated, the more consistent will be the decisions made under it, but nowhere in any of the cases involving entrapment to date is the rationale for the exercise of the power apparent: on what ground of principle is the court enabled to say that the use of some evidence obtained by entrapment, or the wider strategies of trickery and deception, is unfair? It is proposed to seek an answer by considering the application of section 78 to other problems, specifically the exclusion of confessions and identification evidence.

When s. 78 came into force, there were not many who supposed it would make a great deal of difference to the approach of the courts at common law.[59] But when the Court of Appeal in *Mason*[60] held that section 78 was wide enough to include confession evidence, it opened the way to a stream of decisions under which confessions which passed the scrutiny of section 76 with its

---

[56] See e.g. Choo op cit at 63.

[57] Ibid., citing *Ameer & Lucas* [1977] *Crim. LR* 104 and *Burnett & Lee* [1973] *Crim. LR* 748.

[58] Heydon, [1980] *Crim. LR* 129 at 134 speaks of the need to avoid the 'mushiness and unpredictability of a general doctrine of exclusion for "unfairness"'.

[59] Zuckerman op. cit. at 60.   [60] [1987] 3 All ER 481.

twin tests of oppression and unreliability were nevertheless excluded on some other ground (most commonly but not exclusively some breach of rights guaranteed by PACE or its attendant Codes of Practice, such as the suspect's right to legal advice, or of some duty similarly imposed, such as the police officer's duty to record interviews). Not surprisingly after that, the fairness of the proceedings was also held to be jeopardised where the Identification Code, Code D, was not complied with and the evidence tendered in consequence was for one reason or another not of the quality demanded by the Code.[61]

The courts' willingness to enforce the Codes by use of the discretion seems to derive from a sense that the breach of detailed provisions which have been designed with achieving the correct balance of fairness at the pretrial stage in mind must impact on the fairness of the trial itself. This was most clearly articulated by the CA in *Keenan*[62] and *Walsh*,[63] which dealt respectively with the duty to record interviews and the right to legal advice. In both cases the court found a link between the aims of these provisions and trial fairness: recording prevents verballing and secures a record on which the prosecution can reasonably rely; representation both protects the legal rights of the accused and reduces the incidence of unfounded allegations of malpractice. In both cases, the court held that 'significant or substantial breaches' of provisions of this sort must upset the balance and thus affect trial fairness, the only remaining question being whether the impact was so great that justice demanded exclusion.

This notion of 'upsetting the balance', however, fails to provide any obvious general principle which could be employed in other contexts, for example where evidence is obtained by a trick or entrapment but without breaking any written rule. It also suggests that the courts are doing no more than 'policing' the Codes, with the underlying purpose either of disciplining the police, or of safeguarding the rights of the suspect. Neither is of much help in entrapment cases if we are aiming for a discretion which (a) does not operate every time the entrapper breaks the law and (b) cannot be said to safeguard any right of the accused not to be entrapped, as the substantive law recognises no such right. A different basis must be found.

[61] See e.g. *Nagah* [1991] *Crim. LR* 344.
[62] [1990] 2 QB 54.   [63] (1989) 91 Cr App R 161.

Fortunately for consistency, it happens that a different basis needs also to be found to account fully for what the courts have done in cases involving confessions and other Code-regulated evidence. Dennis[64] pointed out that there are some apparent inconsistencies in the way the discretion was exercised in these cases: if the justification for excluding evidence obtained following the suspect's denial of access to legal advice is, as was stated in *Samuel*,[65] the fundamental nature of that right, why should it matter (as it has been said to do in *Alladice*[66] and *Walsh*) whether the right was denied in bad faith (according to *Alladice*, this is a ticket to exclusion) or by some genuine mistake on the part of the authorities, which, again according to *Alladice*, may or may not lead to exclusion, after calculation of a number of other factors which are said to be relevant, in particular whether the defendant has suffered any prejudice as a result of the breach. By behaving in this way, the courts are not exercising their discretion simply to protect the right in question, and they repeatedly disavow any intention to use it to discipline the police. What other rule is in play?

Dennis explains the decisions in terms of the need to guarantee the moral legitimacy of the verdict. Courts are concerned not only to develop rules which promote accurate factual outcomes, though such rules are important enough to justify a starting point that all relevant evidence is admissible. But evidence which is reliable may also need to be excluded if it jeopardises the courts' other main goal, which is to secure a verdict which commands moral authority.[67] This seems to be what has led the courts to employ section 78 to denounce the abuse of powers in bad faith by officers who subsequently expect the courts to turn a blind eye to their refusal to follow the rules of the game, as in the notorious case of *Canale*[68] where officers engaged in 'flagrant' and 'cynical' breaches of the note-taking provisions because they thought their way of doing things superior to that clearly laid down in the Code of Practice. Lord Lane CJ gave them their judicial come-uppance by holding that the confession they thus obtained ought to have been ruled out.

If this is what is happening it is exciting because it yields a promising basis for the exclusion of evidence obtained by tricks

---

[64] 'Reconstructing the Law of Criminal Evidence' [1989] *CLP* 21.
[65] [1988] QB 615.   [66] (1988) 87 Cr App R 380.
[67] A view also espoused by Zuckerman op. cit.
[68] [1990] 2 All ER 187.

and entrapment, but explicit statements embracing the 'legitimacy of the verdict' approach are not to be found in the caselaw. Perhaps the closest we come to it is in *Quinn*[69] which dealt with an out of court identification which had taken place in breach of current English rules in Dublin in 1975 shortly after the murder for which Q only stood trial many years later. The balance of fairness was held to justify making use of the identification, and Lord Lane CJ gave this general guidance:

normally proceedings are fair if a jury hears all relevant evidence which either side wishes to place before it, but proceedings may become unfair if, for example, one side is allowed to adduce relevant evidence which for one reason or another the other side cannot properly challenge or meet, or where there has been an abuse of process, e.g. because evidence has been obtained in deliberate breach of procedures laid down in an official Code of Practice.[70]

What is particularly to be applauded is the way that two types of unfairness are brought out. The first and ultimately reliability-centred example, is the risk of prejudice to one side of not being able to mount a challenge which trial fairness should allow: a risk which may occur quite irrespective of bad faith on the part of the other party. Second, there is the quite distinct unfairness generated by letting one side get away with breaking the rules of the game, which Lord Lane CJ terms an abuse of the process of the court and which is about as close as we have come to acknowledging the need to preserve the respect for and legitimacy of the verdict.

What is the practical application of the two-pronged approach to unfairness outlined above? First, there seems no obvious reason to apply different rules to evidence obtained by entrapment or by other tricky methods. If either type of evidence is to be excluded, it will normally be because it fits under the 'abuse of process' wing of *Quinn*, if not through breach of a Code provision then for some other conduct which means that the court cannot properly condone what was done. This provides a satisfactory explanation for the confession case of *Mason*, in which M and his solicitor were tricked into believing that forensic evidence was available to link M to the bombing for which he was in custody. In fact there was very little direct evidence against M, and misinformation was imparted to create pressure on him to confess, a form of abuse of

[69] [1990] *Crim. LR* 581.   [70] Transcript from Lexis.

the rules of the interrogation game even though the investigator was it seems genuinely of the opinion that if M were not guilty he would not confess. The Court of Appeal considered that the trial judge should in his discretion have excluded M's confession, and hoped 'never again to hear of deceit of this kind being practised on an accused person, and more particularly possibly on a solicitor whose duty it is to advise him'.[71]

If *Mason* is a case of an intolerable trick, the more recent decision in *Bailey and Smith*,[72] another confession case, provides an illustration of a ruse the courts will stomach. B and S had been charged with robbery and remanded into police custody pending identification parades. They had made no admissions at interview, and having been charged could not be interviewed further other than in exceptional circumstances, but a solicitor acting for one of the men warned them that the police might try to 'bug' their conversations, and that was precisely what happened: the two men were placed together in a bugged cell. To allay the men's fears of a trap, the investigating officers went through a charade outside the cell door, in the course of which they pretended that it was against their wishes that the custody officer had decided to put the two alone together. Miraculously, it worked, and the Court of Appeal held that the trial judge was right to admit the taped evidence, which was highly incriminating.

Why was the trickery not susceptible to the same analysis as in *Mason*? Because the trick involved no positive misrepresentation, nor was there any duty to be frank about the desire to use a bugged cell: the court accepted that to announce it would have been to destroy its usefulness. And the argument for exclusion sought to draw an incorrect parallel between an involuntary or pressured confession, such as that in *Mason*, and a voluntary, unpressured statement. The fact that the accused had reached the stage in custody when they could not be questioned did not mean that they had to be protected from any opportunity to communicate voluntarily with one another. (The court also went out of its way to stress that the evidence obtained in this way was perfectly reliable, and that it ill-behoved those who committed serious offences and who have not themselves shrunk from trickery and worse to object to it).

[71] [1987] 3 All ER 481 at 485.   [72] [1993] 3 All ER 513.

Putting these two cases together with *Quinn*, the search for the sort of 'abuse' which will justify exclusion now seems to have two elements: (1) the nature of the trick itself, and whether the court can square it with the rules or its conscience and in effect hold that it was called for by the circumstances of the case; and (2) the extent to which the trick creates pressure on the accused to incriminate himself against his will. If either attracts criticism, the evidence may have to go: so if the police in *Bailey* had used a 'stool pigeon' to ask questions of the men whilst in their cell the trick would then have had more of an appearance of an attempt to circumvent the Code and the right to silence after charge, and that might have been enough to jettison the confession even though the men would still have been free to decline to converse with the stool pigeon.

Implicit recognition of these two elements of unfair trickery may clearly be seen in *Christou & Wright*, the case of the jewellers shop used as a cover for trapping thieves and handlers where, it will be remembered, evidence was admitted. Here, as in *Bailey*, *Mason* was distinguished as a 'very different' case in which the deceit which had taken place as part of the official investigation process was clearly unfair. In *Christou & Wright*, on the other hand, a number of factors led the court to the conclusion that the trick was not conducive to unfairness.

(1) Not all tricks are contrary to the public interest: the court instanced the use of marked money to trap a blackmailer. Such a trick may involve self-incrimination, but not unfairness.
(2) The offences had already been committed: the officers did not act in any way as agents provocateurs.
(3) The appellants applied themselves to the trick by choosing to make use of the facility provided by the officers: they came under no pressure to do so. The officers offered only the market price for the goods, not any special inducements to trade with them.
(4) (Related to (3)) the goods would have been fenced somewhere.

The first item goes to the justification for the trick and the extent to which the court can square it with the rules and its conscience, while the others go to the 'no pressure' point: these crimes would have been committed anyway, and it was fortunate for justice that the accused decided for themselves that it was safe to admit it in front of the officers' video cameras.

There is another aspect of *Christou & Wright* which suggests a further relevant consideration, and which has ultimately to do with the reliability of evidence obtained by trickery, a factor also mentioned in *Bailey*. The evidence in *Christou & Wright* included video tapes of the sales themselves, receipts signed by the accused and bearing their fingerprints, and incriminating statements made to the officers and captured on tape. To the use of these statements the further objection was taken that insofar as they had been procured in response to questions from the officers they were subject to Code C and ought to have been preceded by a caution. The court took a bit of a risk in holding that statement in response to questions within the scope of undercover operations where the suspects believe themselves to be on equal terms with the undercover operative are not covered by the Code, but fired a shot across the bows of anyone tempted to abuse the privilege by stating that an undercover operation could not itself be used as a cover to circumvent the intended protection of the Code. Something like this was held to have happened in *Bryce*[73] in which an officer posing as a potential buyer of a stolen car asked questions of the vendor which went beyond what the Court of Appeal thought he needed to ask to maintain his cover, but which were of great use in a prosecution, such as how long it had been since the car was stolen. This would, it was said, have had 'the effect if not the design' of using the pose to circumvent the Code. Most importantly for our purposes, it was also relevant that the questions and answers were hotly disputed and, unlike *Christou & Wright* there was no recording device to provide incontrovertible evidence.

Playing the criminal at his own game necessarily attracts suspicion. *Christou & Wright* was a scrupulously planned operation in which there was uncontrovertible proof of what was said and done. *Bailey* was a slightly more questionable operation, but again it was backed up by the clearest proof. In *Bryce* the rules were broken to gain an advantage. If tricks are to be played there must be little or no doubt left at the end of the day whether the trick worked: the officer weakens his position by admitting deceit, he weakens it still further by admitting unlawfulness, and it is not

---

[73] [1992] 4 All ER 567.

surprising that the courts will not bend over backwards in support of him if he cannot produce reliable evidence.[74]

So we now have three practical aspects which derive from our theoretical approach in trickery cases: the acceptability of the trick itself and the extent to which it forces the suspect, which go to the legitimacy of the verdict, and the reliability of evidence obtained as a result, which go to its accuracy.

How far, if at all, were these considerations reflected in the two cases considered at the outset, *Williams & O'Hare* and *Smurthwaite*?

In *Williams & O'Hare* the decision of the court to admit the evidence ultimately rested on the lack of any real causal connection between the trick and the taking: the two men 'incriminated themselves, not through any trick, but through their own dishonesty', by taking advantage of an opportunity that would not have resulted in temptation for an honest individual. The outcome might have been different had the police done anything to 'force, persuade, encourage or coerce the appellants to do what they did', but it appeared that the appellants had acted of their own free will and without any pressure. Thus the police were not agents provocateurs, but more importantly there was no unfairness in admitting the evidence.

As there was no dispute as to the reliability of the evidence

---

[74] A clear illustration occurred long after this paper was written in the case of Colin Stagg, who was brought to trial for the murder of Rachel Nickell on evidence obtained by an undercover policewoman. She, by pretending to be disposed to violent sexual behaviour, had pressed Stagg to concoct ever more violent sexual fantasies, and offered him inducements including sex in exchange for a confession to Rachel's murder. No confession was forthcoming, but the details of Stagg's fantasies were relied upon supposedly because they fitted a psychological profile of the murderer. The trial judge, Ognall J, rejected the evidence, castigating the undercover operation as a 'blatant attempt to incriminate a suspect by positive and deceptive conduct of the grossest kind'. It was, indeed, a very unattractive strategem, and one which involved an unacceptable level of pressure. If a confession had been made it would almost certainly have had to be excluded under section 76(2)(b) of the Police and Criminal Evidence Act 1984 on the grounds that what had been said by the officer was likely to render it unreliable. The evidence of fantasy, while not a confession, was hardly more reliable, besides being objectionable (I would have thought) as evidence of disposition. Real difficulty would, however, have arisen had S produced convincing evidence of involvement in the crime: the murder weapon, perhaps. The unacceptability of the strategem would then have had to be weighed against the reliability of the outcome, taking into account the difficulty of detecting the crime and the fact that more conventional inquiries had failed to produce a result. Quite possibly, the evidence would have been admitted.

yielded by the trick, the only factor which the court appears not overtly to have considered is the public interest in setting up Operation Rover in the first place. There was no particular reason to suspect W and O'H: the operation was directed, not at them, but at passers-by in general. Should this be relevant? What if the police had left a purse in the street to see if anyone would be tempted, and a youngster or a homeless person took the bait? My answer would be that putting temptation of this kind in people's way, even if it is not entrapment *stricto sensu*, needs to be justified, and this should normally require either reasonable suspicion of an individual (a concept with which the police are familiar and which should cause no practical problems) or the prevalence of an offence in the locality: the purely random selection of citizens for entrapment is not a proper state function.[75] It might also require a consideration of the extent to which the evidence could be obtained in other ways. Quite probably, Operation Rover complied with these criteria, as does the 'rat-trap car' discussed earlier, but it would have been better if the justifications for the operation had been more clearly articulated. A particular cause for concern is that Wright J assumes that, if the evidence in the present case had been excluded, it would have been necessary also to exclude evidence of a brave young policewoman sent to walk about in the area where a molester of women was known to be operating. Yet it does not follow at all that the justifications for the two traps are the same.

In *Smurthwaite* the Court of Appeal thought it appropriate that the trial judge should consider, amongst other (unspecified) matters the nature of any entrapment used and whether the defendant would have committed the offence but for the enticement. If trickery falling short of entrapment was used, it was important to decide how active the officer's conduct was, how reliable the record of any evidence obtained, and whether there had been an abuse of the undercover role to circumvent the Codes of Practice. And in all cases the courts should remember that 'fairness of the proceedings' means fairness not only to the accused but also to the public.

---

[75] See the Canadian authority of *Mack* (1988) 67 CR (3d) 1. There might be plausible exceptions, e.g. the random testing of those responsible for state security to ensure that security is maintained: *Cf. Murphy* [1965] NI 138, where, however, there were grounds to suspect M of disloyalty.

All these matters having been considered, S's appeal was dismissed. W had not enticed S to an offence he would not otherwise have committed, he took a minimal role in the planning while S made all the running, he used no persuasion, he did not use his pose to circumvent the Codes, and there was a reliable record in the form of tape recordings which proved W's account.

As with *Williams & O'Hare*, *Smurthwaite* does not detail the public interest in the undercover operation, though it may be that it is too obvious to be worth saying: the prosecution case was that S had already made inquiries to find a killer before another police undercover officer arranged the meeting with W, and there was a danger that if the police did not get in on the act, the genuine article might. But undercover work of this type inevitably creates a risk that the accused will go along with any suggestions made by the operative not because of criminal inclination but out of fear that he has fallen in with a really tough customer. If such ruses are permissible, then the need for a reliable record becomes especially pronounced.[76] And it ought to be stressed that there would seem no obvious policy justification for offering a temptation of this sort to individuals who had shown no inclination to avail themselves of it.

The problem with *Smurthwaite* is that it fails to address the key issues directly, hiding them behind a mound of factors for the judge's consideration. It does not tell us what happens if, for example, W had come closer to the role of agent provocateur, and had been guilty of incitement. Would the outcome have been different? Would it have turned or whether S would have committed the crime without the incitement? What if he would not, or might not have done so? Eventually more specific guidelines will have to be worked out.[77]

A tentative suggestion is that, first of all, it should not matter whether the officer is technically guilty of incitement or even of secondary participation if the entrapment is regarded as in the public interest and involves no improper pressure. In *Director of Public Prosecutions* v. *Marshall*[78] undercover police officers purchased

---

[76] Compare the case of *Gill*, reported with *Smurthwaite*, in which the first conversation with the supposed 'hit man' was not tape-recorded and the court looked for and found clear corroboration instead.

[77] The same is true of *Christou & Wright*, where it is by no means clear what happens if a slight inducement had been used, e.g. slightly better than average rates had been paid for jewellery fenced at the shop.

[78] [1988] 3 All ER 683.

individual bottles and cans of alcohol from the respondents who were licensed only to sell by the case. Such a ruse, though it may technically involve the officer in criminal liability, was recognised to be a legitimate method of detection of a crime which did not easily lend itself to other detection methods. The need for extraneous reliable proof that the trick worked, ought, as explained above, not lightly to be dispensed with where the officer has broken the law.

Secondly, the predisposition or otherwise of the accused towards the offence should not be determinative of the outcome. It might provide the justification for the trick (as in the case where there is reasonable cause to suspect D of involvement in like offences) and it might provide the explanation for why D yields to temptation quickly and without pressure being applied, but whereas reasonable suspicion and the application of pressure are measurable concepts, the question of how D might have behaved but for the trick is likely to lend itself to some very subjective responses depending on whether it is thought that D ought to be convicted.

Conclusion

The courts have rightly decided that they have a role to play in entrapment cases. There is every chance that, if appropriate guidelines are laid down, they will function effectively, as operations involving entrapment are often planned in advance and after consultation with the Crown Prosecution Service. But the guidelines will only be as good as the principles underpinning them, and the clearer articulation of those principles should be the courts' first aim.

USING FORCE IN SELF DEFENCE AND THE PREVENTION OF CRIME

*J . C. Smith**
(The J. A. C. Thomas Memorial Lecture)

This is, for me, a very special occasion. When we were both beginning our academic careers at Nottingham in the early 1950's, Tony
Thomas was my closest friend. For some years we shared an office
in the attic of the Law Department's home in a converted house. I
know that a shared room is now generally regarded by law teachers as unacceptable but for us, as it happened, it worked very well.
Tony was a tolerant, humorous, and stimulating colleague. I
missed him greatly when he left Nottingham. It was during those
first years of our careers that we produced our *Casebook on
Contract* and, in our attic room, debated many of those problems
and questions which are still there in the current ninth edition.
Tony went on to achieve great distinction in the field of Roman
Law but he never lost his interest in the law of contract and in our
book. We always enjoyed coming together again for each new edition. The last time I saw him was on the occasion, shortly before
his untimely death, when, here in this college, we settled the manuscript for the seventh edition. It is good that his memory is kept
alive by this annual lecture in the college to which he was so
devoted; and it is an honour to be asked to deliver it.

On the 10th of December 1992, a Mr Osborne, a 40-year-old
music teacher and a law abiding citizen, was told by his wife that
two youths were wandering the streets stabbing a knife into car
tyres. Mr Osborne took a hammer and set out after them. He spot-
ted one of the offenders, Joseph Elliott, on the balcony of some
flats and went up some stairs towards him. Elliott, it seems, was
frightened by Osborne's approach and was hammering on the door
of the flat asking to be let in. When Mr Osborne approached

* Emeritus Professor of Law, University of Nottingham.

Elliott stabbed and killed him. Elliott was charged with murder at
the Old Bailey. His acquittal by the jury caused consternation and,
indeed, outrage, to many members of the public and to the press.[1]
I am not going to express any opinion about correctness of that
verdict. That is not possible because we do not know what facts
the jury found to exist. What I propose to do is to discuss the
principles which apply to this and other cases where force is used
by or against those seeking to enforce the law, or in self-defence. It
is certainly a current legal problem. There is evidence of a loss of
confidence in the ability of the police to prevent crime and of a
consequent trend to reliance on self-help. It is reported that Mr
Osborne said to his wife before setting out on his fatal expedition
that it was pointless to call the police—they had been called before
but had never shown up.[2] If the police appear unable or unwilling
to give protection, law-abiding citizens will inevitably be tempted,
and indeed may think it their duty, to take the law into their own
hands.

The law is complicated by the fact that we have to distinguish
between private defence and public defence.[3] A person is acting in
private defence when his purpose is to defend himself, or another
person, or his own or another person's property, against attack.
He is acting in public defence when his purpose is to prevent the
commission of crime or to arrest an offender. We have as yet no
criminal code and our law has developed in a haphazard way.
Private defence, with one rather small exception, is regulated by
the common law—that is, the decisions of the courts. No statute
has made any provision regulating the right to use force in defence
of one's own or another's person. But public defence is provided
for by s. 3 (1) of the Criminal Law Act 1967:

A person may use such force as is reasonable in the circumstances in the
prevention of crime, or in effecting or assisting in the lawful arrest of
offenders, or suspected offenders or of persons unlawfully at large.

That subsection is now the sole source of the law on these matters
for subsection (2) provides that subsection (1) replaces the rules of
common law on the question when force used for a purpose men-

---

[1] See, e.g., *The Independent on Sunday*, 18 July 1993 and letters to *The Times*,
July 19, 1993.
[2] Article by Nick Cohen, *The Independent on Sunday*, 18 July 1993.
[3] Smith & Hogan, *Criminal Law* (7th ed) 252.

tioned in the subsection (1) is justified by that purpose. The rules of common law, however, still apply to private defence. Fortunately, the effect of these two sources of law is at least broadly the same. The common law is that a person may use such force as is reasonable in the circumstances in defence of himself or another against unlawful attack. This is fortunate because public and private defence are by no means mutually exclusive. If you see your friend being viciously attacked and you go to his assistance it is probable that you will have private defence in mind; but you are also almost certainly acting to prevent crime because your aim is to protect your friend from death or injury, which would be a crime.

When Mr Osborne left the house he probably did so with the intention of protecting property—other cars—which was his right at common law; and of preventing crime and perhaps making an arrest. He was entitled to do that and to use reasonable force. When he went up the stairs after Elliott, it seems he could no longer have been acting to defend person or property for no person or property was any longer in peril; and in that case he was no longer acting to prevent crime. But Elliott had committed an arrestable offence—criminal damage—and Osborne had reasonable grounds to suspect that such an offence had been committed; and so he was entitled to arrest him and to use reasonable force in order to do so. Elliott had no right to resist lawful arrest or the use of reasonable force to effect it. It is an offence under s. 38 of the Offences against the Person Act 1861 to assault any person with intent to resist lawful arrest.

Let us suppose, however—though I am not aware that there was any evidence of this—that Osborne was using more than reasonable force. Then Elliott was entitled to defend himself against it. Suppose Osborne had been about to strike Elliott a violent blow on the head with the hammer, a blow which might cause death or serious bodily harm. It is difficult to imagine that a jury would have regarded that as reasonable force to effect the arrest of petty criminal. Then Elliott would have been entitled to use reasonable force to defend himself; and the question would be whether the use of the knife was, in the opinion of the jury, reasonable force.

The law, however, goes further than this. Suppose that Osborne was not in fact about to strike Elliott; he was carrying the hammer only to frighten, or, perhaps, to use only if necessary in self-defence. He was not in fact using unreasonable or unlawful force;

Elliott was in fact resisting lawful arrest; but he thought, perhaps quite unreasonably, that he was about to be struck with the hammer. Then he must be treated as if the facts were as he believed them to be. The question, which would ultimately have to be answered by a jury, is: was it reasonable to use the knife in the way he did in order to avoid the blow which he believed, or may have believed, (wrongly and possibly unreasonably) to be impending? This is the effect of the important decision in *Gladstone Williams*.[4]

It is, however, for the jury to say, applying their standards, not those of the defendant, whether the force used was reasonable in the circumstances which the defendant believed to exist; but the standard they are told to apply is somewhat relaxed. As O. W. Holmes J put it in a celebrated dictum, 'Detached reflection cannot be demanded in the presence of an unlifted knife'—or hammer; or as Lane LCJ once said, 'one did not use jeweller's scales to measure reasonable force.' Furthermore the fact that a defendant thought the force used was reasonable is to be regarded as cogent, but not conclusive, evidence that it was reasonable.[5] Add to all this the fact that the onus of proof is on the prosecution—unless the jury are satisfied beyond reasonable doubt that the defendant is lying, they have to take it that he believed what he says he believed; and they have to be satisfied that the force used was not reasonable; and it is not difficult to see how a jury may properly acquit in circumstances like those of Elliott's case.

Have we then gone too far in relaxing the standards of self-defence? Before the great case of *Woolmington*[6] in 1935 the onus of proof was almost certainly on the defendant and it was not clearly recognised that he bore only an evidential burden until *Lobell* in 1957; and he had to show that he had reasonable grounds

---

[4] (1983) 78 Cr App R 276. In *Morrow and others* v. *DPP* anti-abortion campaigners demonstrated and used force outside a clinic run by the British Pregnancy Advisory Service. One of their defences to a charge under the Public Order Act 1986 was that they were acting in the prevention of crime namely illegal abortions. It was admitted by the prosecution that the demonstrators honestly believed that abortions were being carried out in contravention of the Abortion Act 1967. It was held that so far as this defence was concerned it was irrelevant whether or not illegal abortions were in fact being carried. Though the defence failed for other reasons it is clear that the demonstrators would not have been guilty of an offence if they had been using only such force as was reasonable to prevent the crimes which they believed, however wrongly and unreasonably, were being committed.

[5] *Palmer* v. *R.* [1971] AC 814, PC.   [6] [1935] AC 462.

for his belief in the necessity for self-defence. Until 1983 it was consistently stated that an honest but mistaken belief by a self defender as to the fact or nature of an attack on himself or another could be no answer to a charge unless it was based on reasonable grounds—an objective test was applied. There were modern dicta in the House of Lords to the same effect but, surprisingly, no direct authority. The Criminal Law Revision Committee (CLRC) in their Fourteenth Report in 1980[7] had accepted the conventional view that only a reasonable belief could excuse and recommended legislation to substitute a subjective for the objective test. In 1983 in the case of *Gladstone Williams*[8] the Court of Appeal boldly rejected those dicta, including the remarks of the Law Lords, and held that defendant in a criminal case who sets up private defence is to be judged on the facts as he honestly believed them to be, whether his belief was reasonable or not—a subjective test. The fact that there were no reasonable grounds for the belief he claimed to have was evidence to be taken into account by the jury in deciding whether it was truly held, but that was all. The law was already as the CLRC had recommended it should become. Some considered this statement to be an obiter dictum, not a binding decision, but it has since been followed many times in the Court of Appeal and has received the approval of the Privy Council in *Beckford* v. *R.*,[9] a decision of a judicial committee so constituted that it probably represented the opinion of the House of Lords of that day. It has yet, however, to be endorsed by the House itself.

As for the onus of proof I have no doubt that the present law is right; a person using reasonable force in self-defence is an innocent person; and it would be entirely wrong to impose on a person accused of murder or other offence against the person the onus of proving his innocence.

The other point may be more debatable. The Australian courts have so far declined to follow the English decisions that the defendant is to be judged on the facts as he believed them be. They still adhere to the rule that a mistaken belief, if it is to afford grounds for self-defence, must be based on reasonable grounds.[10] And it is true that we have the anomaly that reasonable grounds are

---

[7] *Offences against the Person*, Cmnd 7844, 1980.
[8] See fn. 4, above.　　　　　　　[9] [1988] AC 130, PC.
[10] See Yeo, *Compulsion in the Criminal Law* (1990), Ch 6.

required for the analogous defences of duress by threats or by circumstances. If I believe, quite wrongly, that X, is threatening my life with a hammer and I knock down an innocent person, Y, because I believe that that is the only way I can escape the supposed threat, I will have a defence to a charge of assault on Y only if I had reasonable grounds for my belief that my life was endangered. My defence to a charge of assaulting Y, who was not threatening me, is duress of circumstances. But if I knock down X, the person whom I believe to be threatening me, my honest belief is a defence, however unreasonable it might be. It is true that in one case I think I am knocking down a person whom I believe to be a wrongdoer and in the other I know I am knocking down a person whom I know to be innocent; but in both cases the question is whether I should be excused for causing a minor injury to another because I believed my life was in peril. If the House of Lords were persuaded that there was no ground for making this distinction, it is by no means certain that they would decide that the subjective rather than the objective test should apply. It might depend very much on the composition of the court.

In my opinion the subjective test is the right one and should apply to all these defences. In the criminal law we are concerned with the moral culpability of the defendant in respect of the particular act with which he is charged; and a mistake which excludes or reduces his moral culpability should have the same effect whether the mistake relates to an element of the offence or an element of a defence. If negligence is a sufficient fault for the offence in question, then it is certainly arguable that an unreasonable mistake as to an element of a defence should ground liability, as would be unreasonable mistake as to an element of the offence. I shall return to that question in connection with manslaughter by gross negligence;[11] but negligence is not a sufficient fault for murder and the principal non-fatal offences against the person.

I have no doubt that, if Osborne had killed Elliott with a blow of the hammer and been acquitted of murder, the public reaction would have been entirely different. Probably no one would have been disposed to criticise the application of a subjective test—If Osborne had said he thought he was about to be knifed if he did not strike first, there would have been little disposition to question

---

[11] Below, p. 122.

the outcome. If, on the other hand Osborne, the good man trying to enforce the law, had been convicted of murder of E, the knife-carrying bad man, many people would have thought the law was too strict. In my view, the law cannot vary according to whether the reputable or the disreputable party is on trial nor, except, I think, in very limited circumstances, according to who set in train the course of events which culminated in death.

Justification and excuse

The CLRC thought that section 3 of the 1967 Act lays down 'a wholly objective test' and recommended that it should be amended so that, as regards criminal proceedings only, there should be a subjective test as to whether the defendant believed that force was necessary for one of the purposes set out in subsection (1);[12] but the decision in *Gladstone Williams* and cases following it have made it clear that this is unnecessary. However, the acquittal of a defendant who has relied on an honest but unreasonable belief is not a decision that his conduct is 'justified' within the terms of section 3. Rather it is a decision that he is to be 'excused' because he lacks *mens rea*. This is most clearly seen by considering a person who uses force to make an arrest, believing honestly, but without any reasonable grounds, that an arrestable offence is being committed. However reasonable the force may be in the light of his belief, it cannot be 'justified' under section 3 because the section applies only to lawful arrests. The relevant enactment, now section 24 of the Police and Criminal Evidence Act 1984 (PACE), makes it clear that the arrest is lawful only if the arrester has reasonable grounds for suspecting that the arrestee is committing an arrestable offence: and, in my example, he does not. The arrester's conduct is not justified. He may be held liable in civil proceedings to pay damages for false arrest, assault and battery. But if he is charged in a criminal court with those crimes, he must be acquitted—he is excused. Similarly where the defendant is acting in private defence; an honest but unreasonable belief will excuse him in criminal proceedings; but if he is sued, it will be held that there is no justification for his conduct. The question whether the arrester deserves to be punished for his conduct is quite different from the question

[12] Fourteenth Report, 119–21.

whether he ought to compensate the wrongfully arrested person for any injury unjustifiably caused.

Reasonableness: necessity and proportionality

The statute and the common law both allow reasonable force. Reasonableness in this context has two elements: necessity and proportionality. This is well established and was clearly described by the Criminal Law Commissioners of 1879 (Cmd. 2345, 11). Having stated the right to use force in public or private defence, they added:

. . . yet all this is subject to the restriction that the force used is necessary; that is, that the mischief sought to be prevented could not be prevented by less violent means; and that the mischief done by, or which might reasonably be anticipated from, the force used, is not disproportioned to the injury or mischief which it is intended to prevent.

If you have stolen my handkerchief and the only way I can stop you getting away with it is to shoot you with the shotgun I happen to be carrying, that degree of force may be said to be necessary to prevent the crime but it certainly is disproportionate to the mischief; and it is obviously unlawful. On the other hand the use of deadly force would certainly be proportionate to save, say, the Prince of Wales from an assassin's bullet; but if the assassin could easily be disarmed and taken alive, it would not be necessary and therefore could not be justifiable to shoot him. The term 'reasonable' is sometimes used to comprehend both elements and, as Glanville Williams says, to give 'a spurious unity to two questions.'[13] It is so in section 3 and in the authoritative statements of the common law of private defence. 'This', to quote Glanville Williams again, 'saves the trouble of sorting them out, but may lead to regrettable confusion.'[14] On other occasions the word 'necessary' is used to comprehend both elements, as when a court speaks of a person acting 'beyond the necessity of the occasion.'

Before *Gladstone Williams* there was no need to distinguish between the two elements. Both were matters for the jury. They had to ask themselves, was the force used, in their judgment, both necessary and proportionate to prevent the harm which D had reasonable grounds to believe was threatened? The recent case of

---

[13] *Textbook of Criminal Law* (2nd ed) 495.   [14] Ibid., 503.

Scarlett (1993)[15] suggests that it may now be different. While an innkeeper was lawfully expelling a trespasser, the trespasser somehow fell down some steps and was killed. The innkeeper was convicted of manslaughter, on the ground that he had caused death while committing an unlawful act, namely an assault. He was entitled to use such force as was necessary to expel the trespasser, provided it was proportionate to the end in view. Clearly the use of deadly force would not be justified merely to expel a trespasser, even if there was no other way of getting him out. The judge had left it to the jury to decide whether, in their judgment, the force used was necessary and reasonable; and it must be assumed that they were satisfied, either that the force he used was greater than was necessary to expel the trespasser or, if no lesser force would suffice, the force used was disproportionate to the end to be achieved. The Court of Appeal quashed the conviction because the jury had not been directed that they must consider the facts as they appeared to the defendant (thought it does not appear that there was any evidence that he believed the facts to be different from what they were). The court stated the *Gladstone Williams* principle—

[The jury] ought not to convict him unless they are satisfied that the degree of force was plainly more than was called for by the circumstances as he believed them to be . . .

—but then continued:

. . . and, provided he believed the circumstances called for the degree of force used, he was not to be convicted even if his belief was unreasonable.

The final words cause difficulty because it is well-settled that it is for the jury to decide whether the force used was (in the circumstances which the defendant believed to exist) reasonable. The fact that the defendant thought it was reasonable is no more than evidence.[16] To hold the defendant's belief to be decisive would be to add a new, and perhaps unacceptable, degree of subjectivity to the test. The existence of the two elements of necessity and proportionality, however, offers the opportunity for another interpretation of the words cited above which does not go so far. Professor Griew suggests[17]

---

[15] *Scarlett* [1993] 4 All ER 935.   [16] Fn. 5, above.
[17] *Archbold News*, 1993.

What D believed the circumstances called for presumably means what he understood to be necessary because of his perception of the circumstances.

If Professor Griew is right, we must now distinguish between necessity and proportionality. It is no longer for the jury to decide whether the force used was necessary. They must only ask whether the defendant thought it was necessary. For example, the jury think that, in the circumstances known to a bodyguard, an intending assassin could easily have been taken alive. The bodyguard who shot him dead says, honestly, that he thought it was necessary to shoot. He is not guilty. This differs from the recommendations by the Code Team in the Draft Code of 1985, (Law Com. No. 143), cl. 47, and, repeated in the 1989 Draft (Law Com. No. 177, cl. 44), under which it would have been for the jury to decide whether the force used was 'immediately necessary and reasonable' in the circumstances which the defendant believed to exist. However it may not be inconsistent with the Commission's latest proposals. In its Consultation Paper No. 122 and subsequent Report, 'Legislating the Criminal Code: Offences against the Person and General Principles,' (1993) Law Com. No. 218, the Commission have dropped the phrase 'immediately necessary'. The test is to be simply whether the use of force was reasonable in the circumstances as D believed them to be. The Consultation Paper, para 20.10, refers to the CLRC's preference for 'a subjective test as to whether the defendant believed that force was necessary.' The Commission's principal concern was with the—as they decided—undesirability of an express requirement of immediacy. The element of necessity can hardly be dispensed with. It is not clear whether 'circumstances' is to be interpreted to include, not only the facts (e.g., was P armed with a knife?), but also the question whether the facts gave rise to a necessity to act. There seems to be an equal possibility that 'reasonable' might be construed to mean 'necessary and proportionate' so that both these matters would fall to be decided by the jury. *Scarlett*, particularly as interpreted by Professor Griew, points to the need for clarification. If Griew's opinion is thought to represent the desirable state of the law—and there is much to be said in its favour[18]—the Commission's draft clause should be amended to read:

---

[18] Law Com. No. 218 (1993), 105–6.

The use of force by a person for any of the following purposes does not constitute an offence if it is only such as he believes to be necessary in the circumstances as he believes them to be and is reasonable in those circumstances—

Powers of arrest of citizen and constable

Osborne's case illustrates some of the legal and physical hazards which may face the citizen who sets out to prevent crime. I turn now to some other legal traps.

Under s. 24 of PACE, the citizen and the constable both have the same power to arrest anyone who is, or whom the arrester has reasonable grounds for suspecting to be, *in the act* of committing an arrestable offence. Outside that situation, the citizen's power of arrest is more limited than that of the constable. Where a constable suspects on reasonable grounds that an arrestable offence *has been* committed and he arrests the suspected person, the arrest is lawful even though it turns out that the reasonable suspicion was unfounded and that no such offence has been committed by anyone. Where the citizen, having exactly the same reasonable grounds for suspicion, makes the same arrest, it is unlawful. The citizen's power of arrest exists only if the arrestable offence has been committed by someone, though not necessarily the person arrested. If you arrest X, reasonably suspecting that he has committed an offence and it turns out that the offence has indeed been committed, but by Y, not X, the arrest is lawful. If the offence has not been committed at all, the arrest is unlawful. This is the rather strange rule which governed arrest for felony at common law; and its enactment in the Criminal Law Act 1967, and re-enactment in PACE 1984, follows the recommendation of the CLRC in their Seventh Report.[19] The Committee recognised that this rule—

. . . may be a trap to a private person who is careful instead of precipitate about deciding whether to arrest a person. If, for example, a store detective saw a person apparently shoplifting, he could arrest him under clause 2 (2) [of the CLRC's draft Bill, now s. 24 (4) (b) of PACE] on the ground that he had reasonable cause to suspect him of being in the act of committing an arrestable offence, and he would not be liable for unlawful arrest even if it turned out that he was wrong; but if he preferred out of caution

---

[19] Cmnd 2659 (1965), para 14.

to invite the other to the office to give him an opportunity of clearing himself, and then arrested him on being satisfied that he was guilty, the detective would be liable if this turned out to be wrong.

The majority of the committee nevertheless thought that the rule should be retained:

They [the majority] doubt whether it would be desirable, or acceptable to public opinion, to increase the powers of arrest enjoyed by private persons; and they think that there is a strong argument in policy that a private person should, if it is at all doubtful whether the offence was committed, put the matter in the hands of the police or . . . take the risk of liability if he acts on his own responsibility.

This seems to be unsound. If it is the policy of the law that a citizen should be able to arrest a person who has committed an arrestable offence it seems quite wrong that one who acts, believing, perhaps on the most reasonable of grounds, that the person arrested has committed such an offence, should be held to have acted unlawfully. As it is, for the citizen to heed the cry of 'Stop thief' is hazardous, however cogent the reasons for believing that the person fleeing is indeed a thief. In *Self*[20] shop assistants thought they saw S take a chocolate bar from the shop without paying for it. They gave chase and, assisted by a bystander, arrested him. He punched and kicked two of the arresters. Subsequently he was acquitted of the theft but convicted of assault with intent to resist arrest. The Court of Appeal quashed his conviction. The supposed arrestable offence had not been committed. The arrest was unlawful. It does not appear that it was argued, as it might have been, that this was the arrest of a person reasonably suspected to be *in the act* of committing an arrestable offence, for then it would have been lawful. The cases show that theft is not an instantaneous act[21] and the thief may still be in the course of stealing after he has assumed the rights of the owner. Perhaps a better argument would have been that he was reasonably suspected of making off without payment, contrary to s. 3 of the Theft Act 1978, which provides a power of arrest, because, even if the theft was over, he was still 'making off'. But these examples show that the distinction is an unsatisfactory one and surely reasonable suspicion that an offence has been committed ought to be a justifica-

---

[20] [1992] *Crim. LR* 572.   [21] Smith, *Law of Theft* (7th ed.) 2–42.

tion, no less than a reasonable suspicion that the person arrested is committing an offence, or that he has committed an offence committed by someone else.

The second respect in which the powers of the citizen are more limited than those of the constable is that the policeman may arrest anyone who is, or whom he has reasonable grounds for suspecting to be, *about to* commit an arrestable offence. The citizen has no such power. This too stems from a recommendation of the CLRC.[22] They acknowledged that there was some authority that any person might arrest anybody whom he reasonably suspected of being about to commit a felony, but then, without argument or reasons, said they thought it enough to confer a corresponding power in relation to arrestable offences on constables only. Suppose then that you see a man—call him Percy—in the street who is behaving in such a way as to lead you reasonably—and we will suppose correctly—to believe that he is a pickpocket. You see him sneaking up behind a lady with the most obvious intention of stealing from the shopping bag on her arm. You grab hold of him and detain him, calling for the police who arrive five minutes later and immediately recognise Percy as a well-known pickpocket with a long string of convictions. You may be commended for your vigilance; but in fact it appears that you have acted unlawfully. You had no power to arrest him while he was merely 'about to' commit the offence. According to the law of arrest, you were obliged to wait until he was 'in the act' of doing so. There is, however, a possible justification for your act. Section 3 allows the use of force not only to make a lawful arrest but also to prevent crime. By seizing the pickpocket you were preventing the commission of a crime. It looks very odd that it should be lawful for you to detain him by using force; but unlawful if you succeed in detaining him without using force; but it appears to be the case. Section 3 justifies the use of force and nothing but the use of force.[23] However you have used force so, so far, so good. But the crime has been prevented,

[22] Seventh Report, para 16.
[23] Cf. *Blake* v. *DPP* [1993] *Crim. LR* 586, holding that the corresponding provision in the Criminal Damage Act could not excuse damage caused by writing on a wall using a felt pen, because that was not violent. If the appellant (a clergyman) had used a hammer and chisel to carve the letters (causing much greater damage) then it seems he might have had a defence! The Law Commission, however, found 'ample reasons' for confining the proposed codification of this area of the law to the use of force: Law Com. No. 122, 20.4–20.5.

the lady, apprised of the danger, has zipped up her shopping bag and her property is quite safe; and you have detained Percy for five minutes. That, in law, is an arrest; and, as an arrest, it cannot be justified. Can it be justified as force used in the prevention of crime, because, if you had let Percy go, he would have continued on his nefarious way and picked someone else's pocket? I think not. The power to use force in the prevention of crime, I believe, must be limited to the prevention of some foreseen specific offence, not the detention of one who has merely shown a propensity, however dangerous to commit crime. That is a matter to which I shall return in a more serious context.[24] If that is right, as soon as the lady's shopping bag was safe you were bound to let him go.

The difference between the powers of the citizen and those of the police is not so great as appears at first sight. The policeman may arrest because he believes the arrestee is about to commit an offence and he may justify any reasonable force used on the ground that it was used either to effect a lawful arrest, or to prevent crime; but once the crime has been prevented and Percy is no longer about to commit, and has not committed, an offence, the officer's power to detain him is also at an end. The most that he could do is bring him before a magistrates' court with a view to his being bound over to keep the peace and if necessary provide sureties. The officer too might have been well advised to wait until Percy was at least in the act of committing the theft; because then he could arrest him for attempted theft, an arrestable offence, for which he could be prosecuted. A narrow interpretation of the concept of attempt creates problems for both citizen and constable.

In *Campbell*[25] the police had good grounds for believing that an attempt was to be made to rob a sub-post office and kept it under observation. One day they saw C in the vicinity, behaving in a very suspicious manner. They waited until he was just outside the post office door and then arrested him. He was carrying an imitation gun and a threatening note. He admitted that he had intended to commit the robbery but said he had changed his mind, and been about to leave when he was arrested. He was convicted of attempted robbery but his conviction was quashed. A person is guilty of an attempt only if he has done an act which is more than merely preparatory to the commission of the offence attempted.

[24] See below, p 118.   [25] (1990) 93 Cr App R 350; [1991] Crim LR 268.

The jury in this case must have been satisfied that C intended to carry out the robbery and that he persisted in this intention until he was within a yard of the post office door; but the Court of Appeal held that he had not done anything which could be held to be more than merely preparatory to the commission of the offence. Although he was not yet attempting to commit the offence the police had reasonable grounds for suspecting that he was about to do so—and indeed it is clear from the jury's finding that he *was* about to do so—so they could lawfully arrest him. Nevertheless police officers in this situation may feel obliged to wait until the robber has entered the shop and approached the counter before arresting him. The extra danger to post office staff, the public and the officers themselves is obvious. If they arrest the suspected offender before he has done a more than merely preparatory act, no charge will lie against him in respect of the contemplated offence so, unless he is guilty of some other arrestable offence, he will have to be released once the danger has passed. In C's case possession of the imitation firearm was an arrestable offence, but the police were not aware of that until after they had arrested him and it will not always turn out this way. The answer to this is a less restrictive interpretation of the Criminal Attempts Act.

Civil liability further considered

The arresters in *Self* would presumably have been civilly liable for false imprisonment and for battery. It does not follow that they would have been criminally liable. If they believed, reasonably or not, that S was guilty of theft, they intended a lawful act and lacked *mens rea*.

But even in civil proceedings the effect of section 3 is not 'wholly objective'. We are still concerned with the defendant's beliefs, but here, they must be based on reasonable grounds. The matter was considered by the Northern Irish Court of Appeal in *Kelly and others* v. *Ministry of Defence*.[26] In 1985 the plaintiff John Kelly's seventeen-year-old son, Paul, was shot dead by soldiers of the UDR. He had driven a stolen car carrying three other youths through a road block in such circumstances that, as Carswell J. found, the soldiers believed on reasonable grounds that the car contained, not merely drunken, or so-called 'joy' riders, but determined terrorists

[26] [1989] NI 341.

who would probably continue to commit terrorist offences if they made good their escape. John Kelly's action for damages in trespass and negligence failed. The soldiers, Carswell J. found, had to choose between shooting with intent to kill or at least to do serious bodily harm and letting the car escape; and Carswell J. held, and the Court of Appeal agreed, that in those circumstances, it was reasonable to fire. The harm to be caused by shooting was outweighed by the harm to be averted, namely, 'the freedom of active and dangerous terrorists to resume their activities of dealing in death and destruction'. The soldiers were not in fact shooting at active and dangerous terrorists; but they had to be treated as if their reasonable belief were true.

Effecting an arrest or preventing crime?

The sergeant in charge had said that his reason for firing was to effect the arrest of the driver; but the *ratio decidendi* of both the judge and the Court of Appeal was that the force was justified because it was reasonable, not to effect a lawful arrest, but to prevent crime: for the purposes of section 3, the objectives are to be determined, not by the evidence of the perpetrator of the force, but by the court using an objective test. The question is: in the circumstances which the defendants reasonably believed to exist, was it, in the opinion of the court, reasonable to use the force which they had used, either to prevent crime or to effect an arrest? If it was, their conduct was justified.

There was no suspicion that Paul had committed any specific crime before reaching the checkpoint; and the court acknowledged that it could not be reasonable to use deadly force to arrest for reckless driving. The courts did not identify any applicable power of arrest and upheld the use of force solely on the ground that it was justified as being in the prevention of crime. Soldiers on duty in Northern Ireland do have power to arrest anyone whom they reasonably suspect of being *about to* commit an offence;[27] but in

---

[27] The Northern Ireland (Emergency Provisions) Act 1978, s. 14 provides:

(1) A member of Her Majesty's Forces on duty may arrest without warrant, and detain for not more than fours, a person whom he suspects of committing, having committed or being about to commit any office.

This is the only arrest power conferred on soldiers by the Act and it plainly does not extend to the 'unspecific crime to be committed at a remote future time' which

subsequent proceedings before the European Commission of Human Rights[28] it was acknowledged that the force was used here, not to prevent offences *about to be* committed, but unspecified offences which might be committed at a remote future time.

There is something very odd about a decision that force used to prevent an escape is not, or may not be, justified as an adjunct to a power of arrest but is justified as being in the prevention of crime. If it is not lawful to say to a suspect, 'Stay where you are—you are under arrest', how can it be lawful to shoot him in the back of the head in order to prevent him getting away? If laying a hand on his shoulder would be a battery and a false imprisonment, one might have thought that shooting him would be murder. One of the youths, Hegarty, was, the Northern Ireland court held, justifiably shot and wounded as he ran away from the crashed car. Was his subsequent capture then an unlawful arrest? It can hardly be the law that a soldier is entitled to shoot an escaper in the leg but is then bound to stand by while he crawls away to freedom because he has no power of arrest.

Kelly's case and the European Commission of Human Rights

John Kelly applied to the European Commission of Human Rights, alleging that the killing of his son contravened Article 2 of the Convention. This provides that 'No one shall be deprived of his life intentionally'. The Article contains a number of exceptions one of which is when the killing results from the use of force which is no more than is absolutely necessary in order to effect a lawful arrest. As the Commission noted, 'the prevention of crime' does not appear as a justification in Article 2 for killing. They did not find it necessary to examine the concept of prevention of crime but held that the shooting was justified as being absolutely necessary to effect a lawful arrest. They thereby assumed the existence of a power of arrest under the law of Northern Ireland which the courts of that country had not recognised and which, so far as I am able to discover, does not exist.

the complainant alleged and the UK government (by claiming that the point should have been argued in the Court of Appeal) agreed was in issue here. Apart from s. 14 (1) above the soldier's powers to arrest and to use force seem to be the same as those of the citizen.

[28] Application No 17579/90, 13 January 1993.

The Commission thought the arrest was lawful because the harm to be averted by preventing the escape of the supposed terrorists, 'namely the freedom of the terrorists to resume their dealing in death and destruction', outweighed the harm likely to be caused by the shooting. Kelly's application was dismissed. The decision suggests some important questions.

Can anyone shoot to kill in order to arrest?

There is a serious difficulty in the way of justifying shooting with intent to kill as an adjunct to a power of arrest. How can shooting to kill be done with a view to arrest? You cannot arrest a corpse. Apart from that obvious fact, in England and Wales PACE, section 28 (3), restating the common law, provides that no arrest is lawful unless the person arrested is informed of the ground for the arrest at the time of, or as soon as is practicable after, the arrest. In *The A-G for Northern Ireland's Reference (No 1 of 1975)*,[29] a case with facts similar in material respects to *Kelly*, it was stated: 'The choice was either to let [the deceased] get away or to shoot him dead.' The person faced with that choice cannot justify his decision to shoot on the ground that he was using reasonable force to make an arrest. Shooting to kill can be justified, if at all, only as being in self-defence or in the prevention of crime. This appears to cause some difficulty in making sense of Article 2 of the European Convention which appears to envisage an *intentional* taking of life in order to effect a lawful arrest. If 'intentional' were taken to mean, or include, knowing that there is a probability, or high probability, it would of course have a sensible meaning in those cases.

Is it lawful to use force to prevent the commission of 'remote' offences?

This matter is considered in Chapter 4 of the writer's Hamlyn Lectures, *Justification and Excuse in the Criminal Law* (1989). Much depends on the interpretation of Lord Diplock's regrettably ambiguous dicta in *A-G for Northern Ireland's Reference (No 1 of 1975)*.[30] The House disclaimed any intention of deciding a point of

---

[29] [1977] AC 105, at 110, HL.   [30] See above, fn. 29.

law; but more than one passage in the report suggests that a soldier might be entitled to shoot a man whom he believed on reasonable grounds to be a terrorist and who would one day commit
terrorist offences if he escaped, if shooting was the only way to
prevent him from escaping. It is, indeed, arguable that the ratio of
the case is that those circumstances are evidence on which a jury
might properly find that this was a lawful use of force. However,
the question for the House, as it was put by the Attorney-General,
concerned, 'the likely result of the man getting away *in terms of his
committing an immediate act of terrorism.*'[31] Lord Diplock said, on
the one hand, that he would deal with the case on the basis that
the accused reasonably believed the deceased to be—

a member of the IRA who, if he got away, was likely *sooner or later* to
participate in acts of violence;[32]—

and on the other hand that the facts to be assumed for the purposes of the reference were that the accused

had reasonable grounds for the *apprehension of imminent danger to himself
and other members of the patrol* if the deceased were allowed to get
away . . .[33]

My opinion was, and is, that the better view is that the shooting
was lawful if, but only if, it was necessary to prevent *imminent danger* to life. The power of constables and, in Northern Ireland, of soldiers on duty would then come into play and there would be no
objection to using reasonable force. In addition, I agree with
Professor Glanville Williams[34] that, contrary to the view of Lord
Diplock, there would, in the case of an imminent threat, be evidence
to found a defence of self-defence at common law, which would justify or excuse anyone, constable, soldier or ordinary citizen.

Though it seems to have the approval of the Northern Irish
courts and of the European Commission, it is a very dangerous
doctrine that would allow a fleeing person to be shot down
because, if he gets away, *sooner or later*, he is likely to participate
in acts of violence. The Criminal Law Revision Committee recommended[35] that the defence of self-defence should be confined to

---

[31] At p. 110.   [32] At p. 135 (author's italics).
[33] At p. 138 (author's italics).
[34] *Textbook of Criminal Law* (2nd ed) 504, fn. 5.
[35] Fourteenth Report, Cmnd. 7844, para 286.

cases where the defendant feared an imminent attack and that the same principle applied to force used in the prevention of crime. The Draft Code[36] accordingly provided that a person does not commit an offence by using such force as is 'immediately necessary and reasonable' to, *inter alia*, prevent or terminate crime. The latest draft to emerge from the Law Commission[37] omits the phrase 'immediately necessary', leaving the word 'reasonable' to do all the work, although an express requirement of immediacy is included for the related defences of duress by threats and duress of circumstances. This is a matter which perhaps deserves further consideration.

Killing by the use of disproportionate force in self defence or the prevention of crime

Our courts have rejected a doctrine once, though no longer, applied by the Australian courts to this effect—

> . . . if the occasion warrants action in self-defence or for the prevention of crime . . . but the person taking action acts beyond the necessity of the occasion and [sc. intending to kill or cause serious bodily harm] kills the offender the crime is manslaughter—not murder.[38]

Although the defendant has killed with the *mens rea* of murder, he is to be convicted only of manslaughter—a partial defence, analogous to provocation. If *Scarlett* (above) has been correctly interpreted, the defendant who wrongly and unreasonably believes that the force was necessary will have a complete defence, unless the force he used was disproportionate in the circumstances as he believed them to be. So it is only in the context of disproportionate force that there is room for such a partial defence.

The CLRC has recommended[39]—and their recommendation has been endorsed by the Law Commission[40] and by the House of Lords Select Committee on Murder and Life Imprisonment[41]—that the law should be reformed on those lines. The government's failure to implement that recommendation was the subject of some

---

[36] Law Com. No. 143, cl. 47 (1) and Law Com. No. 177, cl. 44 (1).
[37] Law Com. No. 218, cl. 27 (1).
[38] *McKay* (1957) ALR 648 at 649, per Lowe J.
[39] Fourteenth Report, para 228.   [40] Law Com. No. 177, Vol 2, para 14.19.
[41] HL Paper 78–1 (1989), p. 28.

criticism after the Elliott case. The argument was that if this reform had been made the jury, would, or might, have convicted Elliott of manslaughter—the underlying assumption being, of course, that this was the desirable result. The argument assumes that the jury were satisfied, or at least may have been satisfied, (because no one knows) that Elliott did use force which was disproportionate in the circumstances as he believed them to be but, being faced with the choice between convicting him of murder, with the inevitable consequence that he would be sentenced to life imprisonment, and acquitting him altogether, the jury decided to acquit him. That is, the jury reached, or may have reached, a perverse verdict. But, it is argued, if they had had the option of convicting of manslaughter, they would have done so. A leading member of the bar is reported[42] to have said—

Juries agonise. It's very difficult to decide what's necessary and reasonable self-defence. They often come down on the defendant's side because all the law allows them to do is to make an all-or-nothing decision: life for murder or acquittal.

Lord Simon of Glaisdale expressed a similar opinion in the *A–G for Northern Ireland's Reference* [1977]:

... the natural reluctance of a jury to bring in a verdict of murder, with its fixed penalty of life imprisonment, is more likely to lead to a perverse acquittal than if a verdict of manslaughter, which can vary so greatly in culpability (reflected in the sentence) is available as an alternative.[43]

Since the jury's deliberations are a closely guarded secret it is impossible to be sure about this but it certainly seems plausible. There is moreover an argument from principle in favour of the reform. We have two categories of homicide, murder and manslaughter. The only justification for retaining two categories is that murder should be reserved for the worst cases; and a person who is genuinely acting for purposes of private or public defence can hardly be said to fall into the worst category. If he has gone beyond what the law permits, he should be convicted not of murder but of manslaughter.

In the present climate of opinion there is perhaps not much prospect of a reform which would be seen as a relaxation of the

---

[42] *Independent on Sunday*, 18 July 1993, Nicholas Purnell QC, cited by Nick Cohen.   [43] [1977] AC 105 at 152.

law—i.e., it would provide that a killing which, in law, is now murder should be manslaughter—even though the intended practical effect would be to bring about more, not less, convictions of homicide. But I am not convinced that the courts need wait for Parliament. They need to be persuaded that the assumption on which they at present act, namely that the intentional killer in putative self-defence is guilty either of murder or no offence at all, is wrong; and that there is a half-way house, namely manslaughter by gross negligence. Take the case of *O'Grady*[44] (followed, *obiter* in *O'Connor*).[45] O, because he was drunk, believed that his life was threatened by an aggressor and struck a blow which caused death. It was held that the *Gladstone Williams* principle did not apply to a drunken mistake: he was *not* to be treated as if the facts were as he believed them to be. The Court of Appeal approved the argument of the single judge (McCullough J.):

If one allows a mistaken belief induced by drink to bring this [the *Gladstone Williams*] principle into operation, an act of gross negligence (viewed objectively) may become lawful even thought it results in the death of the innocent victim. The drunken man would be guilty neither of murder nor manslaughter.

The proposition is that a person who kills by an act done with intent to kill or cause serious bodily harm which, because of a drunken mistake he believes to be necessary to save his own life, must be guilty of murder, because the alternative is to acquit him altogether. 'Reason recoils,' said Lord Lane, 'from the conclusion that in such circumstances a defendant is entitled to leave the court without a stain on his character'. Quite so; but the recent case of *Adomako*[46] has confirmed that killing by gross negligence is manslaughter. The grossly negligent defendant should be convicted of manslaughter, not murder. The Law Commission, when declining to incorporate the effect of the dicta in *O'Grady* into the draft criminal code said—

. . . it would, we believe, be unthinkable to convict of murder a person who thought for whatever reason, that he was acting to save his own life and who would have been acting reasonably if he had been right.[47]

---

[44] (1987) 85 Cr App R 315.   [45] [1991] *Crim. LR* 135.
[46] [1994] 3 All ER 79, HL.   [47] Law Com. No. 177, para 8.42.

That is surely correct; but it is not a reason why the grossly negligent error should not result in a conviction for manslaughter. And gross negligence may flow from reasons other than drink. So I suggest that there is no reason why, in an Elliott type of case, the propositions in *Scarlett*[48] should not be adapted to direct the jury on the following lines

> If he believed the circumstances called for the degree of force he used you will acquit him of murder even if his belief was unreasonable; but if you think that his belief, though genuine, was so very unreasonable that his conduct in using the knife amounted to such gross negligence as to be deserving of punishment, then you will convict him of manslaughter.

A doctor is guilty of manslaughter if, in the course of treating a patient, he makes a grossly negligent mistake which kills him. An electrician fitting a central heating system is guilty of manslaughter if, by his gross negligence, he creates a danger which kills. Why should not the private or public defender who kills in consequence of an equally culpable mistake be similarly liable? Is there any reason why the act of self-defence should be singled out for special privileges from other lawful acts like treating patients and fitting central heating systems? I suggest there is not and that the law is already there, awaiting recognition and application.

I have raised a number of questions about the complex issues which arise in this area of the law and made suggestions as to how some of them should be dealt with. The case for codification is very strong and it is earnestly to be hoped that the government is looking seriously at the Law Commission's proposals in the matter.

---

[48] Above, p. 109.

THE RULE OF LAW, DUE PROCESS AND PRE-TRIAL CRIMINAL JUSTICE

Andrew Sanders* and Richard Young†

There is, I think, no principle more basic to any proper system of law than the maintenance of the rule of law itself. . .[1]

The 'rule of law' is a fundamental element in the ideology of the common law. Decades have passed since Dicey put the concept centre stage, and its meaning, scope and ramifications are still being hotly debated. Despite this—or perhaps because of it—the rule of law remains a fertile area for academic work.[2] Many Marxists and critical legal studies scholars used to dismiss the 'rule of law' as mere ideology, as a bourgeois facade for the rule of class. Few would do so now, although liberal understandings of the concept are still rejected.[3] But the attention the rule of law still attracts demonstrates its resonance in our notion of the difference between law and authoritarianism (whether rule-based or not). Only recently the House of Lords, in a judgment on the bringing of a criminal defendant into British jurisdiction by unlawful means, stated that the judges must:

---

* Centre for Criminological Research, University of Oxford.

† Faculty of Law, University of Birmingham.

[1] *R. v. Horseferry Road Magistrates Court, ex parte Bennet* (1994) 1 AC 42, per Lord Bridge at p. 67.

[2] See, for instance, I. Harden and N. Lewis, *The Noble Lie*, (Hutchinson, London, 1986); G. Walker, *The Rule of Law*, Melbourne UP, Victoria, 1988; R. Cotterrell, *The Politics of Jurisprudence,* (London, Butterworths, 1989) (where the rule of law is a reference point throughout).

[3] See for a good discussion, H. Collins, *Marxism and Law*, (OUP, Oxford, 1982). Also see, B. Fine (ed) *Capitalism and the Rule of Law*, (Hutchinson, London, 1979). Some of the difficulties faced by Critical scholars are set out in M. Kelman, *A Guide to Critical Legal Studies*, (Harvard UP, Cambridge, Mass, 1987), esp Ch 9. The importance of the Rule of Law from many perspectives is argued by Price, 'Taking Rights Cynically: A Review of Critical Legal Studies', [1989] *Cambridge Law Journal* 271.

oversee executive action and . . . refuse to countenance behaviour that threatens either basic human rights or the rule of law. . .[4]

Nor is the power of the concept restricted to lawyers. Weber, and the work he inspired, is, of course, central here.[5] Some of the most sophisticated discussions within sociology concerning perceptions of legitimacy, and within political science concerning legitimate models of legislative interpretation, take the rule of law as an implicit or explicit starting point.[6]

The concept of the rule of law is, of course, most central for public lawyers. It cannot be avoided when considering, in particular, the relationship between the executive and the citizen. It would be reasonable, therefore, to expect the rule of law to be a key organising concept in discussions of police powers and criminal justice more generally. This is so in Richardson's text on the regulation of prisoners and patients.[7] Yet 'standard' police powers and pre-trial texts rarely, if ever, mention the idea,[8] and even sophisticated discussions where the concept is implicitly problematic throughout rarely give extended treatment to the applicability of it.[9]

If the rule of law is assumed to apply, at least in part, in criminal justice then this most coercive aspect of state power is implicitly legitimised by it. Marshall, one of Britain's leading commentators on the constitutional position of the police, certainly makes this assumption, beginning a recent article as follows: 'The

[4] *ex parte Bennett*, op. cit. n. 1, per Lord Griffiths, p. 62.

[5] See, for instance, F. Neumann, *The Rule of Law*, (Berg, Leamington, 1986); P. Selznick, *Law, Society, and Industrial Justice*, (Sage, New York, 1969).

[6] For a recent example see W. Eskridge and J. Ferejohn, *Politics, Interpretation, and Rule of Law* (unpublished paper, 1993, delivered to the meeting of the Public Choice Society, 1992). Thanks to Steven Whitefield for sight of this paper.

[7] G. Richardson, Law, *Process and Custody: Prisoners and Patients*, pp. 14–17, (Weidenfield & Nicolson, 1993). The relationship between police discretion and the rule of law is discussed also by R. Reiner, 'Policing and the Police', in M. Maguire, R. Morgan and R. Reiner (eds.), *The Oxford Handbook of Criminology*, at pp. 729–731, (OUP, 1994).

[8] Those we have looked at specifically for this purpose do not do so at all, but it would be invidious to identify these when this is an almost universal sin of which we have been guilty ourselves: A. Sanders and R. Young, *Criminal Justice*, (Butterworths, 1994).

[9] Two important examples are D. McBarnet, *Conviction* (MacMillan, 1981) and J. Baxter and L. Koffman (eds.), *Police—The Constitution and the Community*, (Professional Books, 1985). The article by Baxter in this latter collection ('Policing and the Rule of Law') is a rare attempt to evaluate the shortcomings of the rule of law model in this field.

impartiality of the police is one of the main components of the rule of law.'[10] It seems to us to be important to subject this assumption to the scrutiny which Marshall, for instance, does not provide, and this is the task we set ourselves in this paper. We will not attempt to define the rule of law here, nor to evaluate the normative power of the concept in general. We will instead evaluate the applicability of two elements of the concept which seem most relevant to police powers: equality under the law, and the control of state officials.

Due Process and the Rule of Law

The basic idea of the rule of law is, of course, that the executive arm of the State is controlled by law and that its actions are not a product of whim, politics or prejudice. It is put well by Jowell:

The Rule of Law is a principle of institutional morality. . . . It seeks to constrain, though not necessarily to deny, the discretion of the agents of enforcement and implementation. . .[11]

Or, in the words of E. P. Thompson, '. . . the imposing of effective inhibitions upon power and the defence of the citizen from power's all-intrusive claims. . .'.[12] This connects the rule of law in criminal justice closely with the idea of Due Process. The traditional Diceyan view of the rule of law is that '. . . every man, whatever be his rank or condition, is subject to the ordinary law of the realm. . .'.[13] This view encompasses both the 'equality' and 'control' strands but is in need of modification.

Taking the 'equality' strand first, the police (like many other state officials) are not 'ordinary'. They have more power than do ordinary people. Walker comments that 'To treat people in relatively different positions equally is as arbitrary as treating equally placed people differently.'[14] In other words, it is unjust to treat as equal those who are unequal. This is why the American Supreme

---

[10] 'The Police—Independence and Accountability' in J. Jowell and D. Oliver, ed, *The Changing Constitution,* (Clarendon, Oxford, 1989), p. 273. The applicability or otherwise of the concept to the police is not discussed.

[11] J. Jowell, 'The Rule of Law Today' in J. Jowell and D. Oliver op. cit., p. 19.

[12] E. P. Thompson, *Whigs and Hunters*, p. 266, (Allen Lane, 1975). This is a good example of the acceptance by a leading humanistic Marxist that the rule of law is not simply ideology even under capitalism.

[13] A. V. Dicey, *Introduction to the study of the Law of the Constitution*, p. 193, (Macmillan, 1961).

[14] G. Walker, op. cit., p. 26.

Court held that the defendant's constitutional right to legal counsel required financial assistance from the state for those who cannot afford it.[15] As Waldron puts it:

Acting within the state apparatus, officials can do things to citizens which are quite different in character from the sort of things citizens can do to one another. It is a mistake for us to think that the laws we use to deal with one another will necessarily be adequate for our dealings with the officials of the state.[16]

Waldron concludes that where special powers are given to state officials, we need special rules to govern their conduct. An obvious example would be that when the police detain someone involuntarily they take on special duties regarding the welfare of that individual, such as refreshment, health, contact with the outside world and so forth.[17]

The 'control' strand appears at first sight to be less problematic. A superficial glance at the criminal justice system suggests that this element of the rule of law accurately characterises it. Police officers do not, in general, assault suspects; bribes do not need to be offered in order to secure bail; judges do not let sentences depend on the degree of deference shown by defendants. Police violence, perjury, planting of evidence and unlawful detention do occur from time to time but are the exception and not the norm. An important implication of this strand of the rule of law model is that changing the law will change police behaviour. This we may term a 'legal reform model'.

But we make a mistake if we deduce from the fact that state activity is usually legal that it is therefore controlled by law. An alternative explanation of these observed facts is that legal control of pre-trial activity is largely an illusion.[18] Police officers are rarely inhibited by 'due process' from doing what they want to do. They are not ruled by law even though their behaviour can usually be classified as lawful. This situation arises because either:

—the law is a product of State agencies (the police in particular); or

---

[15] *Gideon* v. *Wainwright* 372 US 335 (1963). This is, of course, the principle underlying British legal aid provision too.

[16] J. Waldron, *The Law*, (Routledge, London, 1990), p. 41.

[17] Such duties are provided in Code of Practice C.

[18] We focus here on the police, although our analysis could as easily be applied to other State agencies.

—the law is sufficiently flexible to accommodate what the police want to do.

The research evidence suggests that police behaviour is structured by police working rules more than by legal rules, which does indeed cast doubt on the 'legal reform' model.[19] It follows that it is not enough to simply describe police behaviour. We need an explanation for patterns of conformity and breach if we are to assess the current effect of legal changes (PACE and its Codes of Practice in particular), the likely effect of proposed changes (such as the recommendations of the Royal Commission on Criminal Justice), and the applicability of the 'equality' and 'control' strands of the rule of law.

The argument that laws such as PACE have changed police behaviour rests partly on the view that such laws are significantly different to those that they replaced. However, PACE was introduced at a time when criminal justice—along with most British political and economic structures—was steadily becoming more illiberal. This period has been characterised variously as a drift into a 'Law and Order' Society[20] or a facet of 'Consensual Authoritarianism'.[21] Rather than being an exception to this authoritarianism, PACE has been seen by many commentators as part of it.[22] Conservative Government policies since 1979 have explicitly rejected the 'one nation' toryism which characterised the 'Butskellite' consensus of the 1945–1979 Lab-Con governments. The social and political discontent created within disadvantaged sections of the working class, and the homelessness and disorder thus generated, required the continued development of the 'Strong State' of which PACE was part.[23] In this context it would have been remarkable if PACE had been either able or intended to reduce the ability of the police to deal with crime and disorder.

---

[19] As argued in M. McConville, A. Sanders and R. Leng, *The Case for the Prosecution*, chapter 10, (Routledge, 1991). Some commentators have been particularly critical of this pessimistic aspect of the book. See, for example, D. Dixon, 'Legal Regulation and Policing Practice', (1992) 1 *Social and Legal Studies* 515.

[20] S. Hall, *Drifting Into a Law and Order Society*, (Cobden Trust, 1980). Also see M. Freeman, 'Law and Order in 1984' (1984) 37 *Current Legal Problems* 175, and P. Scraton (ed.), *Law, Order and the Authoritarian State*, chapter 5, (Open University Press, 1987).

[21] A. Norrie and S. Adelman, ' "Consensual Authoritarianism" and Criminal Justice in Thatcher's Britain' (1989) 16 *Journal of Law and Society* 112.

[22] Ibid.; Scraton, op. cit.   [23] Hall, op. cit.; Freeman, op. cit.

And in terms of broad powers—to stop-search, to enter and search property, to arrest even for non-arrestable offences—it did not do so. What PACE has done is to set out, much more clearly than ever before, how those powers are to be exercised and how their exercise is to be accounted for.

In order to evaluate the significance of these controls and mechanisms of accountability we shall use Packer's due process and crime control models.[24] These models are not perfect. Not only are they inadequate at a descriptive level (neither alone describes any real system) but they are also inadequate at a normative level too (as Packer himself says, anyone who wholly advocated either would be a fanatic).[25] They are nonetheless useful in order to provide shorthand descriptions of types of belief-systems. On the key question: 'control *by* the police, or control *of* the police?', crime control prefers the former, due process the latter. Rather than PACE and its form of control of the police being a manifestation of due process, we shall argue that its controls operate within a broader crime control framework. This is because PACE's controls on the police are largely controls exercised by the police. There are, in other words, more laws for the police to conform to (which is why the police find PACE irksome) but they comprise, at best, due process ornaments on a crime control edifice.[26]

We shall also argue that, by means of this apparent paradox, the changes in police behaviour brought about by these laws did not shift the balance of power towards the suspect. This is not to say that, prior to PACE, the legal framework of criminal justice comprehensively embodied due process values. McBarnet, for instance, has showed that it did not.[27] At every level of criminal justice (rhetoric, policies, rules, and practices) due process and crime con-

---

[24] H. Packer *Limits of the Criminal Sanction,* (Stanford University Press, 1968).

[25] For a critical assessment see, for example, A. Ashworth, 'Criminal Justice and the Criminal Process', (1988) 28 *British Journal of Criminology* 111; McConville, Sanders and Leng, op. cit., chapter 9. Sanders and Young, op. cit., chapter 1. One of the many problems of these models is their inability to incorporate any coherent notion of victims' rights.

[26] It might occur to some readers that we are arguing with ghosts. However, many commentators (including, not surprisingly, the Police Service and CPS), argue that miscarriages of the type and scale which nearly overwhelmed the criminal justice system in the late 1980s and early 1990s (many of which derived from the pre-PACE era) could not happen again. See C. Walker and K. Starmer, (eds.), *Justice in Error*, pp. 31–2, (Blackstone, 1993). Some research purports to support this idea of a 'sea change' in police practices. See Dixon, op. cit., for a critical discussion.

[27] D. McBarnet, op. cit.

trol have been intertwined, often in contradictory ways.[28] But it does seem that these conflicts are being gradually resolved by movement in a crime control direction.[29] The police are only governed by the rule of law to the extent that PACE requires them to follow certain routines. The content of those routines, and which routines are adopted, are becoming more and more a matter for the police alone. By this means the police conform to law without being controlled by it, and this conformity provides little protection for suspects.

The rule of law approach is necessarily legalistic. In other words it seeks to control police behaviour by setting standards for specific encounters and establishing accountability in court settings for breach of those standards. This only works if policing really does consist of encounters (as distinct from processes) and if accountability to the courts is a realistic possibility. In practice, we shall see, neither of these legalistic assumptions are valid. Thus we shall argue that the rule of law is negated in both senses in which it was discussed earlier. The law does not apply to all equally, and it does not control the police.

Stop and search

Under PACE, police officers may stop and search if they have 'reasonable grounds for suspecting' (s. 1 (3)) that evidence of relevant offences will be found; and seizure may take place of articles which the officer 'has reasonable grounds for suspecting' to be relevant (s. 1 (7)). These powers are additional to other statutory powers to stop and search (eg for drugs) and therefore represent increased police powers over what had previously existed. Research done prior to PACE showed that there was little control over how the police exercised these powers.[30] As we shall see, research done in the last few years suggests that little has changed since 1984.

---

[28] McConville, Sanders and Leng, op. cit., chapter 9.

[29] For an extended discussion see Sanders and Young, op. cit. The movement towards crime control is implicitly endorsed by the Royal Commission on Criminal Justice. See R. Young and A. Sanders, 'Royal Commission on Criminal Justice: A Confidence Trick?' (1994) 14 *Oxford Journal of Legal Studies* 435.

[30] See, for example, C. Willis, *The use, effectiveness and impact of police stop and search powers*, Home Office Research and Planning Unit Paper 15, (Home Office, 1983); and D. Smith and J. Gray, *Police and People in London*, vol.4, *The Police in Action*, Policy Studies Institute, (Gower, 1983).

This is not surprising. The 'reasonable suspicion' limitation in s. 1 is the same as had generally been used, and it has never been clearly defined by statute or case law.[31] PACE Code of Practice A (paras.1.6–1.7) attempts to address the vagueness inherent in this concept by stating that 'personal factors' and 'stereotyped images' do not create reasonable suspicion. Norris et al, in research carried out in 1986–7, observed police stops by accompanying police officers on patrol duty. In one London borough they observed 272 stops, of which 28 per cent were of black people even though black people constituted only ten per cent of the local population.[32] Each black person was stopped four times as often as each white person, and young males were stopped disproportionately often. This meant that, in that area, between one quarter and one third of white males under 35 would be stopped in one year, while for black males under 35 the figure would be a remarkable nine out of ten. The disproportionate stopping of black people was not based on any objective factor. Although Norris et al did not attempt to assess the justifiability of these stops under s. 1, they did divide the reasons for stops into 'tangible' and 'intangible' reasons. Black people were stopped for intangible reasons much more frequently than were white people.

One reason why race remains as significant now as it did before PACE is that police working practices based on 'instinct' remain as important as ever.[33] 'Reasonable suspicion' plays little part in police officers' thought processes or decision making. This is not just because it is so hard to define. It is, more fundamentally, because it does not chime with the experience of police officers. Experience is valued whereas 'books' or theory are not.[34] The reality of the streets, not a legal text, is what police officers respond to. Clearly, s. 1 PACE is not effective in imposing the rule of law on the police on the street in the sense of controlling police behav-

---

[31] See, for example, *Shaaban Bin Hussain* v. *Chong Fook Kam* [1970] AC 942 at 948–9, and *Sanders* v. *Lodwick* [1985] 1 WLR 382. The basis of the latter decision is not at all clear—see Sanders and Young, op. cit., chapter 2.

[32] C. Norris, N. Fielding, C. Kemp, J. Fielding, 'Black and Blue: An Analysis of the Influence of Race on Being stopped by the Police', (1992) 43 *British Journal of Sociology* 207. An analysis of British Crime Survey data also reveals disproportionate stops among young people and black people, and especially people who are both young and black: W. Skogan, *The Police and Public in England and Wales*, Home Office Research Study No.117, (HMSO, 1990).

[33] McConville, Sanders and Leng, op. cit., p. 27.

[34] See N. Fielding, *Joining Forces*, (Routledge, 1988).

iour. This is not to say that the police generally break the rules, but simply that 'the rules' are too vague to impose restraint on them.

As Dixon et al point out, being where one does not belong—incongruity—often triggers a stop.[35] Examples would include a scruffily dressed young male in a 'posh' area, or someone dressed in a dinner jacket driving around a decaying inner city area. The even-handedness here is more apparent than real. Wealthy people are less likely to be in such areas, will not be offended if the police suggest that they do not 'belong', and generally possess fewer traits (race, previous convictions, and so forth) which would, when added to incongruity, lead to suspiciousness. It is also far easier for the wealthy to avoid incongruity when out of their own area (by dressing scruffily) than it is for the poor. The vagueness of 'reasonable suspicion' allows 'incongruity' to operate as a working rule which treats as equal rich and poor alike, even though they are unequal in the extent to which they are at risk of being incongruous.

McConville et al found that many stops occurred without there being any specific reason to stop those particular individuals or cars, but in some areas and in some contexts the police can safely stop and search any 'suspicious' people, for there are simply numerous crimes waiting to be discovered. Inhabitants of those areas—especially the young black males living in areas like those researched by Norris et al—know that they will be frequently stopped by the police. They reluctantly and resentfully accept this. The police do not generally demand that they submit to this. They ask. Most people agree when asked. This is, at first sight, preferable to more coercive encounters.

Yet although s.1 of PACE provides the power to require citizens to stop and submit to searches it provides no power to ask this of citizens. This is because no such power is needed. Legally, anyone can ask anything of anyone else, whether they be police officers or ordinary citizens. Of course, it would be remarkable if ordinary citizens did go around asking people to consent to be stopped and searched, and few people would consent to such an odd request. Police officers, however, often do ask people if they will consent to

[35] D. Dixon, A. Bottomley, C. Coleman, M. Gill and D. Wall, 'Reality and Rules in the Construction and Regulation of Police Suspicion', (1989) 17 *International Journal of the Sociology of Law*, 185.

be stopped and searched. Such 'consent' searches do not require the exercise of s. 1 powers.[36] Consequently there need be no reasonable suspicion, and the other controls imposed by PACE[37] (which the Royal Commission on Criminal Procedure envisaged would provide the main protection for suspects)[38] do not apply. Dixon et al shows that most stops are 'consensual'. As one officer explained:

I have never had any problems with anyone refusing to be searched . . . so I have never had to fall back on proving my reasonable suspicion.[39]

But when an officer asks someone on the street whether they would mind answering questions this is usually perceived not to be a genuine request, admitting either 'yes' or 'no' as answers, but a polite way of insisting. Suspects assume that officers have a power to search in these circumstances, and they rarely know their rights. 'Such lack of knowledge must mean that their 'consent' has little substance'.[40] This is especially so in a context where it is often the same individuals who are repeatedly being stopped and searched. Stop and search is often not a one-off encounter, but part of a continuing process in which suspects find themselves in a long-term relationship with the police.[41] To do other than submit to an exercise of police authority might result in adverse consequences there and then and/or at some later date.

Thus the formal equivalence between consensual stops by offi-

[36] The Code of Practice emphasises the lawfulness of stop and search with consent: 'Nothing in this Code affects . . . the ability of an officer to search a person in the street on a voluntary basis . . .' (Note 1D (b)).

[37] Sections 2–3. For discussion see Sanders and Young, op. cit., chapter 2.

38 Royal Commission on Criminal Procedure, *Report*, Cmnd 8092, para., (HMSO, 1981).

[39] D. Dixon, C. Coleman and K. Bottomley, 'Consent and the Legal Regulation of Policing', (1990) 17 *Journal of Law and Society*, 345 at 349. This important article similarly analyses several other topics: 'voluntary' attendance and requests for lawyers (both discussed below) and searches of premises and consent to providing evidence (not discussed here). Another important police practice is the caution as an alternative to prosecution. Again 'consent' is required and again this is often meaningless in the context in which it occurs. It is a classic example of control of cases moving out of the judicial sphere and into the police sphere. It both allocates control to the police and obstructs accountability to the courts. The same is true of plea bargaining, of which the Royal Commission on Criminal Justice wishes to see more. See Sanders and Young, op. cit., chapters 5–7.

[40] Dixon et al, 'Consent and Legal regulation. . .' op. cit., p. 349

[41] S. Singh, 'Understanding the Long-Term Relationship between Police and Policed', in M. McConville and L. Bridges (eds.), *Criminal Justice in Crisis*, (Edward Elgar, 1994).

cers and consensual stops by citizens takes no account of social reality. Most people do as officers ask, but would not do the same if other strangers asked them to stop and be searched. The identical treatment by the law of people with different levels of power is a breach of the 'equality' strand of the rule of law. This also means that the police can usually avoid the legal controls and safeguards regarding stop-search, and so avoid the 'control' strand of the rule of law.

Arrest

Arrest has changed its function over a long period since the mid-nineteenth century.[42] Originally it was a mechanism for bringing suspects before the magistrates so that they could decide whether to prosecute or not. This was the only coercive power possessed by the police (stop search being a modern invention and thus its very existence being an example of the movement towards the crime control model). The classic model of arrest was under judicial warrant, reflecting the idea that the police acted purely on the authority in each instance of Bench or judiciary. In reality, of course, warrants were (as they still are) issued on the basis of information provided by the police, but at least some information was required. Important changes gradually took place after summary arrest—that is, arrest without warrant on 'reasonable suspicion'—supplanted arrest on warrant.

The idea that arrest could be on suspicion short of a prima facie case recognised the fact that the police were arresting in the hope or expectation that they would secure enough evidence to prosecute. It is a small step from this to simply arrest on suspicion, whether reasonable or not, and this undoubtedly occurs in many cases.[43] Suspects against whom there is little evidence can be released, and, as long as they are not badly treated, little can be claimed by way of damages, making the risk of a civil action remote. Individuals who turn out to be guilty of offences can be prosecuted with zero risk of a civil action as PACE allows arrest of 'anyone who is guilty of the offence.'[44] Since this applies whether the arrest was on reasonable suspicion or not the end is taken by

---

[42] A. Sanders, 'Arrest, Charge and Prosecution', (1986) 6 *Legal Studies*, 257.
[43] McConville et al, op. cit., Chap 2; Sanders and Young, chapter 3.
[44] PACE, s. 24(5)(a).

the law to justify the means. A better example of non-application of due process and the rule of law would be difficult to find.

The original law of arrest requiring a warrant reflected the judicial control of prosecutions which had characterised the system. By this century, police charging had taken control of prosecutions away from the courts, prosecution decisions now being decisions taken by the police.[45] But at least arrest was still largely a mechanism for facilitating prosecution decisions. Even in 1972 Wilcox was writing that, once arrested, the police felt that they had to charge.[46] And although *Wiltshire* v. *Barrett* [1966][47] decided this was not so (the plaintiff argued that, since he was released with no action after being arrested and questioned, the arrest had to be wrongful), the fact that such an action was brought in the first place shows how seriously this was taken. Cases were 'no further actioned' (NFAd) then, and no crimed, but not on a great scale.[48]

Only 25 years ago in *Shaaban Bin Hussein* [1970] Devlin criticised the police as follows: they 'made the mistake of arresting before questioning. If they had questioned first and arrested afterwards there would have been no case against them.'[49] The way the function of arrest has changed is illustrated by a more recent pre-PACE case. In *Mohammed-Holgate* v. *Duke* [1984][50] the plaintiff did not dispute that she was arrested on reasonable suspicion. But the reason she was taken into police custody for questioning, the police admitted, was purely because they thought that she was more likely to confess under those conditions. This was held to be a valid reason for arrest and detention. This shows that rather than magistrates controlling entry of suspects into the criminal justice system, it was the police who were doing this. This was endorsed by PACE, s. 37 allowing arrest and detention for the purposes of investigation if this is necessary to secure or preserve evidence. It is now enshrined in legislation that arrest need not be the final step before charge, and that a charge need not follow an arrest. And so McConville et al found that, after 1986, around one

[45] D. Hay and F. Snyder, 'Using the Criminal Law, 1750–1850', in D. Hay and F. Snyder (eds.), *Policing and Prosecutions in Britain, 1750–1850*, (Clarendon, 1989).

[46] A. Wilcox, *The Decision to Prosecute*, (Butterworths, 1972).

[47] [1966] 1 QB 312.

[48] D. Steer, *Uncovering Crime: The Police Role*, Royal Commission on Criminal Procedure, Research Study No.7, (HMSO, 1980).

[49] [1970] AC 942 at 949.   [50] [1984] 1 All ER 1054.

third of all adults were NFAd. PACE did not create this change, but simply legitimised it.

Pre-charge detention has been increasingly used by the police in order to investigate. Whereas at one time, evidence sufficient to prosecute was the only justification for detention (which had to be endorsed as soon as possible by a magistrate), now the desire to seek sufficient evidence to prosecute can justify detention. The decision to detain is taken by the police alone, with magisterial oversight only coming into play in the unusual cases where the police wish to detain for extensive periods.[51] Arrest is therefore controlled by no more than the police operation of the vague 'reasonable suspicion' standard, from which deviation nonetheless sometimes occurs. The rule of law is conspicuous by its absence.

The result is a pattern of bias in arrest which magnifies the pattern of bias against the young, male, working class, and black which is produced by stop-search practices. Norris et al estimate that one in three of the black male population under 35 would be involved in a stop resulting in formal police action in contrast to only one in ten white males under 35.[52] Fitzgerald's summary for the Royal Commission on Criminal Justice (Runciman Commission) came to similar conclusions.[53] And Reiner highlights a recent study covering nine varied police stations in which the overwhelming majority of suspects were drawn from what he terms the 'police property' group, comprising the economically and socially marginal (unemployed or in manual work). He comments that, 'These data confirm that the weight of adversarial policing falls disproportionately on young men in the lower socio-economic and least powerful social groups.'[54] This pattern is not primarily a product of law-breaking, but of police working rules facilitated by the law.

The absence of due process standards underlying much use of police power on the street (stop-search and arrest) offends the

[51] The police must seek a warrant of further detention from the magistrates if they wish to detain someone suspected of a serious arrestable offence for more than 36 hours. The question of magisterial oversight does not arise in the case of those suspected of less serious offences since they cannot be detained for more than 24 hours. (Sections 41–43 of PACE).

[52] Op. cit.

[53] M. Fitzgerald, *Ethnic Minorities and the Criminal Justice System,* Royal Commission on Criminal Justice, Research Study No. 20, (HMSO, 1993).

[54] Reiner, op. cit., at p. 727. Also see A. Sanders, 'Class Bias in Prosecutions' (1985) 24 *Howard Journal* 176.

rhetoric of law but not, insofar as it can be determined, the letter. While McBarnet pointed this out some years ago[55] she drew the conclusion that the letter of the law, rather than the police, was to blame. McConville et al argue, though, that the letter of the law is permissive and not prescriptive.[56] In other words, 'the police can choose'.[57] The police choose to deviate from the rhetoric because the working rules they wish to follow are incompatible with any form of legalistic structuring of their work. Either they do not seek evidence of specific offences at all,[58] or they do so inquisitorially, which is incompatible with adversarial due process. Thus in a recent 'Crimewatch File' television programme the police openly admitted that in a rape case they had rounded up the 'usual suspects' for interrogation.[59] The self-confidence with which they did this indicates how standard such practices are. In such situations, the rule of law has no purchase. Due process rules for street policing are simply unworkable.[60]

Detention

Section 30 of PACE requires that suspects have to be taken to a police station immediately after arrest except in exceptional circumstances. Once there, control passes to the custody officer. Unless there is sufficient evidence to charge immediately—which is so in only a minority of cases—s. 37 requires that:

the person arrested shall be released. . . unless the custody officer has reasonable grounds for believing that his detention without being charged is necessary to secure or preserve evidence relating to an offence for which he is under arrest or to obtain such evidence by questioning him.

This provision gives the appearance of incorporating a due process presumption in favour of release from the police station. But the strength of that presumption depends on what is meant by a 'necessary' detention in the context of s. 37. The then Home Secretary said at the time PACE was passing through Parliament that detention would have to be 'not desirable, convenient or expe-

---

[55] Op. cit.   [56] McConville, Sanders and Leng, op. cit., chapter 9.

[57] See J. Lambert, 'The Police Can Choose', *New Society*, 18 September 1969.

[58] On non-prosecution objectives in arrest (and stop-search, detention, and interrogation) see our concluding section.

[59] First broadcast on BBC1 on 29 March 1994.

[60] Further discussed in A. Sanders, 'Controlling the Discretion of the Individual Officer' in R. Reiner and S. Spencer (eds.), *Accountable Policing*, (IPPR, 1993).

dient, but necessary.' This seems to imply that the police could not arrest and detain for the purpose of interrogation merely because they thought that suspects were more likely to confess in the police station than if interviewed elsewhere. If this were so, it would mean the reversal of the decision in *Mohammed-Holgate* v. *Duke*. But this cannot be the correct interpretation since s. 30 of PACE and Code of Practice C prohibit most questioning outside the police station.[61] Once s. 37 is placed within the context of these other provisions it becomes clear that the real question to be posed is 'When is police interrogation 'necessary'?' For whenever police interrogation is necessary, detention is also necessary.

Bevan and Lidstone assert that 'the purpose of detention is clearly to enable the police to obtain the evidence necessary to charge.'[62] But since the question of 'necessity' only arises in situations where the custody officer determines that there is not enough evidence to charge, this interpretation seems to point towards automatic authorization of detention in every case. If this were so the requirement that the custody officer take a decision about detention would be redundant. An alternative view would be that the custody officer should consider whether there are reasonable grounds for thinking that the police would be able to secure sufficient evidence to charge even were the suspect not to be detained for questioning. If this were so then the suspect's detention should not be regarded as necessary, at least not at that stage. This would facilitate due process in that infringement of a suspect's liberty would be kept to a minimum. It would also be consistent with the rule of law in so far as police officers regarded themselves as bound to consider and pursue other means of obtaining evidence short of detention even though they might regard interrogation as the quickest and most effective method of securing that evidence.

There are a number of reasons for doubting the realism of such a due process stance on s. 37. To begin with, most crimes with which the police deal require proof of some mental state of mind on the part of the defendant such as intention to steal, or foresight of a risk of causing injury. It is sometimes possible to infer a state

---

[61] Para.11.1 of the Code of Practice states that 'Following a decision to arrest a suspect he must not be interviewed about the relevant offence except at a police station' subject to narrowly defined exceptions.

[62] V. Bevan and K. Lidstone, *The Investigation of Crime*, p. 299, (Butterworths, 1991).

of mind from surrounding circumstances, but compelling evidence of a mental state can usually only be obtained from the suspect's mouth in the form of a self-incriminating statement. In this sense, it is nearly always necessary to detain for questioning. Similarly, while the police may be able to get evidence from other witnesses to support a charge, they know that in practice many witnesses fail to turn up at court, or withdraw or contradict their earlier statements under cross-examination. The police know that a confession is very hard to retract and usually results in a guilty plea (which negates the need for other witnesses to attend court). But once a suspect has been charged, he or she may not be questioned about the offence in question.[63] Detention for questioning before charge can easily be seen as 'necessary' in this context, since only a confession guarantees the police a successful outcome.

This legalistic analysis is only part of the reason why detention for questioning is generally regarded as 'necessary'. The test for the legality of an arrest is 'reasonable suspicion', not whether detention is necessary within the terms of s. 37. Since the police can usually do nothing after arrest except take the suspect to the police station for detention, the custody officer may be faced with many suspects whose detention may not be 'necessary' in the due process sense. If we conceive of the criminal justice system as a sifting mechanism, this need not be a problem. The arrest would be regarded as having achieved its purpose in arresting what may well have been a course of criminal behaviour, and the suspect would be released without more ado. Whether the police then devoted further resources to investigating the alleged crime through means other than interrogation would depend on the seriousness of the offence.

Culturally, however, an arresting officer would see it as a 'slap in the face' were the custody officer to refuse to authorise the detention of an arrested person. The implication would be that a mistaken arrest had taken place. This would not only undermine the arresting officer's authority, but might expose him or her to disciplinary or legal action. More important, detention is used as a resource in policing, serving broader police objectives in relation to maintaining control over volatile individuals and situations, gathering criminal intelligence and so forth.[64]

[63] Code of Practice C, para.16.5—subject to narrowly defined exceptions.

[64] See McConville, Sanders and Leng, op. cit., Singh, op. cit., and M. Young, *An Inside Job*, (OUP, 1991).

Custody officers are thus faced with the choice of either backing the arrests made by their officers and facilitating police objectives, or following a highly legalistic due process approach to PACE s. 37. In practice, custody officers scarcely acknowledge that there is a choice to be made. All the research on detention has shown that detention is almost invariably authorised, and custody officers have even asked whether they might not be given a rubber stamp with the s. 37 formula on it.[65] The result is the appearance of due process but a crime control reality. The rule of law does not operate over the detention 'decision', because the law encourages the police to do what they have been doing for years and generally wish to do anyway (taking suspects into custody to interrogate them). Allowing detention to be authorised only where 'necessary' serves only to disguise the net result of PACE taken as a whole.

The fact that s. 37 is open to such a wide range of interpretations in itself raises questions about the applicability of the rule of law. If the legal standards are so unclear, can it be any surprise to find that the police opt for an interpretation which suits their own purposes? There have been no reported cases on the meaning of 'necessary' within the context of the detention decision. One should not assume from this that there is no issue to be litigated. As we have tried to show, a respectable black letter law argument can be mounted in support of the due process interpretation of this provision. The fact that no defence lawyer has sought to challenge a police decision to detain says as much about the competence and values of defence lawyers as it does about the ambiguity of s. 37.[66] But this does not let the rule of law off the hook for it is crucial to due process that competent lawyers are made available to suspects in order that effective challenges can be mounted to the exercise of state power. In other words, the rule of law is not just about having a set of clear statutory prescriptions in place, but about providing the means to make legal control of police behaviour a reality. If the system of educating, training and paying for defence lawyers is as defective as it appears to be,[67] the rule of law is bound to be a chimera.

---

[65] I. McKenzie, R. Morgan and R. Reiner, 'Helping the police with their enquiries', [1990] *Crim. LR* 22; Dixon et al, 'Reality and Rules. . .', op. cit.; and McConville, Sanders and Leng, op. cit.

[66] For a study of the work practices of defence lawyers see M. McConville, J. Hodgson, L. Bridges, and A. Pavlovic, *Standing Accused*, (Clarendon, 1994).

[67] See ibid in particular, and R. Young, T. Moloney and A. Sanders, *In the Interests of Justice*, (Legal Aid Board, 1992).

Detention is, of course, time-limited to 24 hours in most cases.[68] This can occasionally cause difficulties for police officers. Many therefore find it convenient to ask suspects to 'help them with enquiries' on a voluntary basis as this does not start the 24 hour clock ticking.[69] 'Helping with enquiries' was common in the days before PACE allowed pre-charge detention for questioning in the way described above and it was hoped that PACE would render it obsolete. No express prohibition on the police encouraging 'voluntary attendance' was included in PACE, however. Instead, s. 29 merely provides that anyone at a police station voluntarily 'be entitled to leave at will' and 'be informed at once that he is under arrest if a decision is taken by a constable to prevent him from leaving at will'. But this provision is as opaque as s. 37 on detention. It could mean that if a constable decides that should a volunteer suspect try to leave the station he or she will be prevented from doing so then that person must be informed there and then that they are under arrest.[70] Or it could mean that a suspect need only be told that they are under arrest once they actually try to leave the station but are prevented by an officer from doing so. Either way, the suspect's status can be left highly ambiguous since s. 29 does not require that a volunteer be told that they are entitled to leave at will.[71] Volunteers may think that they are under arrest even when in reality they are not. The lack of clarity in s. 29 allows the police to drive a coach and horses through the attempt by PACE to regulate police-suspect encounters.

Some compensation is provided by Code of Practice C, paras. 10.1–10.2 which require that volunteers who are suspected of an offence must be cautioned before any questions (or further questions) are put to them. They must also be told that they are not under arrest and are not obliged to remain at the police station for

---

[68] PACE, s. 41. For 'serious arrestable offences' detention may be extended: PACE ss. 43, 44.

[69] One third of all suspects were 'volunteers' in one of McKenzie et al's (op. cit.) three police forces.

[70] This view is adopted by Bevan and Lidstone, op. cit., p. 257.

[71] A House of Lords amendment to the PACE Bill, successfully opposed by the Government, would have required the police to tell suspects that they were free to leave: M. Zander, *The Police and Criminal Evidence Act 1984*, 2nd ed., pp. 66–67, (Sweet & Maxwell, 1990). Even this would have left open the question of whether the police had to tell suspects that they were not free to leave before the point at which this became obvious (ie, on physically preventing a suspect from leaving).

questioning. The courts have held, however, that a failure by the police to tell such volunteers that they were free to leave may not be a sufficiently serious breach of the law to justify the exclusion of evidence thereby obtained.[72] This scarcely seems compatible with the notion that the police are accountable to the courts for any lawless behaviour they indulge in.

The continuing practice of 'voluntary attendance' provides another example of how the police can evade control by the rule of law. Not only does the detention clock not tick for 'volunteers' but the custody officer has no statutory duties in respect of them (since they are not in police 'detention'). Thus the period of their 'voluntary' attendance at the police station is not subject to supervision or review. The law on 'voluntary' attendance also falls foul of the 'equality' strand of the rule of law. As with 'consent' searches, the law creates an equivalence between requests by the police and requests by the public. Anyone can ask anyone else to accompany them somewhere. The law post-PACE continues to treat police officers as 'anyone' and suspects as 'anyone else'. This is despite the fact that most people interpret 'requests' by police officers as orders, and are probably realistic in doing so. One of the authors once commented to a CID officer that the local 'villains' were remarkably co-operative as so many of them helped with enquiries without being arrested. The reply was that this was because they knew that if they did not agree then they would just be arrested anyway.

One response to this might be the crime control claim that all the police seek by detaining suspects is to investigate alleged offences and discover the truth. Police fact-finding is as concerned to exonerate the innocent as to convict the guilty. High NFA rates are evidence of this. This is indeed true up to a point. Neither we nor traditional due process adherents would claim that the police routinely 'fit up' suspects or prosecute them maliciously. Our concern is that these long periods of uncontrolled and unsupervised detention allow the police to work on people who they believe to be guilty in coercive ways which we will consider later. That they are sometimes wrong in their beliefs only adds to the problem.

Arrest and detention is intrinsically coercive, as the Royal Commission on Criminal Procedure (Philips Commission)

---

[72] *Rajakuruna* [1991] *Crim. LR* 458.

recognised.[73] Due process argues that it should therefore be used (in the absence of evidence sufficient to prosecute) only when necessary. This would prevent arrest in the *Mohammed-Holgate* v. *Duke* situation where the police conceded that arrest would simply facilitate confession and was not necessary. The idea that arrest be used only when no other course of action is practical is, of course, not new. The Philips Commission recommended it. Report and summons (or not) would have replaced a lot of arrests. Interviews would be voluntary at the police station or carried out elsewhere. The police would investigate first and summons (or arrest and charge) later, if at all. The people who would be NFAd following coercive restrictions on liberty would be spared this. But the government did not implement this recommendation. It even extended arrest to non-arrestable offences in certain circumstances.[74] Now a lower proportion of prosecutions than ever are by way of summons.[75] Many people are arrested, detained and charged who would previously have been summonsed, which also means that many who are now NFAd would have never been arrested at all (although doubtless some would have 'helped with enquiries').

In this way the drift towards a crime control system was accelerated by PACE. Arrest cannot be controlled by 'reasonableness' rules, because street policing involves intuitive on-the-spot decisions, not the exercise of dispassionate and reviewable judgment. Decisions to detain perhaps can be made subject to review,[76] but are not reviewed in practice, and detention now automatically follows arrest. The choice is between either the current abrogation of due process or prevention of arrest and detention except where there is evidence sufficient to charge.[77] Only the latter position would place the police again under the control of a non-police agency (since the courts could review evidential sufficiency), and only this therefore could restore the rule of law in respect of arrest and detention.

---

[73] *Report*, op. cit.   [74] Section 25, PACE.

[75] McConville, Sanders and Leng, op. cit., chapter 3.

[76] Dixon, op. cit., argues that the prospects for controlling the police in the station are far better than on the street.

[77] One might consider the re-assertion of judicial control by allowing arrest and detention on less evidence but only until an emergency judicial warrant could be sought, this on the basis of substantial evidence.

Legal Advice

The right to advice enshrined in s. 58 of PACE is ostensibly a major step forward in due process terms, one of the few proposed by the Philips Commission, almost the only one in PACE, and one endorsed by the Runciman Commission. In most cases, this is the only independent check on police treatment of suspects detained in custody. However, as is now well known, only a minority of suspects request advice,[78] not all those who ask for it actually receive it, much advice is provided only on the telephone (which does not enable police treatment to be controlled), and when advice is received in person the advisor often does not attend the interview—which is one of the key areas of police-suspect interaction in need of control. Only about thirteen per cent of suspects have a legal advisor in the interview.[79] Even where the interview is attended the advisor is often unqualified and untrained and/or passive.[80]

And so only a very small minority of suspects benefit from the major potential mechanism for the operation of the rule of law in the police station. This has no more to do with the application of rational choice theory to decision making of suspects than it has to machiavellianism on the part of lawyers or police officers. The explanation lies in the nature of the law itself and the institutions of criminal justice.

First, the suspect. Suspects are treated by s. 58 like individuals in any walk of life: if they want solicitors they can have them, but they will not be forced to have them. Suspects are given the choice. But this is not a free choice, for they are not in conditions of their own choosing. The evidence is that most suspects do actually want legal advice, but that, even more than this, they want an early exit from the police station.[81] Is it a sensible trade-off for suspects to achieve an earlier release by not seeking legal advice? If it is

---

[78] Up from around 25 per cent in the late 1980s (A. Sanders, L. Bridges, A. Mulvaney and G. Crozier, *Advice and Assistance at Police Stations and the 24 Hour Duty Solicitor Scheme*, (Lord Chancellor's Department, 1989)) to around one-third after changes to the Code of Practice: D. Brown, T. Ellis and K. Larcombe, *Changing the Code: Police detention under the revised PACE Codes of Practice*, Home Office Research Study No.129, (HMSO, 1992).

[79] Brown et al, op. cit.   [80] McConville et al, *Standing Accused*, op. cit.

[81] Brown et al, op. cit., found that half of all suspects who refused solicitors said that had they been readily available they would have asked for them.

assumed (rightly) that most suspects would benefit from legal advice how can they know the answer to this until they get that advice? Asking what people want when they cannot be expected to know what is best for them is analogous to the problem of asking people to consent to search or detention. In all these cases police power—that is, lawful power to make suspects do as asked by the police—exploits the ignorance and powerlessness of the suspect.[82] Suspects only have to choose between advice and an early exit from the station because they are held in the station against their will in the first place. It is not their free choice that leads most to reject legal advice, but their involuntary detention.[83]

Secondly, there are the police. The use of 'ploys' to dissuade suspects from seeking legal advice is well documented.[84] Whether these are frequent or not, deliberate or not, or misleading or not is of little importance in this context. What matters is that when the police give advice—that, for instance, a lawyer will not be much use to them or that suspects may have to wait a long time—the persuasive power of that advice is a product, again, of the involuntary nature of custodial detention. After all, if the suspect was at home it would not matter how long the solicitor took to arrive, nor how useless he or she might be (given that the advice is free).

Finally, the solicitors. There is no space to discuss the complex reasons why most legal aid solicitors are non-adversarial.[85] However, two factors will be considered here.[86] First, legal aid work, particularly at the station, pays less well than other work. Solicitors routinise it in order to allow unqualified staff to handle it and thus make it pay better.[87] Routinisation requires that advisors adopt a reactive stance rather than proactively seeking to

[82] Dixon et al, 'Consent and the Legal Regulation. . .', op. cit. This is why suspects who are 'officially' vulnerable must have a 'responsible adult' with them, whether they like it or not (COP C para 3.7–3.14). Allowing free legal advice to all suspects is a recognition that all involuntarily detained suspects are, to some extent, vulnerable. See Sanders and Young, op. cit., chapter 4. Thus giving a 'choice' to suspects in this situation verges on the cynical.

[83] For a detailed discussion of factors affecting suspects' choices see Sanders et al, op. cit., chapter 4. This is summarised in Sanders and Bridges, 'The Right to Legal Advice' in C. Walker and K. Starmer, (eds.), *Justice in Error*, (Blackstone, 1993).

[84] Sanders et al, op. cit.; Brown et al, op. cit.

[85] But see the thorough exploration of this issue by McConville et al, *Standing Accused*, op. cit.

[86] Another factor is the nature of the suspect population, which is important in relation to the police too, and which we shall consider in due course.

[87] See also Sanders et al, op. cit., and Young et al, op. cit.

establish a defence, and is based on the expectation that clients will plead guilty rather than challenge the police version of events. Second, it is difficult to advise without knowing what the case is against the suspect. But the police need not disclose the case. They do so to co-operative solicitors. Again, the police hold the aces. Legal advisors have a constrained choice: co-operate and be non-adversarial; or be adversarial but be hampered in that task by being denied information. The right of silence, in particular, becomes a bargaining chip to be bartered for information.[88] Again, by providing the police with the power to detain—and police station detention is one of the most potent threats used against suspects[89]—what appears to be a powerful mechanism for securing the rule of law is effectively neutralised in most cases.

Interrogation

The recent history of the law of interrogation is a history of attempts to protect suspects by control through law. This is the classic rule of law approach. Following the *Confait Affair*, where three youths allegedly confessed to murders they did not in fact commit,[90] the Philips Commission argued that suspects needed more protection from the police and that their rights and the powers of the police needed to be clarified. The government complied with this up to a point in PACE and the Code of Practice for Detention and Questioning. Suspects are now to be informed of their rights by independent custody officers, including free legal advice and the right to make one telephone call, and suspects are not to be kept incommunicado. The right of silence was preserved and, again, suspects must be informed of this through the caution. Notes (and now tapes) of interrogation are to be made whenever possible, and interrogation should only exceptionally take place in conditions where taping is not possible. 'Informal' interrogations are therefore almost always contrary to the Code of Practice. A corollary of this is that, as we saw earlier, the first thing that must happen after arrest is that suspects must be taken into police custody. This ensures that they are delivered into the hands of the

---

[88] M. McConville and J. Hodgson, *Custodial Legal Advice and the Right to Silence*, Royal Commission on Criminal Justice, Research Study No.16, (HMSO, 1993).

[89] Sanders et al op. cit., chapter 4.   [90] Baxter and Koffman, op. cit..

custody officer and that interviews are carried out under the Code's framework of control. These rules are designed to prevent questioning taking place under oppressive conditions, to ensure that suspects are not intimidated into confessing, and to ensure that accurate records are made of what both police officers and suspects say.

There are three particularly striking things about this framework. The first is that it seeks to protect suspects by bringing them off of the street (or their home or place of work) and into the station. It removes them, in other words, from what will often be their territory to police territory. In their territory they are more likely to feel safe, to have witnesses, to have unimpeded access to friends, lawyers and other advisors. In the police station the only witnesses will be police witnesses except to the extent that the police allow access by others. It is true that suspects will sometimes be vulnerable outside the station and that allowing the police access to suspects in private unregulated places could be dangerous. But this will not always be true, and will probably be rarely true. The police station is only safer in general if the controls outlined above work in the way intended. Secondly, the very institution from whom suspects are being protected—the police—is the institution which is responsible for operating those protective mechanisms. It is not surprising that custody officers still, for instance, often inform suspects inadequately of their rights.[91]

Finally, the post-PACE law now virtually requires, in non-trivial cases, the activity which the Philips Commission itself thought was intrinsically coercive and hence to be avoided. This, of course, is detention. This is an unresolved contradiction in the thinking underlying that Commission's Report (and, indeed, Runciman's report since that document accepted the Philips framework unquestioningly). Under this regime the police are allowed to interrogate suspects in order to try to secure confessions.

Once the crime control power to interrogate has been conceded, due process is forced on to the back foot. It adopts the defensive posture of arguing that suspects must only be interrogated in the police station under controlled conditions. But the controls that are thereby imposed on the police (tape-recording, custody officers, access to legal advice and so forth) pale into insignificance next to

---

[91] Brown et al, op. cit.

the control that the police are thereby able to exercise over suspects. Thus, suspects do not see detention as a protection. They fear and loathe detention more than anything else, and do almost anything to get out. Faced with the prospect of a sleepless night in a noisy cellblock stinking of vomit, urine and worse, who can blame them?

Requiring all interrogation to be done in the police station under these conditions has produced a situation as far from due process as can be imagined:

1. All arrests now must lead to detention. This makes arrest more coercive than it would otherwise be.
2. Failure to examine exonerating evidence, even if presented to the police by the suspect at the time of arrest, does not make the arrest unlawful.[92] Restrictions on questioning outside the station prevents much investigation prior to detention.
3. Detention is only allowed when 'necessary', but restrictions on street questioning means that it is almost always necessary to secure further evidence, which can only be done when the suspect is in detention. Even if custody officers did consider detention decisions more carefully the results would usually therefore be the same.
4. Charge sergeants (the predecessors of custody officers) used to ask suspects if they had anything to say once they had been brought in. An exonerating reply could lead to an immediate 'refused charge' and release, although this rarely happened. Such an exchange would now be unlawful, as it would be classed as an 'interview'.[93] Conversations at the custody officer's desk now take place at the police's peril. Of course it is desirable that interviews with suspects be witnessed and controlled, and this is a consequence of that principle. But the problem only arises because the suspect is taken into custody in the first place.
5. These formalities have lengthened detention at the less serious end of the criminal spectrum.[94] The longer the period of

[92] See especially *Castorina* v. *Chief Constable of Surrey* (1988) 138 NLJ 180 discussed in Sanders and Young, op cit, chapter 3.

[93] See, for example, *Matthews* (1990) 91 Cr App R 43 discussed in Sanders and Young, op. cit., chapter 4.

[94] See, for example, A. Bottomley, C. Coleman, D. Dixon, M. Gill and D. Wall, 'The detention of suspects in police custody', (1991) 31 *British Journal of*

detention the more agitated suspects become and the more they are pressured into saying whatever is needed to secure release.

6. This anti-due process framework is a creation, in large part, of the desire to prevent uncontrolled interrogation. Yet the absence of non-police controls in the police station allows informal interrogation to take place easily there. Solicitors, for instance, do not stay between interviews, and tapes do not stay switched on. Interviewing is not confined to specific set-piece encounters, but can occur at any point in the process of detention. Contested 'confessions' arise therefore not just from 'scenic routes'[95] but also cell visits[96] and unauthorised codas to taped interrogations.[97] In any event, the police still informally interview outside the station in at least a sizeable minority of cases on their own admission.[98] The police can, as in other situations, choose. The suspect cannot.

The legal framework surrounding interrogation enables the police invariably to detain after arrest, but informally to interrogate if they wish and almost when they wish. It prevents suspects from being encouraged to exonerate themselves prior to detention. And detention in minor cases has been lengthened, thus enhancing the pressure to answer police questions. This framework does little to control the police and does rather more to facilitate and recognise existing crime control practices of isolation and the creation of powerlessness and pressure. It clearly fails the rule of law's 'control' test.

The Right of Silence

The Code of Practice retains the caution enshrining the right of silence. It also says, in Note 1B, that the police are:

Criminology 347; Brown et al, op. cit.; and M. Maguire, 'Effects of the PACE provisions on detention and questioning', (1988) 28 *British Journal of Criminology* 19.

[95] See, for example, *Khan* (1990) 23 February, Court of Appeal, unreported. Discussed by Sanders and Young, op. cit., chapter 4.

[96] Sanders et al, op. cit.

[97] See, for example, *Dunn* (1990) 91 Cr App R 237 and M. McConville, 'Videotaping interrogations', [1992] *Crim. LR* 532.

[98] S. Moston and G. Stephenson, *The Questioning and Interviewing of Suspects outside the Police Station*, Royal Commission on Criminal Justice, Research Study No. 22, (HMSO, 1993); Brown et al, op. cit. The methodology of these studies leave a lot to be desired, and their estimates of informal interviewing are very likely to be underestimates. See, for a critique, Sanders and Young, op. cit., chapter 4.

entitled to question any person from whom he thinks useful information can be obtained . . . A person's declaration that he is unwilling to reply does not alter this entitlement.

There is no right to refuse to be interrogated. And there is no right to object to the way one is being interrogated. The police are allowed to try to persuade people to do that which they do not want to do—confess. Much interrogation is therefore necessarily manipulative. This is no criticism of the police. How else are the police to persuade suspects to do something that which they have the right not to do, and which is contrary to their interests? The police do this by using a range of tactics varying from deception to intimidation.[99] The legality of tactics in the 'middle range' (accusation, persuasion, repetition, threat of custodial conditions, leading through false logic, etc) is completely open to debate. The Philips Commission called for a code of practice which would take 'realistic account of the pressures upon police and upon suspects',[100] but neither Code C nor PACE specifies what is, and is not, oppressive. The police play on this ambiguity. After the release of the *Cardiff 3* the Chief Constable of South Wales called for 'a full debate on what constituted oppressive questioning',[101] and after a murder trial where the judge refused to accept alleged confessions secured after the police 'pounded him with sexual allegations' the head of CID for the force in question said 'it is a matter of interpretation as to what is oppressive . . . It is rather difficult to establish the truth by pussyfooting about.'[102]

Once again the rule of law is more apparent than real. Suspects are given a choice to answer questions or not, just as anyone in 'normal' life may answer questions, or not, asked by any stranger. And the police, just like anyone in normal life, have the right to ask questions of anyone, including suspects in custody. The equivalence here is as false as it is in relation to consent searches, voluntary attendance, and requests for legal advice. Suspects who refuse to answer questions are subjected to further tactics and further interrogation. Continued detention can only be justified if it is 'necessary' to do so in order to secure evidence by questioning; but if a suspect refuses to answer police questions then it clearly is necessary to continue detention if that goal is to be achieved. As we

---

[99] See, for example, McConville and Hodgson, op. cit.
[100] *Report*, op. cit., para 4.111.   [101] *The Guardian*, 17/12/92.
[102] *The Guardian* 22/11/93.

have seen, the attempt to provide the protection of the rule of law by bringing interrogation into the police station has had the opposite effect. The increased use of detention also has a massive impact on the choices made by suspects about whether to answer questions. Suspects do not have a free choice about whether to answer questions. Their choice is structured by police tactics, the brute facts of detention, and the control which the police have over the length of detention. By treating police officers and suspects as equal—each may ask and each may answer questions, and neither need do either—the law creates the conditions under which it is inevitable that few suspects will exercise their rights.[103]

And so in judging the applicability of the rule of law we need to recognise that, insofar as we can determine police compliance with the law on interrogation, compliance is not a product of the law. Rather, the law allows the police to put as much pressure on most suspects as they wish and as they need to do. This explains why cases like the *Cardiff 3*, where the Court of Appeal condemned oppressive tactics, or David Blythe, where a young man allegedly confessed to a murder which he certainly did not do, are rare. It is not because the police are usually reined in by the law. It is because they rarely have to go beyond the law to achieve their objective.[104]

It follows that the focus should not be on the right of silence, which we have seen is a 'right' with little meaning.[105] Instead, the acid test of the rule of law hinges on the police power to interro-

---

[103] Realistic estimates of the extent to which silence is exercised vary between five per cent and 14 per cent. It is impossible to be more precise than this because 'silence' is a far more problematic concept than it might seem, although the most useful definitions would estimate levels nearer the bottom than the top end. The most sophisticated discussions are R. Leng, *The Right to Silence in Police Interrogation*, Royal Commission on Criminal Justice, Research Study No.10, (HMSO, 1993), and D. Brown, 'The Incidence of Right of Silence in Police Stations', (1994) 35 *Home Office Research Bulletin* 57.

[104] Thus when Evans finds that in the majority of cases juvenile suspects confess without prior use of police tactics (in formal interrogations at least) he misses the point in arguing that tactics are of less interest than 'normal' interrogation (R. Evans, *Conduct of Police Interviews with Juveniles*, Royal Commission on Criminal Justice, Research Study No.8, (HMSO, 1993)) Of course the police do not use tactics when they do not need to do so. The question is what the police can get away with when confessions are not readily forthcoming.

[105] It is not even meaningful at a formalistically legal level, as there is no remedy for breach. See A. Sanders, 'Right, Remedies, and the PACE Act', [1988] *Crim. LR* 802.

gate. The police have special power over suspects in involuntary custody. The simple provision of choice to suspects about whether to answer questions fails to recognise the power inequality of the two parties. The rule of law would only operate if suspects could choose whether or not to listen to police questions. Even then the pressures of detention would undermine this. The ultimate position would be to refuse to let the police interrogate at all unless suspects were either with the police voluntarily or, perhaps, with legal advisors throughout the period of detention. In reality the police cannot be prevented from interrogating. But the point of their so doing would be reduced if, as a corollary of a prohibition on interrogation, there was an absolute exclusionary rule relating to the products of interrogation.[106]

Again, as with arrest and NFA it could be argued that it is better to interrogate in controlled conditions than elsewhere. This is doubtless true, at least to some extent. But if interrogation is uncontrollable (which is, in effect, our argument) it is not where or how interrogation takes place that determines the applicability of the rule of law. It is whether it is allowed at all that matters, and whether its products are useable in court. The rule of law is compatible with allowing interrogation only if there is a firm exclusionary rule. This would allow the police to secure confessions in order to help identify guilt, but then require them to prove it by getting other evidence. This is in effect an argument for a corroboration rule. It is certainly no guarantee against wrongful conviction,[107] but the rule of law does not require such a guarantee. All the rule of law requires is that the system is directed at the protection of the innocent (which all suspects are presumed to be), while recognising that mistakes and individual rule breaking will occur.

---

[106] The purpose would be twofold in relation to the rule of law. First, it would recognise the lesser power of the suspect by abandoning notions of 'voluntariness', 'inducements' and 'oppressiveness' which are simplistic within the context of coercive involuntary detention. Second, it would create extra legal control over the police, deterring them from breaching the law. The issues involved are, of course, far more complex than this, but there is no space to discuss them in more depth or to discuss the other merits and demerits of exclusionary rules. See, however, I. Dennis, 'Reconstructing the Law of Criminal Evidence' (1989) *Current Legal Problems* 21; and Sanders and Young, op. cit., chapter 9.

[107] I. Dennis, 'Miscarriages of Justice and the Law of Confessions' (1993) *Public Law* 291. But, contrary to the view of the Runciman Commission, it would certainly help: R. Young and A. Sanders, 'The Royal Commission on Criminal Justice: A Confidence Trick?', (1994) 14 *Oxford Journal of Legal Studies* 435.

Criminal Justice and Social Order

We have argued that the rule of law does not, in general, operate in relation to police powers, and that this is at least as much a product of the applicable rules of law as it is of rule breaking by the police. If this is true we should try to understand how two Royal Commissions, numerous committees of enquiry and Parliament on several occasions could have allowed these fundamental principles to be fatally undermined without acknowleging that this was happening. We think that there are two main reasons. First, our conclusion could not have been reached through traditional legal analysis of the law 'in the books' alone. The operation of the rule of law is about control of the state (in this case, the police) and balances of power. These are empirical and sociological matters, as well as being 'legal' in the traditional sense. The two Royal Commissions did commission empirical research, but only of a limited kind. Most of it measured the extent of compliance with rules rather than the reasons for compliance and deviance.[108] To understand criminal justice we need a better theoretical understanding of the relationship between criminal law and social processes than is usual in the socio-legal field.

The second reason concerns which sections of society suffer from this undermining of the rule of law. The Runciman Commission said:

. . . there is a potential conflict between the interests of justice on the one hand and the requirement of fair and reasonable treatment for everyone involved, suspects and defendants included, on the other. . . . Our recommendations serve the interests of justice without diminishing the individual's right to fair and reasonable treatment.[109]

Taken literally, this makes little sense. For what can the 'interests of justice' encompass over and above everyone being treated fairly and reasonably? This appears to be a false dichotomy. Reading

---

[108] It would be invidious to single out particular studies as epitomising this tendency, particularly as our own past work—for example, Sanders et al, op. cit.—has fallen into this trap at times. We would, however, single out some work as not falling into this trap, especially McConville and Hodgson, op. cit. and M. Maguire and C. Norris, *The Conduct and Supervision of Criminal Investigations*, Royal Commission on Criminal Justice, Research Study No. 5, (HMSO, 1992).

[109] Royal Commission on Criminal Justice, *Report*, Cm 2263, p. 8, (HMSO, 1993).

between the lines, it seems to hark back to the Philips Commission, whose terms of reference enjoined it to have:

regard both to the interests of the community in bringing offenders to justice and to the rights and liberties of persons suspected or accused of crime . . .[110]

Surely persons 'suspected or accused' have as much interest as anyone else in bringing actual offenders to justice, for they are all innocent until proven to be guilty, just as it must be in the interests of justice to treat suspects fairly.[111] And all members of the 'community' are potential suspects. The question which requires consideration is whether the community as a whole should be subject to the interference with liberty which crime control powers involve.

At this point these apparently false dichotomies begin to make sense. For as we have seen, police powers are not exercised against all sections of the community equally. The rule of law is undermined primarily in relation to 'police property'.[112] The police, along with many others, tend to divide society into 'rough' and 'respectable'.[113] The former are fair game for stops and so forth, but are in turn divided into those who are submissive and those who are 'obnoxious', 'slag', or 'toe-rags' who are regarded as unworthy of rights either because of their perceived ways of life or their attitude to the police.[114] As Reiner points out, the 'police property' group within society is larger now than ever before as mass unemployment, low wages and deskilling have become entrenched features of the economic landscape.[115] While, in his view, the duties of the police in our divided society must include 'keeping the lid on underclass symbolic locations' he also believes that the police must do this 'in an effective and just way, or forfeit popular and political support.'

The problem, as we see it, is that the political community (and, indeed, the majority of the population) has little interest in ensuring that the police act in a 'just way', but a vested interest in ensuring 'effectiveness'. For decision makers and decision formers

[110] *Report*, op. cit., (1981), p. vi.

[111] From a due process point of view. The Royal Commission, though, was not thinking on due process lines.

[112] To quote Reiner, op. cit., again.

[113] See, for example, S. Holdaway, *Inside the British Police*, (Blackwell, 1983); Smith and Gray, op. cit.

[114] Young, op. cit.; J. Foster, 'Two Stations', in D. Downes (ed.), *Crime and the City*, (Macmillan, 1989) and Singh, op. cit.

[115] Op. cit., p. 756.

are rarely suspects and are never regarded as 'toe-rags'. They have no experience of being held overnight in police cells and thus no sense of the intimidation it creates. They cannot imagine feeling that the police are enemies of one's community.[116] They are not at the receiving end of the contempt which the police display for some sections of society.[117] One section of society makes the laws and reviews the policies (for the two Royal Commissions have been almost exclusively white middle aged and middle class too) which bear down on the other. It is easy for the decision making community to decide that it is in 'society's' interests for suspects to have their liberty compromised when those suspects are mainly drawn from the non-decision making community.

In a real sense due process does not, and cannot, apply to the policing of 'rough' communities. Reiner's reference to the police 'keeping the lid on' means that they are as concerned to gather criminal intelligence, dispel disorder and provide an authority 'presence' as they are to prosecute particular offences.[118] In the context of a sharply polarised society the choice would seem to lie between the just but ineffective policing of those who are fundamentally alienated, or the relatively effective but repressive policing of such groups and individuals. It is the latter which the law allows and encourages and it is the latter towards which the majority of us appear prepared to turn a blind eye. But to accept this is to accept the most fundamental undermining of the rule of law of all. It denies that the protection of the due process of law applies in equal measure to everyone, regardless of age, race, class or gender. The task for those who believe in the rule of law must be to consider afresh the kind of society within which such a notion could be made meaningful for all.

[116] This perception emerges clearly from the 'race and police' literature. See, for example, E. Cashmore and E. McLaughlin (eds.), *Out of Order ?*, (Routledge 1991). This literature, and the general issue of policing communities, as against policing incidents, is reviewed in Sanders and Young, op. cit., chapter 2.

[117] See, for instance, 'insider's' accounts by Young, op. cit., and R. Graef, *Talking Blues*, (Fontana, 1990). Again, some of this material is discussed in Sanders and Young, op. cit., chapter 2.

[118] It is because of the irrelevance of law to such fluid indefinable processes that we are not necessarily advocating rigorous due process laws aimed at controlling the police. However, if we recognise the limitations of the rule of law we are more likely to accept that the miscarriages of justice which have prompted much of the current debate are a predictable product of the system as it operates in our society and not merely the result of lax laws or 'bad apples'.

EQUITABLE PROPERTY*

Kevin Gray **

*Take note of the meaning of the ancient song: that what there is
shall belong to those who are good for it*
(Bertolt Brecht, *The Caucasian Chalk Circle*)

Not so long ago I was talking with a couple of Martians at one of
those seminars in Oxford organised by Professor Peter Birks. The
visitors explained that they were engaged in a piece of joint
research on the terrestrial concept of property—a mode of thinking
which apparently finds no parallel within their own jurisdiction.
The present paper is prompted in some measure by the conversation which I had with the Martian lawyers, for I was stimulated to
look afresh, from perhaps a wider perspective, at the strange way
in which we humans make claims of 'property' or 'ownership' in
respect of the resources of this world. My concern is to share an
essentially descriptive, rather than normative, view of the phenomenon of property, whilst bearing in mind how readily the descriptive and the normative can merge.

My Martian interlocutors reminded me of the highly anomalous
nature, unparalleled within our own galaxy, of the terrestrial
impulse to view external resources as belonging properly or exclusively to particular members of the human race. Social psycholo-
gists like Ernest Beaglehole used to speak of 'the hidden nerve of
irrational animism that binds the individual to the object he appropriates as his own'.[1] My Martian colleagues were especially
intrigued by the fact that, in one of the earliest phrases articulated
by almost every human child, there lies the strongest affirmation of

---

* This paper was written during the author's tenure of a Senior Research
Fellowship at St John's College, Oxford. The author also gratefully acknowledges
the invaluable help given by Mrs Joycey Tooher of the Faculty of Law, Monash
University and Mr Lawrie Tooher of the Department of the Premier and Cabinet,
Melbourne, Victoria.

** Professor of Law, University of Cambridge, and Fellow of Trinity College.

[1] *Property: A Study in Social Psychology* (London 1931), p. 23 et seq.

this internalised concern to appropriate.[2] The phrase, 'It's mine!', is, of course, literally untranslatable into any of the Martian languages.[3] Yet, as my friends pointed out, even our own judges and legislators seem obsessed with the need to formulate human perceptions of the external world in the intangible terms of individualised ownership and 'private property'. Our lives are in every respect dominated by an intuitive sense of property and belonging.

This insistent allocation of private rights of ownership is not without its own subtlety: it is widely recognised that claims of ownership may sometimes transcend the superficial evidences of formal title. Even if a resource does not belong to someone in any formal or officially recorded way, there is a whole branch of jurisprudence devoted to the proposition that the same resource may 'belong in equity' to a particular claimant. I still remember the curious thrill of opening up the year books to read the poignant plea of the cestui that, when the stranger with notice comes to purchase the entrusted land, he is bound because 'in conscience he purchases my land' (*en conscience il purchase ma terre*).[4]

Legal history similarly pulses with timeless discussion of the extent to which underlying but nevertheless substantial claims of

---

[2] 'Even with animals one finds the recognition of *meum* and *tuum* . . . With children this impulse develops very early. It must be considered as an innate tendency' (L. Litwinski, *Is there an instinct of possession?* 33 British Journal of Psychology 28, 36 (1942–43)). There is a substantial literature on the peculiar status of the child's 'first treasured object' (see e.g. D. W. Winnicott, 'Transitional Objects And Transitional Phenomena: a study of the first not-me possession', 34 *International Journal of Psycho-Analysis* 89 (1953)). It is argued that such transitional phenomena, by reinforcing the self-other distinction, are particularly significant in promoting successful individuation and the construction of self-identity in very young children (see O. Stevenson, 'The first treasured possession', 9 *The Psycho-Analytic Study of the Child* 199 (1954); J. Newson and E. Newson, 'Seven Years Old in the Home Environment' (London 1976), p. 128; L. Furby, 'The origins and early development of possessive behaviour', 2 *Political Psychology* 30 (1980); L. Levine, 'Mine: Self-definition in 2-year-old boys', 19 *Developmental Psychology* 544 (1983)).

[3] In the possible absence of a Martian dictionary, see H. Dittmar, *The Social Psychology of Material Possessions* (Hemel Hempstead 1992), p. 49, for reference to the 'astonishing feat' involved in the 'comprehension and verbal expression of possessive relationships [as] one of the very first stages in children's language development.' See also C. Cooley, 'A study of the early use of self-words by a child', 15 *Psychological Review* 339 (1908); F. W. Rudmin, 'Historical Note on the Development of Possessive Pronouns', 50 *Journal of Speech and Hearing Disorders* 298 (1985); Rudmin, 'Dominance and children's use of possessive case', 61 *Perceptual and Motor Skills* 566 (1985).

[4] YB 11 Edw IV, fol 8. See *The Collected Papers of Frederic William Maitland* (ed H. A. L. Fisher, Cambridge 1911), Vol III, p. 345.

private ownership may be maintained in such elusive assets as swarms of bees,[5] wild animals,[6] wounded whales,[7] and shipwreck treasure[8]—all in the course of their active pursuit. Their modern equivalent, the fugitive or maturing commercial opportunity, was said in *Cook v. Deeks*[9] to belong 'in equity' not to the aggressively opportunistic company directors concerned in that case but rather to their company.[10] Deep in the human psyche is some primal perception of an inner rightfulness inherent in certain kinds of private proprietary claim—even where the claims in question relate to incipient or inchoate opportunities of exploitation and enjoyment. We are continually prompted by stringent, albeit intuitive, perceptions of 'belonging'. Accordingly there is widespread recognition of the wrongfulness of certain *mis*appropriations of resource and opportunity. In this context we are still not far removed from the primitive, instinctive cries of identification which resound in the playgroup or playground: 'That's not yours; it's *mine*.'

This constant labelling as *meum* and *tuum* is perhaps inevitable. As Blackstone said, '[t]here is nothing which so generally strikes the imagination, and engages the affections of mankind, as the right of property'.[11] Neither, ironically, is there any concept quite so fragile as this right: property is not theft but fraud.[12] Almost all of our everyday reference to the property concept is unthinking, naive and relatively meaningless. Property talk is generally careless and vacuous; property talk is mutual deception. In our crude way we are seldom concerned to look behind the immediately practical

[5] *Bl Comm*, Vol. II, p. 393; *Kearry v. Pattinson* [1939] 1 KB 471, 481 per Goddard LJ. See also *Young v. Hichens* (1844) 6 QB 606, 611, 115 ER 228, 230; (1939) 17 Can Bar Rev 130; G. W. Paton, *Bees and the Law*, (1939–41) 2 Res Judicata 22.

[6] *Pierson v. Post*, 2 Am Dec 264, 265f, 3 Caines 175 (1805).

[7] *Littledale v. Scaith* (1788) 1 Taunt 243(n), 127 ER 826; *Hogarth v. Jackson* (1827) Moo & M 58, 173 ER 1080; *Skinner v. Chapman (ex rel Alderson)* (1827) Moo & M 59(n), 173 ER 1081; *Baldick v. Jackson* (1911) 30 NZLR 343, 345.

[8] *Treasure Salvors, Inc v. Unidentified Wrecked and Abandoned Sailing Vessel*, 640 F2d 560, 567 (5th Cir 1981).

[9] [1916] 1 AC 554, 564.

[10] Thus a fiduciary's undisclosed profit 'belongs in equity' to the fiduciary's entrustor (see *Hospital Products Ltd v. United States Surgical Corporation* (1984) 156 CLR 41, 108f per Mason J.). For further reference to the way in which the operation of fiduciary principles 'appropriates' unauthorised gains for the benefit of the entrustor, see *Chan v. Zacharia* (1984) 154 CLR 178, 198 per Deane J. See also *Fraser Edmiston Pty Ltd v. A.G.T. (Qld) Pty Ltd* [1988] 2 Qd R 1, 11.

[11] *Bl Comm*, Vol II, p. 2.

[12] *Property in Thin Air*, [1991] Cambridge LJ 252.

or functional sense in which the term is employed. Thus, for example, we tend, almost as a reflex response, to think of property as the *thing* or *resource* which is owned. It was, however, Jeremy Bentham who long ago pointed out that 'property' is what we have *in* things, not the things that we think we have.[13] 'Property' is the name given to a legally (because socially) endorsed constellation of power *over* things and resources. Property is not a thing at all, but a socially approved power-relationship in respect of socially valued assets.

Criteria of 'proprietary' quality founded on transmissibility and permanence are, moreover, merely circular and self-fulfilling.[14] Invariably, on closer analysis, the language of property collapses back into communal perceptions of the boundary between liberty and privacy. Property talk is ultimately reducible to a dialogue about moral space, about the mutual frontier between autonomy and vulnerability. Thus, argues Loren Lomasky, property rights 'demarcate moral space within which what one has is marked off as immune from predation.'[15] Given the relativity of this moral space, 'property' is not static, but dynamic. 'Property' is not absolute but conditional. I may have 'property' in a resource today, but not necessarily tomorrow (as is amply demonstrated by the case of copyright). There are distinct limits, practical, moral and social, upon the amount of property which I may claim in any resource.[16] Thus, for instance, I cannot demand to build a sky-scraper on 'my' suburban block of land, any more than I may use

[13] Bentham indicated astutely that 'in common speech in the phrase "the object of a man's property", the words "the object of" are commonly left out; and by an ellipsis, which, violent as it is, is now become more familiar than the phrase at length, they have made that part of it which consists of the words "a man's property" perform the office of the whole.' See *An Introduction to the Principles of Morals and Legislation* (ed by W. Harrison, Oxford 1948), p. 337, note 1 (Chapter XVI, section 26).

[14] [1991] Cambridge LJ 252, 292 et seq. See, for instance, the assertion of Lord Wilberforce in *National Provincial Bank Ltd* v. *Ainsworth* [1965] AC 1175, 1247G–1248A, that before a right can be admitted within the category of 'property' it must be 'definable, identifiable by third parties, capable in its nature of assumption by third parties, and have some degree of permanence or stability.'

[15] L. E. Lomasky, *Persons, Rights, and the Moral Community* (Oxford 1987), p. 121.

[16] '[P]roperty may be better understood, both historically and legally, as the result of a balance struck between competing individual and collective goals, the private and the public interest' (Tim Bonyhady, 'Property Rights', in Bonyhady (ed), *Environmental Protection and Legal Change* (Sydney 1992), p. 44).

'my' meat cleaver or 'my' wood-chopping axe to make large holes in a neighbour's head.

On this view we can perhaps say that my 'property' in any given resource is best represented by a continuum along which varying kinds of 'property' status shade finely into each other. Property has an almost infinitely gradable quality. It was, for instance, Blackstone who distinguished 'absolute' from 'qualified' forms of property.[17] The *Restatement of Property* is likewise careful to differentiate 'complete property' from lesser configurations of the property notion.[18] The amount of 'property' which I may claim in any resource thus varies—along some sort of sliding scale—from a minimum value to a maximum value, and it becomes feasible to measure or calibrate the quantum of 'property' which I have in a particular resource at any particular time.[19] Under such analysis casual lay concepts of 'ownership' dissolve into differently constituted aggregations or bundles of power exercisable over particular resources. 'Ownership' of a resource breaks down into distinct quantums of 'property' which are capable of distribution to a potentially vast range of persons; and popular ascriptions of 'ownership' serve at best to indicate merely the current allocation of a predominating or strategic quantum of 'property' in the resource in question. It becomes rapidly apparent both that I can have 'property' in assets supposedly 'owned' by someone else and that our shorthand attributions of 'ownership' conceal only superficially the constant and comprehensive interpenetration of 'property' in the resources of the earth. It is an inevitable fact that all 'property' references have about them an utterly *interdependent* quality.

---

[17] Blackstone pointed to the way in which, along the continuum of 'propertiness', there often occurs a subtle gradation between 'absolute property' and 'qualified property' in a disputed resource. At common law this relativity has long been recognised in relation to such resources as wild animals (see *Bl Comm*, vol. II, pp. 391, 395). Even the landowner's 'qualified property' in wild animals persists only so long as he 'can keep them in sight' and has 'power to pursue them'. See also *Blades* v. *Higgs* (1865) 11 HLCas 621, 631, 11 ER 1474, 1478f; *Walden* v. *Hensler* (1987) 163 CLR 561, 565f; Tim Bonyhady, *The Law of the Countryside: the Rights of the Public* (Abingdon 1987), p. 215ff.

[18] American Law Institute, *Restatement of the Law of Property* (St Paul, Minn 1936), Vol. 1, p. 11 (s. 5, comment e).

[19] For an elaboration of this argument, see Kevin Gray, *The Ambivalence of Property*, in G. Prins (ed), *Threats without Enemies* (London 1993), p. 158 et seq.

1. The doctrinal origins of equitable property

Where then does 'equitable property' fit into all of this? If general notions of property are so fragile and febrile, it must be difficult indeed to isolate the nature of *equitable* property. The task is made even more problematical because, in normal usage, the word 'equitable' more usually qualifies the word 'rights' (as in the phrase 'equitable rights of property'). It is with the origin and function of such equitable rights that much recent discussion has been concerned. To what extent, if any, should English law adopt innovative approaches from other jurisdictions which emphasise, for instance, the formative role of doctrines founded on unjust enrichment or unconscionability? The debate has enjoyed the benefit of many contributions, not the least being made by Lord Browne-Wilkinson who, in his address to the Holdsworth Club in 1991, cautioned against any broad or comprehensive application of such formulae in the solution of contemporary problems of English property law.[20]

But it is not on such issues that I wish to concentrate here. My concern is to take perhaps a more institutional view of the regime of equitable property and to suggest several directions or nuances of approach which have already begun to impact upon the law both in this jurisdiction and overseas. As will become obvious, my recent encounter with the Martian observers has encouraged me to seek a more clearly extra-terrestrial vantage-point in viewing the regime of 'equitable property' as a distinctively human or global institution. My concern is less to argue for the adoption of certain positions than to highlight the fact that certain movements are already underway in what we may call the law of equitable property. It may be that, in this wider perspective, the distinction between enacted and judge-made law dwindles towards relative insignificance and equitable property begins more assuredly to fulfil the primary call of equity—recognised so long ago by Aristotle—that equity must be the corrective of legal justice.[21]

Our starting point is *Commissioner of Stamp Duties (Queensland)* v. *Livingston.*[22] Here the Privy Council denied forth-

---

[20] *Constructive Trusts and Unjust Enrichment* (Holdsworth Club of the University of Birmingham 1991).

[21] See *The Ethics of Aristotle* (transl by J. A. K. Thomson, London 1955), p. 166 et seq.   [22] [1965] AC 694.

rightly that, where the 'whole right of property' is vested in one person, there is any need to suppose the separate and concurrent existence in this one person of two different kinds of estate or interest, ie the legal and the equitable.[23] Merger in one owner of the totality of entitlement renders such a distinction unnecessary and indeed impossible.[24] The absolute owner has no separate equitable estate since this is 'absorbed in the legal estate'.[25] The Privy Council proceeded to point out that equity 'calls into existence and protects equitable rights and interests in property only where their recognition has been found to be required in order to give effect to its doctrines.'[26] In this sense, equitable interests, as and when they arise in response to the dictates of equitable doctrine, are not so much 'carved out of' the legal estate as 'engrafted' upon it.[27] An equitable right of property finds its origin not as a pre-existing component of some larger interest which is then hewn free as a block of equitable entitlement; instead it represents the result of a doctrinally-driven movement which impresses new rights upon the pre-existing estate under the mandate of the controlled conscience of equity. Equitable rights of property thus derive from conscientious obligations to deal with an asset or resource in a certain way. In seeking long ago to express what he termed 'historically the right point of view', Maitland spoke of the way in which, in equity, 'the benefit of an obligation has been so treated that it has come to look rather like a true proprietary right.'[28]

---

[23] [1965] AC 694, 712C–D per Viscount Radcliffe. See also *D.K.L.R. Holding Co (No 2) Pty Ltd* v. *Commissioner of Stamp Duties* [1978] 1 NSWLR 268, 278B–E per Sheppard J, (1982) 149 CLR 431, 463 per Aickin J.; *Re Transphere Pty Ltd* (1986) 5 NSWLR 309, 311D–E per McLelland J.; *Grey* v. *IRC* [1958] Ch 690, 708 per Evershed MR.

[24] *Corin* v. *Patton* (1990) 169 CLR 540, 579 per Deane J. For this reason an absolute owner is often said to be incompetent to transfer a bare legal estate whilst purporting to retain the absolute beneficial interest (see *D.K.L.R. Holding Co (No 2) Pty Ltd* v. *Commissioner of Stamp Duties (N.S.W.)* (1982) 149 CLR 431, 442 per Gibbs CJ, 463f per Aickin J, 473f per Brennan J.).

[25] *D.K.L.R. Holding Co (No 2) Pty Ltd* v. *Commissioner of Stamp Duties (N.S.W.)* (1982) 149 CLR 431, 442 per Gibbs CJ.

[26] [1965] AC 694, 712E. See also *D.K.L.R. Holding Co (No 2) Pty Ltd* v. *Commissioner of Stamp Duties* [1978] 1 NSWLR 268, 278D–E.

[27] *D.K.L.R. Holding Co (No 2) Pty Ltd* v. *Commissioner of Stamp Duties (N.S.W.)* (1982) 149 CLR 431, 474 per Brennan J; *Re Transphere Pty Ltd* (1986) 5 NSWLR 309, 311E–F per McLelland J.

[28] *Equity* (2nd edn revd by J. Brunyate, London 1936), p. 115. See also A. W. B. Simpson, 'The Equitable Doctrine of Consideration and the Law of Uses', (1965–66) 16 *U Toronto LJ* 1, 7.

For a good demonstration of this process we need look no further than the ruling of Lord Cottenham in *Tulk* v. *Moxhay*.[29] As is well known, this case traditionally marks the emergence of the restrictive covenant as an equitable proprietary interest in land. Yet, in holding that the covenantor's successor was bound by his notice of the original covenant, the Lord Chancellor spoke not in terms of property at all, but rather in terms of obligation. The relevant question, said Lord Cottenham, is not the circular question 'whether the covenant runs with the land, but whether a party shall be permitted to use the land in a manner inconsistent with the contract entered into by his vendor, with notice of which he purchased.' Of course, said the Lord Chancellor, 'the price would be affected by the covenant, and nothing could be more inequitable than that the original purchaser should be able to sell the property the next day for a greater price, in consideration of the assignee being allowed to escape from the liability which he had himself undertaken.'[30] What clearer vision could there be of the 'moral space' which marks out the limits of property? And it will be observed that English law has subsequently found no difficulty in saying that the beneficiary of a restrictive covenant has been allocated some of the 'property' in his or her neighbour's land.[31] The covenantee (or his or her successor)[32] is in a position to control or inhibit activities on the burdened land and, to this extent, owns an important part of the utility—an important quantum of property—in the servient tenement. (Nor is it merely metaphorical to add that the socialisation of private restrictive covenants in modern planning legislation now enables all citizens, in some significant sense, to claim a certain quantum of property in everyone else's land.)[33]

---

[29] (1848) 2 Ph 774, 41 ER 1143. See Kevin Gray, *Elements of Land Law* (2nd edn, London 1993), pp. 149, 1137.   [30] (1848) 2 Ph 774, 777f, 41 ER 1143, 1144.

[31] Under the canon confirmed in Law of Property Act 1925, s 1(1)–(3), the restrictive covenant ranks in English law as an equitable proprietary interest in the burdened land. See also *Commonwealth of Australia* v. *Tasmania* (1983) 158 CLR 1, 286 per Deane J. ('The benefit of a restrictive covenant . . . can constitute a valuable asset. It is incorporeal but it is, nonetheless, property').

[32] See the liberalising impact of the decision of the Court of Appeal in *Federated Homes Ltd* v. *Mill Lodge Properties Ltd* [1980] 1 WLR 594.

[33] For reference to the way in which state regulation of land use enables 'the organized public' to vindicate its 'meta-property', see Carol Rose, 'The Comedy of the Commons: Custom, Commerce, and Inherently Public Property', 53 *U Chi L Rev* 711, 772 (1986). See also R. H. Nelson, 'Private Rights to Government Actions: How Modern Property Rights Evolve', (1986) *U Ill L Rev* 361, 366 ('zoning creates collective property rights').

A further, and indeed quite striking, manifestation of the coalescence of property and obligation is provided by the recent holding of the Privy Council in *Attorney-General for Hong Kong v. Reid*.[34] Reid, who had risen to the rank of Acting Director of Public Prosecutions in Hong Kong, had in the course of the corrupt discharge of his office received bribes which amounted in value to more than HK$ 12 million. There was evidence that some of this illicit profit now lay invested in three freehold properties situated in New Zealand. In the view expressed on behalf of the Privy Council by Lord Templeman, as soon as the false fiduciary received the bribe, he became a 'debtor in equity to the Crown' for the amount of the bribe.[35] He was bound by an obligation to 'pay and account for the bribe' to the person to whom his fiduciary obligation was owed.[36]

Thus far the judgment is, of course, unexceptionable. But Lord Templeman went on to indicate that '[a]s soon as the bribe was received, whether in cash or in kind, the false fiduciary held the bribe on a constructive trust for the person injured.'[37] The bribe, as soon as accepted by the corrupt employee, belonged 'in equity' to his employer, on the strength of the moral imperative that equity looks on as done that which ought to have been done.[38] Quoting from Sir Peter Millett's recently published address on the subject,[39] Lord Templeman pointed out that equity insists on treating the fiduciary 'as having acted in accordance with his duty'.[40] In consequence the dishonest employee, although he takes legal title in the bribe, cannot be heard to say that he retains any equitable property in it. In equity the bribe belongs—has always belonged— to the employer and is accordingly held by the employee on constructive trust. The Privy Council thus considered the New Zealand properties, so far as they represented bribes accepted by Reid, to be held 'in trust for the Crown'[41] and, by upholding the Crown's caveats over these properties, the Privy Council averted the clear risk that the proceeds of their sale might be 'whisked away to some Shangri La which hides bribes and other corrupt moneys in numbered bank accounts.'[42]

[34] [1994] 1 AC 324.
[35] [1994] 1 AC 324, 331C.
[36] [1994] 1 AC 324, 331C.
[37] [1994] 1 AC 324, 331E.
[38] [1994] 1 AC 324, 331D–332A.
[39] *Bribes and Secret Commissions*, [1993] RLR 7, 20 et seq.
[40] [1994] 1 AC 324, 337F.
[41] [1994] 1 AC 324, 339B.
[42] [1994] 1 AC 324, 339D.

The *Reid* case may still contain further difficulties, but I refer to it, for the moment, merely as a good demonstration of the doctrinally-driven nature of equitable property. There was, said Lord Templeman, no inherent incompatibility between the twin analyses of equitable debt and constructive trust, provided that they did not result in a double recovery. The Privy Council accordingly discarded the venerable authority of the Court of Appeal in *Lister* v. *Stubbs*,[43] which for over a century had distinguished so sharply between trust and debt, between ownership and obligation.[44] Argument is certain to rage over this development,[45] but the *Reid* case provides yet another remarkable articulation of the moral space which delimits the linked claims of autonomy and immunity from predation.

Now if equitable property is doctrinally driven, it may be interesting—particularly if one adopts a more remote or extra-terrestrial standpoint—to ask in which direction it is being driven today. Such a question—if answerable at all—requires that we survey a reasonable timescale, that we strive for objectivity, and that we suppress or at least suspend many of our internalised inhibitions in order to perceive more clearly the fullness of the human phenomenon which we know as property.

2. Equitable property as a means of empowerment

1994 marks the 30th anniversary of two pieces of writing whose implications, when taken in combination, foretell in my view some of the future of equitable property. I refer here to the publication in the Yale Law Journal of 1964 of Charles Reich's famous article on *The New Property*[46] and the appearance in the same year of the influential Oxford paperback version of CB Macpherson's *The Political Theory of Possessive Individualism*.[47]

Any attempt to summarise here the import of these two contri-

---

[43] (1890) 45 Ch D 1.

[44] For an interesting exploration of this theme, see Judith Nicholson, 'Owning and Owing', (1988) 16 *Melbourne UL Rev* 784.

[45] See C. Rotherham, 'The Redistributive Constructive Trust: "Confounding Ownership with Obligation"'?, (1992) 5 *Canterbury L Rev* 84; [1994] *Cambridge LJ* 31 (A. J. Oakley).

[46] 73 *Yale LJ* 733 (1964).

[47] *The Political Theory of Possessive Individualism: From Hobbes to Locke* (Oxford 1964).

butions can do but scant justice to the original. It may perhaps be said, however, that Macpherson's account of the emergence of possessive individualism during the 17th and 18th centuries—against the backdrop of the broad Lockean interpretation of 'property' as inclusive of a person's 'life, liberty and estate'—was to lay the foundation for Macpherson's lifelong exploration of the tension between two opposed views of the institutional function of property. On one view, property comprises essentially a right to exclude strangers from privately owned resources while, on an older and more expansive view, property had once consisted of a right *not to be excluded* from participation in the goods of life.[48] It was Macpherson's chosen task to seek out a modern equilibrium between the latter sense of property as a *right of access* and the absolutist sense of property as a *right of exclusion*. In opposition to the exclusory view, which had gained pre-eminence with the advent of market-dominated societies during the past three centuries, Macpherson argued for the reassertion of property as a public right to share in those socially valued resources which enable us to lead fulfilled and dignified lives. Thus, in Macpherson's view, the idea of property is constantly being broadened to secure the right of the citizen to 'that kind of society which is instrumental to a full and free life', and therefore to 'a set of power relations that permits a full life of enjoyment and development of one's human capacities.'[49] Macpherson was later to contend that, without this reinvigoration of the property concept, we risk a disastrous contradiction of the 'democratic concept of human rights'. Only by accommodating the wider perspective can our modern law of property avoid 'an inequality of wealth and power that denies a lot of people the possibility of a reasonably human life'.[50]

I will return to this thesis later, but let me add that, for his part,

[48] Macpherson pointed to the way in which pre-market societies established and maintained 'legal rights not only to life but to a certain quality of life.' Macpherson referred particularly to 'the rights of different orders or ranks—guild masters, journeymen, apprentices, servants and laborers; serfs, freemen and noblemen; members of the first and second and third estates. All of these were rights, enforced by law or custom, to a certain standard of life, not just of material means of life, but also of liberties, privileges, honor, and status. And these rights could be seen as *properties*' (*Human Rights as Property Rights*, (1977) 24 Dissent 72, 77).

[49] See C. B. Macpherson, 'Capitalism and the Changing Concept of Property', in E. Kamenka and R.S. Neale (ed), *Feudalism, Capitalism and Beyond* (Canberra 1975), p. 116 et seq.

[50] *Human Rights as Property Rights*, (1977) 24 Dissent 72, 73.

Charles Reich advocated the recognition of a 'new property' comprising the unprecedented largesse, in the form of welfare payments, salaries, pensions, franchises, licences and subsidies, distributed by the modern administrative state. In the wealth transformation of the 1950s and 1960s the significance of such benefits had, in Reich's view, overtaken that of more traditional property forms. In consequence Reich argued that the 'new property' deserved the same standard of legal protection—largely in the shape of immunity from arbitrary deprivation—accorded in the past to the more conventional entitlements of private property. We must, said Reich, 'try to build an economic basis for liberty today—a Homestead Act for rootless twentieth century man. We must create a new property.'[51]

The Reich thesis today presents something of a paradox. It seems that Reich's article on *The New Property* is far and away the most heavily cited article ever published by the Yale Law Journal.[52] It is clear that the article has exerted an immense influence on all recent thinking about property and the utilisation of social resource. It is also commonly agreed that, apart from a brief flowering in Justice Brennan's Supreme Court judgment on the termination of welfare rights in *Goldberg* v. *Kelly*,[53] the Reichian vision has not been realised and his enthusiastic optimism has proved unfounded.[54] As Reich himself acknowledged recently,[55] the America of Nixon, Reagan and Bush simply did not take the road opened up by *Goldberg* v. *Kelly*, although Reich has no doubt that the nation is the poorer for not having done so.[56]

Charles Reich is nevertheless an unreconstructed Reichian and argues now that he would expand the scope of the 'new property' to embrace not merely such governmental benefits as have survived the rightward drift of the past 20 years but also the benefits dispensed by private employers or quasi-public institutions within the

[51] 73 *Yale LJ* 733, 787 (1964).   [52] See 100 *Yale LJ* 1449, 1462 (1990–91).
[53] 397 US 254, 262, 25 L Ed 2d 287, 295f (1970).
[54] For criticism of Reich's exaggerated concern in 1964 with material well-being, as distinct from more spiritual and less tangible values of human self-realisation, see H. A. McDougall, 'The New Property vs the New Community', 24 *U San Francisco L Rev* 399 (1989–90).
[55] 'Beyond the New Property: An Ecological View of Due Process', 56 *Brooklyn L Rev* 731 (1990–91).
[56] See also C. A. Reich, 100 *Yale LJ* 1465 (1990–91).

modern corporate state.[57] He would also extend the 'new property' to embrace environmental rights.[58] According to Reich, writing in 1991, we live as never before under the shadow of concentrated and authoritarian economic power which threatens gravely to diminish personal liberty within the 'individual sector'.[59] He says, with perhaps less hyperbole than we on either side of the Atlantic might care to admit, that 'we live in a world in which you starve unless you can obtain a contract with an organization'.[60]

Like Macpherson, Reich is unable to 'accept the idea of a propertyless people in a democratic society', which is the result he fears if 'we limit the concept of property to its traditional forms'.[61] In an era in which security in homes, jobs and pensions has proved increasingly fragile, thereby withdrawing from many the possibility of conventional property forms, the 'new property' offers the only property rights that some people will ever have.[62] 'If we are to safeguard liberty in the coming age,' says Reich, 'we will have to create more ownership rights than now exist . . . A society organized into large institutions must rethink and reconceive the idea of property, or the foundation of democracy will disappear.'[63] Reich reminds us, interestingly, that '[a]t the heart of new property philosophy is the concept of boundaries . . . Every person must be able to say, "This is mine, this is yours, this belongs to the community."'[64] Here again we have the demarcation of moral space to which reference was made earlier, a demarcation which may be

---

[57] See Reich, 'The New Property After 25 Years', 24 *U San Francisco L Rev* 223, 225 et seq (1989–90); 'The Liberty Impact of the New Property', 31 *William and Mary L Rev* 295, 296 (1989–90).

[58] Reich, 100 *Yale LJ* 1465, 1468 (1990–91); 24 *U San Francisco L Rev* 223, 226 (1989–90). For a cogent exploration of the 'new property' or 'due process' analogy which links *Goldberg* v. *Kelly* with the requirement of an environmental impact statement prior to decision-making under the United States' National Environmental Policy Act 1969, see M. Herz, 'Parallel Universes: NEPA Lessons for the New Property', 93 *Col L Rev* 1668, 1684 et seq (1993). See also M. C. Blumm, 'Liberty, the New Property, and Environmental Law', 24 *U San Francisco L Rev* 385, 397 (1989–90).

[59] 'Exclusion from the system has become a form of internal exile' (Reich, 100 *Yale LJ* 1465, 1467 (1990–91)). See also Reich, 'The Individual Sector', 100 *Yale LJ* 1409 (1990–91).

[60] 31 *William and Mary L Rev* 295, 299 (1989–90).

[61] 100 *Yale LJ* 1465, 1468 (1990–91).

[62] Reich, 24 *U San Francisco L Rev* 223, 227 (1989–90).

[63] Reich, 31 *William and Mary L Rev* 295, 304 et seq (1989–90).

[64] 100 *Yale LJ* 1409, 1413 (1990–91).

essential if, as Reich would say, '[e]veryone has a right to a share in the commonwealth.'[65]

Now there is much to admire, and perhaps much to criticise, in the broad theses advanced by Macpherson and Reich. Both place a central emphasis on the need to assure access to certain human goods as a vital precondition of securing freedom, dignity and the flourishing of the human spirit. In both there is found a strong resonance of James Madison's statement in 1792 that just 'as a man is said to have a right to his property, he may be equally said to have a property in his rights.'[66] Nevertheless Macpherson and Reich alike court the danger that *all* rights become property rights and, as Duncan Kennedy in fact says, 'all rules are property rules'.[67] Yet this objection (which is doubtless overstated in any event) may merely point to the fact that we should be more broadminded, historically more accurate,[68] and perhaps even more honest in our contemporary use of the property accolade. It may be our preconception of property which is wrong.

But, I hear you say, all this is merely the faded credo of latter-day hippies. Name me one example in the modern era where property rights have been harnessed for the conscious purpose of assuring citizens access to a life of reasonable human dignity. Provide one instance in which a common law-based legal system has dispensed property rights *de novo* as a concerted means of guaranteeing a minimum floor of decent living standards. Where has property ever been recreated in order to fashion a *modus vivendi* for the propertyless and provide all with a share in the commonwealth?

Strange to relate, recent times disclose at least one stunning assertion of precisely this 'access dimension' of property. Remarkable in its legal scope and social impact, this instance of *property as access* will reach deep into the lives of millions of people in this country including, in all likelihood, close on half of all those who read this paper. Pursuant to Part II of the

---

[65] *56 Brooklyn L Rev* 731, 745 (1990–91).

[66] 'Property', in *The Papers of James Madison* (ed R. A. Rutland et al, Charlottesville Va, 1983), Vol. 14, p. 266 (*National Gazette*, 27 March 1792).

[67] D. Kennedy, 'Form and Substance in Private Law Adjudication', 89 *Harv L Rev* 1685, 1763 (1975–76).

[68] See Richard Tuck, *Natural Rights Theories* (Cambridge 1979), p. 16, for a reminder of the way in which the medieval period initiated a process 'whereby all of a man's rights, of whatever kind, were to come to be seen as his property'.

Matrimonial Causes Act 1973, the courts in this jurisdiction are empowered to reallocate the assets and finances of divorcing parties in total disregard of their historic rights of title. The courts are authorised to refashion the living arrangements of divorced spouses—to reorder their beneficial entitlements—in such a way as to open for both parties (and particularly for a custodial parent) a gateway to a better or at least a sustainable lifestyle. Matrimonial legislation effectively confers on the courts a special power of appointment over the available economic resources of disaffected marital partners.[69] In this context the law adopts not 'a painfully detailed retrospect', but rather 'a forward-looking perspective' in which 'questions of ownership yield to the higher demands of relating the means of both [parties] to the needs of each, the first consideration given to the welfare of children.'[70] In this way matrimonial legislation recognises and gives prospective effect to a latent or subsisting equity in the property relations of those who marry.

It is perhaps worth noticing that the historic function of equitable intervention in property matters has always been to ensure, promote and safeguard rights of *access*. Equity's concerns have long focused on the perceived need to preserve, for doctrinal reasons, various forms of access to the beneficial value of desired goods and resources. Thus, for example, the critical duty of the trustee is to deflect enjoyment to the beneficiary. The function of the restrictive covenant is likewise to permit the covenantee access to part of the utility in the land subject to covenant. The principal must be protected in his or her access to the commercial opportunities which the fiduciary might otherwise hijack. In each of these instances equitable property and the notion of stewardship seldom stand far apart. Whereas legal rights, with their stolid and uncompromising character, more clearly connote the exclusory aspect of property, equitable rights more subtly articulate a range of protected access to the benefits derived from profitable guardianship. This is not, of course, to say that the exclusion and access dimensions of property never overlap, for they certainly do. The functions of exclusion and access are never wholly discrete. There is

---

[69] See Kevin Gray, *Reallocation of Property on Divorce* (Abingdon 1977), p. 322 et seq.

[70] *Hammond* v. *Mitchell* [1991] 1 WLR 1127, 1129D–E per Waite J. See the distinction drawn between 'prospective' and 'retrospective' approaches in Gray, *Reallocation of Property on Divorce* (1977), p. 278 et seq.

even a confusing and somewhat unfortunate human tendency to assert access rights precisely in order to claim rights to exclude others from access later.[71] The relevant point is, however, that any set of property relations contains, at any given time, a balance which leans, in some degree, in either an exclusory or an access-related direction.

3. Equitable property as a gateway for rights of access

I want now to suggest just three of the ways in which, across the jurisdictions of the common law world, equitable property is currently being refashioned in order to accommodate increasing claims of access in juxtaposition to those of exclusion. Broad connections link all three instances. Each relates essentially to land-based resources. Each involves the gathering protection accorded to newly emerging claims *not* to be excluded from access to the commonwealth. In each case it is possible to contend that an equitable property is being recognised and extended in order to protect and preserve various kinds of claim to human dignity and rightful participation in the goods or opportunities of life.

(1) EQUITABLE PROPERTY IN 'QUASI-PUBLIC' PLACES

My first example relates to the incipient recognition of rights of access to what we might call 'quasi-public' land. In conventional terms the ultimate prerogative of private property comprises an absolute right to determine who may enter or remain on land. No doctrine of reasonableness controls the grant by the landowner of access to his or her land by way of bare licence. Nor is there normally any legal necessity that in the exercise of this discretion the landowner should comply with rules of natural justice. The legal owner may exclude or evict without giving any notice or assigning any reason, subject only to such constraints as are imposed by doctrines of contract and estoppel or by the legislation prohibiting discrimination on grounds of race or gender. In the orthodox analysis the landowner simply has an unchallengeable discretion to withhold or withdraw permission to enter.[72]

By means of this dogma the common law appears to have main-

---

[71] See e.g. *Gerhardy* v. *Brown* (1985) 159 CLR 70.
[72] See Gray, *Elements of Land Law* (2nd edn 1993), pp. 897–898.

tained a strict dichotomy between rights of access in respect of so-called 'private' and 'public' places. Uncontracted privileges to enter upon private land are almost entirely defeasible in nature, whereas the exercise of public rights (such as a right of passage over the public highway) is generally unqualified and absolute.[73] Nowadays, however, it is strongly arguable that this dichotomy between the private and public domains (although perhaps workable under the social and economic conditions of a different era) no longer wholly accords with the reality of many modern forms of landholding.[74] Although the absolute nature of the landowner's common law right undoubtedly still applies to such 'private' property as the domestic curtilage—an Englishman's home is still, by and large, his castle—its extension today to many other kinds of premises increasingly involves an unacceptable denial of the citizen's just or equitable share in the commonwealth.

The modern world discloses many examples of places, premises and land areas which are heavily invested with a 'quasi-public' character and where a right of arbitrary or selective exclusion is not—and perhaps never has been—exercisable in its unfettered form. Important factors of public policy now urge that, in respect of such 'quasi-public' places, the law should confirm, as a matter of entitlement, the existence of certain carefully delimited rights of equal and reasonable access for all citizens. Particularly in a plural-ist, multicultural society there is nothing quite so alienating as the perception that one is not welcome; that one does not belong; that one has entered a door through which one should not have come.

Many facets of modern living involve our ready access to places which, although strictly the subject of private ownership, are char-acterised by or are quite deliberately intended for general public use. Examples include local parks and leisure areas, railway sta-tions, airports, shopping centres and megastores, public hospitals,

---

[73] As Lord Wilberforce indicated in *Wills' Trustees* v. *Cairngorm Canoeing and Sailing School Ltd*, 1976 SLT 162, 191, 'once a public right of passage is established, there is no warrant for making any distinction, or even for making any enquiry, as to the purpose for which it is exercised. One cannot stop . . . a pedestrian on a highway, and ask him what is the nature of his use.'

[74] For evidence that the boundary between 'private' and 'public' domains has become blurred in recent times, see *Moss* v. *McLachlan* (1985) 149 JP 167. Here a Divisional Court indicated that the public right of passage on the highway may no longer be as absolute as it once was, the Court holding that police officers were entitled at common law to turn back motorway convoys of 'flying pickets' during the miners' strike in the mid-1980s.

museums, libraries, art galleries, community colleges and various other kinds of community facility—sporting, educational and therapeutic. Such premises are only imperfectly described in terms of private ownership; they are underpinned by (and indeed exist only by virtue of) their 'quasi-public' quality. It is no longer feasible to regard premises within this 'quasi-public' category as being governed by the same absolute regulatory power as pertains to the fee simple owner of the private dwelling-house. It is no longer appropriate that the implied non-contractual licence which invites public entry should in every circumstance be revocable on the whim of the landowner. As Murphy J. often pointed out in the High Court of Australia, '[t]he distinction between public power and private power is not clear-cut and one may shade into the other'.[75] It is at precisely this blurred borderline that the exercise of power calls for particularly vigilant scrutiny lest it become unreasonable and oppressive. In the words of Murphy J., '[w]hen rights are so aggregated that their exercise affects members of the public to a significant degree, they may often be described as public rights and their exercise as that of public power. Such public power must be exercised bona fide . . . and with due regard to the persons affected by its exercise'.[76]

Interestingly one of the test-cases in the present context has come to focus on the common areas of the large shopping centre. The modern shopping mall performs a mixture of functions of which the buying and selling of goods represent only one feature. The shopping centre facilitates no less the motiveless appraisal of consumer goods and, with its provision of seating, indoor plants, fountains, open-plan cafés and so on, affords much of the recreational aspect of a meeting-place. The location effectively provides the equivalent, in an enclosed format, of a public park. The very layout of such centres points to a consciously designed versatility as a modern crossroads for the social intercourse of the general public. The shopping centre serves not least as a common meeting-place for the unemployed, the disadvantaged and the discouraged of society—persons whose presence may not be entirely welcome to the private commercial interests which own the shopping centre. Yet arbitrary exclusion of such persons from the precincts of the shopping centre—a practice which is becoming increasingly fre-

[75] *Gerhardy* v. *Brown* (1985) 159 CLR 70, 107.
[76] *Forbes* v. *New South Wales Trotting Club Ltd* (1979) 143 CLR 242, 275 (dissenting).

quent in towns up and down the country—may mean that sizeable portions of down-town areas are being effectively converted into no-go areas for proscribed classes of individual.[77] Are the private security firms which patrol shopping malls indeed entitled to extrude from the premises the jobless, the Rastafarian and the down-and-out? Nothing would epitomise quite so forcefully the growing apartheid between rich and poor as the reservation of exclusive consumerist havens for the relatively affluent of our society. Nothing would underscore so plainly the state of 'internal exile' which Charles Reich feared might become the fate of the unconventional and the unwaged.[78]

Against this background it can be argued that the right to exclude from certain kinds of privately held premises has now become qualified by an overriding principle of reasonableness. The power of arbitrary exclusion no longer comprises an inevitable proprietary incident in respect of land to which the public enjoys entry by general or unrestricted invitation.[79] Within the area of 'quasi-public' property the public's rights of access are supported and constrained by legitimate expectations of reasonable user, and these expectations are, in their turn, indivisible from certain civil liberties of association and assembly and more generally indivisible from freedoms of movement and expression.[80] The recognition of a rule of reasonableness cuts both ways, of course: it provides a clear ground for the exclusion of unreasonable users,[81] but also provides

[77] The scale of some modern shopping plazas may be considerable. See eg *Amalgamated Food Employees Union Local 590* v. *Logan Valley Plaza*, 391 US 308, 20 L Ed 2d 603 (1968) (perimeter of 1.1 miles); *Alderwood Associates* v. *Washington Environmental Council*, 635 P2d 108 (1981) (1 million square feet of store area on 110 acres of land).

[78] See C. A. Reich, 100 Yale LJ 1465, 1467 (1990–91).

[79] It was Henry George who pointed to the unacceptable outcome of private power over land taken to its logical conclusion. '[T]o this manifest absurdity does the recognition of individual right to land come when carried to its ultimate—that any one human being, could he concentrate in himself the individual rights to the land of any country, could expel therefrom all the rest of its inhabitants; and could he thus concentrate the individual rights to the whole surface of the globe, he alone of all the teeming population of the earth would have the right to live' (see H. George, *Poverty And Progress* (New York 1981) (first published 1879), p. 345).

[80] See the original 'company town' case, *Marsh* v. *Alabama*, 326 US 501, 90 L Ed 265 (1946) (private ownership of town could not be asserted to stifle freedom of expression on sidewalk).

[81] See e.g. *The Queen in Right of Canada* v. *Committee for the Commonwealth of Canada* (1991) 77 DLR (4th) 385, 395d per Lamer CJC, Sopinka and Cory JJ concurring.

a guarantee of access during good (ie reasonable) behaviour.[82] In the process it becomes possible to maintain that all citizens have thereby acquired some sort of equitable property in 'quasi-public' places; that all are effectively the beneficiaries in gross of a restrictive covenant implicitly undertaken by the landowner that the visitor shall not be arbitrarily or unreasonably excluded from the tenement concerned.

In recent years it is significant that other jurisdictions have increasingly imposed a requirement of reasonableness on the regulation of entry to and exclusion from 'quasi-public' premises. For instance, in a series of cases culminating in the ruling of the Supreme Court of California in *Robins* v. *PruneYard Shopping Center*,[83] courts in the United States and Canada have upheld claims of reasonable public access to privately owned shopping centres for purposes which extend beyond commercial activity to encompass the peaceful communication of a range of personal and political concerns.[84] The 'quasi-public' nature of such premises has been said to follow from the fact that shopping malls have impliedly been made the subject of an open invitation to the public and therefore represent 'private property having an essential public character as part of a commercial venture'.[85] According to the

---

[82] See Laskin CJC's reference in *Harrison* v. *Carswell* (1975) 62 DLR (3d) 68, 74, to privileged user of public areas which is 'revocable only upon misbehaviour . . . or by reason of unlawful activity.'

[83] 592 P2d 341 (1979), affd sub nom *PruneYard Shopping Center* v. *Robins*, 447 US 74, 64 L Ed 2d 741 (US Supreme Court 1980). See also R. Moon, 'Access to Public and Private Property under Freedom of Expression', (1988) 20 *Ottawa L Rev* 339, 357 et seq.

[84] Later cases have made it clear that the permitted forms of communication include 'nondisruptive speech' such as that comprised in the wearing of a T-shirt or button which contains a political message (*Board of Commissioners of the City of Los Angeles* v. *Jews For Jesus, Inc*, 482 US 569, 576, 96 L Ed 2d 500, 508 (1987) per O'Connor J.). Protected communication may also involve a display or celebration of a particular lifestyle or cultural or political affiliation. See the statement of Tobriner J. in *In re Cox*, 90 Cal Rptr 24, 32 (1970) that a shopping centre 'may no more exclude individuals who wear long hair or unconventional dress, who are black, who are members of the John Birch Society, or who belong to the American Civil Liberties Union, merely because of these characteristics or associations, than may the City of San Rafael'.

[85] R. v. *Layton* (1988) 38 CCC (3d) 550, 568 per Scott Prov Ct J. See also *Harrison* v. *Carswell* (1975) 62 DLR (3d) 68, 73 per Laskin CJC. For further reference to private property which has assumed 'the functional attributes of public property devoted to public use', see *Central Hardware Co* v. *National Labor Relations Board*, 407 US 539, 547, 33 L Ed 2d 122, 128 (1972) per Powell J.

Supreme Court of North Dakota in *City of Jamestown* v. *Beneda*,[86] the shopping mall has come to provide 'the functional equivalent of the city streets, squares and parks of earlier days'—areas which the United States Supreme Court has long declared to be 'held in the public trust'.[87] Perhaps most important, the courts have linked the protection of reasonable shopping mall access to the 'interest of a free society in the highly placed value of open markets for ideas.'[88] As the Supreme Court of Washington made clear in *Alderwood Associates* v. *Washington Environmental Council*,[89] '[t]he ability . . . to communicate ideas would be greatly reduced if access to such centers were denied'.

Although developments in the United States and Canada are often coloured by constitutional or charter considerations,[90] the controlling factor in the emerging jurisprudence is the constant reference to an overarching requirement of reasonableness. Thus, in *Uston* v. *Resorts International Hotel Inc*,[91] Pashman J confirmed that 'when property owners open their premises to the general public in the pursuit of their own property interests, they have no right to exclude people unreasonably. On the contrary, they have a duty not to act in an arbitrary or discriminatory manner towards persons who come on their premises.' Similarly, in *State* v. *Schmid*,[92] Princeton University was adjudged to have violated a defendant's state constitutional rights by evicting him from

[86] 477 NW2d 830, 837f (1991). See also *Alderwood Associates* v. *Washington Environmental Council* 635 P2d 108, 117 (1981) (Supreme Court of Washington).

[87] *Frisby* v. *Schultz*, 487 US 474, 481, 101 L Ed 2d 420, 429 (1988) per O'Connor J. See e.g. *Hague* v. *Committee for Industrial Organization*, 307 US 496, 515, 83 L Ed 1423, 1436 (1939).

[88] See *City of Jamestown* v. *Beneda*, 477 NW2d 830, 835 (1991), citing *International Society for Krishna Consciousness* v. *Schrader*, 461 F Supp 714, 718 (1978). For reference to the importance of 'free trade in ideas', see *Abrams* v. *United States*, 250 US 616, 630, 63 L Ed 1173, 1180 (1919), where Justice Holmes went on to suggest that 'the best test of truth is the power of the thought to get itself accepted in the competition of the market'.

[89] 635 P2d 108, 117 (1981). See also *The Queen in Right of Canada* v. *Committee for the Commonwealth of Canada* (1991) 77 DLR (4th) 385, 449d–f per McLachlin J.

[90] Contemporary developments are not, however, attributable solely to the infusion of constitutional or charter-based norms. As was explained for instance in *R.* v. *Layton* (1988) 38 CCC (3d) 550, 570, the enactment of the Canadian Charter of Rights and Freedoms merely confirmed, in present respects, the common law position already elaborated in Laskin CJC's seminal judgment in *Harrison* v. *Carswell* (1975) 62 DLR (3d) 68, 73f.

[91] 445 A2d 370, 375 (1982) (Supreme Court of New Jersey).

[92] 423 A2d 615 (1980).

university premises and by securing his arrest for distributing political literature on its campus. In the view of the majority of the Supreme Court of New Jersey, 'the more private property is devoted to public use, the more it must accommodate the rights which inhere in individual members of the general public who use that property'.[93] The Court recognised that the owner of private property is 'entitled to fashion reasonable rules to control the mode, opportunity and site for the individual exercise of expressional rights upon his property'.[94] Here, however, the university's rules had been 'devoid of reasonable standards' designed to protect both the legitimate interests of the university as an institution of higher education and the individual exercise of expressional freedom. In the total absence of any such 'reasonable regulatory scheme', the university was at fault for having ejected a defendant whose actions had themselves been 'noninjurious and reasonable'.[95]

Fears that there might be difficulty in delineating the scope of quasi-public premises have proved largely unfounded within the present context. North American courts have been careful to emphasise that the reasonable access rule does not invade the 'property or privacy rights of an individual homeowner or the proprietor of a modest retail establishment'.[96] Central to the reasonable access rule is the demarcation of an area of 'private autonomy'[97] whose parameters comprise, in themselves, the essential defining characteristic of rights of property.[98] Correspondingly the enforcement of reasonable access has been extended to many other kinds of premises which are deliberately laid open to public resort and where the claim of private autonomy has thus been

---

[93] 423 A2d 615, 629.   [94] 423 A2d 615, 630.

[95] For reference to the social value derived from treating as 'inherently public' property which is used for political speech, see C. Rose, 53 U Chi L Rev 711, 778 (1986). According to Professor Rose, the Supreme Court decision in *PruneYard Shopping Center* v. *Robins*, 447 US 74, 64 L Ed 2d 741 (1980) could legitimately be considered to be an extension of public trust doctrine.

[96] *Diamond* v. *Bland*, 113 Cal Rptr 468, 478 (1974) per Mosk J., cited with approval in *Robins* v. *PruneYard Shopping Centre* 592 P2d 341, 347 (1979). See *Johnson* v. *Tait*, 774 P2d 185, 190 (1989) (Hell's Angel in full regalia rightly excluded from Crazy Horse Bar in Anchorage). See also *Amalgamated Food Employees Union Local 590* v. *Logan Valley Plaza*, 391 US 308, 325f, 20 L Ed 2d 603, 616 (1968) per Douglas J.; *Harrison* v. *Carswell* (1975) 62 DLR (3d) 68, 73 per Laskin CJC.

[97] *Johnson* v. *Tait*, 774 P2d 185, 190 (1989) (Supreme Court of Alaska).

[98] See text accompanying note 15.

waived in whole or part.[99] In *The Queen in Right of Canada* v. *Committee for the Commonwealth of Canada*,[100] for instance, the Supreme Court of Canada was entirely prepared to uphold the citizen's right of access—even for the purpose of disseminating political ideas—to the government-owned public terminal concourse at Montreal International Airport. Although agreeing that the government's proprietary rights were the same as those of a private owner,[101] the Supreme Court forthrightly dismissed the government's argument that it was entitled within its absolute discretion to exclude any person it wished from the airport concourse.[102] In the Court's view the airport terminal bore the earmarks of a 'public arena'[103] and was 'in many ways a thoroughfare'[104] or 'contemporary crossroads',[105] a 'modern equivalent of the streets and by-ways of the past'.[106] Such property was 'quasi-fiduciary'[107] and was owned for the benefit of the citizen.[108] Within this forum the Supreme Court was quite prepared to protect civic rights of access

---

[99] See e.g. *In re Hoffman*, 64 Cal Rptr 97, 100 (1967) per Traynor CJ ('a railway station is like a public street or park'). The key notion here is that of 'dedication' to public use (see e.g. *The Queen in Right of Canada* v. *Committee for the Commonwealth of Canada* (1991) 77 DLR (4th) 385, 402*f* per La Forest J.).

[100] (1991) 77 DLR (4th) 385.

[101] (1991) 77 DLR (4th) 385, 402*e* per La Forest J.

[102] (1991) 77 DLR (4th) 385, 393*d–h* per Lamer CJC, Sopinka and Cory JJ concurring, 402*f* per La Forest J, 421*b*–422*b* per L'Heureux-Dubé J, 449*d*–450*c* per McLachlin J. See also *City of Jamestown* v. *Beneda*, 477 NW2d 830, 835 (1991).

[103] (1991) 77 DLR (4th) 385, 426*f* per L'Heureux-Dubé J. The Supreme Court noted, however, that the public forum doctrine expounded for many years in the United States was currently under considerable attack and the Court was not therefore prepared to endorse it in its full form ((1991) 77 DLR (4th) 385, 391*b* per Lamer CJC, 428*d* per L'Heureux-Dubé J, 452*d* per McLachlin J. See now *International Society for Krishna Consciousness, Inc* v. *Lee*, 120 L Ed 2d 541 (1992); *Lee* v. *International Society for Krishna Consciousness, Inc*, 120 L Ed 2d 669 (1992); D. S. Day, *The End of the Public Forum Doctrine*, 78 Iowa L Rev 143 (1992–93).

[104] (1991) 77 DLR (4th) 385, 396*h* per Lamer CJC, Sopinka and Cory JJ concurring.

[105] (1991) 77 DLR (4th) 385, 430*g* per L'Heureux-Dubé J.

[106] (1991) 77 DLR (4th) 385, 459*g* per McLachlin J.

[107] (1991) 77 DLR (4th) 385, 393*d* per Lamer CJC. In the Federal Court of Appeal, Hugessen J had emphasised that the government owns its property 'not for its own benefit but for that of the citizen' and that the government therefore has an obligation to 'devote certain property for certain purposes and to manage "its" property for the public good' ((1987) 36 DLR (4th) 501, 509*f*).

[108] (1991) 77 DLR (4th) 385, 393*f* per Lamer CJC, Sopinka and Cory JJ concurring. ('[I]t must be understood, since the government administers its properties for the benefit of the citizens as a whole, that it is the citizens above all who have an interest in seeing that the properties are administered and operated in a manner consistent with their intended purpose.')

and communication not least because, as McLachlin J. explained, the safeguarding of such rights is integrally linked with the 'pursuit of truth, participation in the community and the conditions necessary for individual fulfilment and human flourishing.'[109] Only through 'the encouragement of a tolerant and welcoming environment which promotes diversity in forms of self-fulfilment and human flourishing' could the Court recognise 'the role of expression in maximising human potential and happiness through intellectual and artistic communication.'[110]

Such developments in the comparative law make it increasingly feasible to contend that the private owner of 'quasi-public' premises may nowadays exclude members of the public only on grounds which are objectively reasonable.[111] The imposition of a requirement of reasonableness is already well established in relation to private owners whose rights of control derive from statutory authority,[112] and there appears to be no good reason why the same approach should not apply to the ownership of premises whose 'quasi-public' status is not fixed by legislation.[113] It is strictly inaccurate, in any event, to suppose that the delineation of special rules for quasi-public property represents a startling innova-

---

[109] (1991) 77 DLR (4th) 385, 457*d*.

[110] (1991) 77 DLR (4th) 385, 457*h*. It was Lon Fuller who identified as the 'central indisputable principle of what may be called substantive natural law' the requirement to '[o]pen up, maintain, and preserve the integrity of the channels of communication by which men convey to one another what they perceive, feel, and desire' (see L. L. Fuller, *The Morality of Law* (New Haven and London 1964), p. 185 et seq).

[111] The standard of objective 'reasonableness' is of course likely to vary in its application over time; exclusion which seemed reasonable in the late 19th century will not necessarily seem reasonable today.

[112] See e.g. *Cinnamond* v. *British Airports Authority* [1980] 1 WLR 582, 588A–E, where Lord Denning MR declared, in relation to a statutorily established airport authority, that '[i]f a bona fide airline passenger comes to the airport, they cannot turn him back—at their discretion without rhyme or reason—as a private landowner can. Nor can they turn back the driver of the car. Nor the friends who help him with the luggage. Nor the relatives who come to see him off.' Lord Denning emphasised, significantly, that the airport authority would have a right to exclude only 'if the circumstances are such as fairly and reasonably to warrant it', although the Master of the Rolls indicated that there were clear examples of circumstances (eg traffic congestion or terrorist alert) in which it might be 'fair and reasonable for the airport authority to restrict or prohibit entry'.

[113] It may be that some similar doctrine of reasonableness provides part of the true explanation of the old 'railway cases' (see e.g. *Perth General Station Committee* v. *Ross* [1897] AC 479; *Barker* v. *Midland Railway Co* (1856) 18 CB 46, 139 ER 1281; *Foulger* v. *Steadman* (1872) LR 8 QB 65).

tion in English law. The clearest counter-example is afforded by the venerable case of the common innkeeper, who, in the absence of some reasonable ground of refusal,[114] has always been bound by the common law and custom of the realm to receive and provide lodging in his inn for all comers who are travellers.[115] For centuries it has been settled law in all common law jurisdictions that 'the business of an innkeeper is of a quasi public character, invested with many privileges, and burdened with correspondingly great responsibilities'.[116] In the discharge of this important calling the common innkeeper is neither entitled to select his guests nor justified in applying any ground of exclusion or discrimination which is itself unreasonable.[117] It is indeed only the dimming of our collective memory which obscures the fact that premises used in pursuit of a public calling have been subjected from time immemorial to special rules curtailing the freedom arbitrarily to turn away all comers.

(2) EQUITABLE PROPERTY IN TRADITIONAL COUNTRY

A second (and rather different) example of the recognition of the 'access dimension' of property is to be found in recent attempts to resolve claims of original or aboriginal title made by the historically dispossessed native peoples of Canada, the United States and Australia. The Australian experience is particularly informative.

[114] See *Hawthorn* v. *Hammond* (1844) 1 Car & K 404, 407, 174 ER 867, 869.

[115] On the compellability of the common innkeeper to admit all comers, see YB 39 H VI 18, 24 (1460); *White's Case* (1558) 2 Dyer 158b, 73 ER 343, 344; *Calye's Case* (1584) 8 Co Rep 32a, 77 ER 520; *Anon* (1623) 2 Roll Rep 345, 81 ER 842, 843; *Newton* v. *Trigg* (1691) 1 Show 268, 269, 89 ER 566; *Lane* v. *Cotton* (1701) 12 Mod 472, 484, 88 ER 1458, 1464f per Holt CJ; *Robins & Co* v. *Gray* [1895] 2 QB 501, 503f; *Lamond* v. *Richard* [1897] 1 QB 541, 547. See also 24 *Halsbury's Laws of England* (4th edn. (Reissue), London 1991), para 1113.

[116] *De Wolf* v. *Ford*, 86 NE 527, 529 (1908) per Werner J. See *Garifine* v. *Monmouth Park Jockey Club*, 148 A2d 1, 2 (1958). See also B. Wyman, 'The Law of Public Callings as a Solution of the Trust Problem', 17 *Harv L Rev* 156, 158f (1903–04); C. K. Burdick, 'The Origin of the Peculiar Duties of Public Service Companies', 11 *Col L Rev* 514, 521ff (1911); N. Arterburn, 'The Origin and First Test of Public Callings', 75 *U Penn L Rev* 411, 424f (1927).

[117] See *R.* v. *Ivens* (1835) 7 C & p. 213, 219, 173 ER 94, 96f per Coleridge J. ('The innkeeper is not to select his guests. He has no right to say to one, you shall come into my inn, and to another you shall not, as every one coming and conducting himself in a proper manner has a right to be received; and for this purpose innkeepers are a sort of public servants, they having in return a kind of privilege of entertaining travellers and supplying them with what they want').

Blackburn J.'s well-known decision in *Milirrpum* v. *Nabalco Pty Ltd*[118] expressly (albeit reluctantly) denied that the Australian Aboriginal's customary intimate relationship with his land—based upon the personal usufructuary right to go walkabout and forage over traditional tracts of country—could ever conform to the essential indicia of proprietary ownership in its common law sense. The standard ingredients of conventional proprietary ownership were notably absent not least because the Aboriginal nomad had no concept of a right to exclude others, still less to alienate lands to a stranger.[119] At the heart of the Aboriginal concept of land has always been the notion of access not of exclusion.[120] Its fundamental feature has been the acknowledgement of a duty to care for the land—to 'look after country'[121]—in the discharge of which responsibility Aboriginal people 'see themselves as caretakers of a relationship of trust deriving from The Dreaming and passed on to them by their immediate forebears.'[122]

As Brennan J was to emphasise in *R.* v. *Toohey; Ex parte*

---

[118] (1971) 17 FLR 141, 272ff.

[119] According to Kenneth Maddock, 'Aborigines regard land as a religious phenomenon. The earth owes its topography to the acts of world-creative powers who appeared mysteriously and moved about on the surface before sinking into the ground or the water or rising into the sky, leaving a formed and populated world behind them . . . The Aboriginal theory is thus that rights to land have to do with the design of the world, not with alienable title' (*The Australian Aborigines: A Portrait of their Society* (London 1972), p. 27). See also *Mabo* v. *Queensland (No 2)* (1992) 175 CLR 1, 51 per Brennan J.

[120] 'Access to the country of one's forebears provided substance for the Dreamtime experience and an identity based on the continuity of life and values which were constantly reaffirmed in ritual and in the use of the land' (D. Bell, *Daughters of the Dreaming* (Melbourne and Sydney 1983), p. 47f). In *Milirrpum* v. *Nabalco Pty Ltd* (1971) 17 FLR 141, 272, Blackburn J. found that 'the clan's right to exclude others is not apparent . . . Again, the greatest extent to which this right can be said to exist is in the realm of ritual. But it was never suggested that ritual rules ever excluded members of other clans completely from clan territory; the exclusion was only from sites.'

[121] 'Responsibility to look after country has always been an imperative for Aboriginal people' (House of Representatives, Standing Committee on Aboriginal Affairs, *Return to Country: The Aboriginal Homelands Movement in Australia* (Canberra 1987), para. 1.20). For the range of meaning invested in the phrase 'looking after country', see G. Neate, 'Looking After Country', (1993) 16 *UNSWLJ* 161, 189 et seq.

[122] G. Neate, (1993) 16 *UNSWLJ* 161, 194 ('The relationship is reciprocal . . . Just as they know and care for their country, they believe that country knows and cares for its people').

Meneling Station Pty Ltd,[123] the connection of the Aboriginal group with the land 'does not consist in the communal holding of rights with respect to the land, but in the group's spiritual affiliations to a site on the land and the group's spiritual responsibility for the site and for the land.' Aboriginal ownership, said Brennan J., is 'primarily a spiritual affair rather than a bundle of rights.' Paradoxically, it is the performance of an amalgam of symbolic, organic and ritual duties which, for the Aboriginal, constitutes the closest approximation to 'land rights' known to his community. Right and responsibility emerge not only as correlatives but as deeply interpenetrating images of the 'proper' association with the resources of the earth. Here 'property' has more in common with 'propriety' than entitlement[124] and the notion of 'right' has more to do with perceptions of 'rightness' than with any understanding of enforceable exclusory title.

It was in the context of this intensely symbiotic relationship with the natural environment that in *Milirrpum* Blackburn J. found that the Aboriginals had 'a more cogent feeling of obligation to the land than of ownership of it'. It was, he declared, 'easier . . . to say that the clan belongs to the land than that the land belongs to the clan'.[125] It thus followed, with brutal clarity, that native claims were incompatible with, were not accommodated within, and were indeed extinguished by, the common law system of property brought by the white settler two hundred years earlier. The Aboriginal relationship with land being essentially religious,[126] the spiritual or ritual evocation of The Dreaming could simply not be comprehended within the impoverished common law notion of property.[127]

It has taken virtually two centuries for the Australian conscience to catch up the inequity that customary native title throughout Australia (as indeed elsewhere in the New World) should be

---

[123] (1982) 158 CLR 327, 357f. See also *Gerhardy* v. *Brown* (1985) 159 CLR 70, 149 per Deane J.

[124] Semantically 'property' connotes the condition of a resource as being 'proper' to a particular person (see Gray, *Elements of Land Law* (1st edn, London 1987), p. 8).

[125] *Milirrpum* v. *Nabalco Pty Ltd* (1971) 17 FLR 141, 270f.

[126] See explicit recognition of this point in *Milirrpum* v. *Nabalco Pty Ltd* (1971) 17 FLR 141, 167 per Blackburn J.; *R.* v. *Toohey; Ex parte Meneling Station Pty Ltd* (1982) 158 CLR 327, 356 per Brennan J.

[127] See *Mabo* v. *Queensland (No 2)* (1992) 175 CLR 1, 178 per Toohey J.

wholly swallowed up by the process of colonisation.[128] During the
1970s and 1980s suggestions began to emerge—and the language is
significant—that government owed some fiduciary obligation to the
indigenous peoples, even that there was an element of trust (public
or otherwise) in the relationship between government and
Aboriginal in respect of native land.[129] This infusion of equitable
terminology was given significant support by Canadian courts
which slowly recognised that native Indians might collectively have
a beneficial interest in their reserved lands.[130] In *Guerin* v. *The
Queen*[131] Dickson J. considered there to be 'no real conflict
between the cases which characterise Indian title as a beneficial
interest of some sort, and those which characterise it a personal,
usufructuary right. Any apparent inconsistency derives from the
fact that in describing what constitutes a unique interest in land
the courts have almost inevitably found themselves applying a
somewhat inappropriate terminology drawn from general property
law.'[132] In the view of Dickson J. and the Supreme Court, the *sui
generis* character of native title, hovering between 'beneficial ownership' and 'personal right', was capable of giving rise to a 'distinctive fiduciary obligation on the part of the Crown to deal with
land for the benefit of the . . . Indians.'[133]

Precisely this fiduciary theme has been taken up in Australia,

[128] It was not until the decision of the High Court in 1992 in *Mabo* v.
Queensland (No 2) that Australian courts fully recognised that the historic assumption of Crown sovereignty could not, in itself, have made the indigenous inhabitants
of Australia mere 'trespassers on the land on which they and their ancestors had
lived' ((1992) 175 CLR 1, 184 per Toohey J.), thereby converting them into 'intrud-
ers in their own homes and mendicants for a place to live' ((1992) 175 CLR 1, 29
per Brennan J.). 40,000 years of prior possession must surely count for something.

[129] Such notions can ultimately be traced to the decision of the United States
Supreme Court in *Cherokee Nation* v. *Georgia* (1831) 5 Pet 1, 8 L Ed 1.

[130] See *Cardinal* v. *Attorney-General of Alberta* (1974) 40 DLR (3d) 553, 568ff per
Laskin J. (dissenting); *Guerin* v. *The Queen* (1984) 13 DLR (4th) 321, 338;
Delgamuukw v. *The Queen in Right of British Columbia* (1993) 104 DLR (4th) 470,
495*h*. See also D. M. Johnston, 'A Theory of Crown Trust towards Aboriginal
Peoples', (1986) 18 *Ottawa L Rev* 307.

[131] (1984) 13 DLR (4th) 321, 339.

[132] See also *Delgamuukw* v. *The Queen in Right of British Columbia* (1993) 104
DLR (4th) 470, 494*f*–4495*b*, 511*a*–*b* per Macfarlane JA, 572*f*, 573*e* per Wallace JA,
650*c*–*e* per Lambert JA.

[133] (1984) 13 DLR (4th) 321, 339. Dickson J. doubted whether, in the strictest
sense, this fiduciary obligation gave rise to a trust, but was quite clear that 'the
obligation is trust-like in character' (ibid., 342). See also *R* v. *Sparrow* (1990) 70
DLR (4th) 385, 408; *Delgamuukw* v. *The Queen in Right of British Columbia* (1991)
79 DLR (4th) 185, 198, 482 per McEachern CJ.

most famously in the controversial ruling of the High Court in 1992 in the second *Mabo* case (*Mabo* v. *Queensland (No 2)*).[134] Here a strong majority in the High Court conceded that Australia, on first colonisation, was not *terra nullius*, and that the settlers' law of property must recognise pre-existing customary native rights in respect of the land.[135] Brennan J. had earlier spoken of the 'sadly familiar' phenomenon of 'landless, rootless Aboriginal peoples'.[136] In dealing in *Mabo (No 2)* with the land rights of the Meriam people of the Murray Islands, Brennan J. forthrightly condemned as 'discriminatory denigration' the theory that indigenous inhabitants of a 'settled' colony lost all 'proprietary interest' in the land which they continued to occupy.[137] Brennan J. was therefore prepared to regard customary claims as comprising a 'proprietary community title' which could be recognised as 'a burden on the Crown's radical title when the Crown acquires sovereignty over that territory.'[138] According to Brennan J. it was 'only the fallacy of equating sovereignty and beneficial ownership of land that gives rise to the notion that native title is extinguished by the acquisition of sovereignty.'[139] Some form of beneficial ownership thus remained vested in the indigenous peoples at least in relation to lands occupied by them at the date of the Crown's assumption of sovereign control.[140]

In *Mabo*'s case Toohey J., another member of the High Court majority, was happy to adopt the reasoning in the parallel Canadian case law in pointing to the existence of a fiduciary

[134] (1992) 175 CLR 1.

[135] (1992) 175 CLR 1, 48ff, 69 per Brennan J., 90ff per Deane and Gaudron JJ, 183 per Toohey J.

[136] See *Gerhardy* v. *Brown* (1985) 159 CLR 70, 136.

[137] (1992) 175 CLR 1, 40.

[138] (1992) 175 CLR 1, 51. Brennan J. (with whose reasons Mason CJ and McHugh J. expressly agreed (1992) 175 CLR 1, 15)) considered that it might be 'confusing to describe the title of the Meriam people as conferring "ownership", a term which connotes an estate in fee simple or at least an estate of freehold.' Brennan J nevertheless analysed native title, in essentially proprietary terms, as being 'effective . . . as against the whole world unless the State, in valid exercise of its legislative or executive power, extinguishes the title' ((1992) 175 CLR 1, 75).

[139] (1992) 175 CLR 1, 51.

[140] Only if the land had been 'desert and uninhabited, truly a terra nullius', would the Crown's assumption of sovereignty have conferred on the Crown not merely a 'radical, ultimate or final title', but also 'an absolute beneficial title' to the land ((1992) 175 CLR 1, 48 per Brennan J.). See *Bl Comm*, Vol II, p. 7; *Attorney-General (NSW)* v. *Brown* (1847) 1 Legge 312, 319, 2 SCR App 30, 35 per Stephen CJ.

obligation in the Crown to protect the integrity of native title.[141] Toohey J. openly admitted that, in the present context, recognition of a fiduciary relationship 'may be tantamount to saying that the legal interest in traditional rights is in the Crown whereas the beneficial interest in the rights is in the indigenous owners.'[142] Although viewing as 'fruitless' and 'unnecessarily complex' any further inquiry as to whether native title is 'personal' or 'proprietary',[143] Toohey J. had no doubt that, for present purposes, 'the kind of fiduciary obligation imposed on the Crown is that of a constructive trustee.'[144] Deane and Gaudron JJ likewise recognised the inappropriateness of forcing native title within conventional common law classifications,[145] but acknowledged nonetheless that the rights of occupation or use conferred by native title 'can themselves constitute valuable property'.[146] Any legislative extinguishment of such rights would thus comprise an 'expropriation of property';[147] and any actual or threatened interference with the rights would normally 'attract the protection of equitable remedies' such as the 'imposition of a remedial constructive trust framed to reflect the incidents and limitations of the rights under the common law native title.'[148]

In so far as 'equitable property is commensurate with equitable relief'[149]—a theme much emphasised in Australian jurisprudence[150] —the approach taken by the High Court majority in *Mabo (No 2)* clearly endorsed the recognition of a regime of beneficial entitle-

---

[141] (1992) 175 CLR 1, 200f.   [142] (1992) 175 CLR 1, 203.

[143] (1992) 175 CLR 1, 195.

[144] (1992) 175 CLR 1, 203. See also *Guerin* v. *The Queen* (1984) 13 DLR (4th) 321, 334 per Dickson J.

[145] Deane and Gaudron JJ regarded the rights conferred by native title as merely 'personal', in the sense that such rights were not 'assignable outside the overall native system' ((1992) 175 CLR 1, 110), but were otherwise content to accept native title as 'sui generis or unique' (ibid., 89).

[146] (1992) 175 CLR 1, 113.   [147] (1992) 175 CLR 1, 111.

[148] (1992) 175 CLR 1, 113. It is significant that native title rights were regarded by Deane and Gaudron JJ as partaking sufficiently of the character of rights of equitable property that the 'rules relating to requirements of certainty and present entitlement or precluding remoteness of vesting may need to be adapted or excluded to the extent necessary to enable the protection of the rights under the native title.'

[149] *Hoysted* v. *Federal Commissioner of Taxation* (1920) 27 CLR 400, 423 per Isaacs J.

[150] See *Trustees, Executors and Agency Co Ltd* v. *Acting Federal Commissioner of Taxation* (1917) 23 CLR 576, 583; *Patton* v. *Corin* (1987) 13 NSWLR 10, 13G–14A per McLelland J.; *Stern* v. *McArthur* (1988) 165 CLR 489, 522f per Deane and Dawson JJ. See also *In re Cunliffe-Owen* [1953] Ch 545, 557 per Evershed MR.

ment as a means of securing access-oriented rights for Aboriginal peoples. Only by accommodating native title—however approximately—within the white man's notion of property could Australia be seen to live up to its international human rights obligations.[151] Only by confirming the right of the indigenous peoples of Australia to reconstruct their traditional relationship with their country could modern law restore the 'everlastingness of spirit' enjoyed by these people in earlier and happier times and buttress their sense of 'spiritual, cultural and social identity'[152] within the commonwealth which, in every sense, is Australia.

In Australia the eighteen months following *Mabo (No 2)* saw a rapid, and at times frenzied, public discussion of the High Court's ruling.[153] This debate culminated on 24 December 1993 in the enactment by the Commonwealth Parliament of the Native Title Act 1993.[154] Containing 253 sections, this legislation is complex and comprehensive in its attempt to institute a new regime for native title alongside existing proprietary and commercial rights of a more conventional kind. The Act confirms that native title is to be 'recognised, and protected' in accordance with the terms of the 1993 Act.[155] The legislation sets up a National Native Title Tribunal to determine the validity and scope of claims of native title[156] and a Native Title Registrar to maintain a public register of claims and decisions on claims relating to native title.[157] Interestingly, in view of our discussion of the links between native title and beneficial ownership, the new Act contains a provision which resembles an almost pure application of the trust principle contained in *Saunders* v. *Vautier*.[158] Section 21 allows native title holders, if they so wish, to join together in an agreement to surrender their native title rights to the relevant government on any lawful terms which they may stipulate.[159] In particular section 21(3) indicates that the condition of or consideration for this surrender may be the grant of a freehold estate or such statutory or other

---

[151] (1992) 175 CLR 1, 42. See Preamble to Native Title Act 1993. See also G. Neate, (1993) 16 *UNSWLJ* 161, 163 et seq.

[152] See *Gerhardy* v. *Brown* (1985) 159 CLR 70, 136 per Brennan J.

[153] For reference to the 'hysteria and even paranoia' generated by *Mabo (No 2)*, see G. Nettheim, (1993) 16 *UNSWLJ* 1, 2.

[154] Act No 110 of 1993. [155] Native Title Act 1993, s. 10.

[156] Native Title Act 1993, s. 107. [157] Native Title Act 1993, ss. 95 et seq.

[158] (1841) 4 Beav 115, 116, 49 ER 282; Cr & Ph 240, 249, 41 ER 482, 485.

[159] Native Title Act 1993, s. 21(2).

interest in the land 'that the native title holders may choose to accept'. Native title holders may, in effect, direct an exchange of their old Australian title for a new Australian one, which, as indicated in the explanatory memoranda accompanying the legislation, 'would facilitate their ability to put the land to commercial purposes.'[160] At this point, of course, the exclusory dimension of property will have begun to dominate over the competing dimension of property as a title to access.

(3) EQUITABLE PROPERTY IN THE NATURAL ENVIRONMENT

For my third and final example I turn to the natural environment. Recent years have plainly witnessed an accentuation of the importance and urgency of global environmental issues. Indeed it is in the context of this emerging range of concern that the twin themes of 'equitable property' in quasi-public places and 'equitable property' in traditional country are finally, and perhaps strangely, brought together. The juxtaposition of these themes lends an unexpected relevance to the way in which legal regimes across the world are nowadays coming to recognise, on behalf of the individual citizen, a significant 'equitable property' in the quality and conservation of the natural environment.[161] Here, perhaps even more clearly than elsewhere, the oscillating ambivalence of the 'property' notion is beginning to ensure that 'property' is not a mere mode of empowering exclusion, but is rather a means of empowering access.[162] Furthermore the evolution of a new regime of environmental 'property' not only confirms a relatively modern dimension of access to the goods of life, but also casts an intense contemporary emphasis upon the interrelation of right and responsibility as

---

[160] *Mabo: Outline of Proposed Legislation on Native Title* (Commonwealth of Australia, September 1993), para 29. See also Parliament of the Commonwealth of Australia, House of Representatives, *Native Title Bill 1993: Explanatory Memorandum*, Part A (1993), p. 6.

[161] For a philosophical argument that public goods (e.g. clean air) can be the subject of individual rights, see J. Waldron, 'Can communal goods be human rights?', 28 *Arch Europ Sociol* 296, 308 (1987).

[162] Gray, *The Ambivalence of Property*, in *Threats without Enemies* (1993), p. 157 et seq. For a contention that traditional philosophical justifications of private property are equally supportive of public rights of unconsented access to private property in land, see W. N. R. Lucy and F. R. Barker, 'Justifying Property and Justifying Access', (1993) 6 *Can Jnl of Law and Juris* 287.

inextricable components of our current conceptualisations of 'property'.

In the elaboration of this new equity in the biosphere, the vital ecological resources of the earth are increasingly seen as governed by a trust for the preservation of environmental quality under conditions of reasonable shared access for all citizens. Meaningful reference can thus begin to be made to the collective beneficial rights of the generalised public in respect of strategically important environmental assets. But—just as with the proprietary title so recently recognised on behalf of the Aboriginal clan—the essential constitutive feature of such beneficial rights is the pervasive awareness of an overriding duty to 'look after country'. In this modern emanation of beneficial title the concepts of right and responsibility are inseparably fused, thereby confirming the vacuity of any supposition that 'property' is ever naturally or intrinsically free of 'obligation'.[163] The social responsibility of caring for land is a fundamental, central and inescapable component of real entitlement.[164] It should never be overlooked that, in the law of the new property, rights of access—when asserted in derogation of rights of exclusion—come at a substantial price measured in the performance of social duty.

There may, of course, be some who detect unacceptable novelty, if not outright heresy, in the adaptation of trust doctrine towards the fashioning of an 'equitable property' in the environment. Such sceptics might do well to trace the steady intrusion of concepts of 'stewardship' into mainstream property discourse in the United States during the last quarter century.[165] Throughout this period the international lawyers have talked shamelessly, for instance, of

---

[163] See 'Property in Thin Air', [1991] *Cambridge LJ* 252, 297 et seq. For evidence of the marked resurgence of 'responsibility' as a key concept in property law discourse, see e.g. G. S. Alexander, 'Takings and the Post-Modern Dialectic of Property', 9 *Const Comm* 259, 260 et seq (1992).

[164] This much has always been apparent in the long history of the law relating to the concept of 'waste'. There is a certain irony in the fact that the historic abolition of the incidents of feudal tenure, by freeing land from archaic and obsolete obligations, contributed towards a more general dissociation of the notions of right and responsibility in landholding. See J. E. Cribbet, *Concepts in Transition: The Search for a New Definition of Property*, (1986) *U Ill L Rev* 1, 39.

[165] See V. J. Yannacone, 'Property And Stewardship—Private Property Plus Public Interest Equals Social Property', 23 *S Dak L Rev* 71 (1978); L.K. Caldwell, 'Land and the Law: Problems in Legal Philosophy', (1986) *U Ill L Rev* 319, 325 et seq; J. P. Karp, 'A Private Property Duty of Stewardship: Changing Our Land Ethic', 23 *Envtl L* 735, 748 et seq (1992–93).

the existence of a global or planetary trust on behalf of future generations.[166] Professor Edith Brown Weiss, perhaps the foremost proponent of this form of 'intergenerational equity', has argued that each generation is burdened by an obligation of trusteeship to conserve the quality and diversity of the natural and cultural resource base for future generations.[167] With some dexterity Professor Brown Weiss has elaborated the notion of trust in relation to environmental resources, detailing with specificity such matters as the nature of the trust corpus, the purposes of the trust and the definition of the relevant beneficiaries.[168]

But talk of an intergenerational equity availing future beneficiaries will inevitably strike some as mere metaphor. For those left unimpressed by the rhetoric of the international lawyers, it may be more compelling to examine the possibility of an environmental trust which confers *contemporary* benefits on *living* beneficiaries. In 1972 Christopher Stone posed his famous question: 'Should trees have standing?'[169] Stone's argument, that the jural rights of natural objects can be represented or defended by a next friend or guardian *ad litem* (ie a concerned environmentalist), was to bear a fruit which he could hardly have dared to expect.[170] Within days of

[166] The Declaration of the United Nations Conference on the Human Environment (the Stockholm Declaration, 16 June 1972) stated, in Principle 1, that humankind 'bears a solemn responsibility to protect and improve the environment for present and future generations' (see 11 ILM 1416, 1417f (1972)). Principle 2 required that the 'natural resources of the earth including the air, water, land, flora and fauna and especially representative samples of natural ecosystems must be safeguarded for the benefit of present and future generations through careful planning or management, as appropriate.'

[167] 'The Planetary Trust: Conservation and Intergenerational Equity', 11 *Ecology LQ* 495, 502 et seq (1983–84). See generally *In Fairness to Future Generations: International Law, Common Patrimony, and Intergenerational Equity* (New York 1989). It has been recognised that in other contexts the rights of future generations have always controlled the validity of present assertions of private property. Richard Lazarus has observed, for instance, that '[p]roperty law has long reflected the need to protect the future from the dead hand of the past' ('Debunking Environmental Feudalism: Promoting the Individual through Collective Pursuit of Environmental Quality', 77 *Iowa L Rev* 1739, 1761 (1992)).

[168] It is likely (and also fortunate) that the charitable nature of such a trust eliminates many of the technical problems which would otherwise arise. See, however, D. Parfit, 'On Doing the Best for Our Children', in M. Bayles (ed), *Ethics and Population* (1976), p. 100; A. D'Amato, 'Do we owe A Duty To Future Generations to preserve the Global Environment?' (1990) 84 *AJIL* 190.

[169] 'Should Trees have Standing?—Towards Legal Rights for Natural Objects', 45 *S Cal L Rev* 450 (1972).

[170] See C. D. Stone, 'Should Trees have Standing? Revisited: How far will law and morals reach? A pluralist perspective', 59 *S Cal L Rev* 1, 2 (1985).

the publication of Stone's historic contribution, Justice William O. Douglas delivered his powerfully dissenting (and highly influential) opinion in the United States Supreme Court in *Sierra Club* v. *Morton*.[171]

In *Sierra Club* v. *Morton* the majority in the Supreme Court denied[172] to the Sierra Club (a venerable wilderness conservation society) the requisite legal standing to seek orders restraining the destructive commercial development of the Mineral King Valley in the Sierra Nevada of Northern California.[173] In his dissent Justice Douglas not only endorsed Stone's argument that environmental objects should have standing to 'sue for their own preservation'.[174] He adumbrated the beginnings of a public trust doctrine specifically relevant to ecologically significant resources,[175] and concluded on this basis that 'the voice of the existing beneficiaries of these

[171] 405 US 727, 31 L Ed 2d 636 (1972). For an environmentally sensitive precursor, see *Gould* v. *Greylock Reservation Commission*, 215 NE2d 114, 121 et seq (1966).

[172] The denial was based solely on the Sierra Club's failure to plead any actual injury on the part of its members. Significantly the Court drew the plaintiff's attention to the facility for amending its complaint (405 US 727, 735, 740, 31 L Ed 2d 636, 643, 646). The Court emphasised that it was open to specific club members to allege individualised injury if they 'have used and continue to use the area for recreational purposes' and could plead, on their own behalf, that 'the aesthetic and recreational values of the area' would be diminished by the proposed development.

[173] Walt Disney Enterprises Inc had won a competition (run by the United States Forest Service) to design and operate a winter and summer recreational resort in the Mineral King Valley, comprising motels, 13 restaurants, swimming pools, a nine-mile access highway, a cog-assisted railway and ski resort complex. For Justice Douglas this ghastly US$ 35 million development, estimated to accommodate 14,000 visitors daily, clearly threatened to 'plow under all the aesthetic wonders of this beautiful land' (405 US 727, 759, 31 L Ed 2d 636, 656). Justice Douglas pointed out that the 'mammoth project' would multiply the visitor rate in the valley by a factor in excess of 70 (ibid., 743, 648), and Justice Blackmun questioned whether the expected vehicle frequency of one car every six seconds along the valley floor could possibly be 'the way we perpetuate the wilderness and its beauty, solitude and quiet' (ibid., 759, 656).

[174] Noting that inanimate entities such as ships and corporations are sometimes parties in litigation, Justice Douglas would have allowed environmental issues 'to be litigated . . . in the name of the inanimate object about to be despoiled, defaced, or invaded by roads and bulldozers and where injury is the subject of public outrage' (405 US 727, 741, 31 L Ed 2d 636, 647).

[175] See e.g. *National Audubon Society* v. *Superior Court of Alpine County*, 658 P2d 709, 719 (1983), where, in the context of the Mono Lake controversy, the Supreme Court of California expressly found the public trust doctrine applicable to 'the scenic views of the lake and its shore, the purity of the air, and the use of the lake for nesting and feeding by birds.'

environmental wonders should be heard'.[176] Justice Douglas favoured the recognition of standing in those persons who have a 'meaningful' or 'intimate' relation with 'the inanimate object about to be injured, polluted, or otherwise despoiled.' In respect of the Mineral King Valley, those who 'hike it, fish it, hunt it, camp in it, frequent it, or visit it merely to sit in solitude and wonderment' were 'its legitimate spokesmen' and 'must be able to speak for [its] values'.[177] Only in this way could all the forms of life represented by the endangered environmental resource be enabled to 'stand before the court—the pileated woodpecker as well as the coyote and bear, the lemmings as well as the trout in the streams.' Only thus could the court avert the risk that 'priceless bits of Americana (such as a valley, an alpine meadow, a river, or a lake)' would be 'forever lost or . . . so transformed as to be reduced to the eventual rubble of our urban environment'.[178] In his own way Justice Douglas was another remarkable exponent of an American wilderness tradition which extends richly from Audubon and Thoreau to Aldo Leopold and beyond.[179]

Now no one would, I think, pretend that the wilderness ethic so eloquently expounded by Justice Douglas in the *Sierra Club* case immediately generated unqualified acceptance of the notion of public equitable ownership of environmental resources. Yet his judgment resonated with coded articulations of the essential core or inner meaning of 'property'. These subliminal 'property' messages emerged in at least two forms.

First, in the same way in which traditional Aboriginal ties to land have now been recognised as constitutive of beneficial rights, Justice Douglas was prepared to accept that an intimate knowledge of wild country is creative of a certain beneficiary status in relation to that land. Justice Douglas knew the writings of John Muir[180]

[176] 405 US 727, 750, 31 L Ed 2d 636, 651.

[177] 405 US 727, 743f, 31 L Ed 2d 636, 648f.

[178] Such was the eventual public outcry against the proposed devastation of the Mineral King Valley that Congress prohibited the project in 1978 by including the Valley within the Sequoia National Park (National Parks and Recreation Act 1978, s. 314 (16 USCA s 45f (St Paul, Minn, 1992)).

[179] See R. Nash, *Wilderness and the American Mind* (New Haven and London, 1967), p. 84 et seq.

[180] For evidence of his deep acquaintance with Muir's journals and other publications, see W. O. Douglas, *Of Men And Mountains* (London 1951), pp. 112, 203. See also J. M. Caragher, 'The Wilderness Ethic of Justice William O. Douglas', (1986) *U Ill L Rev* 645.

and would, of course, have been familiar with Muir's assertion, made a century earlier, that 'the true ownership of the wilderness belongs in the highest degree to those who love it most.'[181] Douglas was no stranger to the idea that immersion of the human spirit in the fierce majesty of wild places causes the land to 'belong' in some deep sense to the adventurer; his own extra-judicial writings gave expression to exactly such thoughts.[182] In this context, as elsewhere, habitual user generates its own form of title.

Second, Justice Douglas understood well that the most important 'property' in any resource is the right to participate in the selective exploitation or 'prioritisation' of its various forms of value. To be recognised as having authority to 'speak for' an asset—to have a dispositive voice or strategic vote in determining its mode of utilisation—is, in itself, to command an intensely significant component of 'property' in the resource.[183] It was ultimately this factor which lent proprietary impact to the argument about standing in *Sierra Club* v. *Morton*, adding piquancy to Justice Douglas's assertion that where the 'inarticulate members of the ecological group cannot speak . . . those people who have so frequented the place as to know its values and wonders will be able to speak for the entire ecological community.'[184] In this respect Justice Douglas came close to describing the ultimate beneficial prerogative of mature persons of right mind to join together in predicating the future disposition of their trust interests.

In the America of the late 1960s and early 1970s Justice Douglas's *Sierra Club* dissent coincided with, and doubtless contributed towards, a fresh realisation that all property rights are

---

[181] R. Engberg and D. Wesling, *John Muir: To Yosemite And Beyond—Writings from the Years 1863 to 1875* (Madison, Wisconsin 1980), p. 8.

[182] 'When one stands on Darling Mountain, he is not remote and apart from the wilderness; he is an intimate part of it . . . These peaks and meadows were made for man, and man for them. They are man's habitat . . . Man must explore them and come to know them. They belong to him . . . ' (W. O. Douglas, *Of Men And Mountains*, p. 90). Douglas did, however, recognise that the resources of the wilderness 'will eventually reclaim [man] and rule beyond his day as they ruled long before he appeared on the earth . . . '

[183] 'If property ownership consists of the right to control use, the Sierra Club and the Wilderness Society are already partners with the government in owning wilderness areas' (see R. H. Nelson, (1986) *U Ill L Rev* 361, 371).

[184] 405 US 727, 752, 31 L Ed 2d 636, 653.

necessarily limited by social values and preferences.[185] Professor
Richard Powell had already spoken of 'a playing-down of absolute
rights and a playing-up of social concern as to the use of
property.'[186] Explicitly adopting Powell's language, the Supreme
Court of New Jersey observed in 1971 that the viewpoint that 'he
who owns may do as he pleases with what he owns' had given
way to a perception which 'hesitatingly embodies an ingredient of
stewardship'.[187] Thus, for Mosk J in *Agricultural Labor Relations
Board* v. *Superior Court of Tulare County*,[188] property rights must
be 'redefined in response to a swelling demand that ownership be
responsible and responsive to the needs of the social whole.'[189]
Donald Large was able to point in 1974 to 'a growing attitude that
there exists an inherent public right in property that transcends the
technicalities of title'.[190] The way was amply prepared for a
broader endorsement of the philosophy of environmental trust.

In more recent years a number of related factors have conduced
in the United States to a gathering recognition of the general social
stake in property.[191] It has even become possible to suggest that all
rights of land ownership should be commuted forthwith to
'socially derived privileges' of use.[192] Indeed, with the proliferation

---

[185] This recognition was itself far from novel. Drawing strength from an essentially Jeffersonian vision of private ownership, American courts have long accepted
that 'all property . . . is held under the implied obligation that the owner's use of it
shall not be injurious to the community' (*Mugler* v. *Kansas*, 123 US 623, 665, 31 L
Ed 205, 211 per Harlan J. (1887)). Accordingly the US Supreme Court had no difficulty in 1934 in postulating that 'neither property rights nor contract rights are
absolute . . . Equally fundamental with the private right is that of the public to regulate it in the common interest' (*Nebbia* v. *New York*, 291 US 502, 523, 78 L Ed
940, 948f (1934)). The approach defined in *Nebbia* was later to play a significant
role in guiding the US Supreme Court to its decision in *PruneYard Shopping Center*
v. *Robins*, 447 US 74, 84f, 64 L Ed 2d 741, 754 (1980).

[186] R. R. B. Powell, 'The Relationship between Property Rights and Civil Rights',
15 *Hastings LJ* 135, 149 (1963–64). See Professor J. E. Cribbet's assertion that 'traditional property rights must now be seen through the prism of an expanded public
interest in land use' ((1986) *U Ill L Rev* 1, 25).

[187] *State* v. *Shack*, 277 A2d 369, 372 (1971).

[188] 128 Cal Rptr 183, 190 (1976).

[189] Mosk J. emphasised that property rights 'cannot be used . . . to cloak conduct which adversely affects the health, the safety, the morals, or the welfare of others'.

[190] D. W. Large, 'This Land is Whose Land? Changing Concepts of Land as
Property', (1973) *Wisconsin L Rev* 1039, 1074. See eg *Marks* v. *Whitney*, 491 P2d
374 (1971).

[191] See J. E. Cribbet, (1986) *U Ill L Rev* 1, 40.

[192] L. K. Caldwell, 'Rights of Ownership or Rights of Use?—The Need for a New

of zoning law and the remorseless intrusion of regulation following the National Environmental Policy Act 1969,[193] the fee simple estate in land may already have been stripped back to a mere usufructuary title heavily conditioned by the public interest.[194] Such developments are readily understood as exemplifying a 'principle of stewardship, under which ownership or possession of land is viewed as a trust, with attendant obligations to future generations as well as to the present.'[195] The steady infiltration of this notion of stewardship inevitably impresses on land tenure a range of social obligations which effectively create a public beneficial entitlement in respect of ecologically critical assets.[196] Meanwhile the advent of this new civic property in strategic environmental resources merges quite harmoniously with other contemporary American social and intellectual themes. The community-oriented aspect of the new environmental property confirms and complements the insights of the ecofeminist movement[197] and also blends easily with the communitarian vision of property advanced in much recent economic and philosophic theory.[198] Additional intellectual sustenance for the current socialisation of property relationships can be derived from the modern rediscovery of the 'land

---

Conceptual Basis for Land Use Policy', 15 *William and Mary Law Rev* 759, 766 et seq (1973–74)). See also E. T. Freyfogle, 'Context and Accommodation in Modern Property Law', 41 *Stan L Rev* 1529, 1530 et seq (1988–89).

[193] 42 USCA ss. 4321–4335 (1977).

[194] According to James Karp, all land is 'owned subject to the implied servitude of the police power' (J. P. Karp, 23 Envtl L 735, 750 (1992–93)). For a recent review of relevant American environmental legislation which effectively converts real rights to mere usufructs, see R. J. Lazarus, 77 Iowa L Rev 1739, 1750 (1992).

[195] L. K. Caldwell, 15 *William and Mary Law Rev* 759, 766. Cf J. E. Cribbet, (1986) *U Ill L Rev* 1, 38 ('All land would be a public trust . . . '). See also D. B. Hunter, 'An Ecological Perspective on Property: A Call for Judicial Protection of the Public's Interest in Environmentally Critical Resources', 12 *Harv Envtl L Rev* 311, 319 (1988).

[196] Alison Rieser has pointed to the way in which federal statutes have 'codified the idea that the public has property rights in the non-commodity values of natural resources' (see 'Ecological Preservation as a Public Property Right: An Emerging Doctrine in Search of a Theory', 15 *Harv Envtl L Rev* 393, 432 (1991)).

[197] See e.g. E. Diamond and G. Orenstein (ed), '*Reweaving The World: The Emergence Of Ecofeminism*' (1990); R. Delgado, 44 *Vand L Rev* 1209, 1222 (1991).

[198] See e.g. A. Etzioni, *The Moral Dimension: Towards A New Economics* (New York 1990), p. 237 et seq; C. M. Rose, 'Property as Wealth, Property as Propriety', in J. W. Chapman (ed), *Nomos XXXIII: Compensatory Justice* (New York and London 1991), p. 240; G. S. Alexander, 9 *Const Comm* 259, 260 et seq (1992).

ethic' first proposed by Aldo Leopold over four decades ago.[199]
Leopold's call for the adoption of a cooperative 'land ethic' was
aimed at enlarging 'the boundaries of the community to include
soils, waters, plants, and animals, or collectively: the land.'[200] For
Leopold it had become imperative to bring about 'the extension of
the social conscience from people to land'.[201]

Civic claims in respect of the environment have received further
significant afforcement in the continuing evolution of the American
version of historic doctrines of 'public trust'. In its original formulation the American public trust doctrine confirmed merely the
state ownership of navigable waters and tidelands on behalf of all
citizens.[202] More recently courts and state agencies have seemed
willing to oversee important extensions of both the character and
the coverage of the doctrine.[203] It is now clear that the purposes of
the public trust doctrine extend no less to the protection of environmental and recreational values than to the preservation of commercial navigation and fishery.[204] It is increasingly apparent that
the ultimate role of the public trust doctrine may lie, not in its traditional function as justifying state taking, but rather in promoting
a public beneficial ownership which is opposable against government itself.[205] Even more radically there is now strong reason to
believe that the doctrine of public trust can relate to objects far
beyond its initial scope,[206] thereby extending to such resources as

---

[199] See 'The Land Ethic', in A. Leopold, *A Sand County Almanac* (New York and
Oxford 1987 (first published 1949)).

[200] Ibid., p. 204.   [201] Ibid., p. 209.

[202] See J. L. Sax, 'The Public Trust Doctrine in Natural Resource Law: Effective
Judicial Intervention', 68 *Mich L Rev* 471 (1969–70); C. F. Wilkinson, 'The Public
Trust Doctrine in Public Land Law', 14 *U C Davis L Rev* 269 (1980–81).

[203] See A. Rieser, 15 *Harv Envtl L Rev* 393 (1991).

[204] *Marks* v. *Whitney*, 491 P2d 374, 380 (1971); *National Audubon Society* v.
Superior Court of Alpine County, 658 P2d 709, 712, 719 (1983).

[205] See R. Ausness, 'Water Rights, The Public Trust Doctrine and the Protection
of Instream Uses', (1986) *U Ill L Rev* 407, 435 (The doctrine 'regards the public, not
the government, as the beneficial owner of trust resources'). See also the insistence
of the Supreme Court of California in *National Audubon Society* v. *Superior Court
of Alpine County*, 658 P2d 709, 724 (1983) that the public trust doctrine is 'more
than an affirmation of state power to use public property for public purposes. It is
an affirmation of the duty of the state to protect the people's common heritage of
streams, lakes, marshlands and tidelands'.

[206] This possibility was originally indicated by J. L. Sax, 68 *Mich L Rev* 471, 556
et seq (1969–70). See e.g. *Matthews and Van Ness* v. *Bay Head Improvement Ass'n*,
471 A2d 355, 365ff (1984).

wild country and parkland,[207] wildlife,[208] and perhaps even areas of general recreational utility[209] or historic interest.[210]

The reinvigorated notion of public trust has clearly become a vital weapon in the battle for environmental protection currently being waged in the United States courts.[211] As Alison Rieser has indicated, the theory of public trust now provides an immensely significant doctrinal vehicle for subordinating both private and government ownership to a 'property interest held by the "unorganised public" in the ecological integrity of natural resources.'[212] Similarly Richard Lazarus has predicted that the likely outcome of modern environmental legislation will be the creation of 'modified property rights' for the citizen in many forms of natural resource not hitherto regarded as susceptible to communal proprietary claims.[213] Even in the vexed area of American 'takings' jurisprudence some commentators have begun to discern the 'hidden influence' of the idea that 'land and natural resources are common property'.[214] It has suddenly become realistic to envisage the creation of a 'new property' which consists, not of individual private property rights, but of 'new collective private property rights'

---

[207] *Paepcke* v. *Public Building Commission of Chicago*, 263 NE2d 11, 18 (1970).

[208] *Wade* v. *Kramer*, 459 NE2d 1025, 1027ff (1984). See G.D. Myers, 'Variations on a Theme: Expanding the Public Trust Doctrine to Include Protection of Wildlife', 19 *Envtl L* 723 (1989).

[209] *Van Ness* v. *Borough of Deal*, 393 A2d 571, 574 (1978). See E. Pitts, 'The Public Trust Doctrine: A Tool for ensuring Continued Public Use of Oregon Beaches', 22 *Envtl L* 731 (1991–92). See also *State ex rel Thornton* v. *Hay*, 462 P2d 671 (1969); M. C. Blumm, 24 *U San Francisco L Rev* 385, 397 (1989–90).

[210] *Commonwealth* v. *National Gettysburg Battlefield Tower, Inc*, 311 A2d 588, 591 (1973).

[211] J. E. Van Tol, 'The Public Trust Doctrine: A New Approach to Environmental Preservation', 81 *W Virginia L Rev* 455 (1978–79); J. S. Stevens, 'The Public Trust: A Sovereign's Ancient Prerogative Becomes the People's Environmental Right', 14 *U C Davis L Rev* 195 (1980–81). Compare, however, R. J. Lazarus, 'Changing Conceptions of Property and Sovereignty in Natural Resources: Questioning the Public Trust Doctrine', 71 *Iowa L Rev* 631 (1986); R. Delgado, 44 *Vand L Rev* 1209 (1991).

[212] 'Ecological Preservation as a Public Property Right: An Emerging Doctrine in Search of a Theory', 15 *Harv Envtl L Rev* 393, 426 (1991). See also the reference to 'social property in the resource commons', in W. H. Rodgers, 'Bringing People Back: Toward a Comprehensive Theory of Taking in Natural Resources Law', 10 *Ecology LQ* 205, 230 (1982–83).

[213] R. J. Lazarus, 77 *Iowa L Rev* 1739, 1759 (1992). See also Lazarus, 71 *Iowa L Rev* 631, 698 et seq (1986).

[214] See T. N. Tideman, 'Takings, Moral Evolution, and Justice', 88 *Col L Rev* 1714, 1728 (1988).

in respect of the common pool resources of the national land base.[215]

Although neither uniform nor free of controversy, the American experience provides strong modern evidence of a substantial reintegration of ownership and obligation within the deep theory of property. The advancement of a generalised public interest in the utilisation of environmental resources appears to have engrafted community obligation as an implicit qualification on title. In turn the gradual infiltration of property by notions of social responsibility has made it feasible to claim, on behalf of all citizens, an 'equitable property' in the 'ecologically imperative' resources of the environment.[216] In effect a novel form of civic ownership is in the process of being created behind a trust of environmentally significant assets.[217] Certain resources are simply perceived as conferring such intrinsic public utility that, regardless of nominal title, their benefits must be retained within some version of the commons. By reason of their irreplaceable moral or social character these assets are ultimately 'non-excludable'.[218] Following an assertion of private exclusory control over them there would not, in Locke's famous phrase, be 'enough, and as good left in common for others.'[219]

The acknowledgement of an environmental trust relationship has, of course, many implications. The entitlements recognised under such a trust include not only rights of appropriate beneficiary access to the environmental goods held on trust, but also the right of each beneficiary to require the orderly administration of the trust conformably with the land ethic mandated by its terms. Such quality assurance is in practice indistinguishable from the

---

[215] See R. H. Nelson, 'Private Rights to Government Actions: How Modern Property Rights Evolve', (1986) *U Ill L Rev* 361, 373.

[216] J. P. Karp, 23 *Envtl L* 735, 745 et seq (1992–93).

[217] 'We should all have a right to a safe, clean, and intact natural environment, a right to be free from toxic threats, a right to participate in the management decisions concerning the public domain. Pollution of the ocean, lumbering of the ancient forests, or commercial development of the natural parks should be held to involve "new property rights" because these actions have a direct impact upon the quality of our lives and are part of each person's share in the commonwealth' (see C. A. Reich, 100 *Yale LJ* 1465, 1468 (1990–91)).

[218] On the concept of 'non-excludability', see 'Property in Thin Air', [1991] *Cambridge LJ* 252, 268 et seq.

[219] See John Locke, *Two Treatises of Government* (2nd critical edn by P. Laslett, Cambridge 1967), *The Second Treatise*, s 27 (p 306).

guarantee of reasonable access. Any meaningful notion of reasonable access must involve not the mere provision of factual or physical access but also the preservation of the wholesomeness of the environment to which this access relates.[220] Inevitably the infusion of trust terminology also requires some remodelling of popular ideas of 'ownership'. In the broader perspective of environmental trust the earth belongs to none absolutely except in the fiduciary sense in which, by analogy, our own Settled Land Act of 1925 grants fee simple ownership temporarily to the tenant for life on trust for the remaindermen.[221] From an environmentalist viewpoint all nominal ownership of land is effectively qualified by a trust to preserve, share and improve an extremely precious and easily depleted pool of ecological resource. Claims of exclusory 'property' are always bounded by juxtaposed claims of public access to those utilities and amenities which are fairly regarded as the 'common heritage of humankind'.[222] Furthermore the environmental trust is incapable of being discharged without a consultation of the interests of its beneficiaries, thereby reinforcing the truism that participation in the allocation or 'prioritisation' of goods is the very stuff of 'property'. Environmental rights are essentially participatory or democratic rights of purposeful access,[223] not exclusive rights of destructive consumption.

The advantages conferred by this trust model may be substantial indeed. For the first time it becomes meaningful to claim on behalf of the citizenry a 'property' interest comprising enforceable access

[220] The first beneficiary of an environmental trust was surely Adam. According to *Genesis* the man whom God had formed was given access to all the fruits (bar one) of the garden which He had planted 'eastward of Eden' and in which grew 'every tree that is pleasant to the sight, and good for food'. God saw everything that He had made and 'behold, it was very good' (*Genesis*, 1:31, 2:8,9, 16, 17).

[221] See Gray, *Elements of Land Law* (2nd edn 1993), pp. 617, 637. It was Thomas Jefferson who contended that '[e]ach generation has the usufruct of the earth during the period of its continuance. When it ceases to exist, the usufruct passes on to the succeeding generation, free and unincumbered, and so on successively, from one generation to another forever' (see P. L. Ford (ed), *The Works of Thomas Jefferson* (1904), p. 298 (letter to J. W. Eppes, 24 June 1813)).

[222] Gray, *The Ambivalence of Property*, in *Threats without Enemies* (1993), p. 161. See also the reference in *National Audubon Society* v. *Superior Court of Alpine County*, 658 P2d 709, 724 (1983) to the state's duty to protect 'the people's common heritage' in natural environmental resources.

[223] See, in this context, the call for '[e]xtensive participation in the process of formulating the goals and criteria of stewardship', in J. P. Karp, 'A Private Property Duty of Stewardship: Changing Our Land Ethic', 23 *Envtl L* 735, 759 (1992–93).

to such inherent public goods as clean air, unpolluted rivers and seaways, ozone regeneration, recreational enjoyment of wild country, and the sustainable development of land and marine areas. The moral parameters which have come to delimit the exclusory dimension of 'property' thus go some way towards converting green politics into relatively good communitarian law.[224] The environmental trust also generates rather less tangible—though perhaps ultimately more important—public benefits. The equitable property conferred by the new trust includes shared rights of access to the regenerative socialising dimensions of public environmental goods.[225] The spiritual quality of exposure to wild country is, for instance, a commonplace of Anglo-American literature over the last two centuries.[226] There is some deep sense in which the mountain-top experience makes us more decent human beings: high and open places lend a certain moral elevation. Whether the venture involves a walk up some country lane or a summer's day amble over Haystacks or an airy ascent of the Buachaille's Curved Ridge in snow, there exists a powerful connection between recreational access and the 'contemplative faculty'.[227] Many have attested to the civilising and educative influence—the 'primordial vitality'[228]— imparted by contact with the natural environment. '[I]n Wildness', Thoreau delighted to say, 'is the preservation of the World.'[229] John Muir captured the seductive intimacy of wild places in a jour-

---

[224] 'Property in Thin Air', [1991] *Cambridge LJ* 252, 297. See also J.P. Byrne, 'Green Property', 7 *Const Comm* 239 (1990).

[225] Carol Rose has confirmed that we should expect 'socialising activities' to 'give rise to inherently public property insofar as those activities require certain specific locations' (53 *U Chi L Rev* 711, 777 (1986)).

[226] See generally R. Nash, *Wilderness and the American Mind* (New Haven and London, 1967). There is evidence that vivid perceptions of ecological and spiritual harmony were even more strongly present in an older tradition of Celtic Christianity. See W. P. Marsh and C. Bamford (ed), *Celtic Christianity: Ecology and Holiness* (Edinburgh 1986), p. 10 and passim.

[227] In the words of Aldo Leopold, '[t]o promote perception is the only truly creative part of recreational engineering' ('Conservation Esthetic', in *A Sand County Almanac*, p. 173).

[228] R. Nash, *Wilderness and the American Mind*, p. 88. See, for example, Henry Thoreau's statement that 'Life consists with wildness. The most alive is the wildest' ('Walking', in H. Thoreau, *Excursions* (London 1914), p. 179).

[229] 'Walking', in *Excursions*, p. 177. This theme formed the basis of one of Henry Thoreau's favourite public addresses. First published in 1862, Thoreau's essay on 'Walking' was destined to become one of the pioneer documents of the American conservation and national park movement (see W. Harding, *The Days of Henry Thoreau* (New York 1967), p. 286).

nal entry in which he recorded that he 'only went out for a walk, and finally concluded to stay out till sundown, for going out, I found, was really going in'.[230] Such highly committed personal engagements with nature reveal not merely an empathy with the earth in its unspoilt state, but also a profound tolerance and humility in the face of a larger unknown.

For Justice William Douglas, too, the encounter with nature had a deeply transcendental aspect. It is interesting to observe that Douglas's descriptions of the wilderness experience are no less powerfully religious in character than, say, the sense of spiritual harmony induced by the Australian Aboriginal's ritual relationship with a very different landscape. A survivor of childhood polio, Douglas had learned to love the high country of his adopted Washington State. Douglas wrote that '[o]ne cannot reach the desolate crags that look down on eternal glaciers without deep and strange spiritual experiences.'[231] Douglas knew that in 'the silence and solitude of the mountains in wintertime . . . man comes closer to God . . . He finds the inner harmony that comes from communion with the heavens. He can draw strength from the austere, majestic beauty around him.'[232] Nor, perhaps, are the social dividends of such experience merely spiritual in quality. Douglas was well aware of the 'citizenship of the mountains' where '[p]overty, wealth, accidents of birth, social standing, race [are] immaterial.'[233] For Douglas the earthscape of mountains, forests and lakes called forth and epitomised the American ideals of freedom and equality.[234] If it is true that wilderness experience 'nurtures the

---

[230] R. Engberg and D. Wesling, *John Muir: To Yosemite And Beyond—Writings from the Years 1863 to 1875*, p. 23.

[231] W. O. Douglas, *Of Men And Mountains* (London 1951), p. 308 ('If he ever was a doubter, he will, I think, come down a believer. He will have faith. He will know that there is a Creator, a Supreme Being, a God, a Jehovah').

[232] *Of Men And Mountains*, p. 278. For Douglas, standing on the summit of Darling Mountain in the Washington Cascades, it was possible to say that '[e]very ridge, every valley, every peak offers a solitude deeper even than that of the sea. It offers the peace that comes only from solitude. It is in solitude that man can come to know both his heart and his mind' (ibid., p. 90).

[233] *Of Men And Mountains*, pp. 293, 211.

[234] *Of Men And Mountains*, p. 211. Douglas often spoke of wilderness encounters as promoting cherished qualities of freedom, courage and strength. 'When man knows how to live dangerously, he is not afraid to die. When he is not afraid to die, he is, strangely, free to live. When he is free to live, he can become bold, courageous, reliant . . . A people who climb the ridges and sleep under the stars in high mountain meadows, who enter the forests and scale the peaks, who explore glaciers

democratic character', then, as Charles Reich noted later, the cutting down of ancient forests may 'properly be seen as a civil liberties issue.'[235]

Strong connections can, of course, be made between heightened recognition of the public values conferred by 'worthwhile human experience'[236] and the appeal made by Professor Macpherson for property rights of access to the 'full and free life'.[237] Access rights promote human fulfilment. Increasingly frequent reference is nowadays made to the need to preserve collective entitlements to the 'non-commodity values' or 'option values' inherent in the resources of the natural environment—irrespective of whether such resources are nominally held in private ownership.[238] Some resources are simply unique or irreplaceable and, on this ground alone, should never be subject to private 'holdout'.[239] For Joseph Sax, a leading commentator on American public trust doctrine, certain interests are 'so particularly the gifts of nature's bounty that they ought to be reserved for the whole populace.'[240] Likewise certain amenities have 'a peculiarly public nature that makes their adaptation to private use inappropriate.'[241] Sax accordingly viewed it as the central purpose of public trust doctrine to prevent the 'destabilizing disappointment of expectations held in common but without formal recognition such as title.'[242] Foremost among such expectations, for Sax, was the 'diffuse public benefit' derived from protection of the ecosystem.[243]

---

and walk ridges buried deep in snow—these people will give their country some of the indomitable spirit of the mountains' (ibid., p. 328). See also M. Sagoff, *The economy of the earth: Philosophy, law, and environment* (Cambridge 1988), p. 128.

[235] C.A. Reich, 100 *Yale LJ* 1409, 1445 (1990–91). See also Reich, 'The Public and the Nation's Forests', 50 *Cal L Rev* 381 (1962).

[236] See D. Linder, 'New Directions for Preservation Law: Creating an Environment Worth Experiencing', 20 *Envtl L* 49 (1990).

[237] See C. B. Macpherson, 'Capitalism and the Changing Concept of Property', in E. Kamenka and R.S. Neale (ed), *Feudalism, Capitalism and Beyond* (Canberra 1975), p. 116 et seq.

[238] See A. Rieser, 15 *Harv Envtl L Rev* 393, 423, 429 et seq (1991). See also J. V. Krutilla, 'Conservation Reconsidered', 57 *Am Econ Rev* 777, 780 (1967); M. Sagoff, *The economy of the earth*, p. 50 et seq.

[239] See e.g. Carol Rose, 53 *U Chi L Rev* 711, 780 (1986) ('unique recreational sites ought not to be private property').

[240] 68 *Mich L Rev* 471, 484 (1969–70).

[241] 68 *Mich L Rev* 471, 485.

[242] 'Liberating the Public Trust Doctrine from Its Historical Shackles', 14 *U C Davis L Rev* 185, 188 (1980–81).

[243] 14 *U C Davis L Rev* 185, 193. For a highly persuasive defence of 'public property rights in ecological integrity', see A. Rieser, 15 *Harv Envtl L Rev* 393 (1991).

It is important to note (and equally easy to forget) that a concern not to destabilise community expectation often plays a potent
role in generating what may be called the 'customary law' of the
natural environment.[244] In 1990, for instance, the Letterewe estate
of Wester Ross in North West Scotland, comprising some 68,000
acres of Europe's last wilderness country, was subjected by its private owner to severe restrictions on public access. These restrictions threatened for a time to place the entire estate—an area of
incomparable beauty and mountainous isolation—out of bounds to
the walkers and climbers who for decades had been accustomed to
roam within it.[245] Public opposition to this exclusion was
mobilised by a community of outdoorsmen, whose protests were
symbolised in the statement of the Earl of Cromartie, a keen
mountaineer himself, that 'You can't own a mountain: it belongs
to everybody.'[246] The dispute was eventually resolved with the conclusion in December 1993 of the 'Letterewe Accord', a document
now being hailed as one of extreme importance in the world of
wilderness conservation.[247] The Accord, drawn up by the good
offices of the Earl of Cromartie between the private owner, the
Mountaineering Council of Scotland, the John Muir Trust and the
Scottish Wild Land Group, sets out an accommodation of interests
designed to reconcile the principle of reasonable public access with
the landowner's particular objective of ecologically sound management of red deer. Underpinning the Accord is a recognition of the
need to 'maintain, expand and enhance the area's biological diversity and natural qualities'. Consistently with this aim, climbers are
asked to visit the estate only singly or in small groups, to use minimum impact camping techniques and to accept the principle of
the 'long walk in' across arduous terrain.[248] The Accord, now

[244] For a salutary reminder of the extreme importance of customary law even in
the context of crystalline property regimes, see R. Ellickson, 'Of Coase and Cattle:
Dispute Resolution Among Neighbors in Shasta County', 38 *Stan L Rev* 623, 671 et
seq (1985–86).

[245] For a fuller account of the Letterewe access dispute, see Gray, *The
Ambivalence of Property,* in *Threats without Enemies* (1993), p. 153 et seq.

[246] *The Independent,* 20 September 1991, p. 8.

[247] For the detailed contents of the Accord, see 136 *High Mountain Sports*
(March 1994), p. 24.

[248] A recurring emphasis in access issues rests upon the point that public or civic
rights of access must be limited by an overriding principle of reasonableness applied
with reference to the particular terrain or context in question. The provision
of access and the preservation of ecological integrity are not necessarily or
always compatible. Excessive or unreasonable exercise of access rights may pose a

available for adoption elsewhere, embodies not only an enlightened approach to wild country access[249] but also a remarkable demonstration of the proposition that collective rights of reasonable access to wild land are ultimately non-excludable.[250]

There is increasing evidence on all sides that we are slowly recognising some concept of social trust in relation to the natural environment. This gathering perception of stewardship emulates something of the greater humility expressed in the Australian Aboriginal's orientation towards land resources. We may be starting to have a more cogent sense of obligation than of ownership, and this realisation is, of course, the necessary precursor of a new equilibrium with our environment. But a law of ecological responsibility which confirms civic property rights in natural resources would certainly impart a new environmental twist to the Lockean notion of a person's 'property' in his 'life, liberty and estate'. Are we really beginning to acknowledge some form of trust relationship which confers public rights of reasonable access and due

substantial menace to environmental conservation. In extreme circumstances the sheer numbers of those who seek environmental access may sometimes jeopardise or sterilise a natural amenity. It may therefore be necessary to impose management strategies on environmental goods (see Carol Rose, 'Rethinking Environmental Controls: Management Strategies for Common Resources', (1991) *Duke LJ* 1). Some far-reaching solutions include the abolition of guides or maps indicating scenic or wilderness areas (see R. H. Nelson, (1986) *U Ill L Rev* 361, 372) or, as is the general practice on Scottish hills, a conscious decision not to signpost the terrain.

[249] It is to be hoped that a similarly enlightened approach will prevail in the interpretation of the Criminal Justice and Public Order Bill 1994, cl. 63, should this provision reach the statute book. Clause 63, which would introduce a criminal offence of 'aggravated trespass', is directed against the activities of such persons as hunt saboteurs, but there seems to be some danger that it may also catch walkers and ramblers who are found to have intended to obstruct 'any lawful activity' (eg farming or sheep rearing?) on the land over which they walk. English law has not hitherto conferred a general right to ramble over open country, but by long tradition the courts have never granted any substantial remedy in respect of nominal and innocent trespass in an area of scenic amenity (see eg *Behrens* v. *Richards* [1905] 2 Ch 614 at 622f).

[250] Access difficulties threaten to become increasingly acute with the privatisation of water authorities and the sale of Forestry Commission lands. Vast areas of open land traditionally available for the walker and rambler may become subject to substantial prohibitions on public access. Even more alarming is the prospect that the shareholders in newly privatised concerns might be given preferential access rights to such areas. Increasing concern over public access to the countryside prompted the recent introduction in the House of Commons of Mrs Margaret Ewing MP's Freedom to Roam (Access to Countryside) Bill. See House of Commons, Parliamentary Debates, *Weekly Hansard* (Issue No 1649), Col 137–139 (22 March 1994).

administration in respect of environmental assets? Inevitably there will remain some who cannot, even in their wildest dreams, envisage such 'equitable property' vested in the community.[251]

Yet there is today one set of institutions which, in this and many other contexts, may convert even your wildest thoughts into present reality. These institutions are, of course, the institutions of the European Community or European Union.[252] It is salutary to remember that the European Court's decision in 1991 in *Francovich* v. *Italian Republic*[253] now imposes on member states a civil liability to compensate individuals for damage suffered by reason of a member state's failure to implement a Community directive. This liability will arise where the result laid down by the relevant directive involves the conferment of rights on the individual, and in many instances the *Francovich* ruling—if it remains good law—offers the individual citizen of Europe a broad and effective means of enforcing Community law.

In this context it is instructive to cast another glance at the litigation in *Commission of the European Communities* v. *Federal Republic of Germany*[254] which also came before the European Court in 1991. Here the Court eventually upheld a complaint that Germany had failed to secure legislative implementation of Community directives aimed at curbing air pollution caused by lead and sulphur dioxide emissions.[255] The German defence had been in part that German practice was already in substantial conformity with the thrust of the relevant directives: there was in fact no air pollution in Germany in excess of the limit values prescribed in these directives. The European Court rejected this defence, pointing out that true implementation of a directive requires not merely de facto compliance but also that each member state must actually set in place a specific legal framework relevant to the directive's subject

---

[251] See, however, Sir Harry Woolf, 'Are the Judiciary Environmentally Myopic?', (1992) 4 *J of Env Law* 1.

[252] It may be significant in this context that continental law (and particularly German law) has always been more sensitive to the social limitations of ownership. Article 14(2) of the German Grundgesetz provides that '[p]roperty imposes duties. Its use should also serve the welfare of the community'. See W. Leisner, 'Sozialbindung des Eigentums nach privatem und öffentlichem Recht', *NJW* 1975, 233; A. J. van der Walt, 'The Fragmentation of Land Rights', (1992) 8 *SAJHR* 431, 442.

[253] Cases C–6/90 and 9/90, [1993] 2 CMLR 66.

[254] Joint Cases C–361/88, [1991] ECR I–2567 and C–59/89, [1991] ECR I–2607.

[255] See Lord Slynn of Hadley, 'The European Community and the Environment', (1993) 5 *J of Env Law* 261.

matter, containing provisions sufficiently precise, clear and transparent to enable individuals to ascertain their rights and obligations.[256] The Advocate General emphasised that the relevant directives were intended to give 'individuals, ordinary citizens . . . the right that the air which they breathe should comply with the quality standards which have been laid down.' Individuals, he said, have the right under Community law 'to rely on those quality standards when they are infringed, either in fact or by the measures adopted by the public authorities'.[257] The Court agreed that without the actual transposition of the directives into specific provisions of the national legal system individuals would not be 'in a position to know with certainty the full extent of their rights in order to rely on them where appropriate'.[258] Only the enactment of 'mandatory rules' by the member state would enable citizens to assert their rights.[259]

Viewed from the objective distance of this side of the Channel, such an approach begins to resemble, as perhaps nothing else, the recognition of a beneficiary's right to insist that trust assets are not merely conserved by chance or fortunate practice but are instead fully subjected to governance in accordance with the terms of the relevant trust instrument. The European Court has come close to conceding the existence of an individual right to the effective and structured management of the ecosystem on behalf of all citizens.[260] Taken in conjunction with the *Francovich* ruling, the stance of the Court in *Commission of the European Communities* v. *Federal Republic of Germany* seems to recognise something which looks awfully like a right in the citizen to demand the proper and conscientious administration of a public trust in which he is regarded as having enforceable rights of a beneficial character.

---

[256] [1991] ECR I–2567, 2601. It is significant that, in enforcing environmental standards, the Court has consistently stressed that environmental protection directives are intended to create rights for *individuals*, not least in order that the persons concerned 'can ascertain the full extent of their rights' (see e.g. Case C–131/88, *Commission of the European Communities* v. *Federal Republic of Germany* [1991] ECR I–825, 867).

[257] [1991] ECR I–2567, 2591.   [258] [1991] ECR I–2607, 2632.

[259] [1991] ECR I–2567, 2601. For further reference to the increasing importance assigned by the European Court to the interest of environmental protection, see M. Zuleeg, 'Umweltschutz in der Rechtsprechung des Europäishchen Gerichtshofs', *NJW* 1993, 31.

[260] For similar advocacy in the European context of an emerging 'right to environment' (i.e. a 'right to the *protection* of the environment'), see American Society of International Law, *Proceedings of the 75th Anniversary Convocation* (1981), p. 41f (A. Kiss, President of the European Council for Environmental Law).

4. Conclusion

In certain respects we have dared in this paper to give expression to the unthinkable. But then again it is worth remembering that almost every legal development is, by definition, just a little unthinkable.[261] It is over 40 years since, in one of the earliest addresses published in the *Current Legal Problems* series,[262] Lord Justice Denning called for the advent of a 'new equity'. Interestingly, he thought that 'the new spirit which is alive in our universities' might have a role to play in pointing the way to what he was to term 'a new age and a new equity.'

The task of the immediate future is, in part, to reconceive the law of property for the 21st century. It must be highly improbable that our current perceptions of property will retain a wholly undiminished relevance in the days to come. This paper has therefore tried to suggest some ways in which wider notions of 'equitable property' are in the process of being impressed on a number of resources to which increasing community value is attached. In a number of legal regimes across the world a more socially oriented vision of entitlement is starting to emerge from the dialectic of property. This new equitable property constitutes a sort of 'meta-property', arising in the historic pattern of equity in order to supplement and fulfil the rules of the law.[263] The new equity seeks exactly what the old equity achieved, and aims to engraft a different or corrective image of entitlement on to pre-existing legal estates. As always equity operates in response to demands of conscience, the sole difference being that the doctrinal force which drives equity here is more palpably the conscience of *community*. Although its full scope has yet to be elaborated, the new equitable property is more heavily committed to the articulation of a civic or social morality relating to the goods of life. In respect of certain publicly defined goods it strongly endorses claims of access in preference to those of exclusion.

The move towards this communitarian vision of property

---

[261] See e.g. *Tulk* v. *Moxhay* (1848) 2 Ph 774, 776, 41 ER 1143, 1144, where counsel pleaded unsuccessfully that the ground on which Lord Cottenham was eventually to base his decision was 'unknown to the principles of law' and therefore vitiated by novelty.

[262] 'The Need for a New Equity', (1952) 5 *CLP* 1, 10.

[263] See F. W. Maitland, *Equity* (2nd edn revd by J. Brunyate, London 1936), p. 17.

relationships is, of course, both controversial and far from complete.[264] By imposing collectively perceived limitations on the exclusory control exercised over important resources, the regime of equitable property points up the intensely correlative nature of rights and responsibilities as incidents of 'property'. The language of 'property' begins to disclose a deep subtext of social 'propriety' in opposition to its once more common connotation of appetitive economic power. The concept of 'property' reveals an inner morality founded upon what, in another context, Paul Finn has called 'two characteristic and inter-related concerns: the first, respect for self; the second, regard for others.'[265] When entitlement and duty intersect, property ceases to operate merely as a vehicle for individual preference-satisfaction and begins to carry 'the authority, but also the responsibility, of a trust to the larger community.'[266]

There is nevertheless nothing quite so dangerous as a vested right, since *any* subsequent contraction of its scope—however justified—inevitably appears as unlawful deprivation. The proposal of any social curbs on private autonomy in the control and exploitation of resources is often apt to be considered an unpleasant communist perversion. There is, accordingly, a need for constant reminder that the operation of equitable property is distributive rather than *re*distributive. The claims of civic property endorsed by the new equity comprise merely the assertion of latent human entitlements which have long been submerged by superficial allocations of formal title. Charles Reich wrote recently of the new property that it does not represent 'value transferred to the needy from another group in society', but represents instead the 'birthright of

---

[264] The recent decision of the United States Supreme Court in *Lucas* v. *South Carolina Coastal Council*, 120 L Ed 2d 798, 112 S Ct 2886 (1992) appeared to strike a stance both anti-communitarian and anti-environmentalist. In the view of some observers, however, the case is not as far-reaching as its rhetoric might initially suggest (see J. L. Sax, 'Property Rights and the Economy of Nature: Understanding Lucas v. South Carolina Coastal Council', 45 *Stan L Rev* 1433, 1437 (1992–93)). See also R. J. Lazarus, 'Putting the Correct "Spin" on Lucas', 45 *Stan L Rev* 1411 (1992–93).

[265] See P. D. Finn, 'Commerce, The Common Law and Morality', (1989–90) 17 *Melbourne UL Rev* 87. If 'regard for others' translates broadly as communitarian and self-regarding as its opposite, Gregory Alexander has pointed out that the 'two visions—self-regarding and communitarian—lead to two different and incompatible understandings of the role of property rights' (see 'Takings and the Post-Modern Dialectic of Property', 9 *Const Comm* 259, 264 (1992)).

[266] See C. M. Rose, 'Property as Wealth, Property as Propriety', in J. W. Chapman (ed), *Nomos XXXIII: Compensatory Justice* (New York and London 1991), p. 240.

every individual' and is, as such, 'inseparable from citizenship and personhood'.[267] Those who entertain dark fears of left wing subversion lack the clarity of vision—or perhaps the wit—to realise that the truly conservative option is in fact the more radical and that, ironically, it is only the more radical vision of property which will preserve the conventional *desiderata* of an ordered society characterised by justice, tolerance and the rule of law.[268]

It is, moreover, a constant of communitarian philosophy that the reinforcement of collectively oriented perceptions of 'property' promotes, rather than inhibits, the preconditions of personal autonomy and individual fulfilment.[269] The controlled dispersal of access to a range of socially valued opportunities and life chances has, almost paradoxically, the effect of enhancing personal liberty. In so far as 'equitable property' contributes to a process of distributive justice, it consolidates both the dignity of the individual and some sense of the reciprocal responsibility which each citizen owes to his or her community. The best path for the future thus lies in a wider recognition of the heavily interdependent nature of our social and economic arrangements.[270] This is a realisation already reached, on the macro level, by the international community of states. In this context there has emerged, in both theory and practice, an acceptance of the long-term prudential value of the cooperative ideal. The contemporary outworking of the concept of state sovereignty reveals, incidentally, much the same ambivalence as currently affects the idea of 'property'. Günther Handl has pointed out, however, that 'sovereignty signals no longer a simple . . . legal basis for exclusion, but has become the legal basis for inclusion, or

---

[267] Reich, 100 *Yale LJ* 1465, 1468 (1990–91).

[268] It is on precisely this basis that Gregory Alexander has emphasised that communitarianism 'should not be understood as abandoning a commitment to individual property rights' (G.S. Alexander, 9 *Const Comm* 259, 273 (1992)).

[269] See e.g. Richard Lazarus's insistence that intensified environmental protection actually enhances individual liberty. By opening up new ranges of amenity for the purposive exercise of individual freedom, environmentalism 'seeks to reformulate, not reject wholesale, property law' (77 *Iowa L Rev* 1739, 1757f (1992)).

[270] Eric Freyfogle has pointed out that in the law of water rights in California '[a]utonomous secure rights of property have largely given way to use entitlements that are interconnected and relative'. Noting that water is, in many ways, 'the most thoroughly advanced form of property', Freyfogle predicts that 'property law future will be a version of water law present.' On this view, 'we should base property law as much on responsibilities as on rights, on human connectedness rather than on personal autonomy' (see E. T. Freyfogle, 'Context and Accommodation in Modern Property Law', 41 *Stan L Rev* 1529, 1530 et seq (1988–89)).

of a commitment to co-operate for the good of the international community at large.'[271]

Our own municipal law of property could usefully adopt something of this conceptual realignment from the 'arrogance of rights' towards the 'consonance of duties'.[272] Even if a heightened awareness of community operated at only a secondary or subliminal level, it would still exert a profound influence on the primary processes of decision-making about the allocation of goods. There is nothing either necessary or inevitable about Garrett Hardin's famous 'tragedy of the commons',[273] but it is quite certain that we shall play out our own tragi-comedy if we continue to desensitise ourselves to an aggressive materialism which ignores the structural interpenetration of individual rights and social obligations.

It may, of course, be asked why the interests represented in the new equitable property are not merely urged as human or civic rights. The answer must be the one given by Professor Macpherson: 'We have made property so central to our society that any thing and any rights that are not property are very apt to take second place'.[274] In adopting the terminology of equitable property we lock into the insidiously powerful leverage of the primal claim, 'it's mine', and we harness this claim for more constructive social purposes. When important assets of the human community are threatened, we are able to say, with collective force, 'You can't do that: these assets are ours.' When you pollute our air or our rivers or exclude us unreasonably from wild and open spaces, we can mobilise the enormous symbolic and emotional impact of the property attribution by asserting that you are taking away some of our 'property'.

A further interplay of concepts is inevitably opened up by this purposive adaptation of property language. Initially, of course, it will seem a little strange that property language should be chosen

---

[271] 'Environmental Security and Global Change', (1990) 1 *Yearbook of International Environmental Law* 3, 32. As Philip Allott has said, the rights that emanate from the concept of sovereignty are not unfettered freedoms but 'are in reality *shared powers*, shared between the holder of the power and the community of states, in which regard for the interests of other states and of all states is of the essence' ('Power Sharing in the Law of the Sea', (1983) 77 *AJIL* 1, 27). See also Allott, *'Eunomia: New Order for a New World'* (Oxford 1990), p. 337.

[272] The phrases are those of Bertrand de Jouvenel. See *Sovereignty* (Cambridge 1957), p. 202.

[273] See G. Hardin, 'The Tragedy of the Commons', 162 *Science* 1243 (1968).

[274] See 'Human Rights as Property Rights', (1977) 24 *Dissent* 72, 77.

to express claims which have hitherto belonged largely within the public law domain. Politically conservative members of a former generation would doubtless find it unfamiliar that claims of civic or social right should nowadays be formulated in terms of the private law institution of property. But this merely goes to underline the fact that, in some important sense, all property rights enjoy an inherent public law character.[275] The constant imposition of social and moral limits on the scope of 'property' necessarily entails that private property can never be truly private. It has always been one of the fundamental features of a civilised society that exclusory claims of property stop where the infringement of more basic human freedoms begins. The history of slavery law provides ample demonstration of this last proposition. The law of property has always said much more than is commonly supposed about the subject of human rights.

Particularly in the modern era there is no unbridgeable gulf between public and private law. Indeed there are certain fairly striking parallels to be drawn, over exactly the same timespan, between developments in the field of public law and the elaboration of the new law of equitable property. The spectacular emergence of the discipline of administrative law during the past 30 years is directly attributable to the infusion of fresh perceptions of 'fairness' and 'reasonableness' in the conduct of civil governance.[276] It is nowadays recognised that there are no unfettered discretions in public law and that 'all power has legal limits'.[277] Principles of 'natural justice' have become applicable wherever administrative action impinges on the citizen's legal rights, liberties or interests or where the citizen has a 'legitimate expectation' that he or she should be treated fairly. Public decision-making which affects the citizen's livelihood or life chances is exposed to an ever closer scrutiny against rigorous standards of both procedural and— less directly—substantive propriety.

Against this background it may not perhaps appear quite so

---

[275] See 'Property in Thin Air', [1991] *Cambridge LJ* 252, 304.

[276] 'The principle of reasonableness has become one of the most active and conspicuous among the doctrines which have vitalised administrative law in recent years' (H. W. R. Wade, *Administrative Law* (6th edn Oxford 1988), p. 398). See also Paul Craig's observation that natural justice is a 'manifestation of a broader concept of fairness' (P. P. Craig, *Administrative Law* (2nd edn London 1989), p. 207).

[277] Wade, *Administrative Law*, pp. 388, 399ff.

strange that principles of 'fairness' and 'legitimate expectation' should begin more clearly to infiltrate the private law realm of property. On the contrary, it would seem rather odd that public power should be increasingly subjected to restraint, while private power—supremely evidenced in the exercise of rights of property—should substantially escape similar social control. After all, as Harold Demsetz once said, property rights 'derive their significance from the fact that they help a man form those expectations which he can reasonably hold in his dealings with others.'[278] The emerging law of equitable property is concerned precisely with the protection of the citizen's legitimate expectation to participate fully in the reasonable enjoyment of communally defined opportunities for the good life. Moreover, the idea that all should have a voice in the making of dispositive decisions concerning vital social goods is wholly consistent with the administrative law concept of entitlement to a fair hearing on matters which uniquely bear upon the citizen's rights, liberties and interests.

There need be nothing terribly shocking or revolutionary in the perception that the underlying philosophy of judicial review is percolating slowly into the law which regulates the discretionary exploitation of privately held resources. Abuse of discretion occurs no less frequently in the private than in the public arena and, paradoxically, its potential impact upon the larger community may be even more devastating. The private commercial enterprise which pollutes an entire community's water supply arguably dislocates legitimate expectations far more comprehensively than, say, the government department or licensing authority whose decisions operate capriciously on the rights of a single citizen.

If 'equitable property' has any meaning, it lies in the fact that a fundamental requirement of 'fairness' is beginning to penetrate the administration of the 'commonwealth'—in both its political and its economic dimension. This now seems to be the message emerging simultaneously from the crowded shopping mall, from the deserts of outback Australia, from the battlegrounds of environmental conflict. That the conceptual apparatus of property should be used to fashion and to articulate legitimate expectations on behalf of citizens may in itself be no bad thing. In days when the individual seems ever more powerless in his confrontation with the faceless,

[278] H. Demsetz, 'Toward A Theory Of Property Rights', 57 *Am Econ Rev* 347 (1967).

effectively unaccountable organisations which order his life and control his destiny, he can assert his right to be treated *fairly* by using the only language which bureaucracies traditionally understand—the language of concentrated economic entitlement—the language of 'property'. In this sense the existence of property-based rights of *access* (in contradistinction to those of *exclusion*) may well go some distance towards providing the compromise structure of 'fall-back' rights which, in Jeremy Waldron's terms, 'people can count on for organizing their lives'.[279]

As matters currently stand, the concept of 'property'—such is its ambivalence—presently offers both the greatest threat and the surest assistance to the survival of a sense of 'community'. In its exclusory dimension 'property' tends to accelerate the insensate rapaciousness of humankind at a cost virtually incalculable in terms of social division and lost social cohesion. In its access-promoting dimension 'property' tends in a contrary direction, endorsing a more communitarian form of participation in a range of publicly valued resources. Even enlightened self-interest points towards the same end as the more idealistic versions of communitarian thinking. The future of 'property' requires that there be a ready public access to the dispersed benefits of the earth's resources.[280] There is a rudimentary prudential utility in placing certain social curbs on soul-destroying greed in order to engineer a wider participation in the goods of life.

By engrafting the *conscience of community* on to existing property relations, notions of 'equitable property' can begin to reconstruct and reinforce a more general *community of conscience*. Our own times have witnessed the steadily diminishing force of most traditional sources of teaching on conscientious obligation. It may be that Equity's greatest historic challenge now lies in preserving its original role as the conscience of a nation, keeping alive a

[279] See J. Waldron, 'When Justice Replaces Affection: The Need For Rights', 11 *Harv JL & Pub Pol'y* 625, 634 (1988). Waldron argues that there is still a place for individual rights even in the context of the communitarian society or 'affectionate *Gemeinschaft*'. 'It matters to people that they and their loved ones have enough to eat, it matters to them that they have access to at least some of the resources necessary for the pursuit of their own projects and aspirations, and it is likely to go on mattering sufficiently for them to want some greater *assurance* of that other than merely the affections of their fellow citizens' (ibid., 639f).

[280] See J. W. Singer and J. M. Beerman, 'The Social Origins of Property', (1993) 6 *Can Jnl of Law and Juris* 217, 242 ('A property system only works if lots of people have some').

socially diffused awareness that obligation is, and always has been, an intrinsic component of entitlement. The pressing call is for social education on a grand scale; the process of learning, osmotic; the ultimate lesson, that conscientious obligation takes priority over strict legal right. This, after all, is Equity's single most distinctive contribution to our own jurisprudence.

As we launch into the uncertainties of the next century, it may be that claims of 'equitable property' will begin to rival or outweigh the importance of property forms we have known hitherto. Constant recognition of the intensely interdependent character of property relationships may hold our only hope of averting a world overborne by aggressive material acquisition—our only hope of creating a new commonwealth of dignity and equality. If this is the case, then there is assuredly more equitable property waiting to be claimed. If we fail, however, to endorse a broader collective participation in the goods of life, then it seems quite likely that, from the safe distance of their own planet, my Martian colleagues will eventually observe a polarised society participating in its own disintegration.

RECOVERING STOLEN ART

Norman Palmer[1]
(*Inaugural Lecture*)

1. The scope of the problem

Readers of the Raffles stories by E. W. Hornung[2] may recall an exploit involving a Velazquez picture. The Infanta Maria Teresa had been stolen from Sir Bernard Debenham by his son, 'one of the most complete blackguards about town'. Young Debenham sold The Infanta to an 'ill-bred and ill-informed' Queensland senator named Craggs. The senator, knowing that Sir Bernard could not afford the scandal of a legal action, jeeringly dismissed his offer to buy back the picture.[3] Sir Bernard's agent, a solicitor of questionable antecedents named Bennett Addenbrooke, thereupon engaged A. J. Raffles, the amateur cracksman and legendary spin bowler, to recover it discreetly. Retrieval had to be made from the senator's hotel bedroom on the eve of his return to Australia. The task of diverting Craggs in the sitting room while Raffles performed acts of self-help in the bedroom fell to one Bunny, Raffles's

---

[1] Rowe & Maw Professor of Commercial Law at University College London; Barrister. I wish to thank Ian Longworth FSA for his valuable comments on an earlier draft of this paper.

[2] Ernest William ('Willie') Hornung, 1866–1921, the youngest son of a Middlesbrough lawyer, was friendly with Sir Arthur Conan Doyle and married his sister Constance. Conan Doyle once described him as 'a Dr Johnson without the learning but with a finer wit': see Peter Haining's Foreword to *The Complete Short Stories of Raffles—The Amateur Cracksman* (Souvenir Press, 1984), p. 16.

[3] Presumably, Craggs got no title, and it did not occur to him (being Australian) to buy in market overt; cf Davenport and Ross, *Market Overt* in *Interests in Goods* (1993), eds N. E. Palmer and E. McKendrick, Chapter 17, esp. at p. 472 note 20. Raffles's own analysis of the transaction was confused, and his robust view seems to have misled even the lawyer Addenbrooke:

> RAFFLES: 'But . . . surely its a clear case? The sale was illegal; you can pay him back his money and force him to give the picture up.'
> ADDENBROOKE: 'Exactly . . .'.

This exchange (to which Bunny did not contribute) anticipates the approach of the UNIDROIT draft convention: see below, p. 231.

accomplice: an amiable ditherer, to whom the episode offered fertile opportunities for cardiac and other arrest.[4]

This story, 'Nine Points of the Law,' falls some way short of typefying the modern trade in stolen art. In fact, its archaic flavour is the sole reason for its citation. It conjures up a vanished (perhaps mythical) world of privately-educated burglars, devious solicitors and unpolished Australian politicians; a world where the gentleman thief was a familiar social phenomenon and his crimes (however dastardly) were underpinned by a code.[5]

We live in a very different world. It is a world in which art theft is commoner, less discriminate, more violent, less scrupulous, better organised, better paid and more closely linked to organised crime as a whole. If some newspaper reports are to be believed, practices like designer theft (the commissioned theft of selected works of art) and artnapping (the capture of works of art for future ransom) have emerged in consequence.[6] Even allowing for embroidery, there is scant cause to be complacent. Consider some of the facts.

(a) Not even our most venerable institutions are immune from this plague. The British Museum was the victim of a serious theft last year,[7] though the objects were recovered. In February of this year it was the turn of The National Museum of Norway, which suffered the theft of Edvard Munch's The Scream in a thirty-second episode vividly recorded by security cameras; the picture remains at large.[8] In April, an Iron Age sword was stolen from the Peterborough Museum; officials confessed that their security measures were less exacting than those of the British Museum, which had hoped to acquire the sword.[9] In the United States, one museum (the Isabella Stewart Gardner Museum) was so thoroughly ransacked four years ago that it

---

[4] Raffles successfully recaptured the Infanta and collected a £4,000 fee from Addenbrooke. He lived on to plunder many other institutions, including the British Museum, from which he stole a gold Assyrian cup. In a fit of patriotic zeal, however, he relented and posted the object to Queen Victoria in a Huntley & Palmer's biscuit tin: see 'A Jubilee Present'.

[5] As to that code, see George Orwell's celebrated Essay, *Raffles and Miss Blandish*, published in the Complete edition of the Raffles stories, cited at note 1 above, p. 25.

[6] (1993) *Sunday Times*, December 12th.

[7] (1993) *The Times*, *The Independent*, July 24th.

[8] (1994) *The Times*, February 14th.

[9] (1994) *The Times*, *The Independen*, April 18th.

was forced to close (though not permanently). Nothing appears safe, even if nailed or concreted down.

(b) Art thieves are becoming more versatile and less fastidious. Their depredations extend beyond museums, galleries, stately homes and bank vaults (the obvious victims) to private houses, churches, cathedrals, cemeteries, London clubs, Inns of Court, universities and schools. They encompass almost anything of 'heritage' value: a saint's jaw-bone stolen from the Church of St Anthony at Padua,[10] stuffed rats stolen from the Gloucester Waterways Museum.[11] To an extent, the catholic quality of modern theft seems to be inspired by an increasing demand for privately-owned 'heritage items', or instant personal history.[12]

(c) Accompanying this lack of fastidiousness may be an increasing violence towards the objects themselves. Aside from the obvious risks attendant on unsatisfied ransom demands, evidence suggests that handlers are partitioning larger or more readily-identifiable pictures so as to create several marketable works from a single unmarketable parent.[13] There is a chilling prospect that such mutilated fragments as Holbein's Squirrel without a Lady or a Starling, or Van Gogh's Iris, may one day appear on the market.

(d) Art theft is said to be closely linked to organised crime as a whole. At the upper end of the scale, works of art are allegedly used both to provide initial collateral for narcotics transactions and to launder the profits. Of illicit world markets, that in stolen art is said to be second in turnover only to drug-trafficking.[14]

(e) Security problems have almost undoubtedly played a part in reducing public access to certain works of art. One reason why direct public contact with the owners of a conditionally

---

[10] (1991) *The Times*, October 12th.   [11] (1993) *Daily Telegraph,* August 7th.

[12] Quaere, however, whether the acquisition of stuffed rats can be explained on this basis.

[13] Danya Alberge, 'Unkindest Cuts of All; the Thieves Who Trade in Stolen Paintings' (1993) *The Independent on Sunday*, January 31st, which quotes Italian police sources as estimating that as many as two or three per cent of stolen pictures are being cut up in this way.

[14] National Heritage Committee, *Export of Works of Art*, First Report (Draft Directive on the Return of Cultural Objects Unlawfully Removed from the Territory of a Member State and Draft Regulation on the Export of Cultural Goods) H. C. Session 1992–1993, November 1992, para 21 (hereinafter HC First Report), citing evidence from the Council of British Archaeology.

exempt work of art is said to be virtually impossible[15] is the fear that such works (held on private premises) will attract criminals. On the other hand, it is arguable that some works would not be on loan to public collections at all were their owners not motivated by a conviction that the objects are safer there than on private premises, or at least by a desire to deflect the costs of security and insurance.

(f) The general problem is not confined to England. It has been fanned by the political upheaval in Eastern Europe, bringing in its wake an epidemic of theft as well as destruction: icons from Romanian churches, countless objects from Bosnia. In Russia in 1990 burglaries were reported by 1,441 churches, 18 museums and numerous private collections;[16] virtually all the stolen objects went abroad. Massive removals from Kuwaiti museums followed the Iraqi invasion in 1991.[17]

(g) In Europe, reliable statistics are elusive, but the estimates are disturbing. In January 1994, the Arts and Antiques Unit at New Scotland Yard estimated that the annual value of stolen art stands at around £300 million nationally and £3 billion across the world.[18] The Unit pointed out that the rate of theft is increasing at around 10% annually, that for every reported crime there is one unreported crime, and that average general crime detection rates do not exceed 9% in the United Kingdom.[19] In December 1993 *The Sunday Times* reported that in 1992 insurers paid out £500 million in respect of insured works of art alone; many works are uninsured or inadequately insured.[20] In 1992, the Paris-based Yearbook of Stolen Works of Art reckoned that art worth £600 million had been stolen in Europe over the past five years.[21] Given that anything between 50% and 75% of European Community art trade is handled

---

[15] Davison and Hadfield, '£600m Tax Lost in Arts Loophole' (1993) *Sunday Times*, November 21st.

[16] Boduslavij (1994) 3 IJCP 243 (forthcoming).

[17] (1991) *The Independent*, June 1st.   [18] Private interview, January 6th 1994.

[19] Ibid.   [20] (1993) *Sunday Times*, December 12th.

[21] See on this, and on retrieval techniques generally, David Thurlow, 'Chasing the Immovable' (1993) *Daily Telegraph* March 31st, which discusses the question of 'architectural theft'; Anne Caborn, 'Insurers Join Antique Trade in Tracking Stolen Goods' (1993) *The Times*, March 20th; Danya Alberge, 'Art Finds Place on Computer' (1993) *The Independent*, March 20th; Paul Rambali, 'Booming Chronicle of Stolen Art' (1992) *Independent on Sunday*, September 13th;

through London[22] these figures are less than reassuring. Even worse, Geraldine Norman has claimed that some 80% of antiquities which enter the London market have been illegally excavated and smuggled.[23] This figure has been contested,[24] but given that some 85% to 90% of European Community antiquities business is estimated to run through London,[25] a lower figure would scarcely be more reassuring. The spate of thefts has spawned a thriving retrieval industry, mainly in the form of databases: Trace Magazine, the Yearbook of Stolen Art, State of the Art, the International Foundation for Art Research and its associate body the International Art Loss Register, Thesaurus, etc.[26] There is a Council for the Prevention of Art Theft, founded 'To promote crime prevention in the fields of art, antiques, antiquities and architecture'.[27]

And yet some things are unchanged. Virtuoso art theft, attended by the almost ritual embarrassment of museum and gallery officials, is a recurrent twentieth century entertainment: The Mona Lisa in 1911, the Duke of Wellington in 1961.[28] Volumes have been written on the subject, many purportedly autobiographical.[29] The ingenuity of the art thief continues to enthral, and some modern episodes have a Hornungian flavour: for example, the theft of the Renoir 'Vase of Flowers' from Wildenstein's gallery in London, evidently by means of a fishing rod deployed from the street.[30] After every significant theft (particularly where the work is too well-known to be resaleable) the media teem with conjecture about the motive.[31] Clearly, the public are no less fascinated by tales of

[22] HC First Report, para 28.

[23] (1990) *The Independent*, October 27th.

[24] Cf. Chesterman (1991) 65 Antiquity 538.

[25] HC First Report, para 15, citing Mr McAlpine 'one of the world's leading dealers in antiquities'.

[26] See footnote 10, above.

[27] The Council has campaigned vigorously for (inter alia) the abolition of the doctrine of market overt, as to which see below p. 233.

[28] See Milton Esterow, *The Art Stealers* (Millington, 1975).

[29] For example, Edward Moat, *Memoirs of an Art Thief* (1976).

[30] (1992) *The Times*, November 30th.

[31] Chippindale (1993) 67 Antiquity 699: 'Apocryphal stories circulate of crazed collectors whose private and lonely apartments are lined with Manets and Monets, stolen to order. This is the trouble with stuff you know is nicked: you can enjoy it yourself, but you cannot tell the world or let the experts study it.'

purloined art than in Hornung's day, and rather more perturbed.[32] The violence, frequency and sometimes pointlessness of such activity serve only to heighten public concern.

In the light of that concern, it seems important to examine the ways in which United Kingdom law is responding to the challenges of art theft and to ask whether it is serving its constituents. I shall identify some of the legal issues which arise from this modern epidemic and the measures United Kingdom law is taking to combat them.

2. Limits on the inquiry

I plan, so far as possible, to limit discussion to theft in its literal sense: that is, the taking of cultural objects from an owner's possession without the owner's consent, and with the intention of depriving the owner of them permanently. The owner may be a private person, or a commercial entity, or a public museum, or a church, or a local authority or a sovereign State. The object may be taken from a building during a break-in, purloined from a public gallery by a dishonest curator, amputated by ram-raiders from its mounting in a public monument, or clandestinely excavated by 'night-hawks' on publicly- or privately-owned land.[33]

Other forms of activity are often colloquially termed theft by those aggrieved by them, or are (perhaps extravagantly) classed as its moral or legal equivalent. An example in the first category is the unauthorised commercial reproduction of an artist's work, as alleged in the long-running dispute over the Henry Moore Trust;[34] or the sale of a bequeathed painting by an institution contrary to the inferrable wishes of its donor.[35] An example in the second cate-

---

[32] Especially when they are the victims: see, e.g., the letter from a believed victim of the market overt rule in (1993) *The Times* March 25th.

[33] Looting in times of armed conflict raises separate issues which will not be discussed. As to legal constraints, see the Hague Convention for the Protection of Cultural Property in the Event of Armed Conflict (1954) which applies both to movable and immovable property; and recent articles by Clement (1994) 3 IJCP 11; Eirinberg (1994) 3 IJCP 27. For an account of the relation between Napoleon's military expeditions and the Louvre collections, see Gould, *The Trophy of Conquest* (Faber & Faber, 1965).

[34] See, e.g., Danya Alberge, 'Moore Forgeries Flood Market' (1993) *The Independent on Sunday*, October 24th.

[35] Cf. the sale by the Royal Holloway College of the Turner seascape, 'Van Tromp, going about to please his masters' to the Getty Museum for £11 million. In its 39th Report (1992–1993) paras 6 to 11, the Reviewing Committee on the Export

gory is the unlawful export of an object by its owner without necessary authority. While theft and illegal export can of course coexist, and are treated collectively by the recent Regulations drafted in response to the EC Directive on Removal of Cultural Property,[36] unlawful export can raise quite different issues from those which arise from simple theft. The owner is normally the wrongdoer and not the victim, the claimant state was not normally the owner before the wrong was committed. Identifying the difference between theft and illegal export has been one of the most important contributions of United States authors on this subject,[37] influencing both case-law[38] and at least one international instrument.[39] An example which perhaps falls in both categories is the overseas purchase of objects of art or antiquity from officials of an occupying authority.[40] These wider forms of alleged misappropriation raise fascinating questions but they must be set on one side today.

In what follows, I interpret 'art' widely, to include all objects of substantial artistic or historical significance: artefacts of antiquarian interest as well as modern 'flat' art. Confessedly, this is to skate over the problem, perhaps even to emasculate the inquiry. Definition is one of the thorniest issues in this area and perhaps the greatest single impediment to effective international agreement.[41] Even so, I plan to make it a matter of assumption: to take cultural significance for granted. The reader is invited to imagine that the subject of the ensuing discussion is a stolen Cezanne or an illegally-excavated Bronze Age torc: a work of unimpeachable aesthetic quality and undeniable significance to the history of human expression. Part of

of Works of Art expressed profound concern about the implications of this transaction.

[36] Below, p. pp. 228–30, 237–9.

[37] See, most recently, John Henry Merryman, 'The Nation and the Object' (1994) 3 *IJCP* 61.

[38] E.g., *Government of Peru* v. *Johnson and others* 720 F Supp 810 (CD Cal 1989); affirmed by the US Court of Appeals, without reference to this question, in an unpublished decision: 1991 US App Lexis 10385. See Merryman (1992) 1 IJCP 169.

[39] See the UNESCO Convention of 1970 and the UNIDROIT draft convention: below, pp. 231, 236–7, 238–9.

[40] On the Parthenon Marbles, see generally St Clair, *Lord Elgin and the Marbles* (Oxford University Press, 1967); Hitchens, *The Elgin Marbles* (Chatto & Windus, 1987). On King Priam's Treasure, see Easton, *Priam's Gold: The Straightforward Story of a Controversial Treasure* (lecture to the British Institute of Archaeology at Ankhara, January 12th, 1994).

[41] Note, for example, the two tier definition set out in the recent Directive: see p. pp. 228–9 below.

my theme is that, if the law cannot devise effective safeguards for works of that character, what hope is there for the necessary protection of lesser items?

3. The positive signals.

A superficial glance at modern events would suggest that, in the case of major objects at least, there are grounds for believing that art theft is being valiantly, even effectively combated.

(a) Forensic successes.

One positive sign is the outcome of modern international litigation in the field. There are several recent cases, in England and elsewhere, where a court has ordered the return of demonstrably-stolen works of art to a dispossessed owner, be that owner a sovereign State, a Church, a public institution or an individual. Perhaps the most important (and morally least ambiguous) is *Autocephalous Greek Orthodox Church of Cyprus* v. *Goldberg*[42] where, in an action before the courts of Indiana, the Church succeeded in its claim to the mosaics of the Panagia Kanakaria against Peg Goldberg, a dealer who had bought them (allegedly in good faith) in the free port area of Geneva airport. An English judgment presumably encouraging to the advocates of restitution is *Bumper Development Corpn Ltd* v. *Commissioner of Police of the Metropolis and others*.[43] There a bronze Nataraja representing the Hindu God Siva and proved to be the Pathur Nataraja, unearthed at Pathur village in Tamil Nadu, India, by a labourer in 1976 near the site of a ruined 12th Century Temple, and later sold under a false provenance to a Canadian oil company by a London dealer in 1982, was successfully claimed by the Temple itself, which was held to be a juristic entity recognisable by the English courts. The idol was in due course returned to India. A significant American decision where a museum triumphed over a later good faith purchaser is *Guggenheim* v. *Lubell*,[44] a dispute over Chagall's Merchant of the Beasts. The New York court's ruling that it is the date of the

[42] 771 F Supp 1374 (5 D Ind 1989), upheld on appeal 917 F. 2d 278 (1990) US App; noted by Byrne-Sutton (1992) 1 IJCP 151.

[43] [1991] 4 All ER 638, CA.

[44] *Solomon R. Guggenheim Foundation* v. *Lubell* 153 AD 2d 143, 550 NYS 2d 618 (1990), aff'd 77 NY 2d 311, 569 NE 2d 426, 567 NYS 2d 623 (1991); noted by Gerstenblith (1992) 2 IJCP 359.

claimant's demand for the return of goods and the defendant's refusal to return them that triggers the limitation period offers further encouragement to the proponents of restitution.

While reluctant to turn swallows into summers, or geese into swans, one might infer that litigation works—at least, where it is relentlessly pursued and where the object is precious enough to justify the investment. It is notable that in neither *Goldberg* nor *Bumper* was recovery assisted by any international convention.

(b) Agreed recovery.

In addition to these forensic victories, there are many cases where legal claims are settled out of court, or where agreement is otherwise reached, on terms that the object returns to its dispossessed owner. Of their nature, such cases rarely attract public notice, but sometimes the outstanding nature of the object brings it into relief. The Wildenstein Renoir, for example, was retrieved from Japan in 1992 after the insurers took action under their subrogation rights.[45] Recovery was assisted by the fact that someone unwittingly took it for appraisal to the Wildenstein Gallery in Tokyo.[46] The Samuhel manuscript (or Quedlingburg bible) donated by Queen Mathilde to the Cathedral at Quedlingburg in Saxony-Anhalt around the year 1,000, and liberated by Jack Meador, a Texan army officer, in 1945, finally returned to Germany in 1990 after the Federal Ministry of Internal Affairs and the Cultural Foundation of German States paid $3 million to the Meador's heirs.[47] In January 1994, it was announced that the Michael Ward Gallery was to hand over to the Society for the Preservation of the Greek Heritage a collection of some fifty buttons, beads, rings and seals looted from a 3,500-year old tomb in the Pelepponese and previously offered for sale in New York at $1.5 million.[48] Last year, a Swiss

---

[45] Cf. a case reported in (1992) *The Independent* July 16th, where the owner's insurers recovered eight paintings (with a combined value of £150,000) in Sweden. The pictures had been stolen from The Trinity Gallery in London, which had ceased trading some six months before the recovery. The paintings were the property of the insurers (Star Assurance), whose manager reported that, whereas recovered art was normally returned to its owner on repayment of the insurance monies, these pictures would now be auctioned.

[46] (1992) *The Times*, November 30th.   [47] Siehr (1992) 1 IJCP 215.

[48] (1994) *The Times* January 20th; and see Honan (1993) *New York Times* May 26th; *Greece* v. *Ward*, No. 93 Civ 3493, 1993 (SDNY) May 26th, 27th. The return was to be without cost to the Greek nation, though it was understood that the proprietor would be entitled to a tax deduction for the amount (an estimated £150,000)

museum paid a relatively modest sum to recover a plaque stolen from it several decades earlier, which had resurfaced at auction.[49] Such cases are numerous.

Many consensual returns are without admission of any wrong by the party making restitution. They may be accompanied by co-oper-ative agreements. Sometimes the buyer's agreement to return a work to its dispossessed owner is matched by the owner's agree-ment to loan it to the buyer. In October 1993 the Metropolitan Museum of Art in New York agreed to return to Turkey the Lydian hoard: a collection of over 300 ancient silver vessels and utensils, allegedly plundered in digs at burial mounds in the Usak region in 1966, and sold to the Metropolitan by dealers in Switzerland and New York. The decision came after legal proceed-ings instituted by Turkey in the United States District Court had dragged on for some seven years. The compromise was reached as the action approached discovery stage, at which point[50] the Museum's 'own records suggest that some museum staff during the 1960s were likely aware, even as they acquired these objects, that their provenance was controversial'.[51] As part of the settlement, the Museum and the Turkish Government are reported to have agreed to co-operate on future excavations and exhibitions. One commen-tator[52] has stigmatised the benefit to the Museum as nothing more than a sop for losing what never belonged to it in the first place.[53] There are interesting echoes of this criticism in the debate on the compensation provisions of the recent EC Directive.[54]

(c) *Codes of practice.*

Another positive signal is the emergence of professional codes of practice. The contractual acceptance of voluntary professional stan-

paid by him for the objects. A negotiated return usually offers the best solution where a re-emerging object has simply disappeared rather than been stolen. At the end of 1993, for example, the 1834 George Scharf picture depicting the House of Commons after the fire (which disappeared in the 1860's but had lately resurfaced in a shop in South Africa) was repurchased for a 'bargain,' albeit undisclosed, price.

[49] Private information made available to author.

[50] According to Philippe de Montebello, the current Director of the Metropolitan.

[51] (1993) 14 IFAR Reports, Number 10 (October 1993) p. 3.

[52] Chippindale (1993) 67 Antiquity 700.

[53] The Turkish Government's success in this claim has is said to have inspired a series of further claims against Swiss, German, British and US museums; see (1993) *The Times* November 13th.

[54] See below, pp. 238–9.

dards regulating transactions in art and antiquities can be witnessed among two principal groups, dealers and museums.

Dealers.

There are several codes currently in force.

By Article 12.1 of the *Rules of the International Association of Dealers in Ancient Art*[55] members of the Association undertake 'to the best of their ability to make their purchases in good faith'.[56] By Article 12.3 they undertake 'not to purchase or sell objects until they have established to the best of their ability that such objects were not stolen from excavations, architectural monuments, public institutions or private property'.[57]

The IDAA Code is not the first such initiative. As long ago as 1984, representatives of British auctioneers and dealers signed a *Code of Practice for the Control of International Trading in Works of Art*, which provided *inter alia*[58] that 'Members of the UK fine art and antiques trade undertake, to the best of their ability, not to import, export or transfer the ownership of such objects where they have reasonable cause to believe (a) (that) the seller has not established good title to the object under the laws of the UK, ie whether it has been stolen or otherwise illicitly handled or acquired, and (b) that an imported object has been acquired in or exported from its country of export in violation of that country's laws'. Signatories also undertake[59] that, if they come into possession of any article which can be shown beyond reasonable doubt to have been illegally exported from its country of export, they will take reasonable steps to co-operate in the return of the object to that country, subject to three conditions: (i) the country of export must have sought the return of the object within a reasonable period, (ii) where the code has been unintentionally breached satisfactory reimbursement should be agreed between the parties, and (iii) the duty to make restitution applies only where the trader is legally free to do so.

Clause 1 of the *Antique Dealers Association Code* is more starkly phrased. Members undertake 'to use their best endeavours to ascertain that no piece sold has been acquired in any illegal or illicit

---

[55] Accepted by the vote of the Founding Assembly of the Association on 4th July 1993.

[56] The notion of a duty to act in good faith to the best of one's ability suggests interesting opportunities for escape on the part of the ethically challenged.

[57] See also Articles 12.7, 13.   [58] Clause 2.

[59] Clause 4 of the 1984 Code.

way'. The LAPADA Code says nothing specifically on stolen or illegally-exported or illegally-excavated objects. Members of the Society of London Art Dealers subscribe to the 1984 Code.

Museums.

Adherence to the Museums Association Code of Practice for Museum Authorities[60] is a condition of a museum's registration by the Museums and Galleries Commission. Registration brings substantial benefits and the exercise has been adjudged a success. Under cl. 4.5 of the Code, a museum:

shall not acquire, whether by, purchase, gift, bequest or exchange, any work of art or object unless the governing body or responsible officer as appropriate is satisfied that the museum can acquire a valid title . . . and that in particular it has not been acquired in, or exported from, its country of origin (and/or any intermediate country in which it may have been legally owned) in violation of that country's laws.

Clause 4.5 largely conforms with cl 3.2 of the *Code of the International Council of Museums* (ICOM), adopted at Buenos Aires in 1986.[61]

Some museum officials are optimistic that the Code will enhance acquisition standards and cause the questionable practice of acquiring objects without a provenance to be discarded. In an Introduction to the Ashmolean Museum Supplement section on Recent Acquisitions of Greek and Etruscan Antiquities 1981–1990, Michael Vickers, in reference to the lack of provenance of many of the objects, has written:[62]

It is unlikely there will be another Museum Report quite like this one from the Ashmolean. In 1992, the Museum registered with the Museums and Galleries Commission, and as a consequence of this our acquisitions policy is now in line with that laid down by the Museums' Association Code of Practice for Museum Authorities. This is no bad thing, especially in the light of the sleaziness and corruption which has recently come to characterise some aspects of commercial dealing in antiquities, activities for which serious scholars can only be the fall guys.

[60] Hereinafter the MA Museums Code: adopted in 1977 and amended in 1987.

[61] The MA Museums Code further provides that the phrase 'country of origin' includes the United Kingdom, and again there is equivalent provision in the ICOM code. Supplementary provisions (cll. 4.8.2, 4.10, and 4.11) impose obligations of dissemination, co-operation, consultation and return.

[62] Journal of Hellenic Studies cxii (1992) 246.

(d) Professional co-operation.

Professional vigilance is responsible for many recoveries. It was the through the intervention of Dr Marion True at the Getty Museum that the Autocephalous Greek-Orthodox Church located the mosaics of the Panagia Kanakaria. It was also through the Getty that the Kingdom of Spain was able to identify the current holders of the Goya 'Marquesa de Santa Cruz', alleged to have been illegally exported through the use of forged export documents.[63] A later example is the reporting to the police by Sotheby's[64] of the arrival at their front office of two portraits, stolen from Lincoln's Inn in September 1990. The pictures[65] were brought to Sotheby's in a bin-liner by a man claiming to have bought them at Bermondsey market for £145. They are currently in police custody.[66]

Such vigilance reflects, of course, a healthy self-interest. No self-respecting institution (whether museum, dealer or auction house) will risk strict liability in conversion to the owner, or strict liability under section 12 of the Sale of Goods Act 1979 to a later buyer, by dealing in stolen property. Less scrupulous bodies may, of course, favour a more risk-specific approach. They find a ready accomplice in the law of market overt.[67]

(e) The retrieval industry.

The proliferation of practical prevention and retrieval methods has made a valuable contribution to the suppression of art theft. *Trace Magazine* claims responsibility for the recovery of over £25 million worth of insured objects.[68] The value of objects logged on the database of the International Art and Antiques Loss Register stands at over £300 million, of which £29 million was logged over the preceding eighteen months.[69] In the three years since its institution, the Register has been instrumental in the recovery of property

---

[63] *Kingdom of Spain* v. *Christie Manson & Woods Ltd* [1986] 3 All ER 28; for the background, see Agnew and Farrer (1992) 1 IJCP 137.

[64] Following identification of the pictures by the International Art and Antiques Loss Register.

[65] Reynolds's Francis Hargrave and Gainsborough's Sir John Skinner.

[66] (1993) *The Times*, March 6th. Owing to the law of market overt, the resultant delivery of the pictures into police custody does not mean that the Inn's insurers will necessarily regain them: see below p. 233.

[67] Below, p. 233.   [68] See the sources cited in fn. 10, above.

[69] July 1992 to January 1994.

worth over £14 million.[70] Leading professional associations, such as The Society of London Art Dealers, are among its shareholders. Its existence has led to suggestions that the question whether a buyer acted in good faith or with reasonable diligence for the purposes of the various compensation provisions should depend (perhaps exclusively) on whether that buyer consulted an appropriate register of stolen art.[71]

(f) *The EC directive.*

There is now a positive initiative on this subject from Europe. Wide concern was felt that the dawn of the Single Market and the attendant disappearance of border controls on the movement of goods and personal baggage within the Community would encourage the illegal removal of national treasures, making it simpler to smuggle them from one member State to another.[72] The Community's response is a Council Directive[73] on the Return of Cultural Objects Unlawfully Removed from the Territory of a Member State[74] and a Council Regulation on the Export of Cultural Goods.[75]

The statutory instrument which implements the Directive in the United Kingdom came into force on March 2nd 1994.[76] Its central provision is Regulation 6(1), which grants to every member State a right of action to recover certain defined cultural objects which have been unlawfully removed from its territory, provided that removal has not become lawful from the national territory of the member State at the time the proceedings are initiated.[77] To fall within the Directive, the object must simultaneously constitute (i) a national treasure of artistic, historic or archaeological value under national legislation in the context of Article 36 of the Treaty

---

[70] Private interview, January 19th 1994.

[71] Article 4(2) of the UNIDROIT draft Convention would specifically make such consultation a factor to be taken into account in determining whether a possessor has exercised due diligence in the acquisition of a cultural object. See generally below p. 231.

[72] House of Lords, Select Committee on the European Communities, Sixth Report, Session 1992–1993: *Control of National Treasures* (hereinafter HL Sixth Report) Part 1, paras 1–10.

[73] No 93/7/EEC (OJ No L74/74, 27th March 1993).

[74] OJ No L74/74, 27th March 1993.				[75] EEC 3911/92.

[76] The Return of Cultural Objects Regulations 1994, SI No. 501 of 1994.

[77] Reg 6(2).

of Rome[78] and (ii) a cultural object within one of the categories specified in the Schedule to the Directive.[79] The obligation to return is confined to objects unlawfully removed from the territory of a member State on or after January 1st 1993.[80]

The right of action itself is against the possessor or, failing him, the holder of the object.[81] However, the Regulations impose obligations of assistance on the Secretary of State for National Heritage. The procedure required to activate the right of action is closely defined. The normal triggering mechanism is an application by a member State, specifying the object.[82] The document initiating the proceedings must be accompanied by (i) a document describing the object covered by the request and stating that it is a cultural object[83] and (ii) a declaration by the competent authorities of the member State that the object has been unlawfully removed from its territory.[84] In order to place the Secretary of State under any duty at this stage, the application must also include all information needed to facilitate the search and, in particular, information with

[78] Directive, Art 1(1).

[79] In some cases the object must have a monetary value above certain financial thresholds. The financial thresholds applicable to the various categories of cultural objects are set out in sterling in the Schedule to the Regulations: see Reg 2(3). The Schedule categories are:

VALUE: 0 (Zero)
- 1 (Archaeological objects)
- 2 (Dismembered monuments)
- 8 (Incunabula and manuscripts)
-11 (Archives)
£11,900.00
- 4 (Mosaics and drawings)
- 5 (Engravings)
- 7 (Photographs)
-10 (Printed maps)
£39,600.00
- 6 (Statuary)
- 9 (Books)
-12 (Collections)
-13 (Means of Transport)
-14 (Any other item)
£119,000.00
- 3 (Pictures)

An object may alternatively fall within this second category if it is in the inventory of a public collection or ecclesiastical institution: see Explanatory Note to Regulations.

[80] Reg 1(3).   [81] Reg 6(1).   [82] Reg 3(1).   [83] Reg 6(4)(a).
[84] Reg 6(4)(b).

reference to the actual or presumed location of the object.[85] If these requirements are satisfied, the Secretary of State is thereupon obliged to seek the object,[86] to take steps to identify any possessor or holder,[87] to notify the member State if the object has been found in the United Kingdom (whether as the result of a search under para 3(1) or not) and there are reasonable grounds for believing that it has been unlawfully removed from the territory of that State,[88] to take steps to enable the competent authorities of the member State to check that the object is a cultural object,[89] to take any necessary measures, in co-operation with the member State, for the physical preservation of an object which appears as the result of such a check to be a cultural object,[90] and to prevent, by necessary interim measures, any action to evade the return procedures set out in the Regulations.[91] The last three duties are subject to para 3(5), whereby the member State has two months in which to check that the object in question is covered by the Regulations; failing such check by the requesting member State within the time limit, the Secretary of State ceases to be under any duty to preserve the object or to perform these other duties.

The member State will also lose its right of action if (a) it fails to commence proceedings within a year of becoming aware of the location of the object and the identity of its possessor or holder,[92] or (b) it fails in any event (that is, irrespective of such knowledge) to commence proceedings within thirty years of the unlawful removal[93] (or within seventy-five years in the case of objects from public collections or certain ecclesiastical goods).[94] But if the relevant periods are complied with, and the court finds the object (i) to be the cultural object covered by the request[95] and (ii) to have been removed unlawfully from the national territory of the member State,[96] the court shall order the return of the object.[97] Regulation 4 empowers the court to make orders ancillary to the foregoing obligations. Not the least controversial part of the 1994 Regulations is Regulation 5, which confers powers of entry and search: an almost unprecedented event in a piece of subordinate legislation.[98]

---

[85] Reg 3(2).   [86] Reg 3(1)(a).   [87] Reg 3(1)(b).   [88] Reg 3(3).
[89] Reg 3(4)(a). [90] Reg 3(4)(b).   [91] Reg 3(4)(c).   [92] Reg 6(6)(a).
[93] Reg 6(8).   [94] Reg 6(7).   [95] Reg 6(5)(a).   [96] Reg 6(5)(b).
[97] Reg 6(5).
[98] See the HC First Report, paras 166, 167, and Annex Note by Mr Charles Bird on powers of entry, search and seizure under subordinate legislation.

(g) The UNIDROIT proposals.

In September/October 1993 the third and last session of government representatives and delegates of international organisations met in Rome and prepared a revised version of the draft UNIDROIT Convention on the International Return of Stolen or Illegally Exported Cultural Property. This version will be submitted to a diplomatic conference in 1994 which may formulate a final draft to be opened for signature by the participating States.[99]

Articles 3 and 4 of this instrument deal with stolen objects. Art 3(1) states flatly that the possessor of a cultural object which has been stolen shall return it; for this purpose unlawful excavation or unlawful retention following lawful excavation counts as theft.[100] The right of action can be exercised by individuals and is not limited to States.

Time limits for claims are currently undecided, but there is likely to be a 1-to-3 year limit from the date of the claimant's actual or constructive knowledge of the location of the object and the identity of its possessor, a cut-off 30-year or 50-year limit from the time of the theft irrespective of knowledge, and a special 75-year limit from the time of theft for objects belonging to the public collection of a Contracting State.

By Article 4(1), however, a possessor who is required to return the stolen object, but who (i) neither knew nor ought reasonably to have known that the object was stolen, and (ii) can prove the exercise of due diligence when acquiring the object, is entitled to be paid fair and reasonable compensation by the claimant. In determining whether the possessor exercised due diligence, regard must be had to the circumstances of the acquisition, including the character of the parties, the price paid, whether the possessor consulted any reasonably accessible register of stolen cultural objects, and any other relevant information and documentation which the possessor could reasonably have obtained.[101]

4. The negative signals.

There is, however, a negative side to the modern picture, which calls into question many of the foregoing causes for optimism. If

---

[99] See generally Siehr (1994) 3 IJCP 301 (forthcoming).   [100] Art 3(2).
[101] Art 4(2), and see Art 4(3). Separate provisions of the UNIDROIT draft deal with illegal export: see Arts 5–8.

we rub hard at some of these initiatives, some of the shine comes off.

(a) Common law and domestic legislation.

Not even the most partisan observer could claim that English law unequivocally promotes the prevention of art theft. The laws which conduce to the protection of cultural property in England are, for the most part, permissive and general. Leaving aside the 1994 Regulations,[102] we have very few rules of statute or common law specifically designed for this task. The absence of special provision can be beneficial but it can also be pernicious.

Consider, first, our domestic protection of indigenous cultural objects. It has been said[103] that England has the worst antiquities laws in the world. Although harsh,[104] this criticism is not without substance. The Crown's acquisition of discovered antiquities through the doctrine of treasure trove is a mediaeval lottery,[105] and will remain so until reforms comparable to those prescribed in the Earl of Perth's Treasure Bill 1994 are enacted.[106]

An antiquity which fails to qualify as treasure trove is normally private property. Its preservation is therefore at the mercy of the private law owner: occupier, finder, finder's employer, as the case may be.[107] The owner is, in turn, at the mercy of the thief and of

---

[102] Above, p. 228; below, p. 237.

[103] Peter Addyman, Director of the Jorvic Museum at York, speaking at a Conference on *Conservation and the Antiquities Trade,* organised by the Department of Archaeology at University College London and held at the British Academy in December 1993.

[104] For example, the current reward system has its virtues. It compares favourably with the lack of incentive to disclose finds under the laws of some other countries.

[105] Incidentally, national acquisition through the doctrine of treasure trove can result in the rewarding of a finder who has been guilty of trespass and/or theft in recovering or removing the find. See further fn. 106, below.

[106] Since this was written, the Government has adopted and substantially amended the Treasure Bill. There is now a serious prospect of legislation during the present Parliament. Among other amendments, the Bill now specifies the parties to whom rewards may be granted in respect of finds of treasure (under current provision, rewards for treasure trove are given only to finders) and indicates the potential division and destination of rewards.

[107] One cannot be certain that the land-owner will succeed against the finder. For a recent case where the land-owner's claim failed and the object (a gold Tudor brooch worth £35,000) was awarded to the finder, a metal detectorist, see *Waverley Borogh Council* v. *Fletcher* (1994) unreported, February 17th, Judge Fawcus QC; discussed by Owen Dyer (1994) *Sunday Times,* February 20th.

any later innocent purchaser, at home or abroad. If the thief knows his business, the object will be spirited to London or the Continent. If to London, there may follow the surreal charade of a sale in market overt, or even worse, the irrefutable allegation of one. The effects of this doctrine need not be dwelt on.[108] Though nominally committed to the principle of *nemo dat quod non habet*, English law permits a sale in market overt to extinguish ownership in favour of a good faith buyer.[109] In so doing, it sanctions a preposterous loophole, feared by private owners and opposed by the reputable market (who are themselves increasingly the direct victims of theft). It is gratifying that the Government now proposes to support Lord Renton's Sale of Goods Act (Amendment) Bill 1994, which will expunge the market overt exception.[110] It is said by some that abolishing market overt will reduce crime at no public cost; Lord Renton has claimed that the reform could even reduce public expenditure by saving police time.[111]

In cases of cross-border theft, we encounter yet another general rule of the common law, applicable to cultural goods and commercial commodities alike, which has the capacity to trump the original owner. That is the *lex situs* rule, under which a title validly acquired in England will be lost if a later sale to a good faith buyer when the object is situated in an overseas country has the effect under that country's law of giving the buyer a good title.[112] The earlier title defers to the later, and becomes inexigible even if the cultural object later returns to this country. The object can then be sold under the nose of the original owner.[113] The consequences of the *lex situs* rule were averted in *Goldberg*[114] only, perhaps, at the cost of some intellectual rigour.

---

[108] See generally Davenport and Ross, loc. cit. *supra* note 3.

[109] Section 22(1), Sale of Goods Act 1977. The sale must take place between the hours of sunrise and sunset: *Reid* v. *Commissioner of Police of the Metropolis* [1973] 2 All ER 97, CA.

[110] Earlier governmental reaction was less enthusiastic: HL Deb 12 Jan 1994 (Second Reading) cols 219–221 (Lord Strathclyde, Minister of State, Department of Trade and Industry).

[111] HL Deb 12 Jan 1994, col 222 (Second Reading).

[112] See generally Lyndel V. Prott, *Problems of Private International Law for the Protection of the Cultural Heritage*, Recueil des Cours 217 (1989–V) 219–317.

[113] *Winkworth* v. *Christie Manson & Woods Ltd* [1980] Ch 496.

[114] Above, note 42.

(b) Forensic difficulties.

We would do well not to be too sanguine about cases like *Goldberg* and *Bumper*.[115] Success was achieved there only at the cost of massively expensive litigation, involving intricate questions of fact and law. Consider, for example, counsel's description of the expert evidence as to the identity and source of the idol which it was necessary to accumulate in the Bumper case:[116]

Experts in stylistic comparison, metallurgy, statistical analysis, soil analysis—even an expert on termite workings—were all involved in this complicated and difficult inquiry, some of them spending considerable time 'in the field' in Tamil Nadu in order to pursue inquiries . . .[117]

Factual issues of even greater complexity confronted the court in the *Sevso* case,[118] where the Trustee of the Marquess of Northampton recently defeated claims by Hungary and Croatia (Lebanon having lately withdrawn) to the celebrated Sevso hoard: a collection of 4th and 5th Century silver plates, amphorae, buckets and pitchers, which the Marquess had bought through dealers and later offered through Sotheby's for US$ 70 million. The evidence supporting each national claim was remarkably meticulous. The following account is taken from IFAR Reports:[119]

This summer, the parties . . . agreed to a physical inspection of the treasure. The examination yielded slivers of wood, traces of soil, and tiny organic particles. Each of these samples was divided four ways among the parties and sent to forensic laboratories for analysis. A lab in California identified the slivers as oak, and not the cedar wood more common to Lebanon. Part of the soil samples were irradiated in Missouri, and part in London on behalf of Lord Northampton. Dr Louis Sorkin at the American Museum of Natural History in New York identified the organic particles as caterpillar remains of a moth species that probably nested in the cloth in which the silver was wrapped.

Even where place of origin and original ownership are readily proved, the juridical defences may prove no less complex and dis-

---

[115] Above, fn. 43.   [116] See fn. 43, above.

[117] Text of an unpublished paper delivered by David Calcutt QC, counsel for Bumper, to members of the art trade: October 1990, p. 10.

[118] *Republic of Croatia and Republic of Hungary* v. *The Trustee of the Marquess of Northampton 1987 Settlement* (1993) unreported, November 18th (Supreme Court of the State of New York, New York County).

[119] October 1993, p. 5 (International Foundation for Art Research).

couraging. Consider, for example, the hurdles which the Church in *Goldberg* had to surmount in order to regain its property.[120] The case involved a minutely-detailed forensic debate about the legal characterisation of the claim, the applicable conflict of law principles, the governing law, an alleged abandonment of title, the state of mind of the purchaser, the pertinacity with which the Church had prosecuted its claim and whether that claim was statute-barred.[121] One is tempted to ask whether anyone, other than a State, a State-supported party, an oil company or an private citizen of enormous wealth, could seriously contemplate litigation on this scale.[122]

In the light of these considerations, it is hardly surprising that John Browning has relinquished his claim to the Icklingham Bronzes. Mr Browning has consistently maintained that these were illegally removed from his farm over a decade ago and smuggled abroad. He bases that conviction on the assurances of archaeologists and others.[123] But neither the question of title nor that of exacavatory origin has been judicially tested. Under an agreement made in 1992, announcing the termination of the pending litigation in the US District Court for the Southern District of New York, 'Leon Levy and Shelby White have agreed to bequeath the Bronzes to the British Museum upon the latter of their deaths'. The other terms of the settlement are confidential.

The statement announcing this agreement[124] recounts that the agreed termination is 'satisfactory to all parties'. It may also, of course, be highly satisfactory to the public, which will eventually have access to the Bronzes. But such benefits are largely adventitious.

---

[120] Above, fn. 42.

[121] Limitation period defences are a standard feature of cultural property litigation and a particular scourge to claimants. Time bar defences were raised both in Bumper and in *Solomon Guggenheim Foundation* v. *Lubell* (fn. 44, above).

[122] One estimate puts the legal fees incurred by Turkey in eight-year claim against The Metropolitan Museum of New York at £1.3 million: (1993) *The Times*, November 13th.

[123] Private interview with Mr Browning, December 1st, 1993. In his evidence to the House of Commons Select Committee on National Heritage (1992–1993), Lord Renfrew of Kaimsthorn decsribed the bronzes as a glaring example of looting and illegal exportation: see HC First Report, paras 228 et seq, and HC Deb October 27th 1993, cols 944–947 (Richard Spring MP).

[124] The statement was publicly read for the first time by Mr Browning at a conference on Conservation and the Antiquities Trade at the British Academy on December 2nd 1993, held under the auspices of the Department of Archaeology at University College London.

Had the action proceded to trial and Mr Levy chosen to stand on his strict rights, the chances of a return to the United Kingdom may have been less than certain. In theory, the Bronzes could have remained in private custody indefinitely. The episode also holds some sobering lessons for Mr Browning. He has spent over £100,000 to no personal avail, and considers that he has been ill-served by the United Kingdom authorities.

(c) *Non-subscription to UNESCO.*

The EC Directive is the only international instrument for the return of cultural objects which has passed into United Kingdom law. In contrast to the USA, Canada, Australia, New Zealand and 64 other countries, but in common with (inter alia) France, Germany, Switzerland, Japan and the Scandinavian countries, the United Kingdom has declined to implement the 1970 UNESCO Convention on the Means of Prohibiting and Preventing the Illicit Import, Export and Transfer of Ownership of Cultural Property. This Convention, unlike the Directive, makes an explicit distinction between stolen objects and objects which have been illegally exported. Article 7(b)(i), which deals specifically with stolen cultural property, requires States which are parties to the Convention to prohibit the import of cultural property stolen from a museum or a religious or secular public monument or similar institution in another State party after the entry into force of the Convention, provided the property is properly documented as appertaining to the inventory of that institution. Article 7(b)(ii) requires the relevant State, at the request of the State Party of Origin, to take appropriate steps to recover and return any such cultural property imported after the Convention has entered into force.

Over the past five years, the United Kingdom Government has given a wealth of reasons for declining to adhere to UNESCO:[125] the bureaucratic burden of implementing it, the preference for relying on the dealers' and museums' codes, the breadth of the relevant definition of cultural property, the inexpediency of a national inventory, the problems of verification and compilation of registers, the need to enact legislation, the general resource implications, and the consequent interference with rights of ownership. It is interesting to speculate how many of these inhibitions remain plausible

---

[125] See, e.g., HC First Report para 188; HL Sixth Report paras 19–22.

after enactment of the EC Directive.[126] Perhaps the most commonly-invoked justification is the preferred reliance on codes of practice, a view perhaps fortified by proliferation of such codes in recent years. We consider later whether they go far enough.[127] For the present, it is right to point out one advantage for claimants which the Directive has over UNESCO: that it gives a positive right of recovery of illegally-exported objects.[128]

(d) Limitations of the Directive.

The Directive is a supplement to and not a substitute for those restitutionary rights of action which arise from ordinary private ownership of a cultural object. The statutory right of action is conferred only on member States, not on private citizens.[129] In consequence, the Directive 'does not affect any civil proceedings that may be brought under the national law of the Member States by the owners of the cultural objects that have been stolen' and 'in no way prejudices the rules governing the ownership of cultural objects'.[130] So, in a case which falls within the 1994 Regulations, the right of action conferred on the member State from which the object was unlawfully removed does not extinguish any title acquired by a good faith buyer under a post-theft sale of the object when the object was located in a country which regards that sale as conferring a good title. If, under normal rules of private international law,[131] the post-theft sale extinguishes the original owner's title and confers a good title on the buyer, that second title prevails. The *lex situs* rule does not give way where the EC Directive applies.

The EC Directive is of restricted scope for reasons other than that it cannot be invoked by private owners.

(a) It applies only among member States of the Community. It can, however, apply not only to an object which is unlawfully removed from one member State to another, but also to an object which, having left the Community following an unlawful

---

[126] The Government has an open mind on implementation of the draft UNDROIT Directive, when finalised: HC Deb October 23rd 1993, col 950 (Ian Sproat MP, Parliamentary Under-Secretary of State for National Heritage).

[127] Below, p. 239 *et seq.*   [128] HL Sixth Report para 20.

[129] Reg 6(1). Contrast the UNIDROIT rules on stolen goods, which give a dispossessed owner a direct right of action.

[130] HL Sixth Report para. 23.   [131] Above, p. 233.

removal from the territory of a member State, has re-entered
the Community and is now situate on the territory of another
member State). On the other hand, UNESCO is, and
UNIDROIT is designed to be, worldwide.

(b) It is questionable whether the Directive is likely to play a significant role as an instrument of cultural retrieval. Its machinery is elaborate and the bureaucracy may be discouraging. The
Minister himself, noting the cost and other factors likely to
deter member States from claiming under the Directive,
appears to accept that on a 'pragmatic view . . . very few relevant cases' will arise.[132]

(c) A successful claimant State may have to compensate the current possessor.[133] The duty to compensate is limited to cases
where the court is satisfied that 'the possessor exercised due
care and attention in acquiring the object',[134] but it seems to
apply regardless of the fact that, under ordinary rules of private international law, the requesting member State can establish an enduring title, unimpaired by any later sale to a good
faith buyer as in *Winkworth*.[135] In short, the successful member State may find itself buying back its property if it follows
the Directive path. Other heads of indemnity are also payable:
(i) the requesting member State[136] must bear the expenses
incurred in preserving an object under para 3,[137] and (ii) the
requesting member State must bear the expenses incurred in
implementing a court order for the return of a cultural object
under the Regulations.[138]

The obligation to compensate the possessor has been vigorously defended,[139] and it is hard to see how agreement could
have been reached among the member States without it.
Moreover, the obligation must be seen in context: the main
thrust of the Regulations may be against objects which are not

[132] HC First Report para 220 (Rt Hon Peter Brooke MP, Secretary of State for
National Heritage). Cf. HC Deb 14 February 1994 col 722 (Iain Sproat MP,
Parliamentary Under-Secretary of State for National Heritage).

[133] Cf. the compensation provisions contained in the draft UNIDROIT convention: above, p. 231.

[134] Reg 7(2); and see Reg 7(1).   [135] Above, fn. 113.

[136] Or, where no application has been made, the member State to which relevant
notification is made and which seeks the return of the object.

[137] Reg 3(6).   [138] Reg 8.

[139] For comment as to its operation, see HC First Report paras 178 et seq; HL
Sixth Report para 97.

stolen from owners but are unlawfully exported by owners, and here the reciprocal rights of action given to member States in the courts of fellow member States is a vast advance on normal rules of private international law, whereunder one State may refuse to enforce the fiscal, penal and public laws of another (even, in certain cases, where these laws are underpinned by confiscation provisions).[140] That advance may not have been achieved without the counterbalance of the compensation provisions. Moreover, comparable compensation rules apply under the UNESCO Convention[141] and the draft UNIDROIT convention.[142] Even so, it would be hard to imagine that the Directive is the dernier cri. Both the existence, and the necessary limitations, of the 1994 Regulations fortify the case for adoption of the UNIDROIT draft convention in due course.[143]

(e) Professional codes of practice

The professional codes (however well-intentioned) are of questionable value.

A. DEALERS' CODES.

Having (at most) purely contractual force, these codes can be enforced only by and against members of the relevant group or their disciplinary body. They give no direct rights to third parties such as dispossessed owners. They may not, however, be legally insignificant to buyers: proof of purchase from a dealer who subscribes to a code may, for example, assist in establishing the buyer's good faith or due attention under one or other of the international restitutionary regimes.[144] That consideration alone may hardly reassure the dispossessed owner.

It is also objected that the codes may be narrowly construed within their constituencies. A complaint of differential interpretations by dealers and museologists of the phrase 'reasonable cause'

---

[140] See, generally, *King of Italy and Italian Government* v. *De Medici Tornaquinci* (1918) 34 TLR 623; *Attorney-General of New Zealand* v. *Ortiz* [1984] AC 1.

[141] Art. 7(b)(ii).

[142] Art. 4; and see Art. 8 (unlawful export).

[143] Note further the draft Mauritius Scheme for the Protection of Cultural Heritage within the Commonwealth, as to which see O'Keefe (1994) 3 IJCP 259.

[144] HC First Report para 183.

in the 1984 dealers' Code, for example, was made by Brian Cook two years ago.[145] Three years earlier he had argued that, despite the 1984 Code, the traffic in looted or illegally-exported antiquities was continuing largely unabated.[146] In *Kingdom of Spain* v. *Christie Manson & Woods Ltd*,[147] Christie's evidently contended that the duty under the 1984 code to abstain from transferring the ownership of an illegally-exported artefact did not apply to any artefact entrusted to the trader for sale by a purchaser in good faith, who had acquired such artefact innocently of any involvement in the illegal export. It seems that, in Christie's view, a springing title (or even a purchase in good faith which does not create a springing title) expunged the illegal export and neutralised the normal embargo on handling its trophies. One might be forgiven for inquiring how such objects cease to have been illegally exported simply because someone buys them in good faith after the export. Whether textually justifiable or not, however, the *Kingdom of Spain* construction hardly strengthened the Code. The question may also arise as to the basis of fact on which a dealer must satisfy himself as to the seller's good faith in this context.

Other codes are arguably too flabby and platitudinous to present an effective challenge to illicit traffic in cultural objects. A possible example is the one-line treatment of the subject in the Antique Dealers Association Code.

B. MUSEUM CODES.

All responsible museums and galleries have or are in the process of adopting an acquisitions policy. The standard policy debars the museum from receiving in any manner an object acquired by any illegal means. A leading example, already noted,[148] is the MA Museums Code, first adopted in 1977 and amended in 1987.

The MA Museums Code is highly influential because, as we have seen,[149] registration of a museum with the Museums and Galleries Commission (hereinafter MGC) depends on its adoption of a policy in line with the Code.

We have observed the optimism with which at least one museum official has greeted the MA Museums Code.[150] There seems no rea-

---

[145] *Antiquity* (1991) vol 65 p. 535.
[147] [1986] 3 All ER 28 at 32.
[149] Above, p. 226.

[146] *The Sunday Times*, 28th August, 1988.
[148] Above, p. 226.
[150] Michael Vickers; above, p. 226.

son to doubt that it will play a part in marginalising illicit traffic. Even so, the Code is not without its legal and textual shortcomings. This is not the occasion for a detailed textual analysis, but a few criticisms may be adumbrated.

(a) Privity.

The MA Museums Code appears no more capable of direct invocation by a dispossessed owner than the dealers' codes.[151]

(b) Self-interest.

At first sight, the primary part of cl. 4.5 seems better designed to protect the museum from liability in conversion than to marginalise illicit trade as such. Acquisition is forbidden unless 'the governing body or responsible officer as appropriate is satisfied that the museum can acquire a valid title' to the object. As we have seen,[152] it would be a foolhardy institution that courted the risk of liability in conversion to the real owner. But what of cases where the need to avoid liability in conversion and the refusal to touch illegally-procured objects do not coincide? Such divergence may occur where a former owner has lost his title before the object is offered to the museum. Suppose a museum official knows that, immediately before its offer to the museum, the object in question was stolen from a museum abroad and then sold by the thief to a good faith purchaser in a country which gives such purchaser good title? Or suppose the official knows that the object was stolen from a Cotswold church and then sold to an innocent purchaser in market overt? However clear the museum's capability to acquire good title, there are cogent arguments for saying that it should decline to buy.

It is believed that, at least where the object is known to have been stolen from another museum, an offeree museum will indeed refuse to acquire it.[153] Thefts from overseas cathedrals, schools and private gardens may be a different matter. There is much to be said for the view that a museum's acquisition policy should not confine itself to the necesary self-protection involved in a refusal to acquire objects in which the museum cannot be sure of getting a good title.

---

[151] Above, p. 239.   [152] Above, p. 227.
[153] Private conversations with author, 1993–1994.

(c) Illegal export.

Museum officials may well reply that most cases which do not fall literally within the first part of cl. 4.5 will be prohibited by the second part. It will be recalled that, by this, members must satisfy themselves 'in particular' that the object 'has not been acquired in, or exported from, its country of origin (and/or any intermediate country in which it may have been legally owned) in violation of that country's laws.'

A lawyer might detect a certain ambiguity in the Code's definition of a museum's responsibility in cases of 'pure' illegal export. The use of the connecting words 'and that in particular' in cl. 4.5 implies that the second part of the clause is merely a manifestation of (and is therefore limited by) the first. That may be thought to be the normal effect of an explicit descent from the general (in the first part) to the particular (in the second part). On that analysis, prior illegal acquisition and/or export of an object would not be a separate ground on which a museum must refuse to acquire. Prior illegal acquisition and/or export would be relevant only in so far as they disabled the museum from gaining title; they would be irrelevant where they did not affect title or where events following them (such as a good faith transaction conferring title under the *lex situs* rule) enabled the museum to assert an overriding title.

There may be grounds for inferring that museum officials would adopt a broader analysis of cl. 4.5, which would treat the prior illegal acquisition and/or export of an object as an independent ground for refusal to acquire, regardless of whether the acquisition would grant the museum a good title.[154] Some intention to produce a broader effect might be inferred from other provisions of the Code. These include:

(a) The general endorsement 'in principle' in cll. 4.2 and 4.3 of the provisions of UNESCO. The return provisions of UNESCO apply, subject to restrictions both to illegally exported and to stolen objects, regardless in either case of whether someone has after the illegal act acquired good title. But the Code's endorsement of UNESCO falls short of outright adoption.

(b) The provision in cl. 4.7 that museums should not acquire by purchase British or foreign archaeological antiquities (including

---

[154] Private conversations with author, 1993–1994.

excavated ceramics) in any case where the governing body or responsible officer has reasonable cause to believe that the circumstances of their recovery involved 'a failure to disclose the finds to the owner or occupier of the land, or to the proper authorities in the case of possible Treasure Trove (in England and Wales) or Bona Vacantia (Scotland).'

(c) The drawing by cl. 4.8 of the Code of 'special attention' to the undertaking by each Contracting Party to the European Convention on the Protection of the Archaeological Heritage, under Article 6(2)(a) of that Convention, 'as regards museums and other similar institutions whose acquisition policy is under State control, to take the necessary measures to avoid their acquiring archaeological objects suspected, for a specific reason, of having arisen from clandestine excavations or of coming unlawfully from official excavations.'

These extensions do not, however, cover every case where a prior illegal acquisition and/or export has no adverse effect on the museum's ability to acquire title. The result of this patchy coverage may be to place the museum in a dilemma in cases where it can potentially gain a good title but feels it should not because of some episode in the object's history. The gaps in the Code are at best productive of uncertainty and at worst likely to lead to its evasion. To a lawyer some of its provisions also appear hopelessly vague and ill-coordinated.

Despite the ambiguity of cl. 4.5 of the MA Museums' Code, it is understood that a museum would refuse to acquire an illegally-exported object, whether the illegal export affected title or not. It may be that this spacious interpretation of cl. 4.5 owes as much to political as to legal or moral considerations: offend the State from which illegal export took place and you jeopardise future excavations there.[155]

The ambiguous approach of the MA Museums' Code to illegally exported objects may be contrasted with two other codes.

The policy of the Council of American Maritime Museums (CAMM)[156] states shortly that members should not

---

[155] Ibid.

[156] The CAMM policy applies to misremovals which have occurred from 1990 onwards. In 1993 it was adopted by the International Congress of Maritime Museums.

knowingly acquire or exhibit artifacts which have been stolen, illegally exported from their country of origin, illegally salvaged or removed from commercially exploited archaeological or historic sites.[157]

The Code's outright opposition to the purchase by its members of illegally-exported objects, irrespective of whether the illegal export casts any shadow on the vendor's title, is both clearer and, it is submitted, more satisfying than the corresponding provisions of the MA Museums Code.

The same may be said of another Code much closer to home. Not infrequently, museums acquisition codes are supplemented by codes of practice governing those who work in museums. An example is again afforded by the Museums Association. Clause 3.12 of its Code of Conduct for Museum Professionals[158] states that museum professionals 'must not evaluate, accept on loan or acquire by any means an object which there is good reason to believe was acquired by its owner in contravention of the UNESCO Convention . . . , or by any other illegal means'. Museum professionals are enjoined, in consequence of this provision, to take reasonable steps to ascertain the relevant laws, regulations and procedures of the country or countries of origin.

The MA Professionals' Code therefore appears to declare a general ban on obtaining illegally-acquired objects. Again, the prohibitions on acquiring illegally-exported goods appears stronger than in the MA Museums' Code. The MA Professionals' Code positively requires the non-acceptance by museum professionals of any object if there is good reason to believe that it was acquired in contravention of the UNESCO Convention. This is much more compelling than the references to UNESCO in the Museums' Code. The Professionals' Code acknowledges that UNESCO has not been ratified by the United Kingdom but declares that UNESCO is nonetheless 'supported by the Museums Association'. As we have seen, the Museums' Code does not expressly demand conformity with UNESCO.

It may be that the duplicated constituency of these two MA codes means that the deficiencies of one are automatically repaired by the other. It is, after all, the museum professionals who will be

---

[157] The CAMM policy applies to misremovals which have occurred from 1990 onwards. In 1993 it was adopted by the International Congress of Maritime Museums, cl. 3.

[158] Hereinafter 'the MA Professionals Code'.

acquiring objects and will be charged with implementing both codes. Even so, one might have preferred to see a greater co-ordination or correspondence between the two sets of provisions. Lawyers know the perils of using different phrases to mean the same thing.

(d) The divergent treatment of loans.

The Professionals' Code is not confined to acts of buying and selling. If an object has been illegally-acquired, cl 3.12 also forbids a Museum to accept it by gift or bequest, or on loan, or for purposes of evaluation. Tainted objects are therefore cast into a general outer darkness and made untouchable for all practical purposes.[159] The outer reaches of the embargo may perhaps attract reservations.

There is, again, quite a sharp contrast between cl. 3.12 and cl. 4.9 of the Museums' Code, whereby 'If appropriate and feasible the same tests as are outlined in [*paragraphs 4.5 to 4.8*] should be applied in determining whether to accept loans for exhibition or other purposes'. While the latter provision lacks certainty, some might argue that the less compromising stance taken by the Professionals Code (though intellectually more satisfying) threatens to frustrate one of the greatest advantages of international art loans, that they encourage cultural exchange by marginalising questions of title. Others would reply that this objection is naive. Where an object was once stolen from a private individual in a country to which it now returns on loan, the safety of the object from judicial recapture while on loan would require national legislation depriving that individual of his normal property rights: an improbable (though not unknown)[160] accompaniment. Where the object was illegally removed from State custody or ownership, and has been persistently claimed by that State during its absence abroad, a proposal that the State borrow the object for a limited period or purpose is unlikely to be seen as a diplomatic solution. No-one who has put this suggestion to a Greek museum director is likely to forget the response.

---

[159] Quaere, as to something bailed to a museum for restoration.

[160] The United States has had such legislation since 1965: Immunity from Seizure Statute, 22 USC Para 2549.

(e) Sales by non-owners.

The prohibition in cl. 3.12 of the MA Professionals' Code applies to objects reasonably believed to have been illegally-acquired by their 'owner'. This pre-supposes that the prior illegality has not inhibited the getting of title by the prospective seller, donor, lender or entruster for evaluation. On the interpretative principle *expressio unius est exclusio alterius*, it might be objected that cl. 3.12 does not inhibit a museum professional from accepting illegally-acquired objects where the other party to the transaction is not the 'owner'. Of course, any such anomaly is unlikely to be exploited, even by the most cynical museum official, since a museum which buys from someone who is not the owner at the time of purchase buys at its peril. Even so, the temptation may not always prove irresistible, given the prohibitive costs of cross-border litigation. One might have preferred to see the cl. 3.12 embargo more widely stated.

(f) Where pragmatism must prevail over principle.

Sometimes a museum's policy is publicly explained by its officials. Such clarification can be extremely interesting and helpful.

The *Report of the Trustees of the British Museum* for 1990–1993 flatly declares the Museum's refusal 'to acquire objects which have been illegally excavated or exported from their countries of origin'.[161] The relevant cut-off date for identifying an unlawfully-removed object is the date on which the overseas country imposed the relevant export or excavation control.[162] Cyprus, for example, introduced relevant laws in 1935, so the British Museum will refuse to acquire objects which have been illegally removed from Cyprus from 1935 onwards.[163] In one sense, the embargo is therefore retrospective, in that it covers objects unlawfully exported before the date on which either the Museum's policy or the UNESCO Convention (1970) was promulgated. But this must be put in context.

1. It does not follow that the British Museum will return *any* object currently in its collection which is shown to have been illegally acquired in the past. In this sense, the policy is not retrospective. The return of past acquisitions appears to depend purely on the legal viability of the claim and (perhaps in

---

[161] Report, p. 24.   [162] Brian Cook, op. cit., note 145 above.
[163] Brian Cook, ibid.

extreme cases) on case-sensitive diplomatic factors. A legal claim, as we have seen,[164] can require the claimant to negotiate the domestic and cross-border implications of the *nemo dat* and *lex situs* rules, the complexities of the law of limitations, and the general practicalities of civil litigation. Most potential claimants will give up, and wisely so.

In 1989 Sir David Wilson, then Director of the British Museum, wrote that there were 'good philosophical reasons' for letting sleeping dogs lie.[165] Foremost among them was curatorial responsibility: the need to maintain the universal role of the Museum and the integrity of its collection. Other reasons touched upon by Sir David Wilson were:

(a) the 'domino effect' on other museums if the British Museum were 'the first to give in',

(b) the fact that the acquisition culture of the eighteenth and nineteenth centuries was different from our own ('History . . . moves on: laws change; views of morality are altered'),

(c) the Museum's need to deal with dealers, whether it likes it or not,

(d) the scrupulous care now taken to avoid illegal acquisitions, and

(e) the fact that while our nation, no less than any other, has suffered grievous losses of heritage in the past, we have taken it on the chin: so 'What is sauce for the goose is sauce for the gander'.

Collections in national museums and galleries are legally inalienable, subject only to narrow powers of disposal in the Museums and Galleries Act 1992[165a] Section 5. or other legislation.[166] It need scarcely be said that the Act does not list among the grounds for disposal the fact that an object is reasonably believed to have been stolen or otherwise illegally acquired prior to its acceptance into the collection. In his book on the British Museum in 1989, however, Sir David Wilson declined to rely on the fact that restitution of currently-held objects would

---

[164] Above, pp. 232–6.

[165] *The British Museum: Purpose and Politics* (1989), pp. 116–17.

[165a] For example, British Museum Act 1963, s.4; National Heritage Act 1983, ss. 7, 15, 21, 28; Museum of London Act 1965, s. 9.

[166] See generally Forder (1994) 3 IJCP 131.

contravene the Museum's governing legislation: 'Acts of Parliament can be repealed or amended'.[167]

2. The British Museum distinguishes, for the purposes of its acquisitions policy, between objects of domestic origin and objects of overseas origin. Here again, the approach is pragmatic. For example, the Museum may acquire domestically-excavated items of treasure trove though their excavation has been accompanied by the commission of a civil or criminal offence.[168] Illegal excavation by a trespasser is no barrier to acquisition by the Museum, or to the grant of a reward to the finder. It is understood that no reward has ever been reduced on account of trespassory behaviour alone.[169]

The fact that there is so slender a line between legal and illegal acquisition is tacitly admitted in a British Museum Trustees' Public Policy Statement:[170]

The British Museum deplores the deliberate removal of ancient artefacts from British soil other than by properly directed archaeological excavation, especially when the context of those artefacts is thereby left unrecorded and severely damaged. However, although the unauthorised excavation of such material from a scheduled monument is illegal and can never be condoned, much of what is discovered elsewhere is brought to light lawfully; persons in possession of it often have a legal title to dispose of it as they think fit. In these circumstances, the Museum has an overriding duty to try to acquire such finds as it considers to be appropriate to the national collection. To refuse to follow this course would entail a serious loss to our heritage, since we would then lose the chance to see and record a great many objects. The Museum understands, and shares, the concern of the archaeological world, but since there is a ready market both here and abroad, the situation will not be remedied by a museum embargo. Selective acquisition remains, in our view, not only the practical, but also the proper course.

The policy of selective acquisition which the Museum here defends seems to be limited to legally-excavated objects whose disposers have good title. But, of course, the Museum may also

---

[167] Op cit, note 165 above, at p. 115.

[168] See generally Palmer (1993) 2 IJCP 275, at 282–288.

[169] The position here would change by virtue of cl. 8 of the Treasure Bill 1994, following amendments introduced at Report Stage in the House of Lords (April 20th 1994). The Bill has since failed in the Commons.

[170] Report of the Trustees, 1987–1990.

acquire things unearthed by a trespasser who does not have title.

In the case of treasure trove, this is to an extent defensible. Since treasure trove is Crown property, its acquisition by the British Museum or some other museum does not give the Crown a new title in substitution for a title formerly vested in another.

The Museum's acquisition of other, non-treasure trove objects may suggest a more resourceful interpretation of its policy. An example is the recent agreement for the bequest to the Museum of the Icklingham Bronzes.[171] Wherever the Bronzes were buried and excavated, it was certainly not the United States; they must have been illegally exported from somewhere.[172] On what ground, then, can their acquisition be justified?

It is, of course, arguable that the bequest to the Museum is entirely beneficial and vindicates a policy of privately-agreed solutions, reinforced perhaps by tax incentives.[173] Moreover, Mr Levy may have acquired title by virtue of a good faith purchase outside the United Kingdom, rendering an agreed acquisition from him the only viable solution. Even so, the Museum's acceptance of the Bronzes does not appear immediately compatible with a policy of declining objects 'illegally excavated or exported from their countries of origin'.

One possible interpretation is that the Museum's policy is qualified by some form of 'rehabilitation of offenders' rule, whereby a later acquisition of good title under the *lex situs* rule purges any original illegal excavation or export from the country of origin. An exception of such breadth could substantially neutralise a prohibition on the fruits of illegal excavation, especially if objects are presumed to have been lawfully discovered unless the contrary is shown. Such an interpretation may, however, be simplistic in that it pays insufficient regard to the original *situs* of the Bronzes and the identity of the parties to the agreement. It might be argued that the case of the Icklingham Bronzes is so exceptional in those two respects as to justify the position taken.

---

[171] Above, p. pp. 235–6.
[172] See the observations by Lord Renfrew of Kaimsthorn, above fn. 123..
[173] Cf. the case of the Michael Ward Gallery; above, p. 223.

First, the bequest agreement under which the Museum is to acquire the Bronzes[174] is one to which the possessory claimant was party. John Browning[175] consented to the arrangement and his consent can be assumed to be legally binding. There is a clear difference between a museum acquisition which occurs without reference to the interest of the dispossessed owner and one derived from an agreement to which that owner is privy. Whether or not that distinction is immediately clear from the Museum's policy, it may be thought to carry a certain ethical weight. Of course, there is also a difference between a possessory owner whose participation in an acquisition agreement is unaffected by the costs and hazards of litigation, and one who feels obliged to make a commercial decision as to whether a pending legal claim shall be pursued.

Secondly, it can be assumed that the Bronzes are, by virtue of the bequest agreement, to return to the country in which they were originally deposited and from which they were allegedly removed. Again, there is a clear distinction between this result and that occurring where (say) a Philadelphian museum acquires from a United States citizen a private collection of illegally-excavated Turkish objects.

Given these exceptional factors, the Museum may claim not only to have secured a bargain which advances the cause of scholarship and indigenous public access, but to have maintained intact the spirit, if not the letter, of its policy. The same factors perhaps lend perspective to the words of Lord Renfrew of Kaimsthorn:[176]

I was . . . shocked, on visiting the exhibition of Leon Levy and . . . Shelby White at The Metropolitan Museum of Art in New York a couple of years ago, to find the most extraordinary treasure store of looted antiquities from all over the Ancient World. Life-sized Roman statues from Turkey jostled with Cycladic figures, which competed for space with gold from Mesopotamia. No respectable museum, I felt (and continue to feel), would give space to such a store of loot, however attractive—certainly the British Museum has a policy that would prevent it from doing so.[177]

---

[174] See above, p. 235.

[175] The land-owner from whose land the Bronzes were allegedly taken.

[176] *Archaeology Magazine* (1993) vol 46 No 3 p. 199.

[177] It is perhaps worth noting that the agreement for the bequest of the Bronzes, as set out in part above p. 235, does not record the British Museum as a party.

7. Conclusion

This is a realm of vivid contrasts and wildly-conflicting ideals. There is the contrast between the art-rich nation and the market nation: a contrast sharply reflected in their respective laws. There is the contrast between the ex-colonial power and the new nation, anxious to consolidate its identity. There is the contrast between the collector who maintains that, without his intervention, many chance finds would be abandoned by their finders,[178] and the museologist who contends that collectors stimulate illegal excavation.[179] Less obviously, there is the contrast between the scholarly value of an excavated antiquity (robbed of its provenance by detachment from an unknown site) and that (say) of an eighteenth century European painting, whose provenance and appreciation are less likely to be subverted by buying and selling.

Above all, there is the diversity of interests among those involved in the field: scholars, nations, collectors, dealers, investors, insurers, governments and public. To each of them, a work of art may mean something peculiar. The mosaics of the Panagia Kanakaria, for example, may be a saleable commodity to some, a national icon to others. To some (like the landless Indian labourer who discovered it in 1976) the Pathur Nataraja represents subsistence or survival, to others the common heritage of humankind, an unfit subject of national, let alone private, property.

Perhaps the sharpest contrast lies in national attitudes. Some countries make resounding declarations of the importance of promoting and sustaining national ownership of national treasures. The tendency is not confined to politicians, nor to ancient civilisations. In *Webb* v. *Ireland and the Attorney General*[180] the Supreme Court of Ireland invoked the fact that the Derrynaflan chalice and other ecclesiastical treasures were among 'the keys to our ancient history' to justify a judge-made doctrine of treasure trove notable

---

[178] E.g., Mr George Ortiz, at a forum on Legal Issues in the Antiquities Trade chaired by Professor John Merryman, New York, May 15th 1991. Cf. the story of the illegally-excavated Afghan silver coin hoard, rumoured to be at risk of being melted down because, in the light of ethical considerations, no museum will acquire it: (1994) *The Independent*, April 27th. It is understood that the story has been greeted sceptically by some archaeologists.

[179] Cf. Chippindale, op. cit. supra, fn. 31.

[180] [1988] IR 353.

for its unsentimental view of precedent.[181] A similar view was taken by Noland J at first instance in *Goldberg* towards the Cypriot Republic's standing to sue (alongside the Church) for the return of the Panagia Kanakaria mosaics.[182] Shortly before the 1990 general election in Australia, Mr Hawke, then Prime Minister, pleaded for this country to return his nation's birth certificate (the original copy of its Constitution).[183] Whenever entry charges for the British Museum are debated, critics can be relied on to ask why Greeks and Egyptians should pay a foreign museum for the privilege of seeing their own past exhibited.

United Kingdom authorities are less prone to attitudes of national property or cultural nationalism. Our art export laws are clement and (subject to funding) largely effective; their balance and moderation are much praised.[184] We seldom find ourselves in the position of asking other nations to return our blood and soul, or to restore the keys to our ancient history. Our museums (no doubt for good reasons) are likely in ambiguous cases to interpret their new acquisition rules by reference to broad institutional interests rather than according to abstract notions of right and wrong.

Such attitudes are shared in other, non-source nations. The list of non-subscribers to UNESCO is not, in general, a catalogue of countries whose cultural resources outstrip the economic resources needed to safeguard them. Even critics outside the market are not unanimous in approving the automatic return of unlawfully-removed objects to their countries of origin. Some, like Professor Merryman,[185] maintain that in certain cases the search for truth and the preservation of the object or of the integrity of its parent monument should prevail over national claims.[186] Others like Richard Elia[187] and (semble) Lord Renfrew of Kaimsthorn[188] see

---

[181] See esp [1988] IR 353 at 388 et seq, per Finlay CJ; see also at 390–391, per Walsh J.

[182] See above, note 42, for the reference to this case. Noland J. thought that the Republic had a 'legally cognizable interest in the mosaics sufficient to confer standing', but he considered further analysis of this interest unnecessary since return was requested was to the Church.

[183] (1990) *The Times* Feb. 13.

[184] For a modern account, see Maurice and Turnor (1992) 2 IJCP 273.

[185] Sweitzer Co-operating Professor of Art and Law Emeritus at Stanford University.

[186] See, e.g., 'The Nation or the Object' (1994) 3 *IJCP* 61 (forthcoming).

[187] Director of the Office of Public Archaeology at Boston University.

[188] Disney Professor of Archaeology at the University of Cambridge.

the acquisitive demands of collectors as the true villainy: 'collectors are the real looters'.[189] Some who see collectors as the source of the evil would abolish private collecting, and with it the market; fashions change, and at least one critic has suggested that the private antiquities trade may eventually attract the same ostracism as the fur trade.[190] Collectors, in turn, may point to the fact that their collections may come to rest in public museums (or are frequently loaned to such institutions) as justifying tolerance of their activities and those of their suppliers.[191] It will be interesting to see whether, in the light of the new codes of practice, museums accept such benisons.[192]

Our national restraint may have its virtues, not least for the economy. Four years ago, the value of the London art market was gauged at over £3 billion a year.[193] Some argue vigorously that a legitimate market is vital to the control of illicit excavations.[194] Others believe that a market will exist somewhere for as long as there are collectors, that to drive it abroad would be economically insane, and that no overall compensating benefit would result.

Whatever the merits of these positions, our clemency to the market and to private property law are not without price. Such attitudes can puzzle and alienate those in England who, believing themselves the possessory owners of national treasures, are obliged to fight a lonely battle for their recovery, without overt official support. And they may impede our understanding of others who regard such objects with greater passion. Some of those responsible for policy in this area have not been reticent about characterising certain national claims as 'unthinking' and 'emotional', albeit 'understandable'.[195]

At the end of the day, it is hard to deny that a preference for pragmatism has its advantages: that the relaxed tone of our policy on national treasures is its strength, and that our system achieves more than those which take a head-on approach. However murky

---

[189] The phrase is Elia's, in a book review of Lord Renfrew's 'The Cycladic Spirit': *Archaelogy Magazine* (1993) vol 46 issue 1. Lord Renfrew himself seems inclined to accept the aphorism: see the reference cited above, fn. 176.

[190] Chippindale, op cit, above, fn. 31.

[191] Cf. Chesterman, op cit, above, fn. 24.

[192] Cf. Lord Renfrew in the article cited above, fn. 176.

[193] Cultural Trends 8, 1990, p. 33.

[194] See, e.g., Editorial, *Art Newspaper*, December 1993, p. 1.

[195] Wilson, op cit, p. 116.

their recent history, and whatever the ethical scruples, the Icklingham Bronzes seem set to return. Those inclined to self-congratulation might see in our stance reflections of the national character: a proclivity for minimal regulation, a keen regard for trade, a jealous eye on the public purse, a tendency to be embarrassed by rhetoric (domestic or external) and a haphazardly-derived system that, against all the odds, works. Our national creed might almost be that of our most pragmatic Prime Minister this century: 'you know it makes sense'.

More importantly, in this context, it also makes dollars and pounds and yen.

LANGUAGE AND THE LAW OF PATENTS

'Now, the idea that leads to an invention is, in my opinion, no part of the invention.'

Buckley J.[1]

'. . . you are losing grasp of the substance and seizing the shadow when you say that the invention is the manufacture as distinguished from the idea. It is much more true to say that the Patent is for the idea as distinguished from the thing manufactured.'

Buckley L.J.[2]

I. Introduction

In the recent patent case of *Gale's Application*[3] the Court of Appeal took the opportunity to re-examine some basic notions of the law of patents in what was otherwise largely unremarkable litigation.[4] The case prompted the Court to examine *Hickton's Patent Syndicate* v. *Patents and Machine Improvements Co. Ltd.*,[5] a

* Lecturer, University College London.

[1] *Reynolds* v. *Herbert Smith* (1903) XX RPC 123 at 127.

[2] *Hickton's Patent Syndicate* v. *Patents and Machine Improvements Co. Ltd.* (1909) XXVI RPC 339 at 348. A description of the invention is given in the text to note 37 below.

[3] [1991] RPC 305.

[4] The core of the decision was that putting a program for calculating square roots into the read-only memory of a computer was not an invention entitling the applicant to a patent. A 'program for a computer' is excluded by section 1(2)(c) of the Patents Act 1977 from the notion of 'invention.' The latter is not defined as a term of art; instead the conditions for an invention to be patentable are set out in the Act (see text to notes 21 to 24 below). See also *Wang Laboratories Inc.'s Application* [1991] RPC 463 where a patent was refused for a computer programmed to produce a system yielding expert advice. The computer remained separate even when programmed and did not combine with the program to form a new machine.

[5] (1909) XXVI RPC 339 and see text to note 2 above and to notes 28, 29 and 30 below.

turn-of-the-century case about what it is that patents are supposed to protect.

The emphasis in *Hickton* was on the role of an 'idea' in combination with a means of carrying it out as the basis for a grant of a patent. In other cases judges have put the emphasis on the 'discovery' made by the patentee. These words have been deployed in varying modes in other recent cases, though both the notion of 'idea' and 'discovery' as being central to patent protection can also be seen as contrary to themes present both in case law and statute.[6]

In the light of uncertainty as to what it is that is protected by patent law (both in the sense of what required element of inventiveness is central to patentability and the extent of what the patent actually protects),[7] readers of the Reports of Patent cases might well reach the conclusion that the state of the law in this field depends on how key words and concepts at any crucial moment strike the judge hearing a case or fit the line of reasoning. More charitably, such a reader might conclude that the judicial mind is unavoidably influenced by the words to which it is ineluctably led in the context of the inquiry that has to be made in these cases.

'Invention', 'idea', 'ingenuity' and 'discovery' are used by the courts in conjunction with 'novelty' and the notion of what is 'inventive' or 'not obvious' in unpredictable ways. These terms, if each were given a single clear meaning by the courts, could leave judges, faced with the simplicity of the language of the Patents Act 1977, looking like Humpty Dumpty when he said: 'When *I* use a word it means just what I choose it to mean—neither more nor less;'[8] but the judges' approach seems in fact more like the little girl who, being told to be sure of her meaning before she spoke, said 'How can I know what I think till I see what I say?'.[9]

---

[6] See note 13 and text to notes 47 and 78 below.

[7] This formulation combines the required inventiveness with what the European Patent Office describes as the extent of protection conferred when distinguishing that from the extent of protection in the sense of rights conferred:

. . . in general terms, determination of the 'extent of protection conferred' by a patent under Article 69(1) EPC is a determination of *what* is protected, in terms of category plus technical features; whereas the 'rights conferred' by a patent are a matter solely for the designated Contracting States, and are related to *how* such subject-matter is protected. *MOBIL/Friction reducing additive* [1990] EPOR 73 at 81.

[8] Lewis Carroll, *Through the Looking Glass*, Ch. VI.

[9] Graham Wallas narrates this as a particular problem for poetry, but does so in

There is scope, therefore, for examination of the rules of discourse in patent law cases. Are these rules properly governing the way in which judicial thought is clothed or do they (or, worse, haphazard variants of them) tend to become the master and direct the judicial mind where it may not intend to go? Perhaps the result is on the lines of Pascal's: 'le coeur a ses raisons que la raison ne connaît pas' which Koestler puts more scientifically as:

The controls of a skilled activity generally function below the level of consciousness on which that activity takes place. The code is a hidden persuader.[10]

The principal question addressed here is whether the correct persuader is in use in patent cases. Do the words used in the case law reflect a coherent set of principles for grant of patents and protection of patent rights?

There is a particular reason why it is an appropriate moment to address this. The lag in litigation and the life of a patent combine to result in cases under the 'new' law (the Patents Act 1977) only now starting to come before the courts in appreciable numbers.[11] Further, the increasingly significant operation of the European Patent Office and growing awareness of the European dimension are beginning to have an effect on judicial thinking and utterance in this country.

UK patent law is currently contained in legislation derived from law developed in the European Community[12] and of wider

the context of the effect of 'foreconscious processes for conscious ends'—which is perhaps an apt description of the precursory influence of words on judicial conclusions that is suggested here. See Graham Wallas, *The Art of Thought* (1926 in reissue 1931) at 101 and 106.

[10] Arthur Koestler, *The Act of Creation* (1964), at 42. Koestler characterises his description as 'more abstract', a difference which itself illustrates how linguistic usage, rules of discourse and individual perception are not always open to uniform differentiation.

[11] Patents granted under the Patents Act 1949 ran for sixteen years from the filing date. Those already eleven years old on 1 June 1978 could be extended on the existing grounds up to the maximum life of twenty years, while those under eleven were automatically extended to a maximum life of twenty years. This means that 'old' patents are still very much around as the subject of litigation.

[12] The basis for current UK law in treaties of general international, as well as European, participation is most conveniently described in W. R. Cornish, *Intellectual Property*, Second Ed., 1989. The Patents Act 1977 was based on the Community Patent Convention, Luxembourg, 1975, as well as on the European Patent Convention, Strasbourg, 1973 ('EPC'), even though the former has encountered problems requiring its revision and preventing its entry into force for one and

European application, as well as, to some extent, from instruments of broader international application. Adapting English concepts and applying some of them in parallel with decisions of the European Patent Office (itself treading new ground in applying provisions whose words are sometimes reluctant to yield their meaning) indicates a need for review and adjustment.

Thus the problems over the law in this area arise from existing difficulties in the law of patents, those attendant on new legislation and from the fact that the new system is in part beholden to legal notions hailing from other legal systems. Existing case law in this country shows how English courts have treated the first category of problem. It may provide some pointers to how the 1977 legislation is likely to be approached and in a few cases specifically tackles the third area in cases where some attempt has been made at alignment with approaches of other European jurisdictions.

SOME ASPECTS OF THE LANGUAGE PROBLEM

Problems presenting as language problems in areas of patent law may be taken as indicators of unresolved issues. For example, the 1977 Act excludes from patentability a discovery when claimed 'as such.'[13] This reflects earlier case law which viewed as invalid any claims relating to 'mere discovery and mere novelty of purpose'[14]:

Patents are not granted for the mere discovery that a particular thing has hitherto unknown properties . . . a mere new use for an old thing is not patentable . . . there must be a new way of using it as distinct from merely use with a different end in view. (Unfortunately, the distinction is often *more a matter of language than of reality*.)[15]

In addition, however, to the linguistic difficulty of describing a particular distinction, there is the possibility of judicial thinking being prejudiced or affected by the language to which the judges may feel drawn in any particular case. In some cases, when

a half decades since the Act. Nevertheless, the changes in patent legislation, the established applicability of the EPC and the increasing activities of the European Patent Office provide ample material for the present investigation.[13] Patents Act 1977, section 1(2)(a).

[14] T. A. Blanco White, *Patents for Inventions and the Protection of Industrial Design*, Fourth Ed., 1974, at 1–208.

[15] Ibid. with emphasis added. As to 'merely use with a different end in view,' see now *BAYER/Plant growth regulating agent* [1990] EPOR 257 and text to note 45 below.

describing the sequence of events in which an inventor has made the invention, the judge will almost inevitably indicate that the inventor 'discovered' something. There is no direct harm, in the sense that provided the claim is not to a patent for the discovery 'as such,' the statutory exclusion does not apply; but if the inventive concept that is being protected is the 'idea' with which the discovery is equated by the judge, the potential for confusion as to what it is that patent law protects is apparent.

Thus in the assertion that 'The uninventive expert . . . should not be supposed to be attempting to discover something new, that is, to be striving for inventiveness', Buckley LJ seems to equate discovery with the essence of invention to an extent somewhat of the order ascribed by his earlier namesake to the 'idea'.[16]

Language is crucial to the extent of patent protection in another, much more obvious, sense. If the invention or inventiveness truly lies in the idea, the language in which that idea is encapsulated (in the patent specification) is a key to its bounds or extent. Until recently this has shown up in English case law as the uniquely 'Chancery' approach.[17] The vestiges of this approach are likely to prove hard to eradicate. This particular type of language problem is, of course, a major contributor to the field of patent litigation and is investigated briefly below.[18]

THE SUBSTRATUM

Presentation of the issues in terms of language should not lead to ignoring the changing context in which patent protection is given. Though written some forty years ago and about the situation in the USA, the following description may be quite apt for the current state of affairs in England:

The law of invention is particularly well endowed with unreal legal premises in the interstices of which the smaller negatively phototropic fauna of the courts may take refuge. To begin with it is based on a misapprehension. It accepts a theory of invention which may have been

[16] Per Buckley LJ in *Beecham Group Ltd. (Amoxycillin) Application* [1980] RPC 261 at 290. And see text to note 53, and following, below.

[17] Cornish, op. cit. at 3–008, (referring to the position after the legislation of 1883): 'The question whether the defendant was infringing . . . ceased to be weighed upon a private moral balance in the jury room and was instead subjected to that nice form of linguistic inquiry so natural to the Chancery mind.'

[18] See text to notes 77 to 85 below.

reasonably valid in the older days of the small workshop and the inge-
nious artisan, but which represents a process less and less common at the
present time.

In the early days of the engineering discipline, any new discovery was
largely a matter of seeking new combinations and required ingenuity, but
no particular understanding. . . However, as the several fields of science
received more thorough and better investigation, their structure and out-
lines began to emerge in strokes of greater clarity. . . At such a stage, the
next step is likely to clarify a whole field simultaneously. In the language
of the Patent Office, this new step will be, not an invention extending the
previous set of inventions, but discovery of a law of nature. . .

In other words, an invention is only an invention if it is based on a not
too complete understanding of its subject matter . . .[19]

In this can be seen elements of the problem addressed here. The
nature of invention may most often be the perception or idea of
combining known things or processes to produce something new.
Is entitlement to patent protection to be found in the inspiration or
idea of making the combination, in the labour of discovery, in the
ingenuity employed in overcoming an obstacle to making the combination work or elsewhere? These are issues considered below,
though clothed in the aspects of wording attributed to them.

II. Some key words

'INVENTION'

'Invention' can readily be put in the frame as one of the linguistic
problems of patent law because the 1977 Patents Act does not
attempt a definition 'as such'.[20] It does, however, provide one in
the sense of indicating the requirements for an invention's
patentability, using these requirements to construe references to

---

[19] L. Wiener, *The Human Use of Human Beings*, 118–119 (1950).

[20] The phrase 'as such' is used in section 1(2) of the Patents Act 1977, to qualify
certain exclusions from being inventions for the purposes of the Act, e.g. 'a discovery, scientific theory or mathematical method' is excluded; but this is to prevent
anything being treated as an invention 'only to the extent that a patent or application for a patent relates to that thing as such.' This use of 'as such' invites questions such as when is a mathematical method not a mathematical method (see I. H.
Donner *Should Some Algorithms be Patentable?* . . . [1993] 5 EIPR 162 and *Vicom
Systems Appn* [1987] EPOR 74; but the latitude which the Act allows the judges,
who can interpret these words in the sense of 'alone' or 'without more', is parallel
to the freedom the Act allows in identifying an invention on the basis of criteria for
patentability rather than a single, formula type of definition.

'patentable invention' in the Act and listing specific (or, rather, some specific and some less clear) exclusions from its meaning.

Thus only in the larger sense can it be said that the fact that patents are granted for inventions, that the requirements for patentability are set out in the Act and that the provisions of the Act lead to grant of patents, do along the way add up to an indication of what is to be dubbed an invention.[21]

The previous law ascribed the monopoly privilege granted to 'the true and first inventors' as being for 'any manner of new manufacture.'[22] This formulation was substantially followed in the Patent Acts before 1977 as a definition of 'invention,' with some expansion.[23]

The term 'any manner of new manufacture' clearly needed review and replacement. For though the words might seem most apt to refer to a process of making, their original meaning was articles and substances produced by manufacture, the manufacturing processes themselves being only included 'by long usage.'[24]

More important, however, is that what seems necessary is to distinguish between 'invention' as describing the thing or process which is the subject of a patent, or of related legal assertions or litigation, and the element of 'inventiveness' which is a component of invention and is sometimes subsumed in a particular use of the shorter word.

Fletcher Moulton LJ recognised the necessity of making these distinctions:

. . . I wish to point out that the word 'invention' is used in at least three senses in connection with these subjects, and that these three senses are quite distinct. First of all we say that to support a Patent there must be

---

[21] See Patents Act 1977, ss. 1–4. See also D. I. Bainbridge, *Intellectual Property* (1992), at 264:

Schmookler gives a more rigorous definition and subdivides inventions into process inventions and product inventions. The former are new ways of producing something old and the latter are old ways of producing something new. Every invention can be thus considered to be a 'new combination of pre-existing knowledge which satisfies some want'.

[22] Statute of Monopolies 1623, 21 Jac.1, c. 3, s. 6. See further E. W. Hulme, 'The History of the Patent System,' (1896) 12 *LQR* 141 and R. K. Gardiner, 'Industrial and Intellectual Property Rights: Their Nature and the Law of the European Communities' (1972) 88 *LQR* 507.

[23] This was to include any new method or process of testing and 'an alleged invention.' See Blanco White, op. cit. at 1–201 and W. Aldous, *Terrell on the Law of Patents*, 13th Ed (1982), at 2.02–2.04.

[24] Blanco White, op. cit. at 1–201.

'invention.' There it means an inventive act. Then we talk about a person getting a monopoly for an 'invention.' There it means a thing which is new and that has required an inventive act to produce it. There is also an intermediate sense in which it is used, that is to say, you sometimes speak of a patentee's 'invention' meaning the particular inventive act which this inventor has performed. . . You are speaking generally as if you were giving a history of the subject, and saying,—"So-and-so's invention was that for the first time he applied electricity for such and such a purpose."[25]

It is the first and third of these usages which are the chief cause of conceptual problems in patent decisions, while the second raises questions of interpretation of the words used to define the invention claimed. Thus the first meaning leads to inquiry into the particular inventive step; the third concerns the contribution to the advance in the state of the art (sometimes described as the 'teaching' of the patent specification); while the second meaning is a matter of 'ring-fencing' or 'sign-posting' the invention in the specification.[26]

IS THE 'INVENTION' TO BE FOUND IN THE 'IDEA'?

In the passages which the Court of Appeal quoted from *Hickton* in *Gale's Application*,[27] 'inventiveness' was coupled with the 'idea' in the mind of the inventor as the warrant for the grant of a patent:

'In my opinion, invention may lie in the idea, and it may lie in the way in which it is carried out, and it may lie in the combination of the two; but if there is invention in the idea plus the way of carrying it out, then it is good subject-matter for Letters Patent.'[28] (*Per* Fletcher Moulton LJ)

'I think you are losing grasp of the substance and seizing the shadow when you say that the invention is the manufacture as distinguished from the idea. It is much more true to say that the patent is for the idea as dis-

---

[25] *British United Shoe* v. *Fussell* (1908) XXV RPC 631, at 651. And see the expanded but more concise list of meanings in Blanco White, op. cit., at 1–202, footnote 33:
1. The embodiment which is described, and around which the claims are drawn.
2. The subject-matter of a claim—especially that of the broadest claim.
3. The inventive step taken by the inventor.
4. The advance in the art made by the inventor.

[26] The distinction is between a narrow 'Chancery' approach using linguistic analysis of the specification and the 'continental' attitude of drawing from the specification the essence of the invention or its 'inventive concept.' Though the EPC ordains a middle course, some English judges have shown an ability to treat the latter approach as if it were the former: see, e.g., text to notes 97 to 98 below.

[27] See notes 2 and 3 above.   [28] Loc. cit. at 348.

tinguished from the thing manufactured. No doubt you cannot patent an idea, which you have simply conceived, and have suggested no way of carrying out, but the invention consists in thinking of or conceiving something and suggesting a way of doing it.'[29] (*Per* Buckley LJ)

In addition to this emphasis on the 'idea' as central to the invention for patent purposes, the notion of 'discovery' and the possible relevance of 'use' or 'purpose' was part of the thinking of the Master of the Rolls:

Was that a new idea, was it a meritorious idea, was it a useful invention? I think it was upon the evidence plainly a new idea . . . it had never been discovered before. . . When once the idea of applying some well-known thing for a special and new purpose is stated, it may be very obvious how to give effect to that idea, and yet none the less is that a good subject-matter for a Patent.[30] (*Per* Cozens-Hardy MR)

Similar thoughts are to be found in much more recent case-law:

If there is any inventive step to be found in the appellant's claim it is in the idea of using a known, but recently developed, flocculating agent in a known filtration process in which it had not been used before. This idea, when put into practice as indicated in the specification, with the necessary but unspecified adjustments to the plant, does produce substantial economies of manufacture. If the idea was not obvious, the invention claimed is patentable.[31]

These passages do less than full justice to the difficulty of identifying precisely what it is that the patent is intended to protect. The development of English law in this field rather staggered from emphasis on importation to rewarding inventiveness. Originally intended to encourage foreigners to bring their skills to this country (with a monopoly being granted in exchange for the

[29] Ibid.

[30] Loc. cit. at 346–7, where the Master of the Rolls also said of the previous use of the process in issue that 'it was not a use so analogous to that which is found here as to render the thing so obvious as to compel us to state that there is no subject-matter in the Patent.'

[31] *Johns-Manville's Patent* [1967] RPC 479 at 493, *per* Lord Diplock. See also *Carroll* v. *Tomado* [1971] RPC 401 at 407: 'An invention can lie in the idea and here claim 1 quite clearly sets out in terms the necessary features of the combination which achieves the result.' (per Graham J). Contrast the characterisation by the Court of Appeal in *Re Gale*: '. . . it is helpful to have in mind the principle of patent law, well established before the Act that an idea or discovery as such is not patentable. It is the practical application of the idea or discovery which leads to patentability.' (per Nicholls LJ loc. cit. at 323).

import of technology and know-how which was to be disclosed
and transmitted to the indigenous people), the law switched
emphasis to encouraging inventors to make public the inner workings of their achievements and thus provide a base for further
innovation.[32] Along the way, English patent law developed its own
techniques for identifying and defining what it is that should be
protected by legislation.[33]

IS THE 'INVENTION' TO BE FOUND IN THE 'SUBJECT-MATTER'?

The emphasis in *Hickton's* case on the idea, coupled with an indication of a method of carrying it out, as providing 'subject-matter'
for a patent is consistent with the usage of judges in older cases
when refusing a patent for want of 'subject-matter', that term
being equated with the claimed matter being 'obvious' or lacking
an 'inventive step.'

It has been noted that the phrase 'lack of subject-matter' has not
been used in English patent legislation and is 'more appropriate to
express the absence of any quality of a nature such as to make the
invention inherently patentable than the absence of the quality of
'inventiveness'.'[34] Accordingly, one finds that by statutory provision 'a new filing system or a new game of cards, however inge-
nious, is not patentable and could appropriately be described as
lacking in subject-matter for invention.'[35]

Thus the usage of this term 'subject-matter' can be seen to be a
source of confusion. It might reasonably be thought to have various possible roles: first, it could indicate anything that comes
within any legislative definition of 'invention'; second, it could
refer to categories or classes of that which is patentable; or, third,
the term could refer to what is patentable by reference to prescribed characteristics.

A single definition of 'invention' of the kind that might appear
in a dictionary risks being unduly limitative for legislative purposes. Yet the second option, formulating categories or classes of
inventions as yet unmade by reference to 'subject-matter', is a task
equally difficult or just as likely to lead to unduly restrictive
results. Hence the 1977 Act adopts the third option by pointing the

---

[32] See E. W. Hulme, op. cit. note 22 above.
[33] See Cornish on the 'Chancery' approach, note 17 above.
[34] Terrell, loc. cit., at para 5.82.   [35] Ibid.

inquiry to whether an asserted invention is 'new' as well as having the essential ingredient of being 'inventive' or 'non-obvious.' This is coupled with elements of the second approach in a negative form so that exclusions are listed, eg that a scheme, rule or method for performing a mental act or a discovery, scientific theory or mathematical method are excluded as such.[36]

IS THE 'INVENTION' TO BE FOUND IN 'NOVELTY'?

Investigating whether something is new is commonly put under the heading of 'novelty' in the law of patents. Since one of the early English language uses of 'novelty' was to signify 'innovation,' that heading for this element of patentability carries with it the risk of leading one away from the purely factual question of whether the thing or process has been made or used before towards the thought of whether it is original, in the sense of denoting the presence of some mental effort or ingenuity in its devising. Yet in the law of patents these latter notions fall within the separate inquiry into whether the asserted invention involved an 'inventive step' or was 'obvious.' In the case of both 'novelty' and of 'inventive step' there is a difficult relationship with the notion of 'discovery'.

Although the test of novelty can be put in the simple form of the legislation (whether the invention is new) this can mask the more difficult issue of what it is that must be new. In the case of *Hickton's* patent[37] the idea and method of carrying out the advantageous process concerned saving thread when making lace. The more elaborately worked part of a lace pattern uses more thread than the plain background. By operating the lace-making machine in a particular way the demand for thread from different bobbins could be equalised throughout the pattern. The patented method of operation had been used on a different type of lace-making machine and for a different purpose. On that other machine it had the same beneficial result without being used deliberately to achieve that end. Thus the patent appears to have been granted essentially for the idea of using the technique on the different type of machine to produce the particular result of saving thread though there was nothing intrinsically new in the mechanical process used or the result achieved.

[36] For the listed exclusions see Patents Act 1977, section 1.
[37] See specification, loc. cit. at 340–343.

Nevertheless some literally 'new' elements can be seen, a known process being transposed to a new environment for a new purpose. It may, however, be asked whether this could be better described as 'a new use of an old technique for a new purpose' or 'an old use of an old technique for a new purpose?'

This distinction was addressed by a tribunal of the European Patent Office in cases where the application of a chemical to plants to control fungi was later claimed to have a new use for controlling the height of the plants.[38] Very similar was the case of an additive to lubricating oil which was found to reduce friction but which was exactly the same as one previously used to inhibit rust formation. The tribunal said in relation to the question above:

In reply, the respondent submitted . . . that a distinction should be drawn between a claim for 'a new use of an old thing for a new purpose' and a claim for 'an old thing for a new purpose'. While the former kind of claim could be novel, the latter kind of claim should never be held to be novel, because the only novel 'feature' of such a claim was a 'mental novelty' devoid of technical effect.[39]

The rejection of 'mental novelty' as devoid of 'technical effect' may seem to leave out in the cold the perception that formed the basis of what was found to be inventive in *Hickton's case* (the mental link between the mechanism in one machine, its by-product of saving thread and the problem to be solved on another machine)[40] and the observation in *BAYER/Plant growth regulating agent*[41] (that the process patented for the one beneficial result also produced a different one).

The result, however, in the European Patent Office's ruling was the exact opposite. Initially the reasoning of the Enlarged Board seems unpromising for the prospective patentee:

If the new purpose is achieved by a 'means of realisation' which is already in the state of the art in association with the known entity, and if the only technical features in the claim are the (known) entity in association with

---

[38] *BAYER/Plant growth regulating agent* [1990] EPOR 257.

[39] *MOBIL/Friction reducing additive* [1990] EPOR 73 at 85. Contrast the English case *In the matter of Esso and Shell* [1960] RPC 35 concerning fuel additives (including tri-para-tertiary butyl phenyl phosphate) suggested by one manufacturer for its 'anti-knock' properties and for its 'anti-corrosion' use by the other.

[40] This mental link is Koestler's 'bisociative' thought, the root of creativity. See *The Act of Creation* (1964) *passim*.

[41] See note 38 above.

the (old) means of realisation, then the claim includes no novel technical features. In such a case, the only 'novelty' in the claimed invention lies in the mind of the person carrying out the claimed invention, and is therefore subjective rather than objective, . . .

It follows that . . . the claim contains no novel technical feature and is invalid under Article 54(1) and (2) EPC (because the only technical features in the claim are known).[42]

However, the Enlarged Board did not leave the matter there. Pointing out that the exclusion of a 'discovery' from patentability only applied to a discovery claimed 'as such', the Board saw the whole issue as turning on the words used in the patent specification and whether the result should be viewed as an integral part of the process:

Depending on the particular wording of a particular claim, the above construction is not the only possible construction of a claim concerning the new use of a known compound, however. . .

In relation to a claim whose wording clearly defines a new use of a known compound, depending upon its particular wording in the context of the remainder of the patent . . . the proper interpretation of the claim will require that a functional feature should be implied into the claim, as a technical feature; for example, *that the compound actually achieves the particular effect*.[43]

Thus, on the facts in issue, the results or 'functional features' (namely control of fungi in one case and influencing growth in the other) of applying the same compound to plants in exactly the same way were each viewed as 'technical features', implied into the claim, and therefore independently patentable:

In other words, when following the method of interpretation of claims set out in the Protocol,[44] what is required in the context of a claim to the 'use of compound A for purpose B' is that such a claim should not be interpreted literally, as only including by way of technical features 'the compound' and the 'means of realisation of purpose B'; it should be interpreted (in appropriate cases) as also including as a technical feature the function of achieving purpose B, (because this is the technical result).[45]

That the compound actually achieves the particular effect claimed for it seems a strange basis for awarding a patent. That

---

[42] *MOBIL* loc. cit. at 85.   [43] Ibid. at 86, emphasis added.

[44] This Protocol explains the rules for interpreting the European Patent Convention.

[45] Loc. cit. at 87.

something does not work to achieve what is claimed for it has been a sure ground for refusal or invalidity of a patent in English law. However, that the procedure does work gives no guide on patentability; it does nothing to resolve issues of novelty and inventiveness.

Further, making the issue turn on the wording of the claim and whether a 'functional feature should be implied into the claim, as a technical feature' seems largely a verbal device and one which leads to unpredictability of the same order as is to be found in the (older) approach of the House of Lords to specifications (albeit in a somewhat different context).[46]

IS THE 'INVENTION' TO BE FOUND IN THE 'DISCOVERY'?

Of course the difference between discovery and invention is very familiar. Discovery adds to the amount of human knowledge, but it does so only by lifting a veil and disclosing something which before had been unseen or dimly seen. Invention necessarily involves also the suggestion of an act to be done, and it must be an act which results in a new product, or a new result, or a new process, or a new combination for producing an old product or an old result.[47] (*Per* Buckley J.)

This quotation, like many of the utterances in this field, is beguiling in the apparent ease of the distinction it puts forward. There is nothing, however, inherent in the word 'invention' or in the statute law relating to it that necessarily leads to the conclusion of Buckley J.[48] Both the latin origin of the word and the primary connotation in the English dictionary equate the term more closely with finding or discovery rather than the added attributes listed by Buckley J. Further the early development of English law on patents owes as much to the notion of discovery in the sense of *disclosure* of a technique (the monopoly being to encourage import of foreign skills or 'know-how' in exchange for revealing their secrets) as to any suggestion of a newly developed product or process.[49]

There is another contemporary problem which lies in the assertion that 'invention necessarily involves also the suggestion of an act . . . which results in . . . a new result.' If the act itself is identi-

---

[46] See text to notes 77–81 below.
[47] *Reynolds* v. *Herbert Smith & Co. Ltd.* (1903) XX RPC 123 at 126.
[48] For the exclusion of 'discovery as such' see notes 13 and 20 above.
[49] See references to historical origins in note 22 above.

cal with one already being performed to produce a particular effect, is there a patentable invention in the 'mere' discovery (or description of observation) that, as well as the known effect, it produces another beneficial result? English law has traditionally tended to refuse protection.[50] Cases in the European Patent Office now indicate that there is a basis for a patent if a new 'teaching' is revealed (and if the process of implying functional features into the claim as technical features is gone through).[51] Against the background of the developing law, therefore, the judicial approach to 'discovery' shows some confusion.

Before considering the EPO's approach, however, judicial language used to explain the inventive process is worth examining for its reference to the role of 'discovery'.

Although 'mere discovery' under the old law, or 'discovery as such' under the new, is excluded from patentability, the element of discovery clearly has a significant impact on what judges consider inventive. A fairly thorough consideration of this was made by Buckley LJ[52] in the context of obviousness when he considered the differing situations of the person who was trying to solve a particular problem and the person who was simply researching:

Obviousness and inventiveness are antitheses. What is obvious cannot be inventive, and what is inventive cannot be obvious. . .

It is clearly established that for a particular step to be obvious . . . it is not necessary to establish that its success is clearly predictable. It will suffice if it shown that it would appear to anyone skilled in the art but lacking in inventive capacity that to try the step or process would be worthwhile. Worthwhile to what end? It must, in my opinion, be shown to be worth trying in order to solve some recognised problem or meet some recognised need. The uninventive expert should not be supposed to be *attempting to discover something new, that is striving for inventiveness.* Having been shown what was disclosed by the prior art, he must be supposed to be attempting to solve some problem or fulfil some need which has not been resolved or satisfied by the prior art but which appears to his uninventive mind to be possibly capable of solution or satisfaction by taking the step or doing the thing under consideration.[53]

---

[50] See Blanco White, op. cit. at 1–208; but it is difficult to see all cases in quite such categorical terms. See *Hickton's case* at text to note 37 and following above.

[51] See text to notes 42 to 46 above and note 96 below.

[52] The learned judge was giving judgement some seventy years after the observations by his namesake quoted in the epigraph above.

[53] *Beecham Group Ltd.s (Amoxycillin) Application* [1980] RPC 261 at 290 with emphasis added and the judge's supporting citations omitted.

That the judge equated 'attempting to discover something new' with inventiveness has already been noted.[54] This in itself is indicative of a need for clarification. For the fact that something is new is only one of the requirements for patentability, though (subject to the more recent pronouncements in the EPO on new functional and technical features) it is not sufficient alone. That something is a discovery is sufficient to exclude it from eligibility for a patent where the claim is to the discovery as such. The judge appears to be trapped by the difficulty of finding language which is not already imbued with particular significance in patent law.

In what follows he seems to view the happy, and largely chance, lighting upon something useful as inventive. In contrast, exercise of ingenuity to overcome a particular problem he sees as uninventive, though it may be that in grappling with the particular facts the judge rather lost his grip on the words he used.

This, it seems to me, must involve the uninventive but skilled man having a particular problem in mind. If on carrying out his test he finds that the new step has the sort of consequence he had hoped but in an unexpectedly high degree, this would or might not mean that the new step was inventive or other than obvious; it might merely mean that a new and obvious step has solved the problem or met the need unexpectedly well. If, on the other hand the new step produces some unexpected result productive of an improvement or benefit of an unexpected kind it may well be held to be inventive, the association of the new step with its result not having been obvious.[55]

There are contrasting thoughts in this passage. The view that there may be inventiveness in 'the association of the new step with its result' can be read as locating inventiveness in the idea or mental process of conceiving a new step and linking it with successful implementation in practice (the *Hickton* role of 'idea'); or it may be a case of appreciating the significance of a discovery (using that word as in common parlance).

Either way, Buckley LJ viewed the chance element in the discovery as indicating a greater certainty that the new step was inventive, while ingenuity at overcoming a problem was seen as a mere application of technical skill.[56] This is confirmed in the final extract from this part of the judgment:

[54] See text to note 16 above.   [55] Ibid.
[56] On 'ingenuity' see text to notes 61 to 63 below.

Where, however, the skilled man has no particular problem or need in mind but merely regards some part of the known art as giving a good lead for further research, which may result in the discovery of some useful further knowledge, can the result of that research and its ascertainment by carrying out the research be obvious in the relevant sense? I think not, although this also may be a question of degree. By selecting the research, the researcher is, in my view, demonstrating that he is not wholly devoid of inventive capacity. He is not merely employing an obvious technique to get round an awkward corner; he is seeking to extend the field of human knowledge. The distinction is between *a mere exercise of ingenuity and a voyage of discovery*.[57]

This would lead to a rider to Wiener's assertion that 'an invention is only an invention if it based on a not too complete understanding of its subject matter'[58] to the effect that it is also more likely to be held to be a patentable invention if the inventor discovers something, in the sense of alights on it unsought.

This approach is supported by philosophical investigation of creativity:

Seek not and thou wilst (*sic*) find . . .

Chance only favours invention for minds which are prepared for discoveries by patient study and persevering efforts . . .

pour inventer il faut penser à côté . . . One sometimes finds what one is not looking for. For instance, the technician who set out to find a way to synchronise the rate of fire of a machine-gun with the revolutions of an airscrew discovered an excellent way of imitating the lowing of a cow.[59]

In his analysis of 'Nomenclature and Classification', Bentham largely favours the first category of inventiveness identified by Buckley LJ as warranting the description 'invention', that is where there is some pre-determined problem to solve or some end in mind:

Invention . . . is *imagination*, taken under command by *attention*, and directed to the accomplishment of some particular *object* or *end in view*.[60]

Thus a conclusion on the approach adopted by Buckley LJ is that both his categories of invention (sought and chance discovery) have some basis in philosophical approaches to inventiveness. So

---

[57] Ibid., with emphasis added.   [58] Op. cit. note 19 above.
[59] Narrated, with attributions, by Koestler, loc. cit. at 145.
[60] J. Bentham, *Chrestomathia*, (Smith & Burston eds., Oxford, 1983) 166, emphasis in the published edition.

do some of the words he uses, particularly 'discovery'; but this is discovery in the general usage and such use does nothing to overcome the difficulty of the relationship between discovery and invention in UK patent law.

IS THE 'INVENTION' TO BE FOUND IN THE 'INGENUITY' EMPLOYED?

In his exploration of inventiveness (in the sense of 'not obvious') Buckley LJ concluded that the distinction was between a mere exercise of ingenuity and a voyage of discovery, the latter alone meriting the accolade of patentability for its demonstration of inventive capacity.[61] In the judge's thinking this test seemed effectively to underlie the case where there was a particular problem to be solved since to be held inventive, rather than merely solving the problem exceptionally well, the new step had to produce some unexpected result or be associated with that result in a way which was not obvious.[62] That process, associating a new step with a result, equates more with a 'voyage of discovery' than with 'mere ingenuity.'

Yet there is judicial utterance whose language suggests that 'ingenuity' is the core of inventiveness, very much the opposite of the view just examined but widely supported by textbooks:

1. A patent for the mere new use of a known contrivance, without any additional **ingenuity** in overcoming fresh difficulties, is bad . . .
2. On the other hand, a patent for a new use of a known contrivance is good, and can be supported if the new use involves practical difficulties which the patentee has been the first to see and overcome by some **ingenuity** of his own. . .

If, practically speaking, there are no difficulties to be overcome in adapting an old contrivance to a new purpose, there can be no **ingenuity** in overcoming them, there will be no invention, and the first rule will apply. The same rule will, I apprehend, also apply to cases in which the mode of overcoming the so-called difficulties is so obvious . . . and admit of no sufficient **ingenuity** to support a patent.[63]

---

[61] See quotation in text to note 57 above.   [62] See text to note 55 above.
[63] *Gadd and Mason* v. *Mayor etc of Manchester* 9 RPC 516 at 524 per Lindley LJ, with emphasis added. See also: Terrell, op. cit., text to note 35 above; and D. I. Bainbridge, op. cit., at 268 where English patent law's uninventive person skilled in the art (see text to note 66 below) is equated with a technician rather than an engineer because 'engineers are trained in problem-solving by the application of ingenuity, the very word 'engineer' sharing a common origin with the word 'ingenuity'.'

That the predominant view is that 'ingenuity' aptly describes an aspect of inventiveness seems clear. A deeper investigation is needed, however, of the terminology of the element of inventiveness required for patentability. For this is the ingredient which is hardest to pin down. The 'inventive step' is spelt out in the 1977 Act in terms of the invention being 'not obvious to a person skilled in the art.'[64] This is the area of patent law which may be most open to influence from 'continental' notions, looking in particular to the 'inventive concept' as the core of the patent. Accordingly, this is considered in the next section, along with judicial approaches to words used in patent specifications.

III. Interpretation and Development

By examining words used in judgments in patent cases it is easy to give the impression that the judges have failed to give coherence to the law and have in many cases largely followed their own impressions, clothing these in the words that come most readily to mind. To some extent valid, that criticism must be balanced by acknowledging that law on patents has been statute-based for more than the last hundred years and that the guidance given by Parliament in key aspects of patentability has not been sufficient to avoid a continuing struggle by the judges to give effect to the policy underlying the law while attempting to be faithful to its words.

Foremost among the areas of continuing difficulty is identifying the element of inventiveness required for a patent to be granted. Whether this category of inquiry is dubbed 'non-obviousness', 'inventive step' or 'subject-matter', any such terms need elaboration to be practically applied. The standard laid down and identification of the person to apply that standard are factors given judicial clarification.

Taking the latter element first, the judges emphasise that this is a jury question, though juries long ago departed from the patent litigation arena. Given the complexity of the fields of scientific expertise to be investigated, often at the very frontiers of development, it would be difficult to envisage revival of actual jury evaluation of inventiveness. Judges may occasionally have help from an expert assessor;[65] but such assistance could not be effectively extended to make trial by a randomly selected jury a realistic proposition.

---

[64] Section 3.   [65] See e.g. *Genentech's Patent* [1989] RPC 147.

There is the further difficulty that the substantive standard of inventiveness involves another absent person as well as the hypothetical juryman. This other person is the 'person skilled in the art', patent law's specialist equivalent of the man on the Clapham omnibus:

'Obviousness is to be judged by the standard of a man skilled in the art concerned: competent, 'good at his job,' but not imaginative or of an inventive turn of mind.'[66]

This essential individual may seem easier to reproduce in hypothesis than are the members of a jury. For evidence from people actually fitting the specification of the skilled man can be adduced. Yet this still leaves the matter ultimately to judicial evaluation and impression.

An example of a judge's approach to what is obvious (though not solely in the sense of non-obvious inventiveness) can be found in *Johns-Manville's Patent*.[67] In the course of a challenge to the validity of a patent an issue was whether a step not specified in the patent was obviously necessary if the invention was to work. The patent involved a cement-pipe making process which would only work if the machine was operated at a higher speed than usual. This speeding up was not indicated in the patent. Though a research worker in the relevant industry, who seems to have been a virtual clone of the 'skilled man', gave evidence that he had abandoned his experiments on the same process for several years because he had not found out the need for speeding up the process until after the appellant's patent application, this was not viewed by the judge as an indication that the step was not obvious. The judge thought that the witness' 'glimpse of the obvious was spasmodic' and 'to this extent he was atypical of the skilled worker.'[68]

---

[66] Blanco White, op. cit., para 4–210.   [67] [1967] RPC 479.

[68] Ibid. at 494 per Diplock LJ. The judges' view of this evidence seems in part to have been the result of concessions by counsel; but, though stigmatising the witness as 'atypical', the court was nevertheless happy to accept his evidence as supporting their view, and that of the inferior tribunals, that the whole process was obvious. See also *No Fume* v. *Pitchford* (1935) LII RPC 231 where the Court of Appeal upheld a patent for a smokeless ashtray which did not give the precise proportions necessary to make the ashtray smokeless because these were obvious. The allegation of infringement nevertheless failed because the alleged infringer's ashtray did not work as it used the wrong proportions, a result which goes some way to suggest that the required proportions were less than obvious.

In other cases judges have sought to elaborate criteria or para-
phrases for obviousness or inventive step. Here too, however, this
may be as much a case of lip-service to a number of criteria developed through case law, though the apparent need for such tests
shows that the meaning of 'obvious' is not itself obvious.[69]

Some judicial awareness of the dangers of paraphrase is shown
by Lord Diplock:

I have endeavoured to refrain from coining a definition of 'obviousness'
which counsel may be tempted to cite in subsequent cases relating to different types of claims. *Patent law can too easily be bedevilled by linguistics*
and the citation of a plethora of cases about other inventions of different
kinds. The correctness of a decision upon an issue of obviousness does not
depend upon whether or not the decider has paraphrased the words of the
Act in some particular verbal formula. I doubt whether there is any verbal
formula which is appropriate to all classes of claims.[70]

Although the wisdom of not expanding confusion by unnecessary paraphrase may be readily apparent, the problem of identifying the meaning and test of obviousness does not lie solely in the
word 'obvious'. The statute uses 'not obvious' in identifying
whether the invention involves an 'inventive step'.[71]

A key element in the process of assessing whether something is
obvious is identifying that something. It will be seen that the
'European' approach to evaluating patentability by looking at the
'inventive concept', rather than the more verbal based study of
drafting of the claims attached to the specification, has already
begun to find its way into English case law through use of the very

---

[69] See e.g. *Johns-Manville's Patent* loc. cit., whether likelihood of success of the
invention as if not yet made would be sufficient to warrant its actual trial;
Technograph v. *Mills and Rockley* [1969] RPC 395, if substantial advance in the
state of the art, why was it not done before; *Parks-Cramer* v. *G. W. Thornton*
[1966] RPC 407, whether the invention satisfies a long-felt want; *Longbottom* v.
Shaw (1891) 8 RPC 333, whether the invention is merely the application of a well-
known product (or process) for a well-known purpose; *Parks-Cramer* (above),
Technograph (above), and *Windsurfing International* [1985] RPC 59, whether the
invention is commercially successful; *Williams* v. *Nye* (1890) 7 RPC 62 and *Hickman*
v. *Andrews* [1983] RPC 147, whether the invention is merely a collocation of features which already exist in the prior art; for this list see Phillips & Firth,
Introduction to Intellectual Property Law (Second Ed.), 46–48.

[70] *Johns-Manville's Patent* [1967] RPC 479 at 493, emphasis added.

[71] Patents Act 1977, section 3.

words 'inventive concept', though in a manner which preserves more than vestiges of the old approach.[72]

The notion of 'inventive concept' may, however, already have been in the law in the form of the significance attached by some judges to the 'idea' as an essential ingredient of invention claimed to be patentable. In parallel with thought about the role of the idea behind the invention was consideration of the 'inventive act' and whether this should be required to be stated in the claims. This has been touched on in the context of identifying the meaning of 'invention' but needs further consideration as a possible precursor to the notion of 'inventive concept'.

You sometimes speak of a patentee's 'invention' meaning the particular inventive act which this inventor has performed. . . Mr Terrell would have us say that in order to make a Patent valid a patentee must state, not only what he claims to be his monopoly, but also the inventive act by which he arrived at it. In my opinion that would be useless and in many ways impossible. (*Per* Fletcher-Moulton LJ)[73]

In addition to arguing that the law did not require any such statement of the 'inventive act', Fletcher-Moulton LJ reasoned that the inventive act would be difficult to pinpoint as there would be many different ways of employing existing knowledge of the art as a base from which to reach the invention.

So that to say what is the inventive step from the point of view of the totality of human knowledge is impossible, because there are fifty different lines of approach, and the step to the invention from one is a wholly different step to that from another. As I pointed out, to take the words 'inventive step' from the history of the inventor himself is equally useless. So that to suggest that you have got to state the inventive step—that wherein consists the novelty of the new thing which you have claimed—in addition to stating what is the invention for which you have claimed a monopoly, is, in my opinion, to put a useless, and an impossible burden on the patentee . . .[74]

In this second extract, and the passage leading to it, Fletcher-Moulton LJ shifts from the term 'inventive act' to 'inventive step', conflating the latter with 'novelty'. In his examination of the prior art and the advance made by it, he seems concerned to identify the

---

[72] See text to note 97 below.
[73] *British United Shoe* v. *Fussell XXV* (1908) RPC 631 at 651.
[74] Ibid. at 653.

essence of the invention, in the sense of the inventiveness, rather than confirming that the patentee had not merely done what had been done before. This is, therefore, close to some more modern approaches to inventiveness and the quest by courts to identify the inventive step in terms of the non-obvious element of the invention.

What Fletcher-Moulton saw as an impossible task for a patentee is scarcely any easier for judges. Yet identifying and describing the inventive step may resolve issues of obviousness or be a crucial step in that direction. The solutions reached by judges in the United Kingdom can be described as adopting one of two approaches characterised in the one case by employing a broad conceptual approach (such as fastening upon the 'idea' in *Hickton's case*[75] or, more recently, the 'inventive concept')[76] or the complete opposite, that is hiding behind an extremely literal approach to the words used.

The latter approach is in English patent law the older and the stronger tendency. Probably the most notorious example, albeit in the context of deciding whether a patent had been infringed, is in *Van der Lely* v. *Bamford*.[77]

In *Van der Lely* v. *Bamford* the patent was for a machine which could function both to rake hay together and to turn swathes over. For the latter function the patent directed that the 'hindmost' wheels were to be dismountable and relocated 'adjacent to the foremost rake wheels'. The alleged infringer made the front wheels dismountable and ranged them alongside the rear wheels. The result appears to have operated in exactly the same way whichever set of wheels was made dismountable. The House of Lords, rather than looking to the 'inventive concept' or essential elements of the invention, held that the patentee by specifying the dismountability of the hindmost wheels had identified this as 'the very element of his idea that makes it an invention'.[78] Accordingly, by making the same machine with the foremost wheels dismountable, the respondent had not infringed the patent.

Speculating that the patentee had simply not realised that one could equally easily construct the machine the other way round, Viscount Radcliffe thought it 'not unfair to say that the

---

[75] Loc. cit.
[76] See text to note 96 below.
[77] [1963] RPC 61.
[78] Ibid. per Viscount Radcliffe at 78.

respondents' device of bringing the foremost wheels back contains an element of inventive ingenuity.'[79]

The first point to make is that the statement that by specifying the hindmost wheels the patentee had made dismountability of the *hindmost* wheels the very element of the idea that made the device an invention seems actually to be avoiding identifying the real idea of the invention and saying that one is simply to read the words of the specification literally. If the majority view was based on penalising a patentee for specifying some detail with unwarranted particularity (though the rationale of the majority is far from clear) it seems bizarre to conclude, or presume, that that detail was the very essence of the invention. It also pre-empts the well-established principle of distinguishing essential and non-essential integers.[80]

A second point is that in viewing the respondents' reversal of the stated sequence of rake wheels as containing an element of inventive ingenuity, Viscount Radcliffe seems unconcerned to ascertain the view of someone skilled in the art (though he did not regard his own speculation on this matter as the key to the case).[81]

Particularly telling are the observations of Lord Reid (dissenting on this point):

If the specification of the hindmost wheels were the important part of claim 11 or the only novel feature in it I cannot imagine how it could be held that claim 11 involved any inventive step. Nothing could be less inventive than selecting the hindmost as against the foremost wheels when the selection makes no practical difference as regards efficiency.[82]

---

[79] [1963] RPC 61.

[80] This principle was explained by Lord Reid (dissenting from the majority conclusion on the claim in issue) as being that 'you cannot be held to have taken the substance of an invention if you omit, or substitute something else for, an essential integer.' Lord Reid's analysis of the majority view (that the appellants 'have deliberately chosen to make it an essential feature of the claim that the hindmost wheels should be detachable') seems unassailable. For he said that if this 'meant that there is something in the specification to show that they deliberately refrained from including the foremost wheels or went out of their way to make the hindmost wheels an essential feature I cannot find anything on which to base such a conclusion.' That this was not the intended meaning could be deduced from the acknowledgement that the appellants did not appreciate the possibility that the foremost wheels might be moved. Lord Reid therefore concluded that what must have been meant was 'that the mere fact that they [the appellants] only mentioned the hindmost wheels was sufficient to make the limitation to the hindmost wheels an essential feature of the claim. But if that were right, then I cannot see how there could ever be an unessential feature or how this principle could ever operate. And I think that the principle is very necessary to prevent sharp practice.' Ibid. at 76–77.

[81] Loc. cit. at 78.   [82] At page 76.

It may be justly observed that evaluating inventiveness is a different activity from identifying what it is that is to be evaluated in the first place. The approach taken in the hayrake case was part of an investigation whether someone had violated the protection given by a patent to an invention described in the specification.[83] That distinction, however, masks the underlying question of what it is that the patent is intended to protect. Is the monopoly reward to be attached to the core of the inventiveness? If so, the *Hickton* approach identifies the subject-matter and pedantic adherence to words used in the specification seems out of place.

The counter-argument, that the potential infringer is entitled to know exactly what the boundaries are of the patented invention, does not stand up to support an extreme literal approach in the face of the doctrine of essential integers or infringement by taking 'the pith and marrow' of the invention.

What is needed is a clear line on interpretation of patent specifications. This is attempted in the Protocol on interpretation of the European Patent Convention which proscribes limiting the protection of a European patent to the strict, literal meaning of the words in the specification's claims and, while equally saying that these are not merely guidelines, the principle is to reach an interpretation at the point between the two extremes 'which combines a fair protection for the patentee with a reasonable degree of certainty for third parties.'[84]

At this point it is appropriate to make the contrast between the British tradition and what may be loosely described as the 'continental' approach. As regards identifying the invention, the continental approach employs the words of the specification as

---

[83] The case of *Lyle & Scott* v. *Wolsey* (1954) LXXI RPC 395 provides another clear example of a patentee being held to unduly limiting words in the specification in the course of infringement proceedings, without the court using the idea or essence of the invention to determine whether there had been an infringement by that being taken. The patentee of men's underwear 'Y-fronts' had spelt out in the specification a detail of construction of Y-fronts with precision going beyond what was needed to describe the inventive elements. Hence when they avoided that inessential detail the alleged infringers, manufacturers of 'X-fronts', though manifestly using the same inventive concept, were held *not* to have infringed the patent. Cf. *The Proctor & Gamble Co.* v. *Peaudouce (UK) Ltd* [1989] FSR 180 where precision in the test of stiffness for the absorbent material of nappies resulted in the patent being invalid. In the standard applied, measurements from precisely five samples were to be used; in fact more than five samples would have been needed to obtain accurate measurements and the patent was found invalid for ambiguity.

[84] Protocol on Interpretation of Article 69 EPC.

'signposts' rather than 'fenceposts'. This leads to identification of the 'inventive concept' which could serve both as the element to be evaluated for assessing patentability and as the indication of the extent of the field protected by the patent. From the standpoint of common sense, if it is the inventive concept that justifies the grant of a patent why is it not by reference to that concept that the alleged infringement is assessed?

To some extent courts in the United Kingdom can be viewed as working towards a similar approach in the context of reading specifications for deciding questions both of infringement and patentability. However, progress is patchy.

A good example of a non-literal interpretation is *Catnic Components* v. *Hill & Smith*[85] where a specification indicated that a component of a lintel was to be vertical. A similar lintel with that component at an angle a few degrees off the vertical was nevertheless found to infringe. Lord Diplock stated the principle:

A patent specification should be given a purposive construction rather than a purely literal one derived from applying to it the kind of meticulous verbal analysis in which lawyers are too often tempted by their training to indulge.[86]

In saying this, Lord Diplock was upholding an established principle that a person infringes by taking the essential features of the invention.

It is those novel features only that he claims to be essential that constitute the so-called 'pith and marrow' of the claim.[87]

Lord Diplock is probably here using 'novel' to refer to the essentially inventive features of the invention, that is to say, not the parts that are merely new but the core of the patented thing or process. This use of a term that has a special and different use in the law of patents he matches with a reference to what is 'not obvious' in the ordinary sense, rather than the patent law sense of containing an inventive step. For in examining variants to see whether they fall within the patent's claims he says:

The question, of course, does not arise where the variant would in fact have a material effect on the way the invention worked. Nor does it arise unless . . . it would be obvious to the informed reader that this was so. Where it is not obvious . . . the reader is entitled to assume that the paten-

[85] [1982] RPC 183.   [86] Loc. cit. at 242.   [87] Ibid.

tee thought at the time of the specification that he had good reason for limiting his monopoly.[88]

The potential for confusion was noted by Hoffman J.:

I think that Mr Young has been misled by Lord Diplock's use of the word 'obvious' into thinking that he must have been intending to refer to the rule that an obvious improvement is not an inventive step.[89]

The essential point remains, however, that Lord Diplock avoided an excess of literalism and it is difficult to account for the obviously incompatible outcomes in the lintel and hayrake cases. If 'vertical' was not to be interpreted literally why was 'hindmost'? If the test is whether the 'pith and marrow' has been taken, it most clearly was taken in the hayrake case.

Since, however, words are generally the major part of a specification language inevitably has a role in defining concepts, such as the pith and marrow of an invention. Perhaps it is the lack of a clear objective when analysing a specification, the failure to keep identification of the pith and marrow as the target, which leads linguistic analysis to be preferred in some cases as if that were an end in itself. The matter may, however, be complicated by the differences among technologies and the peculiarities of the linguistic and conceptual matrix which each technology may import into the inquiry.

An example may be found in the contrast between a recent case which revolved around the word 'spheroidal' and an old case in which the specification used the word 'conoidal.' In *Rediffusion Simulation* v. *Link Miles*[90] the defendants has used a 'spherical' mirror in the production of images for a visual system in a flight simulator. The patentee's specification included at different points: 'Preferably the mirror is substantially spheroidal in shape' and a 'spheroid'; used 'substantially spheroidal' in a claim which it was agreed had not been infringed; and had drawn up general claims which were sufficiently wide to cover visual systems using spherical mirrors. Holding that these claims were infringed but invalid (as not being fairly based on disclosures in the specification), the judge also found that there had been a lack of reasonable skill in framing the specification.

---

[88] Ibid.
[89] *Improver Corp.* v. *Remington* [1990] FSR 181 at 192.
[90] [1993] FSR 369.

Linguistically 'spheroidal' may refer to anything which is like a sphere. The suffix '-oid' is defined as 'having the form of' or 'like'.[91] The first definition is apt to fit a sphere, which might be viewed as the best or closest example; but to avoid identity with 'spherical' an element of 'like' must be present in the notion of 'spheroidal' to produce the result similar to a sphere though not truly spherical. This is the same principle which leads pleaders to use the phrase 'on or about' a specified date of an accident 'or whatever', as use of 'about' alone would allow for error but not for accuracy.

Plainly the position is more complex where optics are involved and may magnify the importance of distinctions; but given that the specification disclosed such variation in the description of the spherical nature required, it is difficult to take this element as the essential integer (see Lord Reid's argument in note 80 above) if reasonable experiment would show the more easily produced sphere would produce the desired result.[92]

Were the plaintiffs being punished for drafting which, though poor, disclosed the essential inventive features? Was this a lack of foresight equivalent to that of those who described the hayrake? The linguistically comparable term 'conoidal' was indicated in a footnote to the report of *Watson, Laidlaw & Co* v. *Potts, Cassels and Williamson*[93] as being used to denote 'conical or approximately conical'. This precedent for word formation does not appear to have been considered in *Rediffusion*, the impossibility of 'spheroidal' including spherical having been accepted by the parties in relation to the third claim. Possibly this was because the technology involved was quite different or because the claims in *Watson* (in marked contrast to the drafting in *Rediffusion*) were prudently introduced by a defining provision.[94]

It is, therefore, difficult to predict which angle of approach a judge will select. The principle of purposive construction exemplified in

---

[91] See *Shorter Oxford English Dictionary*.

[92] This is, however, slightly different from the conclusion in the smokeless ashtray case (*No Fume* v. *Pitchford*, cited in note 68 above). To allow a patentee to omit details which can be readily supplied without the need for inventiveness does not provide precisely for the case where it is necessary to decide how liberally a given detail should be interpreted.

[93] (1909) XXVI RPC 349.

[94] 'The term "conoidal" is used to indicate either surfaces truly conical, or surfaces more or less curved but at the same time approximating the conical, or surfaces which, while, in a measure, irregular yet approximate the generally conical.' Loc. cit. at 352.

Catnic was only mentioned *en passant* in *Rediffusion*, and was not applied to the notion of 'spheroidal.' If it would have been indulging in the 'meticulous verbal analysis' (of which Lord Diplock warned) to have considered the word against the linguistic background indicated above, perhaps a case could have been made for suggesting that, in contrast to the hayrake case, there could be read in the specification a stated requirement to adhere to the precise description.[95] Yet this specific analysis is not reflected in the judgment.

At all events, the approach taken by Lord Diplock avoids extremes of literalism and allows for the 'pith and marrow' principle to be developed towards an 'inventive concept' approach. This notion of 'inventive concept' has been contrasted by the European Patent Office with the approach used in the United Kingdom:

In some countries, in particular Germany, in practice the protection conferred by a patent depended more upon what was perceived to be the inventor's contribution to the art, as disclosed by the patent, by way of the general inventive concept, than upon the wording of the claims. In other countries, in particular the United Kingdom, the precise wording of the claims was regarded as crucial, because the claims were required to define the boundary between what was protected and what was not, for the purposes of legal certainty.[96]

The notion of 'inventive concept' has in fact been used in at least one English case involving a patent pre-dating the 'Euro-driven' legislation in 1977. Curiously, the use of these words achieved rather the opposite effect from what one might have expected.

The patent was for windsurfers or sailboards. The Court of Appeal said that the first stage in examining obviousness was to ask what was 'the inventive concept embodied in the patent in suit'.[97] Holding that the inventive concept was the 'free-sail'

---

[95] The specification included a paragraph:

The collimating mirror 7 of the visual display arrangement of Figs. 1 and 2 has a special concave shape which forms part of the surface of a spheroid, or ellipse of rotation. This design is *required* to present a correct geometry picture with tolerable optical distortion . . . (Patent Specification 1385908, page 5, with emphasis added)

However, the 'design' includes elements other than just the spheroid; and the judge does not appear to have viewed these words as having been crucial to making that element of the design an essential feature prescribed by the patentee as obligatory.

[96] *BAYER/Plant growth regulating agent* [1990] EPOR 257 at 260.

[97] *Windsurfing International* v. *Tabur Marine* [1985] RPC 59 at 73. See also J-M. Claydon, The Question of Obviousness in the Windsurfers Decision, [1985] *EIPR* 218.

concept, the court rejected the view that the invention lay in a combination of three components, *viz* an unstayed spar (held in place by a universal joint and free to move under the control of the user), a sail attached along the length of the spar and use of 'arcuate' booms. Though only viewing the first element (the so-called 'free sail' concept) as the inventive concept, the court nevertheless examined the three elements. With the inventive concept thus limited and the elements taken to bits in this way, the components could be shown to be obvious (as well as not new). Thus the court held the patent was bad on grounds of obviousness, even had it not been anticipated.

Not only does this appear to offend the established approach of not dissecting combinations to demolish an invention piecemeal,[98] it is also a narrow, if not obtuse, application of the term 'inventive concept'. Here, if ever, the invention lay in the idea or perception, namely that a rig of this kind could be made to work effectively to produce a windsurfer. The Court of Appeal's approach more closely resembles the reciprocal of Cole Porter's 'Physician' who expressed his love for each anatomical feature of his beloved but never for the whole person.

A contrasting case, in which the 'inventive concept' was implicitly used to uphold a patent, concerned the 'Workmate'.[99] This convenient 'Do It Yourself' aid included a folding workbench, devised to function in part as a vice and a sawing horse, with several other features combining to make it so successful. Plainly the invention lay in the idea and its effective implementation. Nevertheless, much of the judicial examination of it was directed to the narrow issues of the meaning of the general term 'workbench' and consideration of particular features. However, the Court of Appeal endorsed the view of the judge at first instance that 'workbench' had an ordinary meaning; it was to be construed in the context of the specification as a whole and that despite the breadth of the first claim it 'covered a useful article which the plaintiff ought fairly to be able to cover'.[100]

---

[98] See e.g. *Carroll* v. *Tomado* [1971] RPC 401 at 409.

[99] See *Hickman* v. *Andrews* [1983] RPC 147. At first instance the judge referred to his own description as 'inadequate to convey the merit of the inventive concept', loc. cit. at 161.

[100] Loc. cit. at 172, per Graham J. Contrast the approach taken in the *Rediffusion* case above on 'fair basis.'

IV. Conclusions

The language used by judges when resolving disputes over patents needs closer attention; but the problems lie deeper in the law and in particular in what the law uses as the basis for granting the monopoly and defining the things which are covered in any instance.

It is unfortunate that the use made by the Court of Appeal of the 'inventive concept' so far does little justice to that term. Adoption of the 'continental' usage would enable the 'Hickton' role for the 'idea' to be brought up to date and combined with a clearer approach to assessing patentability and infringement.

It is easier to show the flaws in existing terminology than to point the way to improvement. There remains considerable difficulty, and subjectivity, in applying the words 'not obvious'. There remains great scope for uncertainty over 'discovery' and 'ingenuity'.

Equally, it seems that even if a balanced view of the inventive concept is adopted, there are other aspects of the law to which the European Patent Office is introducing verbal complexity. In particular, this looks to be the case with 'technical features' being implied as 'functional features' to allow a newly discovered result to be the subject of a patent. It would be better if this were allowed explicitly rather than disguised by a verbal sleight of hand.

Care in use of terms and avoiding using terms in a different sense from their established meaning in the law of patents will eliminate some of the problems; examination of other notions, however, reveals language as a mask for deeper difficulties in the law. As the Patents Act 1977 comes increasingly into play as 'old' patents expire, there will be more opportunities to abandon the difficulties in the 'old' case law and to take up the sensible elements of the 'continental' approach, a development which could help make patent protection less of the lottery that it is.

THE SELLAFIELD LITIGATION AND QUESTIONS OF CAUSATION IN ENVIRONMENTAL LAW

*Jane Holder**

Introduction

Residential housing in the United Kingdom is often located near industry. This is a nineteenth century legacy; many employers built housing for workers close to mills, printworks, alkali works, mines and so on. This of course left workers subject to the effects of industrial processes—noxious gases, corrupted water, and dangerous accumulations of manufacturing waste—but economic dependency upon their employers meant taking legal action against them for injury to their health and property was most unlikely.[1] A similar type of dependency still exists today in Seascale, West Cumbria where many members of the community rely upon employment at the nearby nuclear power plant, Sellafield (formerly called Windscale).

In *Reay and Hope* v. *British Nuclear Fuels plc*[2] two families living close to the Sellafield plant brought an action for personal injury against British Nuclear Fuels Plc[3] in an attempt to establish

* Lecturer in Laws, University College London.

[1] J. P. S. MacLaren, 'Nuisance Law and the Industrial Revolution—Some Lessons From History', (1983) 3 *Oxford Journal of Legal Studies*, 155–221, at 161–3, concludes that in the period 1770–1870 there were on average one or two actions in nuisance for air pollution every ten years with the record for noise pollution even sparser.

[2] *Reay and Hope* v. *BNFL* (1993) QBD (1993) *Current Law* 2978, *The Guardian*, October 15, 1993; a short precis may be found in *Water Law* (1994) 22–23.

[3] The defendants were referred to as British Nuclear Fuels Limited or BNFL; BNFL was formed as a state-owned limited company in 1971 with shares held on behalf of the government by the United Kingdom Atomic Energy Authority.

that their child's death and their own injury to health from the cancers of the blood, leukaemia and lymphoma, were caused by releases of radiation from the plant; thus that BNFL were in breach of their statutory duty. In October 1993 they lost their claims for damages when the High Court judge, French J. ruled that there was insufficient evidence that the cause, or material contributory cause, of death and injury was radiation emitted by Sellafield. The plaintiffs have not appealed against the decision.

The case was unusual in that, for the first time, the plaintiffs based their claim on genetic links between fathers' exposures to radiation and mutation of sperm, leading to a predisposition to leukaemia or lymphoma in children. This theory is known as parental preconception irradiation (PPI). The plaintiffs also relied upon a more recognised cause of the diseases: exposure to environmental radiation.

The genetic link between radiation and cancer formed the central plank of the plaintiffs' argument. Its failure suggests the parameters of personal injury actions of this type. It also raises a question of significance beyond genetic harm and the nuclear industry: the judicial treatment of scientific evidence of causality in cases of environmental harm. Its failure is likely to have implications for claims currently being brought against Rentokil for aplastic anaemia caused by pesticides; against London Docklands Development Corporation for disturbance caused by dust and noise in the course of construction work; and against ICI and British Steel for respiratory diseases such as asthma.

In this article the breach of statutory duty as a 'toxic tort' is reviewed; the judgment given in *Reay and Hope* and its significance in terms of prospects for future similar cases is then assessed. It is argued that the judicial treatment of evidence—statistical and scientific—in the case was such as to impose an unnecessarily high, and simplistic, requirement of causation, quite unsuited to the consideration of diseases such as cancers, which are characterised by complex aetiology, and are rarely attributable to a single pollutant.

It is suggested that a so-called 'common sense' approach to causation, developed in a number of similar cases, might increase recognition of the complexity of diseases caused by environmental harm. Two possible reforms related to a 'common sense' approach to causation are also considered: the application of the 'precautionary principle'—as yet a principle only of policy-making rather than litigation—in cases such as this; and shifting the burden of proof to the defendant once a prima facie association from which causation might be inferred is established.

'Toxic torts'

Injury caused by environmental harm is an identifiable and discrete area of tort, increasingly labelled 'toxic torts'.[4] It is also a relatively new area within environmental law, with most claims in this category having begun since 1989: *Reay and Hope* is one of the first. Pugh and Day describe the scope and application of this type of tort:

The term 'toxic tort' is a shorthand phrase . . . for any claim that has, at its base, the prospect that an individual has suffered damage to person, property or to the quiet enjoyment of his/her property, or there has been damage caused to the local environment as a result of environmental pollution. The term therefore covers damage resulting from industrial waste pumped into the environment, whether into the air, the sea, the rivers . . . It covers chemical and radioactive waste. It also covers claims for nuisance resulting from noise, dust etc. Finally it covers damage to the environment itself.

The basic starting point for a toxic tort claim is that the person who has suffered the damage is an innocent victim whose only link with the cause of the pollution is likely to be that of living in the vicinity of a toxic source (or having a parent who was occupationally exposed to a toxic substance). Not included are claims by workers in the industry causing the pollution and damage. The reason for the separation is that although the injuries sustained by the workers are often the same or similar there is not usually the same enormous problem of identifying the pathways whereby the pollution has arrived in the victim's body.[5]

Pugh and Day consider that this area has yet to be judicially defined;[6] *Reay and Hope* has begun this process.

The case concerned breach of statutory duty for causing injury by a toxic substance—radiation. The tort of breach of statutory duty was developed by courts willing to interpret industrial safety legislation so as to confer a right of action on injured workmen.[7] Early examples are the breach of statutory rules in failing to fence

[4] C. Pugh, M. Day, (1992) *Toxic Torts*; J. M. Williams, (1993) 'Causation in Toxic Tort Cases', *Environmental Policy and Practice*, vol 2, no 4, 331–332.

[5] Pugh and Day, Op. cit., p.2.   [6] Ibid., p. 1.

[7] *Street on Tort*, (1993) 9th ed., pp. 398–413.

machinery set out in Factories Acts.[8] *Reay and Hope* is quite different from these 'workmen' cases in that it represents a concern that
members of the public as well as workers may be at risk from
breach of statutory duty; in this case, in relation to nuclear installations.

As with other torts, damages for breach of statutory duty are
recoverable only when the defendant's breach 'caused' the harm. In
Reay and Hope the plaintiffs' success depended on their proving on
the balance of probabilities that breach of statutory duty by BNFL
caused, or materially contributed to, their injury.[9]

Sellafield and energy policy

Reay and Hope was prepared and heard in the context of the political and legal debate about first, the privatisation of nuclear power
in the UK and, second and more importantly, of the construction
of a number of pressurised water reactors (PWRs) and the granting
of a licence of operation for a thermal oxide reprocessing plant
(Thorp) at Sellafield. The case's preparation began at the time of
the planned privatisation of the nuclear industry; the judgment was
heard some five years later, just weeks before Thorp received its
licence of operation. Privatisation, however, has been abandoned;
moreover no new nuclear reactors are likely to be built in the fore-
seeable future.

Despite the vicissitudes of energy policy, including the withdrawal of the nuclear industry from privatisation of the electricity
supply industry at the last moment, it is arguable that the various
influential proponents of nuclear power transferred their support to
the reprocessing of spent fuel as a commercially favourable activity
for the industry to engage in.[10] Indeed the support granted to
Thorp, the thermal oxide reprocessing plant at Sellafield, in the
early 1990s appears exactly to mirror the government's seemingly
unerring support of the pressurised water reactor programme in
the 1980s.

[8] *Groves* v. *Lord Wimborne*, [1898] 2 QB 402, CA.
[9] *Bonnington Castings Ltd.* v. *Wardlaw* [1956] AC 613, at 620; see *Street on Torts*, at p. 410.
[10] For a comprehensive account of the volte-face on privatisation of nuclear power see J. Roberts et al (1991) *Privatising Electricity: The Politics of Power*, 98–119; see also T. O'Riordan, R. Kemp, M. Purdue, (1986) 'Environmental Politics in the 1980s: The Public Examination of Radioactive Waste Disposal', *Policy and Politics*, vol 14, no 1, 9–25 at 11.

The Sellafield plant is on the Cumbrian coast two miles from Seascale. This village has long been closely associated with the plant and is regarded as unique in the United Kingdom for its combination of a highly mobile, changing population in a remote rural area. Most Sellafield workers, though, live in nearby Whitehaven, Egremont and Cleator Bridge.

The legal framework within which Sellafield and other sites operate was originally provided by the Atomic Energy Act 1954. This established a United Kingdom Atomic Energy Authority, and equipped it with wide powers 'to do all such things . . . as appear to the Authority necessary or expedient for the exercise of the foregoing powers'—to produce, use and dispose of atomic energy. Whilst not permitted to produce any nuclear weapons, the Authority is permitted to 'conduct experimental work which may lead to improved types of explosive nuclear assemblies for atomic weapons'.[11]

The Act provides that radioactive waste may not be disposed of without a licence. Section 5(3) of the Act imposes a statutory duty 'to secure that no ionising radiations from anything on any premises occupied by them, or from any waste discharged . . . cause any hurt to any person or any damage to any property, whether he or it is on any such premises or elsewhere'. This statutory duty was later reformulated in s. 7(1) Nuclear Installations (Amendment Act) 1965. Section 12 of this Act gives a right to compensation where any injury or damage has been caused by breach of this duty.

The duty 'to secure that no ionising radiations cause any hurt to any person or any damage to any property' was narrowly applied in *Merlin* v. *British Nuclear Fuels Limited* [1990] 3 WLR 383. The plaintiffs' house had been contaminated with radiation emanating from the Sellafield plant. In selling it they were so frank about the contamination that it was sold to a Sellafield worker for £30,000 (considerably lower than it would have been sold for in an uncontaminated state). Faced with the question of whether the diminution in value caused by the contamination fell within the definition of 'damage to property', and so amounted to a breach of statutory duty, Gatehouse J., before the Queen's Bench Division, held that damage to property meant physical damage to tangible property

[11] s. 2(2) Atomic Energy Act 1954.

and did not include diminution in value. Pugh and Day state that in light of this case, it is possible that in the event of a failure at a nuclear plant, the local population could neither claim relocation expenses for evacuation, nor for the diminution in value of their properties.[12]

Briefly then, this was the legal and policy background of the case; *Reay and Hope* also took place in the context of anecdotal reports as well as studies about cancers and environmental contamination in the area surrounding Sellafield.

Cancers and environmental contamination

Leukaemia and lymphoma were the cancers of concern in *Reay and Hope*. Leukaemia is a generalised disorder of the bone marrow in the form of an uncontrolled reproduction of white cells in the network of tissue in the cavities of bones. This reproduction interferes with the development of normal cells and is responsible for symptoms such as excessive bleeding. Lymphoma is the group name for cancers of the lymphatic system in which a similar excessive reproduction of white blood cells takes place. Childhood leukaemias and lymphomas tend to be very malignant and unless treated quickly are rapidly fatal.

Scientific knowledge about leukaemia and lymphoma in adults and children is uncertain, though there is a general understanding that, as with other cancers, they are multifactorial diseases which require at least two events or 'hits' before the cancer emerges. So the disease is not solely attributable to a particular pollutant or toxin. The only known cause of these diseases is radioactive plutonium which attacks bone marrow. As with all types of radiation, plutonium produces a disruption of atoms in the matter through which it passes. Radiation can penetrate human skin, doing damage with varying effects on tissues and organs, while remaining undetectable to the senses.

Many radiation releases have occurred at Sellafield. The fuel cartridges within two nuclear reactors ruptured on a number of occasions, releasing large quantities of uranium and uranium oxide and radioactive argon to the atmosphere. In addition to these atmospheric emissions, some of the reactors' contents were released into

---

[12] Pugh and Day, (1992) *Toxic Torts*, p. 130.

groundwater, rivers and the sea. A serious and uncontrolled discharge of radioactive gases and particles into air and water took place in 1957 when there was a fire in one of the reactors; this lasted two days and contaminated generally the area surrounding the plant.

BNFL's figures for radioactive plutonium emissions—the substance primarily linked with cancers of the blood system—from Sellafield were originally 100 grammes; revised in 1984 to 440 grammes; in 1986 to 12 kilogrammes and finally revised in their evidence to the court to 15–20 kilogrammes. The plaintiffs' estimate is nearer 400 kilogrammes. The defendants conceded that, when applying for authorisation to dispose of radioactive gaseous wastes, some records were not taken into account in disclosing discharge figures; it was accepted in court that this omission might make the defendant's emission figures appear four times lower than in fact they had been.

Anecdotal reports of higher than expected levels of cancer in the Seascale area were publicised in 1983 in a television programme, 'Windscale—the Nuclear Laundry'. This reported that childhood leukaemias were nearly ten times as common in Seascale and nearby areas as in the rest of the country. Within weeks of its broadcast, a number of academic and medical studies were commissioned.

In one such study, Professor Martin Gardner established an epidemiological link between radiation and childhood cancers. He examined 52 cases of leukaemia and 22 of lymphoma—all occurring in people born and diagnosed in West Cumbria Health District between 1950–1985 and under the age of 25. Gardner's thesis was that workers' sperm, damaged by radiation exposure, could produce children with a propensity to leukaemia. He asserted that men who received more than 100 milliSieverts (Msv) of radiation over a lifetime stood six to eight times greater chance of producing a child with leukaemia because of mutations to sperm than if they had not been so exposed. The link was particularly strong where fathers had been exposed in the six months prior to conception. Scientific evidence of the heritability of the predisposition to leukaemia and lymphoma—the causal mechanism underlying the association—was not given in the report.

The scientific community had long considered that levels of *environmental* radiation in the area were not sufficient to cause cancers. The Gardner study asserted statistical evidence of a strong association between radiation and the diseases explained by a *genetic* link; this came to form the basis of the plaintiffs' claim for damages.

The litigation

The case against BNFL was brought by Elizabeth Reay, whose daughter, Dorothy, died of leukaemia in 1962 at the age of 10 months, and Vivien Hope who became partially disabled and infertile after treatment for lymphoma. Dorothy Reay's father, George, and Vivien Hope's father, David, both worked as fitters at the plant for more than 20 years. George Reay had suffered one of the highest radiation doses of Sellafield workers.

Elizabeth Reay claimed damages for her daughter's death and for injury to herself and her late husband caused by the trauma of their daughter's death. Vivien Hope claimed damages for past and future suffering, disability and infertility arising from her lymphoma. After ninety days in court, French J. gave judgment before the Queen's Bench Division, that the plaintiffs in the two cases had failed to prove on the balance of probabilities that the cancers were caused by emissions from the Sellafield site. He agreed that although the Seascale cluster could not be put down to 'chance', it could not be said—even on the balance of probabilities—that it was caused by mutation of the fathers' sperm creating a predisposition to the diseases. French J. specified that the Gardner study had a number of shortcomings including grouping leukaemia and lymphoma together as expressions of one disease. The study was also unsupported by other research, notably those of children of atomic bomb victims in Nagasaki and Hiroshima. The plaintiffs' thesis failed, *inter alia*, because it did not explain the association between parental preconception irradiation (PPI) and the diseases.[13] *Obiter dictum*, French J. stated that had he found that PPI caused or materially contributed to the Seascale cases, and that lymphoma and leukaemia were essentially the same diseases, then Vivien Hope's claim would have succeeded.[14] The company was formally

---

[13] p. 203 judgment; see D. Wilkinson, '*Reay and Hope* v. *British Nuclear Fuels plc*' (1994) *Water Law*, 22–25, at 24.

[14] For comment on this point, see Wilkinson, *supra*, at 23.

awarded costs against the legally aided claimants, but these have not been enforced.

Judicial treatment of evidence

The plaintiffs' case was founded on epidemiological evidence. The purpose of epidemiology—the study of patterns of behaviour in large numbers of cases—is to make a statistical assessment of the probability of an association between exposure (in this case, radiation and PPI) and the disease (leukaemia or lymphoma); and that the association, if any, is causal. An expert witness in the case described the discipline:

In the end, it must be recognised that the idea of cause is a probabilistic one. Rarely can we be certain that a causal relationship exists, but by assembling evidence from many different angles we may build a body of support sufficient to convince most reasonable people that it is more prudent to act as though the association were causal than to assume that it is not. The point in the accumulation of evidence at which this decision is reached depends in considerable part on the consequences of the alternative actions to be taken as a result of the judgment.[15]

Epidemiology only shows a correlation; it cannot directly prove any hypothesis. In other words it does not constitute *biological* proof of causation. Nevertheless, in the absence of contradictory biological evidence, statistical associations may constitute proof of *legal* causation. In the medical negligence case, *Loveday* v. *Renton*,[16] epidemiological evidence supported the conclusion that the whooping cough vaccine sometimes caused convulsions. Epidemiological explanations accord exactly with the standard of causation in actions in tort—a balance of probabilities—but such evidence tends to collapse in criminal cases in which the standard is beyond all reasonable doubt.

In *Reay and Hope*, the court had no reservations about basing a finding of causation mainly on epidemiological evidence; rather the court's concerns centred upon the validity of the Gardner study's methodology. This established a strong statistical association between PPI and childhood cancers; but this association was thrown into doubt by a number of methodological irregularities.

---

[15] Professor MacMahon, at p. 35 judgment.
[16] *Loveday* v. *Renton*, *The Times*, 31 March 1988.

For instance Gardner decided to accumulate information only on those born *and* diagnosed in West Cumbria, as opposed to all those diagnosed in the area, *after* he had begun to collect data. In the defendant's view, this alteration of the study's parameters constituted an 'epidemiological sin'.[17]

Concern was aroused that the study treated leukaemia and lymphoma as presentations of the same disease. The defendants submitted that they are essentially different diseases of the blood system, one originating in the bone marrow and the other deriving from lymphoid cells. French J. was persuaded by this argument. Accepting these various shortcomings, he stated:

Such criticisms do . . . diminish confidence in the study's conclusions and serve to underline the good sense of requiring that studies such as the Gardner study should be confirmed by one or more studies of the same or similar subject matter before much reliance can properly be placed on them.[18]

For this reason, and in 'an attempt to systematise common sense', he invoked a set of tests known as the Bradford-Hill criteria, often used to assess the validity of epidemiological evidence.[19] The various shortcomings of the Gardner report enhanced the significance of these criteria in questioning the report's findings.

On the first criterion, strength of association as a suggestion of causality, French J. considered that 'though an arithmetically strong prima facie association is shown to exist, considerable reserve is necessary before placing reliance upon it'.[20] In his view, other criteria of the Bradford-Hill test—consistency and biological plausibility—had considerable bearing on the extent to which the association can properly be regarded as strong enough to suggest causality.

The second criterion, 'consistency', requires that there be studies demonstrating similar results in comparable circumstances and with the same subject matter as the study in question. In this case, the Gardner study had to be found to be broadly consistent with other studies conducted in the Sellafield area, and with studies around similar nuclear installations in the United Kingdom and

---

[17] A further methodological question was posed by the 'Bristol case', in which a resident of Seascale was diagnosed as having leukaemia in Bristol where he had been for just a few weeks; in strict terms the case fell outside the ambit of the study, but Gardner included him.

[18] At p. 194.   [19] At p. 48.   [20] At p. 194.

around the world. Gardner's hypothesis was found to be inconsistent with a large follow-up study of children of atomic bomb victims at Hiroshima and Nagasaki who showed no excess of leukaemias.[21] The plaintiffs explained this inconsistency by recounting Seascale's unique circumstances—an unusually high proportion of incomers to the area, considerable rural isolation and discharges of radioactive material from Sellafield—'the best evidence in respect of West Cumbria remains the West Cumbrian studies'.[22] French J. dismissed their contention that the consistency criterion ought only to arise if the circumstances elsewhere are truly comparable and judged that Gardner's inconsistency with the atomic bomb studies was a serious shortcoming.

The third criterion of 'biological plausibility' raised two questions: the feasibility of the genetic mechanism *per se*, that radiation is capable of causing mutations of sperm and an inherited predisposition to cancer (the 'genetics' question); and, if the genetic mechanism is feasible, whether it can explain the excessive numbers of cancers in Seascale. On the 'genetics' question, the plaintiffs noted that since a number of syndromes known to be associated with an increased risk of leukaemia—Down's Syndrome, Bloom's Syndrome—are heritable, they may be relied upon as evidence that leukaemia or a predisposition to it is capable of being passed through a father's sperm. While accepting the plaintiffs' argument, French J. emphasised that the heritable component in explaining incidence of the diseases was very small.[23]

In light of marked inconsistencies with other studies in the area, particularly the atomic bomb data, the plaintiffs responded by proposing a theory of 'synergy' of genetic (preconception) factors and environmental radiation (postconception) factors. They contended that, though considered too low to account for the cancer cluster in Seascale *alone*, environmental radiation augmented the

[21] Gardner's theory was also inconsistent with Dr Leo Kinlen's 'biological mixing' hypothesis that it was an unidentified virus brought by construction workers and scientists moving into isolated areas to build and staff nuclear plants which triggered the leukaemias in a vulnerable host population.

[22] At p. 71. The plaintiffs also accounted for inconsistencies with the atomic bomb studies: data loss given the very difficult collecting circumstances; and some 'bizarre' results including no increased risk in respect of Downs Syndrome, the difference in leukaemia rates for Hiroshima as against Nagasaki and more recorded malformations in the group receiving low doses of radiation than in the high dose group.

[23] At p. 200.

PPI received by fathers working with radioactive materials, and also the total background radiation, to a level at which a 'second hit' might occur, causing cancer.

This theory explained many of the inconsistencies alleged of the Gardner report, namely that clusters of cancers were not equally apparent in each town in which Sellafield workers lived, and that the occurrence of the diseases declined with distance from Sellafield. The theory also supports the plaintiffs' assertion that the Sellafield circumstances are unlikely to be replicated elsewhere, not least Japan in the 1940s and 1950s.[24] Finally, the theory accords with understandings of cancer as a multi-causal disease.

Notwithstanding its strengths, French J. remained strongly critical of the plaintiffs' hypothesis of PPI acting in synergism with some other factor—most obviously environmental radiation. He dismissed it as 'pure speculation' and 'uncharted waters'[25] because it 'presupposes but does not *explain* the [data]',[26] that is it fails to explain the causal mechanism of PPI underlying the statistical association that Gardner established.

In addition to a broad acceptance of the various methodological shortcomings of the study and a corresponding emphasis upon the Bradford-Hill criteria, an important feature of French J.'s treatment of statistical and scientific evidence was his uncritical acceptance of data submitted by the nuclear industry. In considering conflicting evidence as to plutonium emissions from the plant, he accepted that 'it is probable that the defendants, like any other undertaker whose activities may cause pollution, would prefer uncomfortable facts to be presented in their most favourable light', but decided that the probity and competence of the BNFL scientists called as expert witnesses 'is beyond question'.[27] He stated:

I am satisfied that I can rely on their evidence to the extent that they [experts for the defence] were doing their honest and expert best to put the full picture regarding environmental dose before the court.[28]

Similarly, in the course of the hearing, one expert witness' report had the effect of quantifying the radiation received by Mr Reay and Mr Hope. In response to the plaintiffs' submission, that to correspond with their evidence the quantities received should be multiplied by a factor of three, French J. reiterated that BNFL's

[24] At p. 80.   [25] At p. 203.   [26] Id. (emphasis added).
[27] At p. 28.   [28] At p. 35.

scientific experts were reliable and the figures they gave were likely to be overestimated rather than underestimated.

In his treatment of epidemiological and scientific evidence relating to causation the judge tended to accept unquestionably the defendant's data whilst imposing more restrictive requirements upon the plaintiffs' evidence.

Causation and common sense

Toxic tort cases have a number of features which tend to make proof of causation difficult: injuries often take a long time to develop after initial exposure to the substance and are frequently caused in ways other than by exposure to the 'accused' pollutant or toxin. In addition, statistical and scientific evidence relating to the causal mechanisms between exposure and injury is rarely definitive and commonly at variance.[29] Such cases pose a challenge to the courts to ensure that plaintiffs will not be deprived of relief when justified, by reason of the complexities of proving causation.

In considering causation in *Reay and Hope*, French J. rejected the plaintiffs' synergy thesis as 'pure speculation'. As mentioned, he did so on the ground that the PPI thesis 'presupposes but does not *explain* the [Gardner data]'.[30] The judge has been rebuked for imposing this restrictive test of causation, which, according to one view, stems from his inability to accept causation in the absence of a detailed biological explanation of the PPI/leukaemia/lymphoma association.[31] A review of case law suggests that the higher courts have not found an absence of a scientific *explanation* of the causal mechanism underlying an association fatal to a plaintiff's claim once that association has been prima facie proven. Pugh and Day describe this as 'the use of common sense to fill gaps where scientific understanding is incomplete' and consider that the approach 'has a perfectly respectable legal pedigree'.[32]

Bonnington Castings v. *Wardlaw* [1956] AC 613 is the genesis of a common sense approach to causation. In deciding whether an employee's pneumoconiosis had been caused by silica dust, the House of Lords held that the plaintiff need not establish on the balance of probabilities that the 'accused' material was the only source of injury, that is fulfil the traditional test that 'but for' the

---

[29] J. M. Williams, *supra*, at 331.
[30] At p. 203, (emphasis added).
[31] Wilkinson *supra*, at 23.
[32] Pugh and Day, Op. cit., p. 52.

defendant's tortious conduct, the plaintiff would not have sustained the injury complained of. Rather the plaintiff need only fulfil a lesser requirement that on a balance of probabilities the defendant's act 'materially contributed' to the injury complained of.[33]

The requirement that a defendant's act 'caused or materially contributed to the injury complained of' was interpreted by the House of Lords in *McGhee* v. *National Coal Board* [1972] 3 All ER 1008 as being broadly equivalent to a test that the defendant creates a 'material increase in the risk of injury'. In this case, experts were unable to decide whether the provision of a shower by employers to allow employees to wash their skin of brick dust would have prevented an employee from contracting dermatitis; but they were prepared to find that showering off the dust would have materially *reduced the risk* of the disease. According to Lord Salmon, to decide other than this would mean 'in the present state of medical knowledge . . . an employer would be permitted by the law to disregard with impunity his duty to take reasonable care for the safety of his employees'.[34]

The development of this liberal test for establishing causation was evaluated and arrested in *Wilsher* v. *Essex Area Health Authority* [1988] 2 WLR 557. The plaintiff claimed that medical treatment received by him from the defendants had caused him to suffer excess oxygen as a premature baby; and this had caused or materially contributed to his blindness and impaired hearing. However excess oxygen was not a definite or the only possible cause of injury; a number of conditions from which premature babies suffer may also have caused the plaintiff's injury.[35] The House of Lords found that the test in *McGhee* which approximated an increased *risk* of injury with a 'material contribution' to the injury did not lay down a new principle of law, but rather was a 'robust and pragmatic'[36] approach to the existing *Bonnington* test. It was argued by Lord Bridge that the apparent extension of the test in *McGhee* was based upon the majority's finding in that case that it was a *legitimate inference of fact* that the employer's negligence had materially contributed to the employee's dermatitis.[37]

---

[33] *Bonnington Castings* v. *Wardlaw* [1956] AC 613, per Lord Reid, at 621.
[34] *McGhee* v. *National Coal Board* [1972] 3 All ER 1008, at 1018.
[35] *Wilsher* v. *Essex Area Health Authority* [1988] WLR 557, at 561.
[36] Ibid., at 569.   [37] Id.

Notwithstanding his restrictive interpretation of the test of 'increased risk', *obiter dictum*, Lord Bridge restated the principle set out in *McGhee* that the fact that experts cannot identify the precise mechanism of causation should not preclude the court making an inference on the facts of the case that a defendant's negligence materially contributed to a plaintiff's injury. Referring to the circumstances in *McGhee* he states:

. . . where the layman is told by the doctors that the longer the brick dust remains on the body, the greater the risk of dermatitis, although the doctors cannot identify the process of causation scientifically, there seems to be nothing irrational in drawing the *inference as a matter of common sense*, that the consecutive periods when brick dust remained on the body probably contributed *cumulatively* to the causation of the dermatitis. I believe that a process of inferential reasoning on these general lines underlies the decision of the majority in McGhee's case.[38]

An approach to causation based upon the inference of fact as a matter of common sense has been applied in other jurisdictions. In *Snell* v. *Farrell* [1990] 72 DLR (4th) 289, the plaintiff lost the sight of one eye following an operation on it performed by the defendant surgeon; medical witnesses could not say positively that the surgeon's action was the cause. The Supreme Court of Canada considered that the evidence adduced by the plaintiff was sufficient to support an inference of causation despite the absence of positive medical opinion. In so deciding, the court lent support to the dictum of Lord Bridge in *Wilsher*, describing it as: 'a robust and pragmatic approach to the facts to enable an inference of negligence to be drawn even though medical or scientific expertise cannot arrive at a definitive conclusion'.[39]

It is therefore possible to draw support for a common sense approach to causation from case law on occupational diseases, as in *McGhee*, and medical negligence, as in *Snell*. In *Hanrahan* v. *Merck Sharp and Dohme* [1988] 8 IR 629, the Irish Supreme Court, gives support for its adoption in toxic tort cases. A chemical factory was built one mile from the plaintiffs' farm. Within a few years the plaintiffs began to suffer severe ill-health; their cattle and crops were similarly affected. The court held that the circumstances of the case and the plaintiffs' primary evidence of their

---

[38] Ibid., at 567, (emphasis added).
[39] *Snell* v. *Farrell* [1990] 72 DLR (4th) 289, at 297.

injuries were such that a causal link between the defendant's activities and the plaintiffs' ill-health was proved. Henchy J. stated that the defendant's scientific evidence that damage to the farm animals could not be linked directly to chemicals emanating from the factory should not be allowed to displace the proven facts:

> It would be to allow scientific theorising to dethrone fact to dispose of this claim by saying . . . that there was 'virtually no evidence in this case of injury to human beings or animals which has been scientifically linked to any chemicals emanating from the defendant's factory' . . . the most credible explanation offered for the ailments and abnormalities in the cattle was the toxic emissions from the factory.[40]

Arguably, an approach based upon the inference of fact as a matter of common sense should be applicable only in cases concerned with a (single) known cause. For example, Wilkinson considers that in *Reay and Hope* it would not have been legitimate for the court to infer that PPI 'materially contributed' to the injury since it was not clear that PPI alone had caused the plaintiffs' cancers. His argument is that in *McGhee* there was only one known cause of dermatitis at issue—brick dust; whereas in *Wilsher* many possible causes of injury were present, raising problems in distinguishing between causing an increased risk of the plaintiff's condition and a 'material contribution' to it.[41] On the other hand, whilst clearly relevant, the number of possible causes of an injury must also be considered in light of their potential for cumulative effects: in *Reay and Hope* the factors examined—environmental radiation and PPI—were likely to act *cumulatively*; in *Wilsher* the alternative conditions likely to cause the plaintiff's injury were capable of acting quite independently. On this basis, the factors in *Reay and Hope* acting in 'synergy' distinguish the case from *Wilsher*. As such a broad—some might say liberal—approach to causation premised on a legitimate inference of fact may still properly have been adopted in this case.

---

[40] *Hanrahan* v. *Merck Sharp and Dohme* [1988] 8 IR 629, at 645. See B. McMahon and W. Binchy, (1990) *Irish law of Torts* pp. 142–144, at 144; they consider that under Henchy J.'s approach 'the inferential conclusion has become, in effect, a premise'.

[41] The House in *Wilsher* approved Browne-Wilkinson LJ's dissenting judgment in the Court of Appeal, [1986] 3 All ER 801, at 834–835, which distinguishes *McGhee* on the basis that it was concerned with only 'one possible agent' as the cause of harm.

To summarise, in *Hope and Reay* French J.'s requirement that an *explanation* of the causal mechanism underlying the Gardner association was necessary for the plaintiffs to succeed is wholly out of step with the treatment of questions of causation in occupational disease, medical negligence and toxic tort case law in the United Kingdom and other jurisdictions. In *Bonnington*, *McGhee*, and *Wilsher*, questions of causation were resolved according to whether a 'legitimate inference of fact' may be drawn, even in the absence of a definitive, scientific explanation of the causal mechanism underlying a proven association. Pugh and Day note: 'Courts apply common sense to the issue of causation and the fact that the exact causal mechanisms are not known to science should not be an insuperable hurdle where primary evidence allows a common sense inference to be drawn'.[42]

Epidemiological evidence of causation accords with the civil standard of proof, the balance of probabilities. In requiring a scientific explantion of the association, French J. demanded a higher standard of causation, similar to the criminal standard of proof, beyond all reasonable doubt, in the context of an action in tort. Furthermore, his simplistic appeal to '*explain*' the causal mechanism underlying the association suggests a misunderstanding of the complex and multifactorial nature of leukaemia and lymphoma. In future toxic tort cases, the adoption of a common sense approach to causation might better be secured by the promotion of the 'precautionary principle'.

The precautionary principle

The precautionary principle reverses the traditional understanding that environmental damage must be proved before action is taken; instead, only when there is sufficient proof that no environmental damage will occur should there be a failure to take action.[43] As yet the precautionary principle operates as a general principle of policy and law-making in the European Union[44] and is the subject of a number of declarations in international law.[45] It is clearly applicable

---

[42] Pugh and Day, Op. cit., p. 4.

[43] See N. Haigh, 'The Precautionary Principle in British Environmental Policy', Institute for European Environmental Policy Paper, (1993).

[44] Art. 130r(2) of the Treaty of Rome as amended.

[45] The principle constitutes Principle 15 of the Rio Declaration 1992; see J. Cameron

to the promulgation of anticipatory measures. But its essence, that the lack of full scientific certainty shall not be used as a reason for barring action pursuant to environmental protection, suggests that it might be applied in a number of different respects. These are considered by Hession and Macrory:

> As the precautionary principle has relevance to liability and evidence principles there may here be the germ of a justification for provisions providing for strict liability or an alteration of the rules of evidence in environmental liability and licensing cases.[46]

In the field of toxic tort claims, the precautionary principle might usefully guide judicial treatment of evidence on the basis that, providing an association is established between an environmental harm and an injury, lack of full scientific certainty should not necessarily constitute a bar to a successful action. A parallel might therefore be drawn with the current requirement that absence of scientific certainty in policy making cannot be used as a reason for postponing measures which might prevent environmental degradation.

In *Reay and Hope*, French J. was inconsistent in his treatment of evidence lacking full scientific certainty. On occasion he rejected uncertain evidence; on others he accepted it, albeit cautiously. For example, scientific and medical evidence is divided on whether leukaemia and lymphoma are separate diseases. With no appeal to guiding principles, he declared:

> The evidence on either side [whether lymphoma and leukaemia are to be treated as the same disease] . . . was so evenly balanced that the *question remains an open question*. It may well be that advances in scientific knowledge will enable a definite answer to be given in the future . . . but, as matters stand, I can only say that I am not satisfied that leukaemia and lymphoma are properly to be regarded as a single disease for the purposes of this case.[47]

This finding had the effect of throwing Gardner's methodology into doubt and was fatal to the plaintiffs' claim:

and J. D. Werksman, (1991) 'The Precautionary Principle: A Policy For Action in the Face of Uncertainty', CIEL Background Paper on International Environmental Law; see also P. W. Birnie and A. E. Boyle, (1993) *International Law and the Environment*, pp. 95–98.

[46] M. Hession and R. Macrory, 'Maastricht and the Environmental Policy of the Community: Legal Issues of a New Environment Policy', in D. O'Keefe and P. Twomey (1994) (eds.) *Legal Issues of the Maastricht Treaty*, pp. 151–167, at 156.

[47] At p. 210 (emphasis added).

If NHL [lymphoma] be considered on its own there is virtually no evidence to suggest, let alone prove, an association, certainly not a causal association, between PPI and [lymphoma].[48]

Yet faced with conflicting evidence about whether the cancers were capable of being inherited, he was prepared to find that: 'even though the *evidence* for the proposition was hard to seek . . . for the purposes of this judgment . . . *there is a heritable component* for the two diseases'.[49] This conclusion was not however very useful to the plaintiffs since he qualified it by stating that the heritable component is very small.

Scientific evidence is often so complex and contradictory that judgments might be more *consistent* if made according to an overriding and guiding principle of 'precaution', rather than in a vacuum awaiting 'a definite answer to be given in the future'.[50] Admittedly, the general application of a precautionary approach to the treatment of conflicting scientific evidence in toxic tort cases represents a significant departure from its previous use in policy formation, but it would also represent an acknowledgment that a lack of full scientific certainty or an absence of a scientific *explanation* of a causal link should not constitute a bar to a successful action in the event that a prima facie association between harm and injury is established.

Shifting the burden of proof

Shifting the burden of proof remains a further possible reform in toxic tort cases. Day advocates shifting the burden of proof to the defendant to disprove causation once the plaintiff has established a prima facie association on the ground that it might create a 'decent balance in these cases'.[51] *Reay and Hope* offers a good example of the possibilities of this reform since French J. clearly accepted that an arithmetically strong prima facie association between PPI and the diseases existed.[52]

In civil cases, including action for breach of statutory duty, the burden of proof is allocated according to two broad principles: the onus is on the party who asserts a proposition, usually the plaintiff; and where the subject-matter of the allegation lies particularly

[48] Id.   [49] At p. 200 (emphasis added).   [50] At p. 210.
[51] M. Day, interview, 4 March 1994.   [52] At p. 194.

within the knowledge of one party, that party may be required to prove it. Whilst usually falling upon the plaintiff, the allocation of the burden of proof is not immutable.[53] In *Vyner* v. *Waldenberg Bros.* [1946] KB 50, the Court of Appeal accepted Scott LJ's proposition that, if an employee has proved a breach of statutory duty by his employer and injury to himself, the defendant had the burden of establishing that the precaution would not have averted the accident. Scott LJ stated that this principle 'lies at the very basis of statutory rules of absolute duty'.[54]

This principle was rejected as erroneous in *Bonnington Castings* v. *Wardlaw* [1956] AC 613 in favour of the general rule that, regardless of the type of action, the burden always rests with the plaintiff to prove that the particular precaution would more probably than not have averted the injury. It was, though, resurrected and reasserted by Lord Wilberforce in *McGhee*, in the only speech to advocate a reversal of the burden of proof:

. . . it is a sound principle that where a person has, by breach of duty of care, created a risk, and injury occurs within the area of that risk, the loss should be borne by him unless he shows that it had some other cause.[55]

Lord Wilberforce advocated this as an alternative to the approach adopted by the majority, which, as noted already, is a legitimate inference of fact as a matter of common sense, though described by him as 'something of a fiction'.[56]

Two theories of causation emerge from the speeches of the House of Lords in *McGhee*:[57] the first, expressed by Lord Wilberforce, that the plaintiff need only prove that the defendant created a risk of harm and that the injury occurred within the area of the risk; the second, that in these circumstances, an inference of causation is warranted. The second theory has consistently found favour with the courts, even in cases in which it might be argued that the subject matter of the allegation lies particularly within the defendant's knowledge, such as medical negligence cases.[58]

---

[53] *Snell* v. *Farrell* [1990] 72 DLR (4th) 289, per Sopinka J., at 294.

[54] *Vyner* v. *Waldenberg Bros.* [1946] KB 50, at 55.

[55] *McGhee* v. *National Coal Board* [1972] 3 All ER 1008, at 1012.

[56] Ibid., at 1013.

[57] The two theories of causation are expressed by Sopinka J. in *Snell* v. *Farrell* [1990] 72 DLR (4th) 289, at 296.

[58] For example, in *Wilsher*, Op. cit., at 567, Lord Bridge, delivering the unanimous judgment of the House of Lords, reaffirmed the principle that the burden of

The reluctance to entertain a reversal of the burden of proof in 'workmen' cases, thus imposing on the defendant employer the burden of proving that his or her violation of a statutory duty was not causal, is the subject of criticism. For example, Fleming argues that the failure to accept this 'plausible proposition' has produced inconsistency and incongruity.[59]

Furthermore, the principle of reversal of the burden of proof has been accepted to some extent in the doctrine of *res ipsa loquitur*: this is applied in cases where there is prima facie evidence of negligence, the precise cause of the incident cannot be shown, but it is more probable than not that an act or omission of the defendant caused it and the act or omission arose from a failure to take proper care for the plaintiff's safety.

Prospects for future cases

A number of cases relating to environmental radiation—a more recognised and understood cause of cancers than genetic links—are pending following the publication of studies not available at the time that *Reay and Hope* was heard. In respect of future cases based on genetic links between radiation and cancers, the Gardner thesis has been confirmed by a study conducted by the Health and Safety Executive on leukaemias and other cancers in children of Sellafield workers, published just twelve days after the judgment of *Reay and Hope* was given. The Executive found a statistical link between children with these cancers and radiation doses received by fathers who worked at the plant. As in the Gardner report, it states 'We cannot find any single factor which satisfactorily *explains* what we have seen in West Cumbria . . . all we have is statistical associations'.[60]

Reay and Hope confirmed the acceptance of epidemiological studies as evidence of associations between environmental harms and injury. The case should therefore give qualified hope to plaintiffs in future toxic tort cases. Its judicial validation of epidemiology might

proving causation rested on the plaintiff; this was strictly followed by the Supreme Court of Canada in *Snell* v. *Farell*, Op. cit.

[59] J. G. Fleming, (1983) *The Law of Torts*, (6th ed.), at p. 485.

[60] Health and Safety Executive (1993) *HSE Investigation of Leukaemia and other Cancers in the Children of Male Workers at Sellafield*.

encourage cases to be brought for contamination of water by cryp-
tosporidium and toxic chemicals.[61]

The case highlights the difficulty confronting plaintiffs in toxic
tort actions of proving causation in relation to diseases involving a
complex combination of 'hits' or causes. This difficulty is by no
means surprising given that the legal framework of causation in
actions for breach of statutory duty was developed in the context
of 'workmen' cases in which, typically, there is a single and easily
identifiable source of harm. In future, it is hoped that courts continue to resolve questions of causation according to a legitimate
inference of fact as a matter of common sense even in the case of
complex diseases such as lymphoma and leukaemia, rather than
gloss over this complexity with an appeal to 'explain' the causal
mechanism underlying even a strong statistical association. In such
cases, scientific evidence might be treated more consistently under a
guiding principle of precaution. That would encourage the view
that even in the absence of conclusive scientific evidence, once an
association has been established it is more prudent to act as though
a statistical association is causal than to assume it is not.

Representing a related, but nonetheless distinct, theory of causation, shifting the burden of proof in toxic tort cases might redress
the evidential balance between plaintiff and defendant, not on the
ground of expert and special knowledge, as has been argued in
medical negligence cases, but rather on the basis of the inherent
difficulty of establishing causation in cases arising from environmental harms.

Reay and Hope exposes legal and technical issues of causation
in toxic torts. But it also acts as a reminder that cases such as this
are heard in the broad context of policy. Notwithstanding that
French J. made clear he was not concerned with the merits or
demerits of nuclear power, the case was influenced by energy policy. In turn, the case itself has had significant effects on this area
of policy: the judgment effectively cleared the way for a major
review of nuclear power to begin, planned at the time of the privatisation debacle. Futhermore, the tenor of the judgment lent
approval to the defendant's activities and competence. Thorp's
licence of operation at Sellafield was granted just weeks after the
judgment in *Reay and Hope* was given: arguably, success for the

---

[61] Wilkinson, *supra*, p. 25; see also [1992] *Water Law* and [1993] *Water Law* 115.

plaintiffs on grounds that radiation emissions from Sellafield had caused, or materially contributed to, childhood cancers in the surrounding villages would have rendered Thorp politically untenable.[62]

[62] I would like to thank greatly Jenny Cooksey, Martyn Day and Sue Elworthy for their help and comments.

THE DOCTOR AS FIDUCIARY*

Andrew Grubb†

I. The fiduciary relationship

A fiduciary relationship is a very special legal relationship. It arises when a person (the beneficiary) entrusts another (the fiduciary) with a power which may affect the beneficiary's interests and which is to be exclusively exercised for the beneficiary's benefit.[1] Fiduciary law is a creature of the courts of equity. Even though fiduciary law has frequently been deployed to remedy perceived injustices, the judges have offered no precise definition of when a fiduciary relationship exists.[2] Instead, they have offered indicia of the relationship: for example, it is one of 'trust', 'reliance', 'vulnerability', 'selflessness' and 'loyalty'.[3] It is well nigh impossible to give a comprehensive definition but the judgment of Mason J. in an important Australian case[4] offers a number of relevant factors:

---

* In preparing the lecture for publication I have retained, in large part, the style appropriate to a lecture while taking this opportunity to expand upon a number of points I originally made and by providing citations and further references for the reader.

† Professor of Health Care Law, School of Law, King's College, London.

[1] See discussion in the leading works on fiduciaries: P. D. Finn, *Fiduciary Obligations* (1977) and J. C. Shepherd, *Law of Fiduciaries* (1981). See also, R. P. Meagher, W. M. C. Gummow and J. R. F. Lehane, *Equity: Doctrines and Remedies* (3rd ed) (1992) ch 5 and Goff and Jones, *The Law of Restitution* (4th ed, 1993), especially ch 33.

[2] See, *Ex parte Dale* (1879) 11 Ch D 772 at 778 per Fry J.; *Re Coomber* [1911] 1 Ch 723 at 728 per Fletcher Moulton LJ. More recently see, *Re Craig (deceased)* [1970] 2 All ER 390 at 395–6 per Ungoed-Thomas J.; L. S. Sealy, 'Fiduciary Relationships.' [1962] *CLJ* 69 and 'Some Principles of Fiduciary Obligation' [1963] *CLJ* 119.

[3] See, P. D. Finn, 'The Fiduciary Principle' in T. G. Youdan (ed), *Equity, Fiduciaries and Trusts* (1989) 1 *passim*.

[4] *Hospital Products Ltd* v. *United States Surgical Corporation* (1984) 156 CLR 41 (HC Aust) at 96–7 per Mason J. For similar statements in Canada see, *Frame* v. *Smith* (1987) 42 DLR (4th) 81 (SCC) at 99 per Wilson J. and *LAC Minerals Ltd* v. *International Corona Resources Ltd* (1989) 61 DLR (4th) 14 (SCC) at 28 per La Forest J. and at 62 per Sopinka J.; *Canson Enterprises Ltd* v. *Boughton & Co* (1991)

'relationships of trust and confidence or confidential relations'; 'the fiduciary undertakes or agrees to act for or on behalf of or in the interests of another person . . .'; 'exercise of a power or discretion which will affect the interests of [an] other person in a legal or practical sense' such that the other person is 'vulnerable to abuse by the fiduciary of his position'. In *Reading* v. *R*[5] Asquith LJ illustrated the breadth of circumstances where the special relationship might arise:

a 'fiduciary relation' exists (a) whenever the plaintiff entrusts to the defendant property, including intangible property as, for instance, confidential information, and relies on the defendant to deal with such property for the benefit of the plaintiff or for purposes authorized by him, and not otherwise . . . and (b) whenever the plaintiff entrusts to the defendant a job to be performed . . . and relies on the defendant to procure the best terms available . . .[6]

Fiduciary law imposes high standards of conduct upon fiduciaries when they have control of the beneficiary's property. The distinguished Canadian Chief Justice, Bora Laskin captured the essence of the special nature of the fiduciary's obligation when he said it 'betokens loyalty, good faith and avoidance of a conflict of duty and self-interest'.[7] In particular, the fiduciary will owe the beneficiary a *duty of loyalty*.[8] Consequently, in exercising the power vested in him, the fiduciary must always endeavour to act in good faith and in the 'best interests' of the beneficiary. Fiduciary law seeks to proscribe 'selfish' conduct by the fiduciary and prevent his abusing the trust confided in him.[9] Transactions between the fiduciary and the beneficiary will be closely scrutinised. There will be a presumption that the fiduciary has exercised undue influence which he will have to rebut if the transaction is to stand.[10] More importantly, perhaps, the fiduciary may not put himself in a position where his (or others) interests are allowed to conflict with those of the beneficiary. He may not gain at the expense of the beneficiary.

85 DLR (4th) 129 (SCC) at 155 per McLachlin J., (Lamer CJC and L'Heureux Dubé J. concurring).

[5] [1949] 2 KB 232 (CA); and on appeal [1951] AC 507 (HL).

[6] Ibid., at 236.

[7] *Canadian Aero Service Ltd* v. *O'Malley* (1973) 40 DLR (3d) 371 at 382 per Laskin CJ.

[8] See, P. D. Finn, *supra*, note 3 at 27–31 and J. C. Shepherd, op. cit., at 47–48 and ch 6 *passim*.

[9] See, Goff and Jones, op. cit., ch 33.   [10] See, Goff and Jones, ibid., ch 10.

Hence, the courts may, for example, strip the fiduciary of any profits gained from the use of the beneficiary's property or in dealings with the beneficiary's interests whether honestly[11] or dishonestly[12] obtained. Further he may not take advantage of confidential information received when a fiduciary.[13]

The fiduciary's duty of loyalty is more onerous and more extensive than legal obligations derived from the principles of, for example, tort or contract law.[14] More significantly, the focus of the fiduciary law is distinct from these other areas of the law. The legal rules of contract and tort law are premised on the fact that the parties are at arms length or at least primarily concerned with their own self-interest.[15] The law then seeks to balance the competing interests in setting legal standards, for example, of reasonable care in the tort of negligence.[16] The essential qualities of the fiduciary's obligations are, as we have seen, focused upon the beneficiary. The duty of loyalty exists to protect and further the interests of the beneficiary and the need to avoid or restrain abuse of this obligation by the fiduciary.

II. The doctor–patient relationship

The doctor–patient relationship is a special relationship based upon trust and confidence reposed by the patient in the doctor.[17] The patient seeks treatment or advice from the doctor and as part of the consultation will disclose intimate and personal information

---

[11] For example, *Guiness plc* v. *Saunders* [1990] 2 AC 663 (HL).

[12] *Attorney General for Hong Kong* v. *Reid* [1994] 1 All ER 1 (PC).

[13] For example, *Boardman* v. *Phipps* [1967] 2 AC 46 (HL).

[14] For a discussion of the relationship between tortious, contractual and fiducial obligations see, T. Frankel, 'Fiduciary Law' (1983) 71 *Cal L Rev* 795; P. D. Finn, *supra*, note 3 at 27–31.

[15] *Norberg* v. *Wynrib* (1992) 92 DLR (4th) 449 at 488 per McLachlin J. (SCC).

[16] Hence, the courts in England are less ready, even chary, of recognising a fiduciary relationship exists between commercial entities: see, Goff and Jones, op. cit. at 644. Contrast *Chase Manhattan NA* v. *Israel-British Bank (London) Ltd* [1981] 1 Ch 105. But the reluctance is less marked in Canada (see, Hon Beverley McLachlin, 'The Place of Equity and Equitable Doctrines in the Contemporary Common Law World: A Canadian Perspective' in *Equity, Fiduciaries and Trusts* (ed D. W. M. Waters) (1993) 37 at 40–44) and, though to a lesser extent, in Australia (see, Rt Hon Sir Anthony Mason (1994) 110 LQR 238 at 245–6).

[17] See, for example, *Kenny* v. *Lockwood* [1932] 1 DLR 507 (Ont CA) at 519–20 per Hodgins JA. See generally, J. Katz, *The Silent World of Doctor and Patient* (1984), and especially ch 4.

to the doctor. The doctor uses that information to advise and help the patient with his illness or complaint. The patient relies upon the doctor for help and places his trust in the doctor to act in his best interests. In so doing the patient exposes himself to the danger of exploitation and bad faith dealing. The patient is in a position of vulnerability: he is both trusting and in need of help. An asymmetry in the relationship exists which stems from the imbalance in knowledge and power vested in the doctor through his training and his position as the patient's doctor.

1. A FIDUCIARY RELATIONSHIP?—THE PROPERTY CASES

In fact, therefore, the doctor–patient relationship displays many of the hall-marks of a fiduciary relationship. Is it in law a fiduciary relationship? The quintessential fiduciary relationship is that of trustee and *cestui que trust*. Courts have tended to develop fiduciary relationships by analogy to this paradigm while expanding the range of fiduciary relationships more widely.[18] In particular, professional and other advisers who enjoy a confidential relationship with their client are often held to owe fiduciary duties. Hence, solicitors,[19] bankers[20] and even priests[21] have been held to be fiduciaries. Usually, these relationships will involve the property or financial affairs of the beneficiary. On the whole, of course, the relationship between the doctor and her patient will be concerned solely with more 'personal' interests.

Sometimes, however, the doctor will be dealing with the patient's property. When this has been so English law has long recognised that the doctor will be in a fiduciary position vis-à-vis her patient.[22] Hence, a doctor who receives property from a patient as an *inter vivos* gift will be held to do so in a fiduciary capacity.[23]

[18] See generally, P. D. Finn, *supra*, note 3 and J. C. Shepherd, op. cit., ch 2.

[19] *McMaster* v. *Byrne* [1952] 1 All ER 1362 (PC) (former solicitor).

[20] *Lloyd's Bank Ltd* v. *Bundy* [1975] QB 326 (CA).

[21] *Huguenin* v. *Basely* [1803–13] All ER Rep 1; *Allcard* v. *Skinner* (1887) 36 Ch D 145 (mother superior) and T. Frankel 'Fiduciary Relationship in the United States Today' in *Equity, Fiduciary and Trusts* (ed D. W. M. Waters) (1993) 174 at 186–7.

[22] For example, *Dent* v. *Bennett* (1839) 41 ER 105 and *Mitchell* v. *Homfray* (1881) 8 QBD 587; *Billage* v. *Southee* (1852) 9 Hare 534; *Gibson* v. *Russell* (1843) 63 ER 46; *Adhearne* v. *Hogan* (1844) Dru temp Sug 320; *Radcliffe* v. *Price* (1902) 18 TLR 466. Contrast, *Brooks* v. *Aker* (1975) 9 OR (2d) 409 (dentist not a fiduciary).

[23] The presumption does not arise in the case of bequests made by will: *Hall* v. *Hall* (1868) LR 1 P & D 481 and discussion by P. V. Baker (1970) 86 LQR 447.

As a consequence, a presumption of undue influence will be made against the doctor because of the nature of the relationship being one of trust and confidence. The court will set aside the gift unless the doctor can rebut the presumption by, for example, proving that the gift was freely made after 'full, free and informed thought about it'.[24] The court will take account of all the circumstances including whether the beneficiary has received independent advice before making the gift.[25]

There are many cases in the books in the main dating back to the nineteenth century.[26] However, as recently as last year the House of Lords in *Barclays Bank* v. *O'Brien*[27] (a case concerned with undue influence by a husband over his wife) confirmed that the doctor–patient relationship is *capable* of being characterised as a fiduciary one and giving rise to a presumption of undue influence.[28] The case of *Williams* v. *Johnson*[29] in 1937 illustrates the point. The defendant attended the plaintiff, an elderly widow professionally as her doctor. After she recovered her health she conveyed to him the freehold in some land. Subsequently, she regretted her decision and she sought to have the transaction set aside. The Privy Council held that the relationship of doctor and patient was a confidential relationship whereby a presumption of undue influence arose. However, on the facts, the Privy Council held that the doctor had established that the gift was the free exercise of independent will 'by the plaintiff who was an intelligent, astute and strong-willed woman'.

What the undue influence cases do not tell us is whether the fiduciary relationship may extend beyond property or financial advice cases. The history of fiduciary obligations makes plain that the fiduciary usually did deal with (or have control of) the beneficiary's property. But the law has not ossified there. It is from the nature of the relationship and not its subject-matter which springs the fiduciary duty. Thus, fiduciary law extends to situations where confidential information is entrusted to another and he uses it to his own advantage. No doubt a doctor would be held accountable as a fiduciary if he obtained commercially valuable information

---

[24] *Zamet* v. *Hyman* [1961] 1 WLR 1442 at 1444 per Lord Evershed MR.
[25] See generally, Goff and Jones, op. cit., ch 10 and R. P. Meagher, W. M. C. Gummow and J. R. F. Lehane, *Equity Doctrines & Remedies* (3rd ed) (1992) ch 15.
[26] Ibid., note 22.   [27] [1993] 4 All ER 417 (HL).
[28] Ibid., at 423 per Lord Browne-Wilkinson.   [29] [1937] 4 All ER 34 (PC).

during a consultation which he then exploited for his own gain.[30] But beyond this, in one important respect English law has already accepted the fiduciary duty of a doctor outside the property or financial advice cases. It is in the law of confidentiality. The legal duty to respect a patient's confidences is well recognised and stems from the relationship of trust between confider (the patient) and confidant (the doctor).[31] The action for breach of confidence is an equitable claim.[32] It has all the hall-marks of being an aspect of the fiduciary duty of loyalty owed by a doctor to his patient.[33]

2. A FIDUCIARY RELATIONSHIP?—BEYOND THE PROPERTY CASES

But let me now burst the bubble. English judges have so far been reluctant to impose a fiduciary duty upon a doctor outside of the traditional property-type cases. In *Sidaway* v. *Bethlem Royal Hospital Governors*[34] a patient suffered severe disability following an operation near her spinal cord. She claimed that the doctor should have advised her of the risk that this might happen. The House of Lords dismissed her action because the doctor did not have a duty to advise her of the risk prior to her agreeing to the operation. The precise contours of a doctor's duty of disclosure is not wholly clear from the case.[35] The Law Lords did not speak with one voice but offered four differing approaches. However one matter is clear, the doctor's duty to advise her patient was seen as growing out of the tort of negligence and the standard of the reasonable doctor. Two judges rejected any suggestion that the obligation to inform a patient of risks inherent in an operation was derived from the doctor's fiduciary duty. In the Court of Appeal,

[30] See, *SEC* v. *Willis* (1992) 787 F Supp 58 (SD NY) and T. Frankel, 'Fiduciary Relationship in the United States' in *Equity, Fiduciaries and Trusts* (ed D. W. M. Waters) (1993) 173 at 183.

[31] See, I. Kennedy and A. Grubb, *Medical Law: Text with Materials* (2nd ed) (1994) ch 9.

[32] *Attorney General* v. *Guardian Newspapers (No 2)* [1988] 3 All ER 545 at 658 per Lord Goff.

[33] See, A. Hopper, 'The Medical Man's Fiduciary Duty' (1973) *Law Teacher* 73: 'the most important consequences of the [medical] practitioner's fiduciary duty seems to be that he may not unjustifiably divulge confidential information which he has acquired professionally.' (at 73–4).

[34] [1985] 1 All ER 643 (HL).

[35] See discussion in I. Kennedy and A. Grubb, op. cit. at 173–216 and I. Kennedy, *Treat Me Right* (1991) ch 9.

Browne-Wilkinson LJ (as he then was) restricted the fiduciary duty of a doctor to cases where he 'abused his position of trust to make a personal profit for himself'.[36] This, for him, could have no application in *Sidaway*. When the case reached the House of Lords, Lord Scarman was even more dismissive, declaring that there was no comparison to be made between the relationship of doctor and patient and that of solicitor and client or the other relationships treated in equity as of a fiduciary character. He did this even though he recognised the 'very special' nature of the relationship: the patient 'putting his health and his life in the doctor's hands'.[37] Curiously, no other judge referred to the fiduciary argument made on Mrs Sidaway's behalf.

The judges in *Sidaway* propounded two limitations on fiduciary law which would be significant in doctor cases. First, a fiduciary relationship can only exist in property or financial advice cases. Arguably, this is merely to assert the orthodoxy. One can reflect at this point on the topsy-turvy nature of this area of the law. Generally, the law more jealously protects an individual's interest in his physical integrity than in his property or financial affairs.[38] Here, the normal order of proprieties is reversed. Secondly, Browne-Wilkinson LJ's thought that Mrs Sidaway could not rely upon the fiduciary argument because she was not alleging the doctor *abused* any duty owed to her. But this view surely only reflects one aspect of the fiduciary's duty of loyalty, namely not personally to benefit through a conflict of interest. Another aspect of the duty of loyalty is to act in good faith in the 'best interests' of the beneficiary. Could this not justify a claim by a beneficiary that he has a right or entitlement to some benefit (such as disclosure of information) being conferred upon him by the fiduciary?

III. Moving towards a fiduciary relationship

The reluctance of the English courts to see the doctor as a fiduciary outside of the property cases has not been shared by other common law jurisdictions. It is recognised, for example, in the

---

[36] [1984] 1 All ER 1018 (CA) at 1031–2. Neither Sir John Donaldson MR or Dunn LJ referred to the 'fiduciary argument'.

[37] *Supra*, at 650–1.

[38] *Southport Corporation* v. *Esso Petroleum Co Ltd* [1953] 2 All ER 1204 at 1209–1210 per Devlin J.

United States,[39] New Zealand[40] and Canada.[41] In particular the fiduciary duty is used as a basis for imposing upon a doctor a duty to disclose information to his patient and for respecting a patient's confidences.

It is important to notice that there are two kinds of situation where a fiduciary duty might bite on the doctor–patient relationship: first, where the claim is that the fiduciary has exploited the beneficiary and *abused* his duty of loyalty (this is the usual claim in the property cases); and secondly, even if there is no abuse, where the beneficiary claims a *right* or *entitlement* to a benefit enforceable against the fiduciary, based upon his duty to act in the beneficiary's 'best interests'. The latter is a relatively unusual claim in the property cases but it would be very significant if the doctor were to be seen as a fiduciary. Most importantly, it would be relevant in cases where the patient asserted a right to information held or known by the doctor.

In two decisions of the Canadian Supreme Court in 1992— *Norberg* v. *Wynrib*[42] and *McInerney* v. *MacDonald*[43] the fiducial qualities of the doctor–patient relationship were explored. In neither case was the patients' property or financial interests implicated. In *Norberg* the action was for abuse or exploitation by the doctor. In *McInerney*, by contrast, the patient's action asserted a right or entitlement by the patient against the doctor to access to her medical records.

1. 'ABUSE' CASES

(a) Norberg *v.* Wynrib

In *Norberg* v. *Wynrib* the patient was addicted to pain-killers. She sought drugs from a number of doctors and elsewhere. The defendant, an elderly medical practitioner, prescribed pain-killers for her after she told him that her ankle, which she had broken the previ-

---

[39] For example, *Nixdorf* v. *Hicken* (1980) 612 P 2d 348 (Utah SC); *Cobbs* v. *Grant* (1972) 104 Cal Rptr 505 (Cal SC) and *Moore* v. *Regents of the University of California* (1990) 271 Cal Rptr 146 (Cal SC).

[40] *Smith* v. *Auckland Hospital Board* [1965] NZLR 191.

[41] *McInerney* v. *MacDonald* (1992) 93 DLR (4th) 415 (SCC); *Norberg* v. *Wynrib* (1992) 92 DLR (4th) 449 per McLachlin J. (L'Heureux-Dube J. concurring) and per Sopinka J. (to a more limited extent).

[42] (1992) 92 DLR (4th) 449.   [43] (1992) 93 DLR (4th) 415.

ous year, was hurting. On a number of occasions he prescribed pain-killers on the basis of this and other illnesses she claimed to be suffering from. Although he realised she was addicted, he continued to prescribe pain-killers and after a while he offered to provide drugs only if she agreed to allow him to kiss and fondle her sexually. She initially declined and sought drugs from other sources but eventually her dependence was such that she returned to the defendant and gave in to his demands. The defendant indulged in sexual acts with the patient on a number of occasions although sexual intercourse never took place. The patient sued the defendant seeking damages. She alleged that his conduct amounted to a battery, gave rise to an action in the tort of negligence and was a breach of his fiduciary duty. Her action was dismissed by the trial judge[44] and a majority of the British Columbia Court of Appeal.[45] On appeal to the Canadian Supreme Court, the lower court's judgment was reversed and the patient's claim for damages was upheld. However, the judges did so for different reasons.[46]

Justice La Forest (with whom Gonthier and Cory JJ agreed) held that the defendant had committed a battery on the patient. Although she had consented to the sexual acts, the patient's vulnerability as a drug-addict created a relationship of 'unequal power' between the parties and one which was 'exploitative' of the patient. As a consequence, applying the contract notions of 'unconscionability' and 'inequality of bargaining power', Justice La Forest held that the patient's consent was nullified.

Justice Sopinka, by contrast, was sceptical of applying the contract notions of 'inequality of bargaining power' and 'unconscionability' in a tort case. Crucially, he concluded that when it

---

[44] (1989) 50 DLR (4th) 167. Oppal J. dismissed the plaintiff's action in battery on the ground that she had consented; her claim in negligence on the ground that she had suffered no damage; and while accepting the basis of her claim for breach of fiduciary duty, he held that her conduct fell within the defence of *ex turpi causa non oritur actio*.

[45] (1990) 66 DLR (4th) 553. McEachern CJ and Gibbs JA rejected her claim in battery on the ground that she had consented; her claim for breach of fiduciary duty; and while accepting that she had suffered damage for the purposes of the tort of negligence, held that the defence of *ex turpi causa non oritur actio* applied. Locke JA (dissenting) disagreed with the majority's application of the defence of *ex turpi causa*.

[46] All the judges agreed in rejecting the application of the *ex turpi causa* defence: her conduct was not her fault because of her addition and vulnerability (*per* La Forest J. at 468–9; *per* Sopinka J. at 483–4; *per* McLachlin J. at 496–8). In the words of McLachlin J. '[s]he was not a sinner, but a sick person . . .' (at 496).

was applied, it did not have the effect of vitiating an individual's consent. Rather, it operated to impugn a consensual transaction. It could not, therefore, turn the doctor's conduct into a battery.[47] Instead, Sopinka J. held that the defendant was liable in the tort of negligence. He had clearly breached his duty of care to the patient by not treating her addiction and this had caused her damage in the sense that the addiction was thereby prolonged.

For our purposes the most interesting judgment is that of Justice McLachlin (with whom L'Heureux Dubé J. agreed). She rejected the approaches of the other judges. For her the orthodox claims in tort did not adequately 'capture the essential nature of the wrong done to the plaintiff'.[48] Instead, she relied upon the principles applicable to fiduciaries. Unlike Sopinka J. and the lower courts, she saw no reason to confine a doctor's fiduciary obligations to the duty to respect a patient's confidences.[49] In holding the defendant to be in breach of his fiduciary duty, her analysis followed 4 stages:

1. Was the doctor–patient relationship capable of being a fiduciary relationship?
2. Did a fiduciary relationship exist between Dr Wynrib and the patient?
3. Had Dr Wynrib breached his fiduciary duty?
4. What damages could the patient recovery for the equitable wrong?

Our interest is primarily in the first three stages of Justice McLachlin's analysis.

(1) WAS THE DOCTOR–PATIENT RELATIONSHIP CAPABLE OF BEING A FIDUCIARY ONE?

Justice McLachlin was in no doubt that it was. She remarked that 'the most fundamental characteristic of the doctor–patient relationship is its *fiduciary* nature.'[50] Like other fiduciary relationships recognised by the law, it had at its heart the

trust of a person with inferior power that another person who has assumed superior power and responsibility will exercise that power for his or her good and only for his or her good and in his or her best interests.[51]

---

[47] McLachlin J. agreed with Sopinka J. on this point (*supra* at 494).
[48] *Supra*, at 484.   [49] See, *supra*, at 480–1 per Sopinka J.
[50] *Supra*, at 486.   [51] *Supra*, at 486.

Justice McLachlin was not persuaded that fiduciary obligations should be restricted to the property or financial cases. Fiduciary principles were 'capable of protecting not only narrow legal and economic interests but [could] also serve to defend fundamental human and personal interests ...'[52] However, Justice McLachlin accepted that the doctor–patient relationship need not be a fiduciary one for *all* purposes. As with other fiduciaries it was necessary to ask whether the particular circumstances gave rise to fiduciary obligations.

(2) DID A FIDUCIARY RELATIONSHIP EXIST ON THE FACTS OF THE CASE?

She identified three crucial features of the relationship which made it a fiduciary one: (i) power in the doctor; (ii) that affects the patient's interests; and (iii) the vulnerability of the patient. She concluded:

Dr Wynrib was in a position of power vis-à-vis the plaintiff, he had scope for the exercise of power and discretion with respect to her. He had the power to advise her, to treat her, to give her the drug or to refuse her the drug. He could unilaterally exercise that power or discretion in a way that affected her interests. And her status as a patient rendered her vulnerable and at his mercy, particularly in the light of her addiction ... All the classic characteristics of a fiduciary relationship were present.[53]

Justice McLachlin concluded that as a fiduciary he owed his patient the duties of 'loyalty, good faith, and avoidance of a conflict of duty and self-interest.'[54]

(3) HAD DR WYNRIB BREACHED HIS FIDUCIARY DUTY?

On the facts there could be no doubt: he had abused his duty of loyalty and pledge to act in his patient's best interests by prescribing drugs when he knew he should not have, by taking advantage of her sexually when he should have been advising her to receive treatment for her addiction. Dr Wynrib had exploited his patient by putting 'his own interest in obtaining sexual favours ... above her interest in obtaining treatment and becoming well.'[55]

[52] *Supra*, at 499.   [53] *Supra*, at 489.
[54] Ibid., and at 495.   [55] *Supra*, at 495.

(b) Implications of the case

The analysis of Justice McLachlin is most persuasive. It is a veritable tour de force. It does not, however, provide all the answers and it leaves a number of issues unclear or unresolved. As she herself has subsequently remarked extra-judicially there may still be 'much work to be done in refining the limits' of this new approach.[56] Not least, one might think the nature of the remedies in such cases, including the calculation of compensation for the equitable wrong,[57] how (if at all) the rules of causation and foreseeability are relevant and what (if any) defence such as contributory negligence or illegality may be pleaded by the fiduciary.[58] There are a number of points I would like to make about the decision.

First, in one sense, *Norberg* is not a remarkable case. McLachlin J. herself 'sells' the case as not representing an extension of the law since it concerns a relationship which has long been characterised as a fiduciary one.[59] It is also, what might be called, a 'classic' fiduciary case in that it concerned an abuse of position by the fiduciary. To that extent it is analogous and entirely in keeping with the orthodox fiduciary cases where there has been exploitation by the fiduciary. But, this is to understate the innovative nature of Justice McLachlin's judgment in her willingness to move beyond the confines of property or financial interest cases and apply the fiduciary approach to protect the personal interests of an individual.

Secondly, there is, here, considerable scope for development. Subsequently, the Canadian Supreme Court in *M(K)* v. *M(H)*[60] held that a parent–child relationship was a fiduciary one such that a child incest victim could sue for breach of fiduciary duty.[61] The

---

[56] Hon Beverley McLachlin, 'The Place of Equity and Equitable Doctrines in the Contemporary Common Law World: A Canadian Perspective' in (D. W. M. Waters ed), *Equity, Fiduciaries and Trusts* (1993) 37 at 50.

[57] See the discussion by W. M. C. Gummow, 'Compensation for Breach of Fiduciary Duty' in T. G. Youdan (ed), *Equity, Fiduciaries and Trusts* (1989) 57.

[58] See, D. Davies, 'Equitable Compensation: "Causation, Foreseeability and Remoteness"' in D. W. M. Waters (ed), *Equity, Fiduciaries and Trusts* (1993) 297.

[59] *Supra*, at 501–2.

[60] (1992) 96 DLR (4th) 289.

[61] Quaere whether a fiduciary relationship may exist between spouses such that non-disclosure, for example, by one spouse that he is the carrier of an infectious disease may found a claim for breach of fiduciary duty: *Bell-Ginsburg* v. *Ginsburg* (1993) 14 OR 217 (Ont HC) (HIV transmission: action arguable)? See generally, Note, 'To Have and To Hold: The Tort Liability for the Interspousal Transmission

equitable protection afforded the victim meant that the claim was not subject to the limitation period applicable if the only action that could be brought was one of battery.[62]

If the fiduciary approach were to gobble up all other types of claim against a doctor, the courts might be chary of developing it.[63] Fiduciary duty claims would not subsume all other duties imposed upon a doctor by the law. Actions based upon a failure to exercise reasonable care and skill when diagnosing or treating a patient should still sound in negligence. The peculiar features of a fiduciary relationship are not implicated here—the patient is not alleging a breach of a duty of *loyalty*. Equally, if the patient's claim is that the doctor treated the patient without consent, a claim in battery would be the more appropriate legal action. The bona fides of the doctor's conduct would suggest that the duty of loyalty is not implicated. The fiduciary claims generally relate to wrongs not reached by tort or contract principles. Herein lies the attraction of developing fiducial law. One could, of course, imagine circumstances where the motivations of the doctor were otherwise and when a concurrent claim in battery and for breach of fiduciary duty would not be inappropriate. For example, if the doctor were to remove an organ from a patient without her consent in order to sell it. In this instance, disloyalty and the absence of consent both characterise the nature of the doctor's wrong.

Thirdly, the scope of a doctor's fiduciary duty is left a little hazy by the judge. Justice McLachlin makes it clear that to characterise the doctor–patient relationship as a fiduciary one in principle does not mean that as such a relationship does actually exist. But is this correct? Arguably, the relationship of doctor and patient will always exhibit the indicia of a fiduciary relationship identified by Justice McLachlin. The placing of trust in the doctor, his ability to exercise power and the vulnerability of the patient are surely inherent in the relationship.[64] If so, all sexual relationships between a

---

of AIDS' (1988–89) 23 *New Eng LR* 887 (US law) and R. O'Dair, 'Liability in Tort for the Transmission of AIDS: Some Lessons from Afar and the Prospects for the Future' [1990] *CLP* 219 (English law).

[62] If this approach were to be followed in England, the result reached by the House of Lords in *Stubbings* v. *Webb* [1993] 1 All ER 322 would be reversed.

[63] See the argument of Sopinka J. in *Norberg, supra,* at 480–1 and P. D. Finn, *supra,* note 3 at 25–6.

[64] See, *supra,* at 491–3 per McLachlin J.

doctor and patient would potentially amount to a breach of his fiduciary duty.

Perhaps, this is the right stance for the law to take. It would certainly be justified in cases involving psychiatrists or psychotherapists where the relationship of dependence is most marked.[65] In these situations, it is the inevitable vulnerability of every patient that motivates the law's censure.[66] Adopting the words of Justice McLachlin in *Norberg* '[a] more grievous breach of the obligations, legal and ethical, which he owed [to his] patient can scarcely be imagined.'[67] Where the patient is a competent adult it might be considered unduly harsh and thought that the law's censure is unnecessary, providing always that the doctor makes no inducements and does not apply pressure to the patient. Or, did the fiduciary duty arise in *Norberg* only because the patient was particularly *vulnerable* due to her drug addiction? Justice McLachlin's judgment is not clear even though the particular vulnerability of the patient was referred to on a number of occasions by the judge.[68]

The confusion can be resolved if the vulnerability of the patient is taken into account at the breach stage. The fiduciary duty arose because of the *inherent nature* of the relationship. This would be an important statement for the law to make. However, in deciding whether a doctor has abused his duty the particular circumstances may be taken into account. Perhaps, this is what McLachlin J. meant in *Norberg*. It is certainly consistent with the thrust of her judgment.[69] Thus, there will not be an *abuse* by the doctor of his fiduciary duty unless he takes advantage of his patient or exploits her.[70] It could be said that a sexual relationship is not such *unless*

---

[65] See, T. Frankel, 'Fiduciary Relationships in the United States' in D. W. M. Waters (ed), *Equity, Fiduciaries and Trusts* (1993) 173 at 184–5. See, *Taylor v. McGillivray* (1994) 110 DLR (4th) 64 (New Brun QB)—physician who acted as a psychotherapist breached his fiduciary duty when he engaged in a consensual sexual relationship with a patient.

[66] On this basis, it might prohibit sexual relationships between lawyers and their clients: see, Sir Matthew Thorpe, 'The Relationship Between lawyer and Client' [1993] *Family Law* 681 at 683–4 and D. Pannick, 'When Sex Pleads its Case in Court' (1993) Times, 27 April.

[67] *Supra*, at 497.   [68] For example, *supra*, at 493 and 497.

[69] '[T]he scope of [a physician's] fiduciary obligations can only be determined on a case-by-case basis, having reference to the degree of power imbalance and patient vulnerability present in the relationship under examination.' (*supra*, at 497 per McLachlin J).

[70] *Supra*, at 496 per McLachlin J.

the patient is peculiarly dependent upon the doctor as in *Norberg* or if the doctor is, for example, a psychiatrist. Only in these latter situations is the very basis of the patient's need for the doctor undermined by his actions. In other cases the fiduciary duty would exist but there would be no breach of it.

Finally, in some situations the imposition of a fiduciary duty on a doctor will facilitate communication between the parties. In some instances a potential conflict of interest may be legitimised if the fiduciary informs the beneficiary of the conflict and the beneficiary agrees to it. For example, in *Clark Boyce* v. *Mouat*,[71] the Privy Council held that a solicitor (a fiduciary) could act for both parties when a mother mortgaged her house as security for a loan to her son notwithstanding the obvious conflict of interest when representing two parties to a legal transaction. Lord Jauncey said:

[A solicitor] may act provided that he has obtained the informed consent of both [parties] to his acting. Informed consent means consent given in the knowledge that there is a conflict between the parties and that as a result the solicitor may be disabled from disclosing to each party the full knowledge which he possesses as to the transaction or may be disabled from giving advice to one party which conflicts with the interests of the other. If the parties are content to proceed upon this basis the solicitor may properly act.[72]

Sometimes the degree of conflict is such that the fiduciary cannot act even with the agreement of the beneficiary as *Norberg* itself illustrates. But, in many situations the net result will be that the doctor must disclose any conflict of interest that he may labour under, for example, where he intends to carry out research on the patient.

(c) Financial conflicts of interest

If the lead given by Justice McLachlin in *Norberg* is followed, it would have implications in other situations where a doctor may find herself in a position where her interests conflict with that of her patient. A helpful, and important, illustration can be seen in the Californian case of *Moore* v. *Regents of the University of California*.[73] The plaintiff was treated by the defendant, his doctor for a form of leukaemia. Samples of bodily tissue and fluids were taken from him over a period of time. Cells derived from these

---

[71] [1993] 4 All ER 268 (PC).
[72] Ibid., at 273.   [73] (1990) 793 P 2d 479 (Cal Sup Ct).

were used for research purposes to develop a therapeutic cell-line which it was estimated might be worth over $3 billion. Some of the samples were taken solely for the purpose of developing the cell-line. The patient was never informed of this. He sued his doctor and the bio-tech company which had developed the cell-line under agreement for at least a share of the expected profits. A majority of the California Supreme Court[74] held that the doctor had a duty to inform him of the purposes for which the samples were taken as well as the financial and commercial interest the doctor had in the patient's treatment and body materials.[75] The dissenting Justices,[76] by contrast, considered the duty to inform to be inadequate to allow the patient to share in the exploitation of his tissue through the cell-lone. Instead, they held that the tissue taken from the patient was his property. As a result, its use without his consent amounted to conversion of the plaintiff's property.[77] Of course, the bulk of the profits were made by the bio-tech company. Only the doctor owed the patient a duty to inform him of the use his tissue was to be put to. Therefore, it was not an action which allowed the patient to reach the profits of the bio-tech company. The dissenters chose the property analysis in part because it would reach those profits.[78]

In English law how would the *Moore* case have been decided? It is far from certain that the property analysis would appeal to an English Court and even if it did, it is not without its difficulties particularly in determining how much of the profits the patient could recoup.[79] Although the 'informed consent' analysis of the

[74] Pannelli J. with whom Lucas CJ and Eagleson, Kennard and Arabian JJ agreed.

[75] Notice, the Supreme Court did not go any further than was necessary for the case as a 'conflict of interest' case. A doctor would not be under a duty to disclose information to protect the patient's *financial interests* per se: *supra*, at 485 note 10. Subsequently applied by the Supreme Court in *Arato* v. *Avendon* (1993) 858 P 2d 598 (Cal SC) (no duty to disclose information relevant to a patient's nonmedical interests, for example, his business and investment affairs) discussed (1994) 2 *Med L Rev* 230 (AG).

[76] Mosk and Broussard JJ.

[77] This had been the view of a majority of the Californian Court of Appeal: (1988) 249 *Cal Rptr* 494.

[78] For a discussion of the case, see, R. Hartman, 'Beyond Moore: Issues of Law and Policy Impacting Human Cell and Genetic Research in the Age of Biotechnology' (1993) 14 *Journal of Legal Medicine* 463 and I. Kennedy and A. Grubb, op. cit. at 1102–1133.

[79] See, G. Dworkin and I. Kennedy, 'Human Tissue: Rights in the Body and its Parts' (1993) 1 *Med L Rev* 291.

majority might be more appealing, surely the *Moore* situation is better analyzed as one where the doctor as fiduciary abused his position—using it to further his personal interests.[80] *Moore* is, after all, close to the classic fiduciary cases of financial gain at the expense of the beneficiary all too familiar in the case law. On this analysis the doctor and the bio-tech company (if they are aware of his breach) would be accountable for the profits (or at the very least a share of them).[81] Further, the *Moore* case illustrates that a doctor who wishes to undertake research on a patient cannot do so without the explicit agreement of the patient.[82] Surely it is desirable that the law should require such disclosure by the doctor?[83] It would then be open to the patient to refuse consent, agree unreservedly to the doctor's proposed action or agree on terms of a share in any profits.

It seems, therefore, that the fiduciary approach goes a long way to providing a workable solution to cases of financial conflict of interest. Indeed, to apply fiducial law would, in fact, give legal effect to many of the existing ethical duties of doctors found in the General Medical Council's 'Blue Book'.[84] Potential conflicts of interest loom large in the concerns of the GMC. For example, personal relationships with patients, fee splitting and financial gains from institutions and pharmaceutical companies are all identified as potentially unethical and amounting to 'serious professional misconduct' for which the ultimate sanction of the GMC is removal of a doctor from the Medical Register.[85]

To apply fiducial law to the doctor–patient relationship, would require a doctor who referred a patient to a private clinic to disclose any financial interest he might have (for example, in the

---

[80] It is true that the majority of the Californian Supreme Court did characterise the doctor–patient relationship as a 'fiduciary' one to justify their conclusion that a patient should 'disclose personal interests unrelated to the patient's health whether research or economic, that may affect his medical judgment.' (*supra*, at 485 per Panelli J.). However, the judges did not take the logical step of holding that a doctor (and, importantly any other) might be required to account for any profits made if his conflict of interest was not disclosed.

[81] I. Kennedy and A. Grubb, op. cit. at 1128–1132.

[82] For the current law see, I. Kennedy and A. Grubb, op. cit., at 1045–1051 (therapeutic research); and at 1057–1061 (non-therapeutic research).

[83] For an illustration of such a case from America see, *Estrad* v. *Jaques* (1984) 321 SE 2d 240 (NC CA) (duty to disclose experimental nature of procedure).

[84] *Professional Conduct and Discipline: Fitness to Practise* (December 1993).

[85] Ibid., at 24–25 (personal relationships); at 37–38 (financial relationships).

institution) to the patient.[86] Of course, providing the doctor fully disclosed his interest and the patient understands the implications of the doctor's financial interest, the patient's agreement would undoubtedly exonerate the doctor.[87] But, there are also implications here for general practitioners working within the National Health Service. Since 1990 GPs have been offered financial incentives to provide certain health prevention or promotion services for their patients, for example, cervical smears for women and immunisation programmes for young babies. GPs now undoubtedly have a financial interest in advising their patients to take advantage of these services. How can this be consistent with a fiduciary obligation? It could be said that it is not. However, these are not voluntarily created conflicts of interest; they are imposed by the Government through the GPs' terms of service.[88] Fiducial law is flexible[89] and, in the light of the legislative *imprimatur* given to the financial conflict, no doubt fairness would be achieved if the doctor disclosed her position to the patient.[90]

There are other problematic situations which could arise within the NHS if fiducial law is applied. What of the doctor whose decision about treatment is affected by the limited available resources?[91] Some have labelled the doctor in such a situation as a 'double agent' working both for the patient and for society in allocating (and saving) scare resources.[92] Put most starkly, how could a doctor fulfil his fiduciary duty to two patients when he only has resources available for one, for example, one kidney dialysis machine and two patients in need? One response would be to say

[86] See, M. A. Rodwin, *Medicine, Money and Morals: Physician's Conflict of Interest* (1993) and E. H Morreim, 'Conflicts of Interest: Profits and Problems in Physician Referrals' (1989) 262 *JAMA* 390.

[87] See, T. Frankel, *supra*, note 30 at 185–6.

[88] See, The National Health Service (General Medical Services) Regulations 1992 (SI 1992 No 635) (as amended), Regulation 34 and Statement made by Secretary of State thereunder.

[89] *New Zealand Netherlands Society 'Oranje' Incorporated* v. *Kuys* [1973] 2 All ER 1222 (PC).

[90] An analogy may be drawn with the exception to the *nemo iudex in re sua* rule of administrative law where statutory necessity justifies the 'conflict of interest': see, for example, *Dimes* v. *Grand Junction Canal* (1852) 3 HLC 759 (HL).

[91] See, M. J. Mehlman, 'Fiduciary Contracting: Limitations on Bargaining Between Patients and Health Care providers' (1990) 51 *Univ Pitt L Rev* 365 and M. A. Rodwin, op. cit.

[92] M. Angell, 'The Doctor as Double Agent' (1993) 3 Kennedy Institute of Ethics Journal 279; and response, P. T. Menzel, 'Double Agency and the Ethics of Rationing Health Care' ibid., at 287.

he should not undertake the care of more than one patient in such a situation but this is wholly unrealistic. Another response would be that he fulfils his duty providing he explains the externally imposed dilemma, and each patient agrees to him carrying on as his doctor. This is also not wholly satisfactory since the patient may have no choice; she may be unable to seek out another doctor who has more resources.

Further, limitations may be placed upon a doctor's ability to treat (or offer treatment to) a patient by constraints within the 'internal market' of the NHS.[93] Cost containment provisions or restrictions in an 'NHS contract' between the purchasing health authority (or 'GP fundholder') and NHS Trust provider may compromise the doctor's ability to do what she considers best for the patient. On one view, this is inconsistent with saying that the doctor has fiduciary obligations because limits must inevitably be imposed upon her duty to act in the patient's best interests.[94] Another view would be that the doctor must stand above the systematised limitations such that she must create a 'chinese wall' between herself and the patient (on the one hand) and the managerial and other pressures (on the other hand).[95] Thus, she may still be a fiduciary since her sole consideration must always be the interests of her patient.[96] Probably, it is in these areas of scarce resources and the 'internal market' that the fiduciary approach is most tested.[97]

---

[93] See, C. Newdick, 'Rights to NHS Resources After the 1990 Act' (1993) 1 *Med L Rev* 53.

[94] See, R. Schwartz and A. Grubb, 'Why Britain Can't Afford Informed Consent' (1985) 15(4) *Hastings Center Report* 19.

[95] See, for example, *Wickline* v. *State of California* (1986) 228 Cal Rptr 661 (Cal CA) (cost containment programmes may not corrupt medical judgment). See C. Newdick, op. cit., at 68–70.

[96] There are also implications for doctors who *purchase* health care treatment for their patients, in particular, 'GP fundholders'. It may be difficult to see them as acting as a fiduciary for *any one* patient when exercising their purchasing power: there will be an inevitable conflict of interest between one group of patients and another in making decisions about what 'NHS contracts' are placed for the GP's patients as a whole. Here, it may be that the only legal duty upon the 'GP fundholder' is a tortious duty to exercise reasonable care: see, I. Kennedy and A. Grubb, op. cit., at 429–30.

[97] See the detailed analysis in the context of the United States health care system in M. A. Rodwin, *Medicine, Money and Morals; Physicians' Conflicts of Interest* (1993).

2. THE 'RIGHT' OR 'ENTITLEMENT' CASES

As part of a fiduciary's duty of loyalty, the court could, in addition to preventing conflicts of interest, seek to empower the patient by recognising that he has certain rights or entitlements enforceable against the fiduciary. In particular, the doctor's fiduciary duty may extend to divulging information held by him.[98] Whether a right of access to medical information could be forged out of the doctor's fiduciary duty arose in the second of the Canadian Supreme Court cases.

(a) McInerney v. MacDonald—*access to medical records*

In *McInerney* v. *MacDonald*[99] a patient was treated by a number of physicians over a period of years. When her doctor advised that she should cease a particular treatment which she had previously received from the other doctors, the patient asked to see her medical records. The doctor agreed to provide the records she had prepared herself but refused, out of sense of ethical propriety to the other doctors, to produce any of their records held in the patient's file. The patient brought an action against the doctor seeking an order to direct the doctor to provide her with a copy of the entire file.

The patient's claim required some ingenuity from the Canadian Supreme Court. There was no action in tort, contract or based upon a property interest. The records were not the property of the patient—they were assumed to belong to the doctor or hospital where they were prepared.[100] A majority of the New Brunswick Court of Appeal had held that there was an implied term in the contract between the doctor and patient giving the patient a right of access to material in the records if it related to the treatment or advice provided by the doctor.[101] The Supreme Court was 'not entirely comfortable' with this approach.[102]

---

[98] For the position as regards a discretionary trustee's duty to divulge 'trust documents' to a beneficiary: *Re Londonderry's Settlement* [1965] Ch 918 (CA) and *Hartigan Nominees Pty Ltd* v. *Rydge* (1992) 29 NSWLR 405 (NSW CA).

[99] (1992) 93 DLR (4th) 415 (SCC).

[100] In England, the medical records would belong to the Family Health Service Authority (in the case of GPs) or the relevant Health Authority or NHS Trust (in the case of hospitals).

[101] (1990) 66 DLR (4th) 736 and [1991] 2 Med LR 267 (Hoyt and Ryan JJA; Rice JA dissenting).

[102] *Supra*, at 421 per La Forest J.

Instead, the Court based the patient's right of access to the records and to obtain a copy upon the fiduciary duty of the doctor to act with 'utmost good faith and loyalty'. Justice La Forest (who delivered the judgment of the Court) characterised the relationship as fiduciary because of the 'trust and confidence' which the patient places in the doctor when he chooses to share intimate details about his life in a medical consultation.[103] He said:

The fiduciary duty to provide access to medical records is ultimately grounded in the patient's interest in his or her records ... [I]nformation about oneself revealed to a doctor acting in a professional capacity remains in a fundamental sense, one's own. The doctor's position is one of trust and confidence. The information conveyed is held in a fashion somewhat akin to a trust. While the doctor is the owner of the actual record, the information is to be used by the physician for the benefit of the patient. The confiding of the information to the physician for medical purposes gives rise to an expectation that the patient's interest in and control of the information will continue.[104]

Justice La Forest viewed the patient's right of access as '*prima facie* in the patient's best interests.'[105] In other words, the right grew out of the doctor's duty of loyalty as a fiduciary. The patient was permitted to raise a claim against the fiduciary *even though he was not exploiting the patient.* You will recall the limitation expressed by Browne-Wilkinson LJ in the *Sidaway* case that only a claim for *abuse* of fiduciary duty could lie. Significant though the *McInerney* decision is, the Canadian Supreme Court was careful to limit its ruling.

First, the fiduciary duty of the doctor was conceived in, and limited to, the realm of information. It was the confidential nature of the information provided by the patient to the doctor which triggered the fiduciary obligations. The patient's interest which the court sought to protect was in that information. The fiduciary duty would thus be limited to allowing the patient access to her medical records or preventing the misuse of the information in breach of confidence. Consequently, the scope of the doctor's fiduciary duty is much narrower than that asserted by Justice McLachlin in *Norberg*. In *Norberg*, Sopinka J. similarly restricted a doctor's fiduciary duty 'to improper disclosure of confidential information or

---

[103] *Supra*, at 423.   [104] *Supra*, at 424.   [105] *Supra*, at 426.

something like [it] . . .'[106] Subsequently, however, Justice La Forest
seems to have accepted that the broader approach of McLachlin J.
in *Norberg* is permissible. In *M(K)* v. *M(H)*[107] he held that a
parent owed a fiduciary duty to a child such that a child incest victim could bring a claim in equity. He said: 'the non-economic
interests of an incest victim are particularly susceptible to protection from the law of equity.'[108]

Secondly, the court accepted that the fiduciary duty of a doctor
did not mean that he always had to allow access to a patient's
medical records: the right of access was not absolute. The fiduciary's duty was to act in the 'best interests' of his patient and in
exceptional circumstances this might justify non-disclosure. The
discretion to do so would, however, be closely scrutinised by the
court and the onus would be on the doctor to justify withholding
the information. Disclosure could be withheld where '[t]here is significant likelihood of a substantial adverse effect on the physical,
mental or emotional health of the patient or harm to a third
party.'[109]

(b) McInerney *in England*

McInerney provided the patient a remedy where previously there
had not been one.[110] In England a patient's right of access to his
medical records has been created by statute, in the case of comput-
erised records by the Data Protection Act 1984 and for manual
records by the Access to Health Records Act 1990.[111] However, the
latter only applies, in general, to records created after 1 November
1991. When the issue of access to records created before that date
came before a court in 1993, an argument based upon the doctor's
fiduciary duty was rejected.

In *R*. v. *Mid Glamorgan FHSA ex p Martin*,[112] the applicant suffered psychological problems over a long period of time. During
his treatment in the 1960s, he fell in love with his psychiatric social

---

[106] *Supra*, at 481 (quoting McEachern CJ in the British Columbia Court of
Appeal).
[107] (1992) 96 DLR (4th) 289 (SCC).
[108] (1992) 96 DLR (4th) 289 (SCC), at 325.
[109] *Supra*, at 430 per La Forest J.
[110] See commentary on *McInerney*, (1993) 1 *Med L Rev* 126 at 127–9 (AG).
[111] See I. Kennedy and A. Grubb, op. cit., ch 8.
[112] (1993) 16 BMLR 81 (QBD). See commentary, (1993) 1 *Med L Rev* 378 at
379–381 (IK).

worker. As a result, she withdrew from his care. For many years he demanded to see his medical records in search, presumably, of the cause of her spurning him but his requests were always turned down. Finally, in 1990 he sought to quash the health body's decision. *Inter alia*, he relied upon the *McInerney* decision. Popplewell J. held that in England a patient did not have a right of access at common law. He gave a number of reasons. First, no English case supported the plaintiff's claim. Secondly, a distinction was to be drawn between a doctor's duty to inform his patient before a medical procedure of relevant information and disclosure of a record prepared in the absence of the patient which might be less guarded in its terms. Thirdly, the legislation conferring a right of access would have been unnecessary if the right already existed at common law.

The persuasiveness of these arguments is doubtful.[113] They effectively do nothing more than assert the status quo. But what of the fiduciary argument in *McInerney*, here surely innovation was a possibility? Not so. Popplewell J. specifically rejected the *McInerney* decision as being inconsistent with the views expressed in *Sidaway* where, as we have seen, the notion of a fiduciary relationship between doctor and patient had been expressly disavowed. Perhaps a judge at first instance could do no more given the eminence of the two judges in *Sidaway*. Their *obiter* comments (and they were no more than that) seem to have set English law in stone for the moment. Popplewell J. did make an interesting remark which, it would seem, was crucial to his rejection of *McInerney*. He said

[T]here is a distinction to be made between the information conveyed by a patient for the benefit of the doctor's consideration and the conclusion to which the doctor comes based on that information. The opinion of the doctor is wholly the property of the doctor. It does not seem to me that the fact that the patient provides the original information entitles him subject to exception, to see the conclusion of the doctors based on that information.

Why should this be so? Popplewell J.'s answer was that the doctor owns the copyright in his opinions expressed in the medical records and the court in *McInerney* had failed to draw a distinction between the *patient's information* on the one hand and the *doctor's*

---

[113] See commentary, (1993) 1 *Med L Rev* 378 at 379–81 (IK).

opinion on the other. Leaving aside Popplewell's wrongful characterisation of the issue as one of whose property the information is: this was not the issue in *McInerney* and his reasoning is almost certainly flawed. First, even if the doctor's opinion is amenable to copyright (and it may not be), it is likely that it would be a joint copyright with the patient given the patient's contribution in providing the information upon which it is based. Thus, there could be no breach of copyright if the patient gained access. Secondly, and more importantly, even if this were wrong the law of copyright would only apply if the patient had a right to receive *a copy* of the medical report. Copyright is a law which prohibits unauthorised *reproduction*. To give the patient *access* to the record, i.e. the right to inspect it, would not infringe copyright law. In the end, the strength of Popplewell J.'s rejection of *McInerney* rests solely upon the *dicta* in the *Sidaway* case.[114]

In one situation it could be argued that a doctor's relationship with an individual would not give rise to a fiduciary relationship such as to entitle him to access to his medical records. Often when an individual is seeking life insurance, the insurance company will require that the individual be medically examined prior to its writing the policy.[115] Usually, the doctor will be a stranger to the individual and not his own general practitioner. In a situation of this sort the doctor's legal duties to the patient may be more limited than where he has the continuing care of a patient. Certainly he will owe the individual a duty of care not to cause him injury negligently, for example, whilst taking a blood sample. It has been argued that the doctor's duties go no further than this.[116] He may not, for example, owe a duty to tell the patient of any adverse findings, for example, that he had discovered a tumour or other condition necessitating treatment. Thus, no action could be brought by the patient in negligence for failing to put the patient on notice of his need for further care or treatment.[117] There is

---

[114] The Court of Appeal subsequently dismissed the patient's appeal: (1994) *The Times* 16, August. The judges did not refer to the 'fiduciary argument' but assumed that a patient had a prima facie right of access and held that on the facts it had been permissible to withhold the records. For a criticism of the reasoning see, Commentary (1994) 2 *Med L Rev* (forthcoming) (AG).

[115] A similar problem may arise in the case of an occupational health physician. See discussion in D. Kloss, *Occupational Health Law* (2nd ed.) (1994) at 40–45.

[116] See, ibid.

[117] See, M v. *Newham LBC* [1994] 2 WLR 554 (CA) per Staughton LJ at 582 (Sir Thomas Bingham MR dissenting).

another (and perhaps, better) view which would extend the doctor's duty under the common law and hold him accountable in these circumstances.[118] The law would hold the doctor to have undertaken a minimum degree of responsibility as a doctor.[119] However, given the doctor's obligations to the insurance company that has employed him to examine the individual, it is difficult to say that a fiduciary duty is owed to the patient. One of the most important conditions for the duty to arise is absent: an entrusting of a power by the beneficiary which is to be exercised *only for his benefit*.

Nevertheless, in the case of *Parslow* v. *Masters*,[120] a Canadian court applied *McInerney* in somewhat similar circumstances. In that case the plaintiff was covered by insurance under a group policy provided by his employer. He sought access of the doctor's report and other medical records and notes after his claim for long-term disability benefit was turned down following an examination by an independent doctor. Applying *McInerney*, Hunter J. held that the relationship between the insured and the doctor was a fiduciary relationship. The insured disclosed personal information to the doctor to enable the report to be prepared. Consequently, the insured had a right of access and there was no evidence to establish that disclosure would be harmful to the insurer or insured.

(c) Other information cases

If the fiduciary obligation of a doctor does encompass a duty to grant access to medical information held in a patient's medical records, there are a number of implications which may presage wider duties of disclosure than currently exist. First, it would require a doctor to explain to a patient *after* a medical procedure what has happened to the patient if something went wrong.[121] There is no logical distinction which can be drawn with

---

[118] See, I. Kennedy and A. Grubb, op. cit., at 73–6.

[119] See, *Green* v. *Walker* (1990) 910 F 2d 291 (5th Cir CA). See also cases cited in T. R. LeBlang and J. L. King, 'Tort Liability for Nondisclosure: The Physician's Legal Obligations to Disclose Patient Illness and Injury' (1985) 89 *Dickinson L Rev* 1 at 30–35.

[120] [1993] 6 WWR 273 (Sask QB).

[121] See, T. R. LeBlang and J. L. King, op. cit. at 35–45 and M. Schultz, 'From Informed Consent to Patient Choice: A New Protected Interest' (1985) 95 *Yale LJ* 219 at 260–3.

McInerney. It may be pure chance whether the explanation of the 'accident' is noted in the patient's records or not. Even if it is not, the patient's interest in that information suggests that the doctor has a duty to divulge it. That such a duty might exist has been proposed by Lord Donaldson in the cases of *Lee* v. *South West Thames RHA*[122] and *Naylor* v. *Preston AHA*.[123] However, whatever the merits of disclosure in these circumstances he offered no convincing legal basis for it.[124] Indeed, he has admitted himself that he was 'flying a kite'.[125] A claim in negligence could only arise if the failure to tell the patient *caused* the patient injury after the medical procedure. In *Gerber* v. *Pines*[126] part of a hypodermic syringe broke off during an operation and was left in the patient's body. The patient successfully brought a claim in negligence for the post-operative injury he suffered because he had not been made aware of the need for corrective treatment. Usually, however, the damage will already have been done.[127] The fiduciary claim would explain what Lord Donaldson described in *Naylor* as 'the duty of candour' of the doctor in these circumstances.

Secondly, the doctor's fiduciary duty to divulge information relating to the patient or the patient's condition must extend to disclosing information in order for a patient to decide whether or not to consent to medical treatment.[128] Here, of course, the House of Lords in the *Sidaway* case has already accepted that such a duty exists under the common law. The fiduciary duty would overlap, therefore, to an extent with the duty in negligence. But, there might be a difference and it would be an important one. The duty in negligence arises from the doctor's undertaking to exercise reasonable care when treating the patient. The judges in *Sidaway* saw the doctor's duty as 'a comprehensive one'.[129] As a consequence, the tortious standard of the 'reasonable doctor' applied to information cases as much as in cases where negligent diagnosis or treatment was alleged. In turn, the judges in *Sidaway* linked the

---

[122] [1985] 2 All ER 875 (CA).   [123] [1987] 2 All ER 353 (CA).

[124] See discussion in, G. Robertson, 'Fraudulent Concealment and the Duty to Disclose Medical Mistakes' (1987) 25 *Alberta LR* 215.

[125] Sir John Donaldson (1985) 53 *Medico-Legal J.* 148.

[126] (1934) 79 *Sol Jo* 13.

[127] See, for example, *Stamos* v. *Davies* (1985) 21 DLR (4th) 507 (Ont HC).

[128] See, *Nixdorf* v. *Hicken* (1980) 612 P 2d 348 (Utah SC). See also, T. R. LeBlang and J. L. King, op. cit. Contrast P. D. Finn, *supra*, note 3 at 28.

[129] [1985] 1 All ER 643 at 657 per Lord Diplock.

standard of the reasonable doctor to the standards prevailing in the profession and applied the so-called *Bolam* test. Medical evidence largely (perhaps even conclusively) determines what information a doctor must give his patient. To see the duty to disclose as an aspect of the doctor's fiduciary duty would require the law to rethink this. The standard would now, *prima facie*, be patient-oriented since the duty focus on the patient's interest in knowing the information in order to make a choice rather than the medical profession' practices in telling as *Bolam* does. The court might, therefore, heighten the standard of disclosure to require a doctor to disclose all information that would be material to the patient's decision. The patient's 'best interests' as perceived by him would require nothing less. Of course, as *McInerney* illustrates, the doctor would have a discretion to withhold that information if disclosure would harm the patient—the so-called 'therapeutic privilege'. A rare, but important, exception.[130] The *fiduciary* duty would then reflect that common law duty proposed by Lord Scarman in *Sidaway* but which was rejected by the other judges. Lord Scarman's struggle to explain the basis in law for the patient's right to information would be resolved by recourse to the fiduciary duty of the doctor.

It might be suggested that this application of the fiduciary duty of a doctor would ensure that a court will never accept that the duty exists. The courts have been scrupulously careful not to extend a doctor's duty to provide a patient with information beyond the safe haven of the *Bolam* test.[131] Certainly, in this context the fiduciary duty is not for the faint-hearted. However, there is every likelihood that the judges will be pressed in the near future to re-examine the *Sidaway* decision.[132] The *Bolam*isation of the doctor's duty outside of diagnosis and treatment cases was doubted by Lord Mustill in the *Bland* case.[133] England is increasingly alone in its continued adherence to the *Bolam* test in information cases: the Canadian Supreme Court rejected it in 1980[134] and in 1992 the

---

[130] See, I. Kennedy and A. Grubb, op. cit., at 211–14.

[131] *Gold* v. *Haringey HA* [1987] 2 All ER 888 (CA) (volunteering information) and *Blyth* v. *Bloomsbury HA* [1993] 4 *Med LR* 151 (CA) (answering questions).

[132] See commentary, (1993) 1 *Med L Rev* 115 at 117–19 (AG).

[133] [1993] 1 All ER 821 (HL) at 895.

[134] *Reibl* v. *Hughes* [1980] 2 SCR 880 (SCC).

Australian High Court followed suit in *Rogers* v. *Whittaker*.[135] The bold spirit may yet win the day: the fiduciary duty should provide the means.

3. THE 'BEST INTEREST' CASES

One pocket of medical law cases which has always troubled me— because I have never quite understood the proper legal basis of the cases —is the so-called 'best interest' cases. Seen in the context of fiduciary law, these cases may be explicable.

Judges frequently state that a doctor has a *legal* duty to act in a patient's 'best interests'. In *Sidaway* Lord Templeman stated that '[t]he doctor, obedient to the high standards set by the medical profession impliedly contracts to act at all times in the best interests of the patient.'[136] Most often the duty to act in the patient's 'best interests' is utilised by judges when the patient is incapacitated and unable to make a decision in order to justify the doctor treating without consent.[137] The clearest (and perhaps earliest) judicial expression of this is in the case of *Re F*.[138] It formed the basis of the Law Lords' decision that it could be lawful to sterilise a mentally incompetent adult woman.[139] Lord Goff stated: 'the doctor must act in the best interests of his patient, . . . just as if he had received his patient's consent to do so.'[140] Subsequently, the House of Lords in *Airedale NHS Trust* v. *Bland*[141] affirmed and applied this approach so as to justify withdrawal of artificial hydration and nutrition from a patient in a persistent vegetative state when its continuation would not be in the patient's 'best interests'. Lord Goff again said 'it is now established that a doctor may lawfully treat [an 'incompetent'] patient if he acts in his best interests, and indeed that, if the patient is already in his care, he is

---

[135] (1992) 67 ALJR 47 (Aust HC). See also, D. Chalmers and R. Schwartz, 'Rogers v. Whitaker and Informed Consent in Australia: A Fair Dinkum Duty of Disclosure' (1993) 1 *Med L Rev* 139.

[136] [1985] 1 All ER 643 at 665.

[137] See, I. Kennedy and A. Grubb, op. cit., ch. 4 and A. Grubb (ed), *Decision-Making and the Problems of Incompetence* (1994).

[138] *Re F (Mental Patient: Sterilisation)* [1989] 2 All ER 545 (HL).

[139] For this aspect of the case see, I. Kennedy and A. Grubb, op. cit., at 712–57.

[140] Ibid., at 567. See also, per Lord Bridge at 548; per Lord Brandon at 551; per Lord Jauncey at 571.

[141] [1193] 1 All ER 821.

under a duty to treat him . . .'[142] The other Law Lords all affirmed the 'best interests' approach adopted in *Re F*.[143]

Thus, the doctor's duty is (subject to the consent of a competent patient) to act in the patient's 'best interests'. This much seems axiomatic.[144] No-one seems to have asked *where* this duty comes from. It cannot be founded in the law of negligence. While a doctor does owe the patient a duty in negligence, it is a *duty of care* to exercise reasonable skill and care in his dealings with the patient. The concern of the law of negligence is not with the 'interests' of the patient but rather with the skill and conduct of the doctor.[145]

One can see, however, why the courts in *Re F* and *Bland* adopted the 'best interests' language when formulating the doctor's duty to an incompetent adult patient. They were borrowing from cases which involved the medical treatment of young children.[146] When determining its own duty, or a parent's duty to a child, the court acts in the 'best interests' of the child.[147] But now the 'cat is out of the bag' because these cases either concern the fiduciary duty of a parent[148] or the analogous duty of the court as a judicial parent.[149] The 'best interests' test in the children cases is, therefore, actually founded in the decision-maker's fiduciary duty to the child whether the decision-maker is a court or parent. Thus, there is an unbroken line between these cases and the decisions concerning adult patients. Without appreciating the significance of what they were

---

[142] Ibid., at 868.

[143] Ibid., per Lord Keith at 860; per Lord Lowry at 876–7; per Lord Browne-Wilkinson at 882–3; per Lord Mustill at 893–5.

[144] In some instances, it could be argued that in some circumstances, particularly in the case of an incompetent adult patient, that a doctor ought to act to make the decision the patient *would have made* if competent: the so-called 'substituted judgment' test. In England, this test has not received wide approval: see, I. Kennedy and A. Grubb op. cit., at 282–93.

[145] See, J. C. Shepherd op. cit., at 48–9 (distinguishing the 'duty of loyalty' from the 'duty of care').

[146] See, for example, *Re B (a minor) (wardship: sterilisation)* [1987] 2 All ER 206 (HL) (sterilisation of an intellectually disabled child); *Re J (a minor) (wardship: medical treatment)* [1990] 3 All ER 930 (CA) (treatment of a physically and mentally disabled baby).

[147] For a discussion of the role of the court in medical cases see, A. Grubb, 'Treatment Decisions: Keeping it in the Family' in A. Grubb (ed), *Choices and Decisions in Health Care* (1993) at 37.

[148] That it is so characterised see, *M(K)* v. *M(H)* (1992) 96 DLR (4th) 289 (SCC) (relationship between father and child-incest victim).

[149] As, for example, in *Gillick* v. *West Norfolk and Wisbech AHA* [1986] AC 112.

doing, in the adult incompetent cases the courts have utilised language reflective of fiduciary law.

IV. Conclusion

There is no doubt that the doctor–patient relationship has fiduciary qualities. As the 'best interests' and other cases show the shadow of fiduciary law is cast upon much of the existing law. The crucial question is whether English law will become more explicit and utilise the potential of fiduciary law to redress the imbalance of power between doctor and patient. The Canadian Supreme Court in the *McInerney* and *Norberg* cases has provided a guide for those who wish to follow. Fiduciary law would not replace the legal framework which currently defines the duties owed to a patient but would supplement it. It would, as I have suggested, have a significant impact in imposing acceptable standards of conduct on doctors in their dealings with patients. It could, if used wisely, bolster a patient's rights. It would allow the courts to give content to many of the entitlements we intuitively feel patients should have but cannot find a legal home for, at least currently. But, most of all, it would allow (indeed require) the courts to disengage medical law from the *Bolam* test.[150] The wisdom of recourse to professional practice to determine the legal duties of a doctor outside of medical negligence cases has been questioned in the *Bland* decision by Lord Mustill.[151] In the words of Lord Justice Hoffman in *Bland* rejecting the application of *Bolam*: 'a purely legal (or moral) decision . . . does not require any medical expertise and is therefore appropriately made by the court.'[152] Notwithstanding the strictures of the eminent judges in *Sidaway* the time may have come for English law to reappraise the doctor–patient relationship and recognise the doctor as a fiduciary.

---

[150] See, for example, the criticisms at (1993) 1 *Med L Rev* 115 and 241 (AG).

[151] *Supra*, at 895. See also commentary on *Bland* (1993) 1 *Med L Rev* 358 at 363–4 (IK and AG).

[152] *Supra*, at 858.

ACCESS TO JUSTICE

Lord Woolf*
(The Bentham Club Presidential Address)

It is 40 years on that I stand before you to give this lecture. Forty years since my finals were approaching and I was at last buckling down in a frantic attempt to defeat the examiners. That I had the good fortune to just succeed in doing so means that we have to suffer together before we can dine together in accord with the long established tradition of the Bentham Club, of which I am immensely proud to be this year's President. The only comfort I can offer you, if my experience is anything to go by, is that the dinner should be worth waiting for and there is no risk of my speaking again and spoiling your dinner.

It is hard for me to accept it is as long as 40 years ago. I realise that I know less law now than I did then, but I do not feel that much older. Indeed, not so long ago I was deceived into believing (but only for a matter of moments) that I do not even look that much older as a fellow student whom I had not met for almost 40 years crossed my path and, flatteringly, recognised me! We talked over old times and I could not resist commenting on the remarkable fact that she was still able to recognise me (even though, as I thought to myself, she had changed so dramatically). Her response brought me back to reality. It was not me she had recognised but my old sports jacket. She couldn't believe there were two quite like that. Of course, it's also possible that we had both forgotten that we had met during the intervening years—perhaps at a Bentham Lecture.

I was fortunate enough to attend the 1986 Lecture given by Lord Goff of Chieveley. He assured his audience that he was 'no public entertainer', nor was there any risk of his being thought to be one—unlike my noble and learned friend, Lord Oliver who had been compelled to assume the territorial designation of 'Aylmerton' in order to avoid confusion with Laurence Olivier and the embarrassment of seeing his judgment reviewed, in error, on the theatrical pages of *The Times*.

---

* Lord of Appeal in Ordinary.

If Lord Goff was not an entertainer, he was a spiritualist as over the next 40 minutes or so he was able to convince his fascinated audience that they were hearing a verbatim account of a discussion which he had had with the reincarnated, disembodied spirit of Jeremy Bentham himself. Also, I also lack Lord Goff's qualities as a spiritualist. So the best I can do in order to show a proper respect for our great mentor is to choose access to justice as the subject for my address, a subject of which I believe Jeremy Bentham would approve if I possessed the power to summons him here this evening. He would approve because of his concern with utilitarianism and the need for the demystification of the law. These are fundamental concepts which you need to have very much in mind in determining how you can improve access to justice.

The justice which I have in mind is civil, not criminal. If you commit a criminal offence and you are one of the unfortunately too few who are found out; then usually there is no difficulty in your having access to, and I would hope obtaining, justice. It is in relation to civil proceedings that the problems exist. If you have the means and the necessary patience, I believe that our system of civil justice compares favourably with that in other countries. Although I may not be the most appropriate person to say so, I would suggest that our judiciary is of exceptionally high standard across the board, comparing favourably with the judiciary in both civil and common law jurisdictions. Relative to our population we are remarkably well served by fewer judges than any other developed society.

I can support these boasts by a reference to the fact that if you go into the commercial court, the likelihood is that the case will have at least one foreign party and may well be a dispute where neither the parties nor the subject matter in dispute has any connection with this country. Approximately one-third of the cases fall within the latter category and well over 50% involve one overseas party. This explains why foreign legal earnings for the commercial court in 1992 represented no less than £425 million. Then again, there is the Privy Council. One aspect of my work since my promotion to the Lords is the amount of time I spend in the Privy Council. Approaching 50% of the cases heard by the Law Lords are ones involving the remaining jurisdiction of the Privy Council. Although the number of countries which regard the Privy Council as their final court of appeal has been reduced over the years since the end of the last War, a sizeable number, over 30, of the smaller Commonwealth countries and dependencies are still content to swallow their national pride and accept the jurisdiction of the Privy Council. Most of those Commonwealth countries now have written constitutions which incorporate provisions protecting human rights, equivalent to those contained in the European Convention. Ironically, in the Privy Council, the Law Lords are regularly adjudicating on the protection for human rights provided by a written constitution. This applies in situations as diverse and as important as the death row phenomena in the Caribbean[1] and the obligations of the New Zealand Government to the Maori people under the Treaty of Waitangi.[2] The situation is ironic because while we can protect human rights of citizens who come from Commonwealth countries across the globe, our own citizens in order to obtain the same protection are obliged to make the, admittedly shorter, journey to Strasbourg.

It is worth mentioning in relation to both the examples I have just taken, that it is not only the contribution of the judiciary which should be noted. There is also the contribution of both sides of the profession. Japanese construction firms would not be content to have disputes with Gulf states adjudicated upon in London if it were not for the quality of the legal services which are provided. The quality of those services compares favourably with those provided in competing jurisdictions but the cost of those services is as high, if not higher than those in other jurisdictions. As to those costs, I do believe that both sides of the profession would be well advised to exercise more restraint than they always do at present. I do believe there is a risk, that by extracting the maximum fee the market will bear, they will reduce the volume of work which would otherwise be attracted to this country because it is the ideal neutral forum for resolving international disputes. As against those words of caution I would like to acknowledge the contribution which, largely on a *pro bono* basis, those same lawyers make to enable petitioners from the Caribbean invoke the jurisdiction of the Privy Council. By preparing and appearing on appeals for those who could not possibly afford their services, at least initially without charge both barristers and solicitors demonstrate that the best traditions of the professions are

---

[1] See *Pratt* v. *A. G. of Jamaica* [1993] 4 All ER 769.
[2] See *New Zealand Maori Council* v. *A. G. of New Zealand* [1991] 1 All ER 623.

far from dead. The scale of their service is underlined by the fact that normally they would not choose to be involved in 'crime' even for paying clients.

Whether that counsel of caution is justified or no, it is not my primary concern this evening. My concern is with the home market and in particular with that sector of the home market which services those who fall between the modestly poor and the modestly rich. I include the small firm or company. I have no doubt that the issue of costs provides an increasingly insurmountable impediment to access to civil justice for this large section of the public. A system of justice which a very substantial section of its own citizens cannot afford, is a system which contains a fundamental flaw and leaves them vulnerable to exploitation.

Sir Jack Jacob, who almost single-handed is responsible for establishing the status of this Society, has explained why access to justice constitutes a touchstone of the quality of a civilised community when he said; 'The administration of justice is the life-blood of the civil legal system of any country, and at the same time it is also the life-line which enables its citizens to secure justice and, as Bentham put it, the effectuation of their legal rights.'[3]

Equality before the law has to be a fundamental feature of any respectable system of justice. It requires, as the recent Heilbron Report ('*Civil Justice on Trial—the Case for Change*') points out, that 'all litigants, rich and poor, however large or however small the subject matter of litigation, have access to a fair and impartial system of dispute resolution.' Yet, as the same report also points out:

the recent Government retrenchment in the availability of civil legal aid deprives millions of our citizens of this life-line.

Such a statement may strike some of the audience as an exaggeration. I am afraid that on the contrary it is no more than the unvarnished truth. While in respect of our health, as a country we demand that no one should be prevented because of a lack of means from receiving medical treatment; with regard to civil justice for our fellow citizens our society is prepared to accept a lower standard. The position was made clear by the Lord Chancellor when on the 20th January 1994 his Department announced his new Legal Aid objectives. This is the approach which was described:

[3] '*The Reform of Civil Procedural Law*' 1982.

it has never been intended that the Legal Aid scheme should ensure that every citizen should be put in a position where financially they were able to pursue every *meritorious* case through the courts. The cost of such a scheme would be prohibitive. The Lord Chancellor intends that the money which is available for legal aid should be targeted towards those whose need, arising out of their financial means, is the greatest.

In considering whether that approach is justified it must be acknowledged that the Legal Aid expenditure in England and Wales is already enormous. The budget this year is £1,406 million. By 1996/97 it's expected to be £1,633 million. This is a huge burden for society to bear. Yet, it is the unhappy fact that, despite the State shouldering this burden, fewer and fewer of our citizens qualify for legal aid and as a result in practice are incapable of resorting to the courts to protect their rights. This is a deplorable situation which must be redressed by urgent action. But what is the solution? I am afraid I cannot provide a comprehensive answer to that question this evening. However, what I will seek to do is to indicate the areas we should be investigating in order to find that solution. In order to do this there are two questions, which I believe are related, on which I suggest we should be focusing. They are:

1. Are we targeting legal aid in the most constructive and effective manner?
2. Are we taking sufficient steps to make litigation accessible (including affordable) by those who do not have great personal wealth or an institution or the legal aid fund to fall back on?

On the first question, it is for the government of the day to decide how much of the public purse should be devoted to funding legal aid and my personal views as to the priority which it is given among the competing demands on that purse are of no interest. Where lawyers and perhaps even a judge can help is as to whether there is a better method of focusing the resources which are available.

At present there are two principal hurdles which a litigant has to surmount to be a granted legal aid. The first is a means hurdle and the second is a merits hurdle. What has happened is that the volume, the complexity and the costs of litigation have increased dramatically and though the budget for legal aid has also increased greatly it has not kept up. The result is that the proportion of the cases that are eligible for legal aid and the scale of that aid has continuously fallen so as to meet budget constraints. The principle method by which this has been achieved is by raising the means hurdle so that either an applicant is not eligible at all or only eligible if he is willing to pay a greater contribution towards his own costs than he understandably considers he can afford. The result of the targeting, as the Lord Chancellor's departmental statement indicates, has been to make legal aid the privilege of that section of the community which has the greatest financial need. The results of this policy can be extremely unfair to individual litigants who are just beyond the limits.

But is there an alternative? What I would suggest may not have been sufficiently considered, before the numbers eligible for legal aid were reduced in this way, is whether part at least of the necessary economy could be achieved by introducing a third hurdle based on the difficulty and complexity of the case and its importance to the applicant. The third hurdle might have to be a high one and it would involve, what is becoming anathema to administrators, a degree of discretion, but it could mean for example that a litigant who just failed to clear the means hurdle but could clear the third hurdle would be granted legal aid. If the administrators could not handle this degree of discretion, then I believe the courts should have no difficulty in identifying a third hurdle case for them. The additional cost of such cases could be met by increasing the proportion of cases which it would be practical for the litigant to conduct for himself or with less assistance than he would receive on legal aid today. The full benefits of this could not be achieved overnight because those benefits will involve changing the manner in which we conduct the type of litigation with which the ordinary man in the street is likely to be involved. In the meantime it might be possible to single out areas of litigation where legal aid would not *normally* be available because they are regarded as something of a luxury. (It is to be remembered that already legal aid is not available in respect of defamation.) Again, legal aid might be more difficult to obtain to prosecute an appeal. This could then be another consequence of there being a third hurdle; some of the cases for which legal aid is granted at present would fall at the third hurdle.

Before I move on to focus on how the courts might be made more user friendly to the litigant in person, which provides the link between the two questions I identified earlier, I would like to touch on another consequence of there being an insufficient element of discretion exercised at present in the grant of legal aid. That is the tendency for legal aid to be granted if the two hurdles are surmounted too readily in a small minority of cases. For example it can result in over representation. Recently, we had in the House of Lords a case involving a baby whose mother was also a child and in care. The issue was a narrow but difficult one. From the mother's point of view, it was in her interest she should have contact with her baby, but from the baby's point of view it was not in his interest he should have contact with his mother. Whose interest prevails? As you know, it is the interest of the child in such matters that is paramount, but how do you apply that principle where both mother and baby are children? The Court of Appeal decided the paramount interest of the mother cancelled out that of the baby. We decided that of the baby prevailed. There could only be one of two possible answers but the parties were represented by 5 QCs and 5 juniors and 5 firms of solicitors. The representation was all at public expense. The baby was represented, the mother was represented, her guardian *ad litem* was represented, the father was represented and the council was represented. We caused the legal aid authority to be informed of the situation but it did not wish to make representation on the question of costs so all we could do was indicate that serious consideration should be given in future to whether this scale of representation is necessary.[4] Unless it be thought that the status of the court influenced the representation I can tell you that last week I was told about a case of a similar nature which was heard in the magistrate's court and the representation was on the same scale but without the QCs. In considering the scale of the waste of public money this can cause, it should be remembered that the number of parties represented inevitably increases the length of the hearing and therefore the expense. In our case 3 days before us but 5 days at first instance.

I turn to the second and more important of the two questions I have identified. Here I am considerably helped by the recommendations of the Civil Justice Review, the Heilbron Report, to which I have already made reference, and the recent Hamlyn Lecture of the Lord Chancellor. The Heilbron Report lucidly identifies what I

---

[4] *Birmingham City Council v. H. (a minor)* [1994] 1 All ER 12 cf. *Re S. (a minor) (independent representation)* [1993] 3 All ER 36.

believe is required by stating that 'the legal system must adapt to match contemporary needs and expectations of society', and later that there is a requirement for a change of culture, 'for a radical reappraisal of the approach to litigation from all its participants. It is time for many of the deeply engrained traditions to be swept away and for their replacement by pragmatic and modern attitudes and ideas.' The Report then identifies ten underlying principles or themes which the committee considered would provide the necessary new ethos in the civil courts. These principles are admirable in themselves and, if adopted, together with their related detailed recommendations could substantially improve the present position for litigation in general. In particular I would, as did the Lord Chancellor, commend trying to produce a simple unified procedure in the High Court and the County Court with a single set of rules (which I suggest should be concentrated so that they fit comfortably within the 3rd and thinnest volume of the White Book and could be written in a language a layman might conceivably understand). However, such is the scale of the problem that I suggest the Committee may not have gone anything like far enough to assist the section of the community on which I am focusing. We should at least be considering a more radical model. Like it or not (and I do not like it) we are faced with a situation where litigants frequently have the choice of not engaging in litigation or either appearing in person or using a lawyer for limited purposes only. The position today is still the shaming one referred to in the Civil Justice Review of 1988 where;

The cost of litigation is quite disproportionate to the amount involved in the claim. Thus the costs of both parties to a personal injury case which goes to trial often exceed or equal the damages recovered.

and where the

fear of costs is one of the greatest deterrents to using the Courts . . . [and the problem] is compounded by the fact that there is little or no chance of knowing beforehand what a case will cost or of making price comparisons.

I fully recognise that we cannot change the model of court which we have developed over the centuries overnight. To attempt to do so could do more harm than good. It would risk throwing out the baby with the bath water. I also acknowledge that helpful initiatives have taken place such as the establishment of the Small Claims Jurisdiction in the County Court which have a completely informal procedure. There is also the Deadline listing at Liverpool County Court and the initiatives of the profession such as the Bar's scheme for a fixed fee of £100. However although each of these initiatives assist they do not constitute a radically different model of litigation from that which exists at present. A model which we could over a period of years work towards, so that when it is created, even with the likely scale of the provision of legal aid no citizen should feel he is deprived of obtaining civil justice from the courts.

Reluctantly, I have come to believe that except in the area of specialist litigation such as that conducted in the Commercial Court, we have to accept that the role of courts has to change. The court and particularly the county court has to be organised so that it can take charge of litigation from the outset. When this is required the court will have to be equipped to advise and instruct the litigant on the steps he will have to take to bring his case to trial and supervise and help him to take those steps. For this purpose the court will need the necessary resources. There will have to be available some form of advisory service at the court staffed by a mixture of trained layman and lawyers both paid and voluntary. As happens now with the free representation unit and has happened in the past with the dock brief young men and women in their early days may have to be prepared to take on litigation at reduced fees. We may need a Litigant Support Scheme to match the imaginative initiative of the Victim Support Scheme in the Criminal Courts. The courts will have to try and become user friendly to litigants as well as lawyers. The court must be in a position to give a high priority to assisting the parties settle their differences at the earliest possible stage. Mediation and Alternative Dispute Resolution will have to be available. The judge will have to be much more flexible in the role which he plays. In some cases it will be his traditional one of being primarily the impartial adjudicator of an adversarial system but in other cases it will be largely inquisitorial, perhaps in some cases conducted entirely on written submissions. If there is a medical or other expert issue he should be able to delegate it to others to determine or have the assistance of assessors. An example of what is possible is provided in the field of social security where the delegated medical practitioner determines disputes as to the gravity of a claimant's disability. Somehow we have to find an alternative system for the just resolution of disputes which does not involve the expense and delays of the present system. I suggest there are models in addition to those already referred which do indicate what might be the road we should take.

One solution which I would not endorse, however, is that which provides a decision by applying some pre-determined formula. This would be a possibility for example in the case of quantifying damages for personal injury. From an administrative point of view the approach obviously has much to commend it. However, recent experience has indicated that the inflexibility which is inherent in this approach is inconsistent with achieving a just result in a significant number of cases. This was the problem with the unit fine. The philosophy behind the unit fine is one which had much to commend it. However, it produced too many absurd results. Within a short time of its adoption the system was scrapped. There appear to be similar problems with the attempt to make parents more accountable for making proper financial contribution for the support of children of their former marriage. I suspect that the Child Support Agency is a victim of the formula it has to apply. I fear the same result will follow if the Government insists on implementing the proposed amendments to the present Criminal Injuries Compensation Scheme. The changes should result in claims being disposed of much more expeditiously than at present. However, this will be achieved by sacrificing the need to tailor the award to the particular circumstances of the particular case. The consequences of the same injury to different individuals can vary to a remarkable degree and it is just not possible to ignore, as the scheme proposed will ignore, those differences. I acquit the Government of being only motivated by the desire to save money. However, those who support the proposal would be well advised not to persist in trying to rubbish those who point out the disadvantages of the scheme on the basis that they are lawyers merely motivated by a desire to protect the interest of lawyers. It is lawyers' experience of personal injury litigation which makes them aware why the proposed scheme will not work; and why, with admittedly some defects, the present scheme is infinitely preferable. Indeed, although delays do exist in the existing scheme this is because of the growth in the number of cases with which it deals. The scheme provides an example of the fact that it is possible to dispose of substantial claims relating to personal injuries without retaining more than the residual elements of the conventional civil trial.

Since the importation from Scandinavia of the first ombudsperson in the form of the parliamentary commissioner, there has been the creation of numerous replicas both in the public and private sector. From my own experience, I can vouch for the effectiveness of the Banking Ombudsman. With my involvement, limited to filling out a form and responding to three or four letters, I was provided with a result to my dispute with one of the 'big four' banks within a remarkably short period of time. Of course I am prejudiced because the ombudsman ruled in my favour. However, making all allowance for that, I was provided with a perfectly satisfactory remedy in circumstances where litigation would have been out of the question. The costs of conventional litigation would have been disproportionate to the amount in issue. The principle was one, however, on which I felt strongly and the scheme does provide an appropriate remedy. A remedy which has always been honoured by the member banks although the scheme is voluntary. What I was interested to observe from the Banking Ombudsman's 1992/3 report is the number of cases with which he is dealing (11,000 eligible complaints and 1,100 deadlocked complaints), that the scheme is being extended to the small company, and the way many complaints are resolved by the ombudsman's knowhow enabling him to refer complaints to the appropriate department so that they can be resolved in house. This is achieved at an early stage because complaints are screened at the outset. The handling of a mature claim took 240 days and the target is 6 months. This is achieved by just over 40 staff and an increased budget for the current year of £2.3m (I wonder what could be achieved with such a budget by a Director of Civil Proceedings for whose appointment I have long canvassed). I am sure it makes commercial sense for the banks to fund the scheme because it will raise standards within the banks if they know there is a method by which the customer can and will obtain redress. It also leads to customer satisfaction and it avoids the costs of litigation and provides good value. To work effectively the existence of the Scheme needs to be known by bank staff and customers. That more progress is needed on this front is illustrated by this extract from the report:

The lack of general awareness of the scheme was demonstrated recently after one member bank had distributed our change of address notice to its branches. A number of them promptly wrote or telephoned to say that they could not trace our account and requested more details!

Would it not be possible for an extension of ombudsman schemes and perhaps for an ombudsman option to be available from the courts? It is certainly and economical and effective way in which to provide the individual with a remedy against the big battalions. Could we not develop a close relation between ombudsmen and the courts so the courts could use an ombudsman to ascertain the relevant facts and the courts determine issues of law?

We now have in this country a substantial spectrum of tribunals which deal with a remarkable variety and number of disputes. (Over a quarter of a million cases last year.) In a wide range of situations justice is provided for litigants by Tribunals. Not all have been an equal success. I am afraid, sometimes, they have tended, too closely, to mirror the procedures of the courts instead of concentrating on devising procedures which are appropriate for the type of dispute which they are required to adjudicate upon. However, on the whole, they are a success story. They do illustrate the fact that it is possible to devise methods of dispute resolution which are more effective and give readier access to justice than our conventional courts. They have the advantage that they have expertise in respect of the subject with which they deal. Their procedure is also tailored to the resolution of a particular type of dispute. On the other hand, they have the disadvantage that legal aid is not available and there is now developing disturbing evidence that even with the sort of issues that come before the Social Security Tribunal, that representation, which does not have to be by a lawyer, can materially affect the outcome. There has also developed in one tribunal in particular, the Employment Appeal Tribunal, substantial delays because of lack of judicial resources. On the other hand in the case of the immigration tribunals there is an example provided by the Immigration Advisory Service of how the Government can fund support for litigants on a modest and inexpensive basis. Without the help that these bodies and the C.A.B. can provide, the fairness and the validity of the hearing depends very much on the quality of the chairman.[5]

[5] See Hazel Genn 'The Unrepresented Tribunal Applicant', *Tribunals* Vol I p. 8.

It is because of these problems that I again call on my personal experience to suggest what could be an improvement for many tribunals. I have no doubt as a result of conducting the Prison Inquiry that it is possible to devise methods which can cut through the need for representation and expedite the process of the inquiry in a manner which accords with the requirements of justice. This process is assisted if there is available to the tribunal the services of counsel to the inquiry. In the case of a modest inquiry the 'counsel' need be no more than that of a tribunal presentation officer; in the case of an inquiry on the scale which I conducted there was need for both counsel and solicitors to the inquiry. In both cases, it should be the responsibility of this 'representative' of the tribunal to ascertain the issues, where possible, to secure agreement as to the facts and, in so far as it is not possible to achieve agreement, to call the appropriate evidence in an informal manner so as to enable the facts to be determined. In so far as there are issues of law the representative will place the issues before the tribunal and cite the necessary authorities. However, if either party to the dispute is not satisfied that all the evidence or all the considerations are being brought out by the representative, he or she can be permitted to supplement material provided by the representative. If they do this, the primary responsibility still remains with the tribunal's representative, whose presence will ensure the equality of arms between the parties and act as a filter so as to avoid unnecessary delay or expense. To be successful, the proposal involves the parties to the dispute accepting the impartiality of the representative. However, as far as I'm aware, those who appear before them are well satisfied with the impartiality of our tribunals, made up as they usually are by three representatives, one a qualified lawyer and two appropriate lay individuals. If they are satisfied with the impartiality of the members of the tribunal, I do not see why the parties to the dispute should not also be satisfied with the impartiality of the tribunal's own representative. Certainly in the type of inquiry of which I have personal experience, no one doubted the impartiality of counsel to the inquiry or, for that matter, the Treasury Solicitor, notwithstanding the fact that the Treasury Solicitor was also concerned with the interests of a department of Government whose actions were being investigated by the inquiry. If this role is properly performed, it is my belief that the tribunal in the majority of cases will receive all the assistance which is necessary to achieve a just result without the need for the parties to be represented by lawyers.

Members of the Bentham Club are too astute not to identify what might be said to be at least one snag of the proposal which I am making. That is, who is going to pay for the representative? If it is the Government is this no more than providing legal aid in another form? While I acknowledge that the initial reaction of the Treasury to my proposal may be one of scepticism, I would hope that they would at lest be prepared to countenance a test of what I propose since it is my belief that instead of adding to the costs it would reduce the costs of the tribunal system. It would certainly make them more effective. If the representative performs his role in the manner that I envisage, he would dramatically reduce the length of the hearing before tribunals. One of the difficulties with which the tribunals are faced without proper representation, is finding out what is the nature of the dispute. They also frequently have to listen to evidence relating to issues which are not in dispute. In an adversarial system, it is part of the task of the representatives of the adversaries to agree and limit the area of dispute and only to call evidence which is relevant to resolving those issues which cannot be agreed. Because they are adversaries, sometimes it is difficult for them to perform this task as well as they would like. When an applicant is unrepresented it is difficult for this process at present to take place at all. However the representative which I am proposing, being apart from the parties, would be able before the hearing to find out the issues and ascertain the extent to which they can be limited. The representative can perform these functions when it would not be possible for the members to do so without prejudicing the impartiality of the tribunal. It is always important that those who have the task of making the determination should be, as far as this is possible, above the affray and not involved in it. The representative could also, when this is appropriate, act as a mediator. He would be in the best possible position to know what was the likely outcome of the proceedings and while he would have to exercise discretion to avoid his independence being undermined, he would undoubtedly in many disputes be in the position to facilitate their disposal by agreement. The presence of the representative would also avoid in the case of the social security type tribunal the requirement which exists at present of the Department having to be represented by a qualified member of the Department who is capable of presenting the case to the tribunal. Frequently, the person having that responsibility finds himself compelled to perform some of the functions of the representative which I have identified. He is, however, under the disadvantage when doing this of being seen by the other party to the dispute to be the agent of the Department he represents.

If an approach on these lines can work for tribunals, why should it not also work in the case of some court procedures? To an extent it already happens. The small claims arbitration in the County Courts is an admirable example. In the High Court there is that distinguished office of Master of the Supreme Court which our Chairman holds, following in the footsteps of his predecessor to whom I have already made reference. Because of the pressure which they are under, the Master's role in the smooth running of litigation has had to be more passive than I would regard as desirable. He obviously could not appear as the advocate of the court as would my representative. However, he could readily perform a more extensive role in mediating, limiting the areas of dispute and controlling the evidence which is called than he does at present. It remains, however, within the tribunal system that I believe the representative could play the largest part. In addition possibly to trying to adapt the court system so that it can accommodate a representative, consideration should be given to extending the tribunal system so that it would be able to accommodate certain of the litigation which is now primarily the province of the courts. I have already gone on record, extrajudicially, in proclaiming the advantages of an environmental tribunal which could provide a one-stop shop for resolving environmental disputes. The record in Australia of such a tribunal is quite remarkable. It is expeditious, cheap and effective. It has been able, without any adverse effects, to dispense with the requirements of *locus standi*. That is but one example where a specialist body may be able to perform its role more satisfactorily than can a court. Another, would be in relation to housing disputes. It is inappropriate that litigants who are complaining that they have been the victims of a local authority not doing its duty in relation to the homeless to have to come to London and have their complaints adjudicated upon by a High Court judge on an application for judicial review. The costs of such applications, when they lack merit, inevitably fall on the legal aid fund. They are expensive. They would be much better disposed of by a local tribunal or the County Court, which deals with a broad range of housing problems within the locality. In the case of this type of dispute the representative to whom I referred would benefit both the housing authority and those who have housing needs. If this were to succeed in practice, there would be little difficulty in identifying other areas to which the same approach could be applied.

In this connection it is important to recognise the pressure on the courts that the increase in litigation is causing. You will remember that not so long ago the Lord Chief Justice had to complain in the most dramatic terms about the consequences of the lack of judicial resources. Just last week an article in *The Times*[6] gave a message which I found deeply disturbing. It was pointing out the difficulty which the Lord Chancellor was having in obtaining acceptance from those whom he first approached for judicial appointments. So far as High Court judges were concerned, the position was not quite so grave as it is in the case of Crown Court judges. If the article is correct, since 1992 eight candidates declined and 27 accepted appointments to the High Court Bench, but in the County Court 75 declined and only 45 accepted. I have little doubt that the increased number of appointments which the Lord Chancellor has been called upon to make recently has aggravated the situation. It is most important that we should continue to attract to the Bench judges of the highest calibre. So far those who have been appointed have been of that calibre. Should that cease to be the position, the consequences to the standards of justice in our society could be drastic. The danger is that if it becomes more and more common for appointments to be declined this will devalue the status of the judiciary. Appointments to the bench will cease to be seen as the culmination of a successful career in practice but instead will be seen as a secure haven for the second rate. This would seriously damage the public's respect for the Bench which would in turn make recruitment more difficult and we could find that there was a downward spiral in quality from which it was difficult to recover. In time this would destroy the confidence in the justice system which is essential for its success. I do not believe the problem is due only or primarily to the contrast between a judicial salary and the income of a successful practitioner though the difference can today be dramatic. It is also now a problem of the

---

[6] F. Gibb, *The Times*, 23 Feb. 1994.

extent of the pressures to which the judiciary are being subjected; pressures from overwork and from the media. There is also the effect of the ever increasing number of appointments which has the tendency of debasing the coinage. A beneficial effect of the possibilities which I have touched on in this lecture would I hope be to reduce that pressure. The qualities of a good member of a tribunal are not necessarily those which are required for a judge. The effects of the proposals I have discussed should be to reduce the proportion of cases coming for trial before a judge and to achieve a more effective form of disposal when they do so. Against this there would almost certainly be an increase in the amount of litigation. If you provide a cheap and efficient means of disposing of disputes people will use it. That is something we should all want for this would be consistent with the provision of a more acceptable standard of access to justice.

But what of advocates, what would be left for them? Here I have no concern. Society continues to grow ever more complex and we are increasingly aware of our rights so that we wish to vindicate them, if we can realistically do so. We will increasingly want to employ advocates if we can afford to do so. The changes that are needed will make it easier to afford advocates because the litigation will be more rapidly and effectively resolved. If we can still not afford to employ an advocate under a reformed system we could not have employed the advocate anyway. However in this situation at least under a reformed system a litigant in person will have a better chance of coping with the system.

The skills which may be needed in the future of the lawyer may however change. Here the UCL graduate need have no fear. He will find, as I found when I started out at the Bar, that he has the advantage of a legal education based on Benthamite utilitarian principles that give him a head start over his contemporaries. We all have cause to be grateful to Bentham and UC.

This lecture was given prior to his being asked by the Lord Chancellor to conduct an inquiry into access to justice.

INDEX

Index